Ukrainian, Russophone, (Other) Russian

Postcolonial Perspectives on Eastern Europe

Edited by Alfred Gall, Mirja Lecke, and Dirk Uffelmann

Volume 8

Zur Qualitätssicherung und Peer Review der vorliegenden Publikation

Die Qualität der in dieser Reihe erscheinenden Arbeiten wird vor der Publikation durch die Herausgeber der Reihe sowie durch Mitglieder des Wissenschaftlichen Beirates geprüft.

Notes on the quality assurance and peer review of this publication

Prior to publication, the quality of the work published in this series is reviewed by the editors of the series and by members of the academic board.

Marco Puleri

Ukrainian, Russophone, (Other) Russian

Hybrid Identities and Narratives in Post-Soviet Culture and Politics

PETER LANG

Bibliographic Information published by the Deutsche Nationalbibliothek
The Deutsche Nationalbibliothek lists this publication in
the Deutsche Nationalbibliografie; detailed bibliographic
data is available online at http://dnb.d-nb.de.

Library of Congress Cataloging-in-Publication Data
A CIP catalog record for this book has been applied for
at the Library of Congress

Printed by CPI books GmbH, Leck

ISSN 2192-3469
ISBN 978-3-631-81662-2 (Print)
E-ISBN 978-3-631-82366-8 (E-PDF)
E-ISBN 978-3-631-82367-5 (EPUB)
E-ISBN 978-3-631-82368-2 (MOBI)
DOI 10.3726/b17031

© Peter Lang GmbH
Internationaler Verlag der Wissenschaften
Berlin 2020
All rights reserved.

Peter Lang – Berlin · Bern · Bruxelles · New York · Oxford · Warszawa · Wien

This publication has been peer reviewed.

www.peterlang.com

Acknowledgements

The idea of writing this book first came to my mind when in September 2018 I *unexpectedly* received an invitation to Berlin to join a workshop on "Russophone Literatures in the Post-Soviet Space" at the Center for East European and International Studies (ZOiS)—that would have then taken place six months later. In her email, Nina Frieß, the coordinator of the project, proposed to discuss the theoretical framework, aesthetics and topics of "Russophonia," inviting junior and senior scholars with different regional research focuses (i.e. the Baltics, the Caucasus, Central Asia and Ukraine). My surprise—and enthusiastic reaction to the idea behind the project—was motivated by my previous academic experience in "Russophone Studies": a highly unsystematic and "displaced" research field that first made me revolve around literary studies (namely, "Russian Studies" and "Ukrainian Studies"), and eventually led me to explore the broader cultural, social and political dynamics in Ukraine. To me this was a good sign for the further development of the field, and the long-awaited answer to the "global dispersion" of scholars involved in this extremely challenging research area.

This book reflects almost ten years of research on "Ukrainian Russophonia." It also incorporates and further develops some outcomes of my first monograph in Italian (Puleri 2016)—which resulted from my PhD in Slavic literatures at the University of Florence (2012–2015)—and other publications in scholarly journals (Puleri 2014; 2017b; 2018) and collected volumes (Puleri 2017a)—where I had the chance to further investigate social and political dynamics in Ukraine as a result of my post-doctoral fellowship (2015–2020) at the Department of Political Sciences of the University of Bologna. I am indebted to the editors for their reprint permission. These contributions have been further revisited in light of the latest social and political developments, and integrated with new research findings, in an attempt to reframe the debate on Ukrainian culture and politics in the broader post-Soviet (and global) struggle for meaning.

I am proud that this volume is part of the pioneering book series *Postcolonial Perspectives on Eastern Europe*, and I wish first and foremost to thank the series editors for their support, thorough reading of the earlier versions of the manuscript, and insightful comments. Without their help, the volume would have never had its finished shape. In particular, I owe a debt of gratitude to Dirk Uffelmann, who has strongly believed in this book project since my initial proposal, and has patiently followed every aspect of its realization. Special thanks also go to the Institute of Advanced Studies in Köszeg (Hungary), that has generously subsidized and hosted the last stage of my research, and Alessandro Achilli, who has provided extensive and incisive feedback on the final draft of the manuscript.

My own field research and life experience in Simferopol', Kyiv, L'viv, Kharkiv, Donets'k, Dnipro and Odesa, where I lived for several weeks and months throughout 2010–19, gave me the opportunity to grasp the heterogeneous social and cultural dynamics in Ukraine. As a result of the research fellowship term at the Kyiv-Mohyla Academy (2013), and exchange fellowships at the Ivan Franko National University of L'viv (2018) and at the Odesa I. I. Mechnikov National University (2019), I had the chance to talk with several academics, literary actors and friends, which enriched my knowledge about Ukraine, taking an active part in the search for potential answers to the research questions included in this book. I would like to express my gratitude to them and also to all the people who have shared their insights on the issue in both the academic and extra-academic contexts, in Italy and abroad. Last but not least, I am thankful to Chiara and my family for tolerating the solitary activity of writing and supporting me every step of the way.

Note on Transliteration

The transliteration of Ukrainian and Russian names, terms and geographic locations follows the Library of Congress system, without diacritic signs. In the case of Ukrainian Russian-language authors, I followed the transliteration system from Russian: throughout the book it is possible to find some exceptions, since in most cases these authors are bilingual in everyday life and present their own names also according to the Ukrainian transliteration system. Unless otherwise indicated, translations from Russian and Ukrainian included in this book are mine, as are any errors or misinterpretations.

Contents

Introduction
From (Global) Russian to Ukrainian Culture—and Back Again

> In the contemporary context, diasporization and hybridity have become conditions for novel ways of "translating the world" [...] The question of whether we should talk about one global Russian culture or many finds an answer only provisionally and, paradoxically, locally. (Rubins 2019: 46)

Following a 2017 report based on data on language use from national censuses and the United Nations, collated by Euromonitor International, we witness how significantly "Russian has lost more ground than any other language over the past 20 years as newly independent former Soviet states have attempted to assert their linguistic sovereignty" (Johnson 2017). In his commentary emblematically entitled *Russian Beyond Russia*, Alexander Morrison (2017) observed how "language is harmfully intertwined with politics these days in Eurasia." On the one hand, this followed former president of Kazakhstan Nursultan Nazarbayev's decision in 2017 to move the Kazakh language from the Cyrillic to the Latin script for the sake of national "modernization" (Nazarbaev 2017). On the other, the Kremlin elite is still implementing new policies for supporting "the Russian citizens and compatriots who live abroad, the defence of their rights, including the right to receive education in Russian,"[1] within the framework of the 2015 Concept *Russian School Abroad* (*Russkaia shkola za rubezhom*; Prezident Rossii 2015).

In a wider perspective, these are only some of the measures undertaken in the realm of official policies affecting the public debate in the post-Soviet scene, where over the past decades we dealt mainly with categorical assumptions that rendered national languages and cultures as part of

---

1 "[...] российским гражданам и соотечественникам, проживающим за рубежом, защите их прав, в том числе права на получение образования на русском языке."

the new state ideologies. As highlighted by Sheila Fitzpatrick in her 2005 study *Tear Off the Masks! Identity and Imposture in Twentieth-Century Russia*, after the collapse of the USSR in 1991 we witnessed an intense process of resignification of the old cultural symbols and social practices in the "new Europe." Nonetheless, the new national models emerging from this historical rift have been shaped in the absence of new "proper verbal signifiers" (Oushakine 2000: 994) that have the potential to reflect ongoing social processes in the post-Soviet scene. It was in a "state of post-Soviet aphasia," borrowing Serguei Oushakine's definition (2000), that the culture of (post-Soviet) crisis—"revising the past, depicting the present, and foretelling the future"—became "comprehensive and ubiquitous" (Etkind 2017: 2).

It is especially the contested revision of the role and position of Russian language and culture in the region that still represents the true bone of contention in reframing the configuration of the post-Soviet political, cultural and social landscape. Its definition influences not only the creation of a definite and *territorially bounded* Russian identity, but also affects the emergence of "novel ways of 'translating the world'" (Rubins 2019: 46) in the so-called Near Abroad. As emphasized by Kevin M. F. Platt (2019a: 3) in the introduction to the pioneering volume *Global Russian Cultures*, this is the result of the "process of global dispersion"—of "millions of ethnic Russians and others who identify with Russian language and culture"—that "has produced novel and thorny questions concerning Russian culture and identity," not only in the former Soviet space but even globally.

Nowadays these "Russian" subjectivities, together with their extremely diverse range of political and social positions, lie at the core of an intense process of external *appropriation* or, alternatively, internal *rejection* in the post-Soviet national discourses. As testified by the so-called Crimean euphoria—that is, the dynamics of the public debate in Russia following the contested annexation of Crimea and the war in East Ukraine in 2014—geopolitical clashes in the region served as a catalyst for new political projections of the Russian idea (and cultural space) beyond the borders of the Russian Federation. It is especially the theorization and contested ideological appropriation of the concept of the Russian World (*Russkii mir*), which was "once created as an alternative to nationalism and imperialism in any form" and is now "strongly identified with them" (Nemtsev

2019), that contributes to an understanding of the fluidity of the narratives implemented by political actors in the post-Soviet arena.

As retraced by Mikhail Nemtsev (2019), the origin of the concept is deeply rooted in the late Soviet years, when the historian and philosopher Mikhail Gefter introduced the idea of *Russkii mir* in his analysis of "the Soviet Union's future prospects through his philosophy of world history" as "a possibility for humanity to save itself from self-destruction."[2] Throughout the 1990s, the concept was then "suitable for conceptualizing a 'new Russian-language self-consciousness' [*Russkoiazychnost' myshleniia*] for post-Soviet people" in the work of "humanitarian technologists" in Eltsin's times. It was only in the 2000s that we witnessed the political appropriation of this philosophical concept by the Kremlin, directly affecting its original "universal appeal" and tying it "to the geographical boundaries of the former Soviet Union" (Nemtsev 2019). The Russian world came thus eventually to be externalized *beyond* the borders of the Russian Federation, but *within* the blurred boundaries of the Russian cultural space.

In spite of the highly politicized narratives around *Russkii mir*, it is only through the lens of the dynamic changes occurring in post-Soviet societies that we can still understand where symbolic politics fails to represent a vivid picture of the Russian cultural space. When focusing on the *local* developments of Russian culture—and on its interrelation with *local* cultures, societies and traditions—we clearly witness how today " 'Russianness' [*Russkost'*] is still deterritorialised," or "largely 'broken off' from any geographic boundaries or ethnocultural traditions of the Russian ethnos" (Nemtsev 2019).

Interestingly enough, only in the 2010s did scholars in post-Soviet studies start to reconsider the role of the new Russian cultural phenomena emerging *locally*.[3] In the aftermath of the dramatic political developments in the last

---

2 "Gefter called this alternative the 'world of worlds' [*Mir mirov*], comprising several communities, or 'worlds' which historically formed around large, developed cultures [...] Thus the 'Russian World' [...] can only exist and be understood in relation to other such worlds, the boundaries of which have nothing to do with boundaries of states. In essence, the 'Russian World' cannot be tied to any strictly territorial definition, nor to any specific form of governance" (Nemtsev 2019).

3 Still in 2007, in the concluding section of his *Mapping Postcommunist Cultures: Russia and Ukraine in the Context of Globalization*, Vitaly Chernetsky wondered about the jarring omission of Russian-language literary phenomena

decade, and following the specious misuse of cultural categories in the public debate, new research questions arose: "Could there ever be 'another Russian World'?" (Nemtsev 2019); "Where is Russian culture properly located?" (Platt 2019a: 3), or "How can we even posit a single entity called 'Russian culture as a whole'?" (Platt 2019a: 5). While "rethinking Russianness," today, scholars and observers in post-Soviet studies wonder about "new ways of translating" the *other* Russian world in all of its diversity. This creates the ground for developing new analytical tools not only for an understanding of the new *local* places and shapes of Russian culture in the region, but also for better interpreting the heterogeneity of post-Soviet local scenes through the lens of the *global*—and transnational—location of culture.

From Russianness to Russophonia

Over the past 30 years much attention has been devoted, especially in the social and political sciences, to the role played by such "groups of people who are referred to variously (often interchangeably) as (ethnic) Russians, Russian speakers and Russophones" (Cheskin, Kachuyevski 2018: 3) in the post-Soviet scene (Brubaker 1996; Kolstø 1996; Laitin 1998; Zhurzhenko 2002b; Gorham 2011). Geopolitical developments related to the implementation of new nation-building policies and the formation of new national majorities and minorities in the former Soviet republics, the heritage of the Soviet policies of nationalities and ethno-federal structure, the emergence of new normative measures in the Russian Federation devoted to the protection of the alleged "Russian diaspora" and compatriots, and eventually the rise of migration flows within and beyond the former Soviet Union: all these factors have contributed to the methodological cul-de-sac affecting

---

from post-Soviet research: "Another paradigm of post-Soviet writing that has not received detailed attention [...] is one that, although of utmost importance, is still in its infancy; hopefully it will undergo a prodigious development in the near future. I have in mind postcolonial russophone writing that, in a way structurally analogous to similar developments in anglophone and francophone literature, develops the language medium in ways radically different from the metropolies' national literary traditions" (Chernetsky 2007: 266).

the creation of a solid research framework for the study of this complex mosaic of peoples, ideas and traditions as a whole.

Yet the problematic conceptualization and terminology adopted throughout the last years to define such a diverse and heterogeneous group of people—together with their political and social ideas, activities and behaviours—still deserves further discussion. A constructive point of departure has been proposed by the contributors to the previously mentioned volume *Global Russian Cultures* (2019). While retracing the background behind the title of the book, Platt highlights how the shared stance of the scholars who participated in the research venture is that Russians "have gone global" (or, better, "plural"): "Our use of the plural 'cultures' corresponds to our shared conviction that these formations must be seen as an interconnected web of distinct entities rather than a totality that can be captured in any definition or formula" (Platt 2019a: 4). Yet global Russian cultural life is "a highly complex area of study that varies across time, space, social environment, and the vagaries of individual cases" (Platt 2019a: 5). Focusing on the dialogical relations between cultural production and political forces—in post-Soviet Eurasia and globally—we witness how " 'being Russian' or 'performing Russian culture' is everywhere subject to local constraints, but those constraints, and therefore the content of 'Russianness' as well, are distinct in each new context" (Platt 2019a: 6).

The kind of approach brilliantly described by the scholars who contributed to this research venture can help us deconstruct the multiplicity of labels and categories based on strictly exclusive territorial, linguistic and ethnic terms, especially whereas we understand that paradoxically, as in the case of Central Asia, the "Russophone cultural-linguistic space might continue to function here even without a larger presence of 'Russians' " (Kosmarskaya, Kosmarski 2019: 90). Moving further to an understanding of the complexity of the "Russian-speaking" world, new insights emerge from the analysis undertaken by the Kazakhstani scholars who contributed to the thematic issue emblematically entitled *When Global Becomes Local: Modern Mobilities and the Reinvention of Locality* (2017) in the scholarly journal *Ab Imperio*. At the core of Akbota Alisharieva, Zhanar Ibrayeva and Ekaterina Protassova's research proposal lies the opportunity to study Russian as a polycentric language, following the analogous case of the field of the so-called "World-Englishes," which was first developed in the 1970s in the aftermath of the decolonization process (Kachru 1992; Bolton, Kachru 2006). Here again, "[i]n theoretical and pragmatical terms […] the use of the term 'Englishes' emphasizes the autonomy and plurality of the world varieties of the English language" (Kachru et al. 2006: 4). Similarly, nowadays the "Russian-speaking space" is influenced by the new demographic processes, national cultural standards and language practices which have followed the Soviet collapse since 1991:

> As a result of the collapse of the USSR, the Russian-speaking area has reduced and changed its configuration. Russian speakers live in almost all countries of the world. Diaspora is growing, but it is not subordinate to a single center as before […] Russian philologists working outside the Russian Federation are faced with the question of how to describe new phenomena in Russian language, when this deviates from the previous standard and the interaction with local languages affects its vocabulary, grammar and pronunciation—even among those for whom it was the native language.[4] (Alisharieva et al. 2017: 232)

Research provides preliminary evidence supporting the hypothesis that the Russian language in Kazakhstan, or "Kazakhstani Russian," has acquired autonomy from the "global" Russian language.[5] Such dynamics have been

---

4 "В результате распада СССР русскоязычное пространство сократилось и изменило свою конфигурацию. Русскоязычные живут практически во всех странах мира, диаспора растет, но она уже не подчиняется единому центру, как раньше […] Перед филологами-русистами, работающими за пределами Российской Федерации, встает вопрос о том, как описывать новые явления в русском языке, когда он отклоняется от прежнего стандарта, а взаимодействие с местными языками влияет на его лексику, грамматику и произношение даже у тех, для кого он являлся родным."

5 "Although over 90 % of Kazakhs are proficient in Russian, as a result of a deliberate policy of transition to the Kazakh language and the increasing segment of English language learning, a 'reversing language shift' occurred. In the country the Russian-speakers are mainly non-Russian. At the same time, Russian language absorbs more and more 'kazakhisms' […] Moreover, in Kazakhstan people learn from textbooks written by local groups of authors based on local Russian-language works, use dictionaries and other handbooks published in the country, and here they read local press and watch local television in Russian (that's true, along with the one produced by the Russian Federation)" (Alisharieva et al. 2017: 237–238; Хотя русским владеет более 90 % казахов, в результате целенаправленной политики перехода на казахский язык и увеличения доли английского языка в обучении произошел «обратный языковой сдвиг.» Носителями русского языка в стране являются сегодня преимущественно нерусские. В то же время русский

recognized even in other post-Soviet contexts where the cultural proximity of Russian with the state language, in spite of a "downgraded" official status, is more pronounced (see the Ukrainian case: e.g. Del Gaudio 2011). Yet these reassessments have implications well beyond the sphere of linguistics, as they redefine the terms in which social scientists—and even politicians—contemplate the issue of the "Russian speaking communities" in post-Soviet countries.[6]

The above-mentioned authors of the article "The Kazakhstani Russian: An Outsider's Perspective" ("Kazakhstanskii Russkii: Vzgliad so storony") further emphasize that whereby, on the one hand, "in Russian studies such analyses have just started," today "the study of the variability of the Russian language is still tied to observe the exclusive normative model of Russian supported by the scientific and political resources of the Russian Federation" (Alisharieva et al. 2017: 234).[7] Interestingly enough, on the other hand, here again the main factor affecting the actual and habitual use of the local varieties of Russian language "from below" is "the subjectivity of the speakers: how do people answer the question of who, strictly speaking, owns the language and who has the right to speak it?" (Alisharieva et al. 2017: 235).[8]

язык принимает все больше казахизмов. Тем более что в Казахстане учатся по учебникам, написанным местными коллективами авторов с опорой на местные русскоязычные произведения, используют изданные в республике словари и иные пособия, здесь читают собственную прессу и смотрят местное телевидение на русском (правда, наряду с российским))."

6 As also highlighted by the Polish scholar Tomasz Kamusella in his studies on contemporary language politics: "*Atypically*, Russian is the only 'big' language of worldwide communication shared by numerous countries which (as yet?) is considered *not* to be pluricentric or de-ethnicized. But having recognized the sociolinguistic dynamics of this plural reality of 'world Russians' on the ground, it is possible to reimagine monocentric Russian as a pluricentric language." (Kamusella 2018: 169).

7 "В русистике подобные исследования только начинаются […] работа по изучению вариантности русского языка по-прежнему вынуждена ориентироваться на эксклюзивную и нормативную модель русского, поддерживаемую научным и политическим ресурсом РФ."

8 "[…] субъектность носителей языка: как люди отвечают на вопрос о том, кому, собственно говоря, принадлежит язык и кто имеет право на нем говорить?"

An answer to this question—and to the proliferation of cultural constructs that still tie categories such as "Russian" and "Russian-speaking" to territorially, ethnically or ideologically bounded labels—can be identified in the emerging field of "Russophonia." Yet, as mentioned by Robert A. Saunders, still in 2014 a Google search for Russophonia only produced "a list of pages dedicated to 'Russophobia' or the 'fear of Russians'" (2014: 1). While addressing a necessary practice of reflection on terminology, Dirk Uffelmann (2019: 208) used the term to describe "the global community of Russian language and culture," significantly—and provocatively—switching the focus from the speakers to the set of speech acts. Disembodying language from its carriers, we can consider even the room for "Russophone Russophobia," highlighting how nowadays a "critique of all that is constructed as Russia(n)—namely, Russian politics, mentality, culture, and above all language—if expressed in Russian, can collide with the performance of using the Russian language" (Uffelmann 2019: 214).

Eventually, the term "Russophonia" brings the attention to the performative acts of speaking Russian (and even *speaking back* to Russia), thus laying the ground for a new potential methodological orientation, with the aim to overcome contradictory ideological constructs based on ethnicity, nationality and territory.[9] Most fundamentally, Russophonia highlights the self-conscious and autonomous nature of the performance that carriers of the Russian language are enabled to produce with their individual speech acts, finally switching the focus to the agency of these new cultural actors— thus creating the ground for an extremely interesting field of study aimed at an understanding of the multiplicity of Russian political and linguistic cultures and identities.

In-between (Literary) Russophonia

In the closing lines of the lecture given at the Swedish Academy in Stockholm on the occasion of the awarding ceremony, Sviatlana Aleksievich (b. 1948,

---

9 As Uffelmann (2019: 208) puts it: "[...] both the conspiracy theory about 'Russophone Russophobes' and the metalinguistic deconstruction of this assumption reveal the multiplicity of Russian political and linguistic cultures as well as the fundamental—although mediated—autonomy of culture(s) from nations, state borders, and geographic fixity."

Stanislav—today Ivano-Frankivs'k), the winner of the Nobel Prize for literature in 2015, reflected upon one of the most controversial issues mirrored by the kaleidoscope of post-Soviet identity:

> I have three homes: my Belarusian land, the homeland of my father, where I have lived my whole life; Ukraine, the homeland of my mother, where I was born; and Russia's great culture, without which I cannot imagine myself. All are very dear to me. But in this day and age it is difficult to talk about love.[10] (Alexievich 2015)

In an attempt to define the different cultural, historical and political affiliations of the writer Sviatlana Aliaksandrauna (in Belarusian)/ Svetlana Aleksandrovna (in Russian) Aleksievich, a number of different labels have been adopted: (post-)Soviet, for her historical-cultural background; Belarusian, for her citizenship; Ukrainian, for being born in the Soviet Stanislav, today's Ivano-Frankivs'k; and, finally, Russian, for her native language and artistic-literary instrument. Eventually, this created the ground for the rise of a contested reception of Aleksievich's success in Belarus, Ukraine and Russia, where she was at times appropriated or rejected along the "own/other" divide (Charnysh 2015).

In an article published the day after the awarding of the prize to Aleksievich, the Ukrainian journalist Vitalii Portnikov (2015) offered an interesting key to an understanding of this controversial issue. Reflecting upon the observers' attempts to position the writer's experience within the borders of a single national literary canon, the Ukrainian journalist highlighted how today at the core of the dispute lies "our inability to shift cultural frontiers" (*nashe neumenie razdvigat' kul'turnye granitsy*; Portnikov 2015). For Portnikov, Sviatlana Aleksievich is a Belarusian writer "to the same extent that Joyce and Yates are Irish writers, Mark Twain and Hemingway are Americans, García Márquez is Colombian, and Vargas Llosa is Peruvian"[11] (Portnikov 2015). According to Portnikov, "[i]n the

---

10 "У меня три дома — моя беларуская земля, родина моего отца, где я прожила всю жизнь, Украина, родина моей мамы, где я родилась, и великая русская культура, без которой я себя не представляю. Они мне все дороги. Но трудно в наше время говорить о любви." Translated by Jamey Gambrell.

11 "[…] в той же степени, в которой Джойс и Йейтс — писатели ирландские, Марк Твен и Хемингуэй — американские, Маркес — колумбийский, Льоса — перуанский."

contemporary world the national belonging of a writer is not determined by language, but by a choice of civilization"[12] (Portnikov 2015).

Following Portnikov's reflections, today it is still literature that can show us the path to undertake even while turning the gaze to the *other* "Russian World"—and to the diversity of its *local* historical and cultural experiences. Following the collapse of the Soviet Union, we witnessed the textualization of new speech acts that contributed to developing "new ways of translating the world" (Rubins 2019: 46)—that is, new tools and symbols able to reflect the reshaping of the cultural frontiers of modernity. As highlighted by Maria Rubins (2019: 21), "Russia has been no stranger" to the "global trends that informed much of the world's cultural production in the last hundred years": among these trends, we can mention the fall of multiethnic empires (i.e. the Tsarist empire in 1917) and totalitarian regimes (i.e. the Soviet Union in 1991), revolutionary cycles (i.e. the October Revolution in 1917, perestroika and the fall of the communist rule in 1985–1991), wars (i.e. the two World Wars in the first half of the century, and the Afghan war in late Soviet era, above all), massive migrations and displacement. These events created the ground for the "proliferation of hyphenated, hybrid, translocal and transnational identities" that make up today the so-called "archipelago of Russian culture," borrowing Rubins' definition (2019: 24).[13]

Whereas, following a geocritical approach, Rubins observed how globally "the interdisciplinary study of the archipelago has challenged the binary conception of mainland versus islands, recasting the entire cultural space as an archipelago" (2019: 25), in the 2000s the peculiar "glocalization" (Kukulin 2019: 171) of Russian language and culture in post-Soviet times has been the focus of studies adopting the postcolonial methodology for research on the post-communist region. It is also as a result of this emerging approach that in his review of the latest English editions of Aleksievich's novels *Second Hand Time* (*Vremia sekond-khend*, 2013) and

---

12 "В современном мире принадлежность писателя определяется не языком, а цивилизационным выбором."

13 "A polycentric, nonhierarchical model of global Russian cultures may be visualized as an archipelago, a chain of islands that appear independent and isolated but in fact are interconnected in space, as well as time, often owing their origin to a series of volcanic eruptions" (Rubins 2019: 24).

Chernobyl Prayer (*Chernobyl'skaia molitva*, 1993), emblematically entitled *Neighbours in Memory*, Serguei Oushakine (2016: 12) significantly came to describe Sviatlana Aleksievich as "the first major postcolonial author of postcommunism."[14]

Notwithstanding the historians' enduring reluctance to endorse the *methodological hybridization* between postcolonialism and post-communism, Aleksievich's experience reveals once again the presence of multiple points of intersection between the two "post-": postcolonial linguistic and cultural hybrids, textual and identity deterritorialization, conflictual binary discourses re-emerge in a different form—but, at the same time, akin to classical colonialism—in the cultural contexts of the new countries that have arisen from the ashes of Communism. It was significantly "[t]he opening up of Second world cultures to increased global contacts as a result of the policies of perestroika and glasnost and, even more so, the collapse of communist rule in Eastern Europe and the suddenly former USSR" that "highlighted this jarring omission" (Chernetsky 2007: 7) in postcolonial research.

Among the most productive points of contact between the two "post-," we witness the revision of the so-called "East–West" divide in the heart of Europe, which opened the ground to global contacts and interdisciplinary research perspectives. The studies undertaken by the post-communist scholars who contributed to the volume *Postcolonial Europe? Essays on Post-Communist Literatures and Cultures* (2015), edited by Dobrota Pucherová and Róbert Gáfrik, reflect the original perspectives offered by this methodological orientation. As highlighted by the editors in the introduction to the book, the unifying idea behind all the contributions is to give voice to new actors in the contemporary debate on European identity.[15]

---

14 "With her cycle Svetlana Alexievich has established herself as the first major postcolonial author of post-Communism: the daughter of a Ukrainian and Belarusian who uses the Russian language—the only language in which she is completely fluent—to collect and present, from her own subaltern perspective, subaltern accounts of the traumas inflicted by empire" (Oushakine 2016: 12).

15 "[…] this book uses the term 'postcolonial Europe' in a new way; rather than designating the former West European colonial powers, as it has been used by the postcolonial discourse, it indicates here the Central and East European countries formerly under Soviet domination, pointing to the fact that all of Europe is postcolonial, but in different ways, and arguing that this region should play a

As argued still in 2012 by Dorota Kołodziejczyk and Cristina Şandru, the editors of a special issue of the *Journal of Postcolonial Writing*, here we deal with "an inquiry that does not so much seek some postcolonial status for East-central Europe as it strives to find, theorize, and make productive spaces of difference within similar paradigms of subjection, subalternity and peripheralization" (Kołodziejczyk, Şandru 2012: 116).

Generally, drawing upon the path undertaken by the editors of the volume included in this book series, *Postcolonial Slavic Literatures After Communism* (2016), the proposed framework answers the need for exploring "not only the heuristic potential of postcolonial approaches to postcommunist cultures on the meta-theoretical level," but also "literature's specific contribution" (Smola, Uffelmann 2016: 14) to a broader understanding of post-communist societies. On the one hand, as emphasized by Klavdia Smola and Dirk Uffelmann (2016: 17), "for East and East-Central Europe, it might be useful to stress selected concepts of postcolonial studies such as hybridity or inbetweenness that are compatible with interpretative routines such as deconstruction [...] or global paradigms such as transnationality or world literature." On the other, whereas together with the editors of the volume we argue that "Slavic literatures after communism *are* postcolonial [...] in a no more metaphorical way than the allegedly 'classic' cases of postcolonial literatures," we can still maintain that they "need not, however, necessarily be postcolonial in the same respect" (Smola, Uffelmann 2016: 15). It is exactly following this path that we can go beyond the question posed by David Chioni Moore still at the dawn of the new millennium in his seminal essay "Is the 'Post-' in Postcolonial the Post- in Post-Soviet?" (2001), and eventually create the ground for a new epistemological approach to the post-communist—and, namely, post-Soviet—culture and society. As suggested by Smola and Uffelmann (2016: 14), we should reframe the main research question as follows: "on what levels *are* the literatures of postcommunist countries *postcolonial*?"[16] The complexity

---

major role in the current debates in postcolonial studies on European identity" (Pucherová, Gáfrik 2015: 13–14).

16 "a) Are they postcolonial on the level of socio-political conditions? b) Or are they, alternatively, postcolonial on the level of a (post-) colonial mind? c) Or are they just postcolonial on the level of postcolonial modes of representation with the means of literature" (Smola, Uffelmann 2016: 14).

and heterogeneity of a space where "neighboring cultures with mutual linguistic intercomprehension and cultural and religious similarities" (Smola, Uffelmann 2016: 15) were in a state of constant interaction and exchange prevents us from giving a univocal answer to this question.[17] Nonetheless, the peculiar in-between position which emerges from the diverse historical experiences of Slavic cultures still represents one of the main characterizing traits of the postcolonial setting in Eastern Europe. Paradoxically, shared historical dynamics make the definition of new post-Soviet ethnic and national identities in Eastern Europe—together with the demarcation of the respective fields of national cultures—even more complex and contested than in overseas colonialism.[18]

Most fundamentally, regarding my research focus, the "transnationalization" of Russian culture also seems to regard a broader process taking place in the post-Soviet region as a result of a peculiar (post-)colonial experience in (post-)Soviet times. As emphasized by Susanne Frank,

---

17 As highlighted by Ilya Gerasimov and Marina Mogilner (2015: 718), "the main limitation of modern postcolonial theories stems from their genealogical dependence on the phenomenon of colonizing empire and hence the inability to contemplate a truly postcolonial reality that is indifferent to the imperial past (not obeying imperial legacy or constantly struggling with it)."

18 It is not by chance that recently in a special issue of the Russian journal *The New Literary Observer* (2017), Smola and Uffelmann's attention has been further devoted to the literary construction of postcolonial ethnicity in the yet overlooked field of non-Russian Russophone literatures in the Russian Federation and the Near Abroad: "The literary texts under scrutiny somehow problematise the relationship between Russian and non-Russian, starting with the 'mirror' (according to Lacan) merging in the context of Soviet multinational literature and ending with the models of de(con)struction and parody implemented by the authors of the latest period. By means of rhetoric, tropes, linguistic hybridity and performative analysis of ideological models, the authors under scrutiny critically rethink the same constructions of ethnicity" (Smola, Uffel'mann 2017: 425; Исследуемые нами литературные тексты так или иначе проблематизируют соотношение русского и нерусского — начиная с их «зеркального» (по Лакану) слияния в контексте советской многонациональной литературы и кончая образцами де(кон)струкции и травестирования у авторов новейшего периода. С помощью риторики, тропов, языковой гибридности и перформативного анализа идеологических моделей выбранные нами авторы критически переосмысляют сами конструкции этнического).

the ambivalent multinational Soviet literature "that emerged as a project of cultural and literary policy in the mid-1930s can be seen as not the least important part of political enterprise of nationalities policy in the Soviet Union" (Frank 2016: 193). This project, proclaimed as anti-imperial, still had some characteristics that allow identifying it as imperial: "the dominance of Russian as lingua franca and the language into which all (relevant) literary texts had to be translated was only one feature, others being dogmatism of one aesthetic doctrine—Socialist Realism—and universalism" (Frank 2016: 193). According to Frank, the heritage of this transnational project—that forged "a literary reality of dense intercultural entanglement" (2016: 201)—comes to still influence the "post-imperial" developments of post-Soviet literatures. Especially, when identifying its "unintended result" for "the space of Russian-language literature," Frank recognizes that "nearly everywhere [...] there are authors today who use Russian as their writing language" (2016: 213). This is "a group and a tendency in-between" (Frank 2016: 213), living at the crossroads between the processes of "nationalization and/as de-Sovietization" in former Soviet republics and "nationalization in Russia itself" (Frank 2016: 212). Recent literary developments in post-Soviet cultures could be thus included "on the one hand in the context of current global tendencies of literary transnationalization, and on the other in a historical perspective as effects and consequences of the project of Soviet multinational literature" (Frank 2016: 214).

Interestingly, it is also through the lens of the global decentralizing process of literary and cultural studies that the US scholar Naomi Caffee, in her dissertation "Russophonia: Towards a Transnational Conception of Russian-Language Literature" (2013), proposed the introduction of a new framework "for discussing literary works from past and present communities of Russian speakers regardless of citizenship or ethnic identity, both within and outside of the Russian Empire and its successor states" (2013: 20). On the one hand, Caffee identifies "Russophonia" as "the totality of social, linguistic, and geo-political environments in which Russian-speaking authors write and live," while on the other—"taking a cue from postcolonial literary studies" and "especially from the disciplines of Francophone and Sinophone studies"—considers "Russophone" as describing "literature written in the Russian language" (2013: 20). Caffee defines "Russophone" as "the most accurate term available," mainly in light of the misuse of ethnic and linguistic labels in public discourse.[19]

Even if the research area still remains quite vague in temporal and spatial terms, following Caffee's proposal, the potential discipline of Russophone studies answers the need for providing "the crucial interdisciplinary space" for the analysis of "pressing contemporary issues" (Caffee 2013: 24). Among these, Caffee mentions "a preoccupation with establishing identity, and also with categorizing and hierarchizing identities" (2013: 36), which emerges quite clearly as a central theme in "Russophone literature": this includes works that "often belong to more than one literary tradition concurrently," and authors who "are acutely aware of this gap between traditions, between identities and between locations" (2013: 36).

In an attempt to analyse the dynamics characterizing "the very essence of culture's 'in-betweenness'" (Caffee 2013: 36) as experienced by Russophone authors today, we need to be aware that in the archipelago of Russian culture "each center" presents "a unique combination of local and global factors," giving rise to "hybrid island identities" which are "subject to continuous redefinition" (Rubins 2019: 25). It is exactly these blurred dynamics in the field of *global* Russian culture that makes the investigation of its *local* centres and *provisional* status an extremely compelling field of research.

Today, the contested encounters of the Russian language and culture with *other* languages, cultures and traditions in the post-Soviet space raise "pressing contemporary issues" related to—and affected by—political and social developments, the presence (or, alternatively, the lack of) cultural institutions and, eventually, market dynamics. This reflects global tendencies affecting cultural practices in contemporary multicultural societies. It is no surprise that still in 1997, in his study *Translating and Resisting*

---

19 "[...] first, because it is descriptive, rather than prescriptive; and second, because the term is not ethnically, politically, or geographically specific. Its only central criterion for inclusion is the participation in Russian-language discourse. As such it provides a space for viewing authors of a variety of cultural backgrounds and historical periods. Above all the introduction of Russophonia is an attempt to step away from the classification of literature by nationality (so beloved by the Soviets), and instead to rely on the social and linguistic realities inherent in the production of texts and the multi-faceted structuring of identity." (Caffee 2013: 20–21).

Empire: Cultural Appropriation and Postcolonial Studies, Jonathan Hart could question the ambivalence of global cultural processes: "Can all the claims of different cultures find expression in a community or nation?" (1997: 138). The classification of subjectivities and cultural phenomena that do not necessarily respond to a knowledge paradigm based on the demarcation between the centre and the periphery, the superior and the inferior, discloses the need for new analytical criteria able to understand the complex dynamics of today's cultural métissage.

As emphasized by Hart in his analysis of the developments of Francophone literature in the 1990s, the emergence of new narratives built around the cultural negotiation between centre and margin are the outcome of the global experience of migration, diasporization and hybridity.[20] Looking at the rise of transcultural subjectivities in the post-Soviet space through the prism of global cultural dynamics, we may assume that cultures "based on a model of penetration and interconnectedness are to be understood as externally networked and internally hybrid, dynamic, and fluid constructs" (Hausbacher 2016: 417). It is not by chance that, while describing the globally emerging literary narratives through the lens of "transculturality," Arianna Dagnino (2013: 4) comes to the conclusion that "what makes this kind of writing different is first and foremost its resistance to appropriations by one single national canon or cultural tradition."

In this book I will focus on the case of the contemporary Ukrainian cultural process, in an attempt to understand the result of the interplay between literature, politics, market and identity. Most fundamentally, focusing on the perspective of Russophone intellectuals and literary actors, I will try to go beyond the binary opposition in the Ukrainian intellectual environment between the *local* Ukrainian-language and Russian-language literatures as separate realms, thus positioning the latter within the *global* developments in post-Soviet culture and society. Following these lines, the purpose and the core research questions of this study are threefold:

---

20 "Cultural appropriation in the Francophone world is not simply a matter of assimilation of the Francophonie to France, of mimicking or imitating the colonizer. The local and the global are interrelated, and the old opposition of center and margin is no longer tenable" (Hart 1997: 157).

a) What are the different ways that Ukrainian literature and culture can be defined in 2019? Literature and culture produced in the Ukrainian territory? Literature and culture produced by citizens of Ukraine in any language (and, namely, also in Russian)?

b) What is the role and position of Russophone/Russian culture in Ukraine? How can the dynamics of Ukrainian culture lend insight into the possibility of a global Russian culture, or multiple Russian cultures, in the contemporary world?

c) And, eventually, may hybridity as an analytical tool help us address the global "pressing contemporary issues" that have arisen as a result of political and social developments in the post-Soviet space?

Recasting "Ukrainianness" through the Prism of "Russianness"

Framing Ukrainianness and Russianness: following the dissolution of the Soviet Union, the national question has been at the core of the intellectual and political debate in Ukraine and Russia since the 1990s. As emphasized by Igor' Torbakov, in post-Soviet times the ambivalent directions of nation-building policies in Ukraine and Russia reflected a complex process of "rebounding" the contested legacy of their historical encounter, revealing both symmetric and diverging features:

> Not surprisingly, both Ukraine and Russia find themselves in a kind of postcolonial condition, because their histories had been closely entangled throughout the imperial and Soviet eras, and both have been struggling to adapt to the postimperial realities after 1991 [...] The pattern of Ukraine's and Russia's hybridities and ambivalent behaviours during the postimperial period seem to be similar but one might also observe a crucial difference: "Ukraine is only a subaltern, whereas Russia is both subaltern and an empire." (Torbakov 2016: 91)

Taking into account the historical dynamics of the contested Ukrainian–Russian encounter, the duplicity of the role of Ukraine in the imperial ventures—"as the core of the Russian and Soviet projects, on the one hand, and as the center of the anti-imperial and anti-Soviet resistance on the other"—and its special status as "a contested borderlands" (Hrytsak 2015: 733–734) between empires makes the postcolonial "not enough" to describe its complex dynamics. Though assuming that "Ukraine was not a classical colony of the Russian Empire" (Kappeler 2003: 178)—whereby it lacked most of the classical attributes of colonies, such as "geographic, cultural, and racial distance"—the paradox still lies in the fact that here, as emphasized by Georgii Kas'ianov, "[i]t is possible to consider Ukraine as an example of postcolonial syndromes without colonialism"[21] (Volodarskii 2017a): these syndromes include the reframing of diverging memories, cultural categories and identity markers along rigid binary lines.

The cultural specificity of the Ukrainian postcolonial condition was thoroughly theorized already in the early 1990s by Marko Pavlyshyn, who highlighted how modern Ukrainian tradition "had been built up on a binary opposition between the self and the other, where the other was the intruder, the colonizer, the enemy" (1992: 48). Even today we can understand the historical complexity of Ukrainian postcoloniality only through the lenses of its oppositional relation with the external "hegemonic discourse" taking shape in the contemporary Russian Federation, where "[Belarusians and] Ukrainians are still regarded among the ethnic groups of the 'near abroad' as particularly close relatives, with whom one gladly cooperates and to whom one is ready to make certain concessions, but whom one does not recognize as socially and culturally equal or accept as independent nations with national states" (Kappeler 2003: 181). Interestingly enough, whereas on the one hand this kind of narrative shows how in the case of contemporary Russia "the postcolonial discourse has not undergone a social process of deconstruction" (Berg 2004) yet,[22] on the other this also helps us

---

21 "Украину можно рассматривать как пример постколониальных синдромов без колониализма."

22 As Mikhail Berg noted already in 2004: "For the Russian consciousness, the process of colonisation was more than controversial, since Russians, who saw themselves as an imperial nation, still nowadays feel not so much like colonisers as liberators (of European countries from the fascist yoke, of the countries in the Far East and Africa from the advancing American imperialism, and—even earlier—of the former Soviet republics in the Caucasus and Central Asia from the aggressive politics of Turkey [...] in other words, the postcolonial discourse has not undergone a social process of deconstruction, and for this reason in the future we will also talk more often about a post-imperial, rather than postcolonial, situation—although they structurally and chronologically coincide in many respects" (Berg 2004; Для русского сознания процесс колонизации был более, чем противоречивым, так как русские, ощущавшие себя имперской нацией, до сих ощущают себя не столько колонизаторами, сколько освободителями — стран Европы от ига фашизма, стран Дальнего Востока и Африки от наступающего американского империализма, еще раньше бывших советских республик Кавказа и Средней Азии от агрессивной политики Турции — [...]

clarify how still nowadays Ukrainian postcoloniality and "postcolonial syndromes" paradoxically emerge from the conflicts engendered by cultural proximity. Mykola Riabchuk puts it in historical perspective,

> The simple truth is that Ukrainians were not discriminated against as *Little Russians*, i.e., as loyal members of a Russian regional subgroup, who recognize their subordinate position and do not claim any specific/equal cultural rights. But as *Ukrainians*, i.e., as members of a nationally self-aware and culturally self-confident group, they were not merely discriminated against, but also politically persecuted as dangerous "nationalists." (2010: 12)

Here we may grasp the peculiar historical continuity of post-Soviet narratives with imperial and Soviet "hegemonic discourses," which today still come to affect contemporary cultural and political dynamics in the region. Following these lines, according to Roman Dubasevych (2016: 38), the "term 'post-imperial' thus seems for several reasons to better match the complex reality of the Ukrainian-Russian encounter."[23] Most fundamentally, the postimperial frame creates the ground for discussing the case of Ukrainian–Russian cultural relations in light of the contested annexation of Crimea to Russia (March 2014) and the armed conflict that erupted in Donbas (April 2014), since even "if before 2014 the anti-imperial tendencies in Ukraine never led to interethnic violence, they manifested themselves in symbolic struggle over cultural hegemony, embodied in the reluctance to recognize Russian as a second official language, and in multiple 'memory wars' " (Dubasevych 2016: 136). According to Dubasevych's insights, the present conflict could be thus interpreted "as an effect of a long-term alienation between Ukraine

---

Иначе говоря, постколониальный дискурс не подвергся общественной процедуре деконструкции, поэтому в дальнейшем мы также будем чаще говорить о постимперской, а не постколониальный ситуации, хотя они структурно и хронологически во многом совпадают).

23 "First of all, it accounts for the spatial and historical proximity of both cultures, epitomized in the highly controversial Russian topoi of 'bratskii narod' ['brother nation'] and Malorossiia ['Little Russia']. In addition and chronological continuation, it correlates with the involvement in the Soviet project where both, Russians and Ukrainians, undoubtedly stood much nearer to its foundation and the center of power, and were 'more equal' than any other representatives from the Asian, Caucasian or Baltic periphery" (Dubasevych 2016: 138).

and Russia, Ukrainophiles and Russophiles, that has been growing since Ukrainian independence in 1991" (2016: 134).

In the Ukrainian intellectual environment these dynamics intensely affected the conceptualization of the national canon: today the litmus test for the meaning of Ukrainianness and attitudes towards it still remains the language question. The problem stems from the fact that in contemporary Ukraine, besides the people who identify themselves as ethnically Russian, there is also a large community of Russian-language Ukrainians.[24] In light of the very complex and fluid ethnolinguistic pattern of contemporary Ukraine, the definition of the cumbersome nature of Russian language and culture in post-Soviet times thus continues to play a central role in the debate around the definition of the national identity.

In September 2017, while discussing the recent developments in defining "Ukrainianness" in the national debate, Ukrainian philosopher Serhii Datsiuk significantly declared that "in the coming decades the solution of the Ukrainian question is not possible without the solution of the Russian question"[25] (Datsiuk 2017). This followed the publication of controversial commentaries by Galician intellectuals, such as Taras Prokhas'ko (2017), Iurii Andrukhovych (2017a; 2017b; 2017c) and Iurii Vynnychuk (2017), debating the Ukrainian question on the online platform *Zbruch*. In these commentaries, the Russian language was depicted as an attribute of the "enemy," "a language of violence" (*mova nasyl'stva*), which is embodied by those Ukrainians who are not able even "to sleep" in the national language, that is, the "Ukrainian Russians" (*Ukraïns'ki rosiiany*)—the term used by Prokhas'ko (2017) in his column entitled "Do You Sleep in Ukrainian?" (*Chy ty spysh ukraïns'koiu?*) to address indiscriminately both ethnic Russians and Russian speakers in Ukraine. Paradoxically, in his analysis of the problematic relationship between literary text and territory within

---

24 "As the last national census of December 2001 indicated, more than 17 % of the population, that is, 8.5 million inhabitants, classified themselves as ethnically Russian. There is, apart from the Russians, the largest group of non-Russians, declaring Russian their mother tongue, mostly Ukrainian (14.8 % of all Ukrainians, that is about 5.5 million people), but also members of minorities other than Russian" (Besters-Dilger 2009: 7).

25 "вирішення українського питання без вирішення російського питання в найближчі десятки років неможливе."

Russia, Il'ia Kukulin similarly came to the conclusion that "in an era of regret and anxiety over Russian state collapse and turmoil around its (re) expansion, the cultural problem of Russianness—whether conceived as an overarching matrix of many cultures and people, unique ethnic identity, or nation wrapped in an imperial destiny—has yet to be resolved" (Kukulin 2019: 181). Here we may witness the persistent entanglement between the solution of the "cultural problem of Russianness" (Kukulin 2019: 181) and the creation of a shared and inclusive "Ukrainianness" in the post-Soviet space.

Yet the developments of the national question should be viewed and interpreted within the broader context of the search for new self-identification in post-Soviet societies. Interestingly, it was only in the aftermath of the Euromaidan revolution in 2013–2014—the wave of protests starting in Maidan Nezalezhnosti in Kyiv on the night of November 21, 2013, after the Ukrainian government's decision to suspend the signing of the association agreement with the European Union—that scholars and observers in post-Soviet studies started to highlight the emergence of a "civic turn" in codifying the national identity in Ukraine (Gerasimov 2014; Goble 2015; Kulyk 2015, 2016; Pavlyshyn 2016a). From this vantage point, Ukrainian "hybridity" (Gerasimov 2014: 32) appeared to be a new form of collective subjectivity, as it offered new terms to describe "Ukrainianness [...] as an attribute freely chosen by people favourably disposed to the Ukrainian nation-state without regard to ethnicity or cultural orientation" (Pavlyshyn 2016a: 76–77). The (re)emergence of this language of self-description in post-Soviet societies is the result of a long-term process, which still lacks a full-fledged explanatory model. According to the Ukrainian historian Andrii Portnov: "To define this new language, the new Ukrainian studies needs to analyze the specifically post-Soviet Ukrainian hybridity as a distinctive and autonomous subjectivity and fully accept that Ukraine is a complex and dynamic society, which requires nuanced inquiry" (2015: 730). Conceptualizing Ukrainian hybridity, we deal with "a fundamentally interdisciplinary research field in which history meets anthropology, economics, sociology, literary studies, political philosophy, and art history" (Portnov 2015: 731).

Indeed, it is especially the field of "literary politics" that since Ukrainian independence has seemed to privilege "the plurality and hybridity of national and cultural identities" (Rewakowicz 2018: 2). As suggested by Maria Rewakowicz in her recent work titled *Ukraine's Quest for Identity: Embracing Cultural Hybridity in Literary Imagination*, "the issue facing literary critics (which till now has not been adequately addressed) is to decide how to arrive at the body of texts that form a national literature" (2018: 2). And here the debate comes to emblematically include the ongoing negotiation around the actual content and shape of Ukrainianness.

Following Rewakowicz's stance, it is the space of Ukrainian literature that in the long term better reflects the room for hybrid forms—and their contestation—in the post-Soviet space.[26] Especially in the aftermath of the revolutionary cycles experienced by Ukrainians throughout the last decades (i.e. the Revolution on Granite in 1990, the Orange Revolution in 2004–2005, and the Euromaidan Revolution in 2013–2014), we may use and readapt the postcolonial categories to Ukraine as a post-Soviet (and post-Maidan) society for creating new tools for translating the new *local* dynamics. The proposed approach is aimed at creating a productive path to disembodying *nation-ness* in the post-Soviet space and, especially, at achieving an understanding of how, paradoxically, an answer to the eternal question on the role and position of global Russian culture can be found "only provisionally and, paradoxically, locally."

The Long Road to Post-Soviet Transition: A Russophone Perspective

This book is aimed at deeply rethinking and better understanding the different approaches to the "Russian question" in Ukraine, by analysing both the political and cultural narratives that emerged before and after the Ukrainian–Russian clash of discourses which followed the contested annexation of Crimea to Russia and the military aggression against Eastern Ukraine in 2014. My study is based mainly on the results of a research carried out from 2012 to 2019, including interviews with prominent cultural figures

---

26 "In the aftermath of the fall of the Soviet Empire, the issue of the social role of the literary work and its creators has reemerged, primarily in the context of a newly earned freedom and the state's seeming attempts at nationalizing agenda, forcing writers and intellectuals alike to negotiate cultural positions" (Rewakowicz 2018: 2).

(cultural journal/magazine editors, publishers, writers, scholars) conducted in Kyiv, Donets'k and Kharkiv on the eve of Ukraine's Euromaidan. Through the lens of the intertwining of political and cultural developments in post-Soviet Ukraine (and parallel dynamics in Russia), throughout the sections of the present book it is possible to retrace the origins of the debate on hybridity and hybrid subjectivities in post-Soviet times.

Under the umbrella of the global decentralizing process of traditional literary and cultural studies, I mainly devote my attention to the provisional status of a "displaced transition" experienced by cultural actors and phenomena emerging "in between" national languages and traditions. The category of hybridity discussed in this research (and its variegated vocabulary in theoretical discourse, such as métissage, transculturation and creolization) was developed mostly by postcolonial studies to problematize the discourse of empire, by revealing the "in-between space" where the "meaning of culture" takes shape. By going further in defining the rather generalizing theory famously advanced by Homi K. Bhabha,[27] I will follow Anjali Prabhu's further theorization of hybridity. Turning to the legacy of Frantz Fanon and Édouard Glissant,[28] she attempted to reframe the concept by highlighting the need to demarcate "a particular framework or closing-off of an historical moment, action or geographical space *as* hybrid by also specifying the terms between or among which such hybridity occurs or is called up" (Prabhu 2007: 5):

---

27 "Terms of cultural engagement, whether antagonistic or affiliative, are produced performatively. The representation of difference must not be hastily read as the reflection of pre-given ethnic or cultural traits set in the fixed tablet of tradition. The social articulation of difference, from the minority perspective, is a complex, on-going negotiation that seeks to authorize cultural hybridities that emerge in moments of historical transformation" (Bhabha 1994: 2).

28 "Hybridity as it can be identified in Fanon is tied to revolutionary social change [...] while most postcolonial theories of hybridity, in their wish to be revolutionary, tend to overstate the ability of hybridity to dismantle power structures. Glissant's hybridity brings together reality and thought and challenges Marxian informed thinking to engage more consequentially to the idea of 'difference.' In this way, hybridity, as it can be gleaned from the thought of Frantz Fanon and Edouard Glissant [...] reconnects more credibly to the impulse for the formation of postcolonial studies as a discipline" (Prabhu 2007: xiv).

> I therefore think it is important to provisionally, but clearly distinguish between hybridity as a theoretical concept and a political stance that we can argue, and hybridity as a social reality with historical specificity [...] For me, the most productive theories of hybridity are those that effectively balance the task of inscribing a functional-instrumental version of the relation between culture and society with that of enabling the more utopian/collective image of society. (Prabhu 2007: 2)

Following Prabhu's analytical theory of hybridity, and adapting it to the case of post-Soviet Ukraine, we will see how hybrid subjectivities are first a product of a cultural debate that emerged in Imperial and Soviet times, and then the result of a political clash of national paradigms in post-Soviet times: nowadays these are subjected to a constant internal and external delegitimizing process, influencing the transitoriness—or provisionality—of this "third space," as alternatively being subject to processes of cultural appropriation or peripheralization. In the proposed analytical framework, Ukrainian hybridity appears to be "tied to revolutionary social change," and "linked to contingency and [...] time-bound."[29] More importantly, Ukrainian hybridity entails *practices of dis-identification*, by providing "a way out of binary thinking," (Prabhu 2007: 1) and responds to the possibility of a third space of enunciation, whereas it represents "a completely new political community that cannot rely on any preexisting 'national' structures to sustain itself" (Gerasimov, Mogilner 2015: 720). Finally, it is *deterritorialized*, whereas—in spite of the misuse of language categories in the political debate—Russian in Ukraine is becoming an ex-territorial language, which is not necessarily linked to a particular territory or entity and a particular ethnicity.

To my knowledge, this is the first book to investigate contemporary Ukrainian cultural developments through the lens of Russian-language literary production and the Russian-language intellectual community's position. While Russian and Ukrainian cultural developments have been framed as the outcome of the Soviet collapse and the embrace of globalization (Chernetsky 2007), recent studies tend to privilege only one of the two aspects of the issue, which is here analysed in light of a constant

---

29 "That is, the analysis of hybridity (and of specific instances of it) is obliged to account for historicity, while at the same time the impulses of this process are to valorize synchrony over diachrony" (Prabhu 2007: 5).

dialogue between Russian and Ukrainian Studies. Furthermore, while in the volume authored by Maria G. Rewakowicz (2018) the focus seems to rely mostly on pre-Maidan developments, here I draw an analysis of the long-term outcomes of the debate on cultural hybridity, considering both "the phase of distinctly post-Soviet and transitional dynamics of the first two decades of independence" (Rewakowicz 2018: viii) and the subsequent crystallization of these dynamics in post-Maidan realities. Whereas Chernetsky (2019: 58) identifies the Orange Revolution of 2004 as the true starting point for "the process of rethinking and reclaiming identities by Ukraine's Russian-language writers in the newly independent Ukraine," in my opinion it is worth analyzing the phenomenon in a broader perspective, going from the early years of Ukrainian independence to the outcomes of the Euromaidan in 2013–2014 that "kicked into higher gear" (Chernetsky 2019: 59) the dynamics of the previous revolutionary cycle.

Here the prehistory of the phenomenon, which was the subject of my previous study (Puleri 2016), has been deliberately assigned to a marginal role, in order to privilege a focus on the present situation and to prevent any attempts at formulating historical and ideological projections. This book is not a history of Ukrainian Russian-language literature, nor does it include all its contemporary variants and actors: rather, the premise of this study is that, while looking at these plural literary phenomena, it is worth focusing on the profoundly diverse and heterogeneous range of positions, identities and forms emerging from their provisional status, and on the need to analyse them through the lens of the global tendency towards the transnationalization of cultural practices. This helps us describe Ukrainian hybridity as a "time-bounded" condition that, on the one hand, is deeply rooted in the Ukrainian social and political experience in post-Soviet times and, on the other hand, still answers to and follows global cultural dynamics and trends.

In this study I hence propose the use of new analytical tools for translating the recent social developments in Ukraine through the lens of literature.[30] On the one hand, it is postcolonial multilingualism, symbolic

---

30 Amongst the most relevant Ukrainian cultural and social phenomena that are beyond the scope of this book, we should certainly mention the case of national minorities in the territory of Ukraine (i.e. among them, Bulgarians, Crimean

"interstitiality" and pluricentric counternarratives to established social conceptions of identity, nation and culture that prominently emerge in the Russophone literary production. On the other, the "minor paradigm" elaborated by Gilles Deleuze and Félix Guattari (1975) works as a useful methodological approach to interpret the "collective enunciation" conveyed by these cultural actors working in an intermediate space between the Ukrainian and Russian "great (or established)" literatures and narratives. As for the selection of the literary texts under scrutiny, I have opted for prose works by Andrei Kurkov, Aleksei Nikitin and Vladimir Rafeenko. The reasons behind this privileged focus are twofold: on the one hand, prose works by the mentioned authors are revealing for the heterogeneous evolutionary, regional, sociopolitical and market dynamics affecting the creation of full-fledged cultural discourses and narratives in post-Soviet Ukraine; on the other, the peculiar focus of Russophone prose on "the crowding out and displacement of experiences that are painful to protagonists and narrators alike and that compromise the integrity of their sense of self" (Kukulin 2018: 60) still represents an overlooked field of analysis in literary criticism.[31]

Finally, this is the framework for developing the two intertwining sections of the book, focusing respectively on the pre- and post-Maidan periods. In the opening chapter, after providing a brief overview of the historical background of the postcolonial situation in present-day Ukraine, I focus on the complex positioning of the Russophone literary phenomenon in the Ukrainian post-Soviet national canon. Analysing the conceptualization of the hybrid cultural elements in the post-Soviet area, it is possible to observe the rise of a contrast between the cultural "exclusivist" and "inclusivist" attitudes in the Ukrainian intellectual debate. It is the product of the renewed social and political clash between the Ukrainian and Russian

---

Tatars, Romanians, Hungarians) and the role of the Ukrainian diaspora. This certainly deserves attention as well and demands different studies.

31 In light of the recognized "role reversal" in modern Russian literature, poetry has been described as more able to have global contacts and transnational connections. More often, literary scholars have devoted their attention to the peculiar concern of Russian-language poetry of the 2000s for analysing "the historical traumas of the contemporary mind" and "pointing to ways those traumas may be healed" (Kukulin 2018: 60).

"national systems" at the dawn of the Soviet collapse. The ideologization of the ethnolinguistic factor in the post-Soviet area gives birth to competing ideologies, which draw new "imagined borders" in the Ukrainian literary space, as being the result of the polarization of the Russian and Ukrainian respective national historical narratives.

The second chapter provides readers with a challenging reconstruction of the most widespread attitudes concerning the role of language for the definition of the boundaries of national culture among the foremost Russian-language writers and critics in contemporary Ukraine and Russia. The last part of the chapter is dedicated to a discussion of the role of anthologies, publishing houses and literary prizes in the process of cultural negotiations between Ukraine and Russia, Ukrainian culture and Russian culture. At the crossroads between these seemingly binary juxtapositions, new cultural phenomena emerge under the sign of hybridity.

In the third chapter I propose a new understanding of the heterogeneous framework of enunciations conveyed by contemporary Ukrainian Russian-language writers. By reading and interpreting Andrei Kurkov's (*Death and the Penguin*, 1996; *The Good Angel of Death*, 1998), Aleksei Nikitin's (*Istemi*, 2011; *Mahjong*, 2012) and Vladimir Rafeenko's works (*The Moscow Divertissement*, 2011), we may see a new artistic attempt to recompose the fragments of the existential mosaics left unbound in the aftermath of the Soviet collapse.

In the fourth chapter, which opens the second section of the book, I move to the recent cultural developments in the aftermath of the so-called "Ukraine Crisis" (2013–2014). The chapter approaches literary processes in Ukraine as emblematic for the general epistemological (and hence political) crisis in the country, and as an important litmus test allowing a diagnosis of the crisis. Deconstructing "Russianness" and "Ukrainianness," I highlight the emerging positioning of Russophone authors in the aftermath of the Euromaidan "revolution of hybridity."

The aim of the fifth chapter is to rethink the different approaches to "value-based" politics—and social subgroupings' reactions to it—in the post-Soviet area through the lens of the post-Maidan Ukrainian scene. An accurate tracking of the policies normativizing the field of culture on the one hand, and of blurred cultural boundaries on the other, helps us question the fixed constructs of national and cultural identity when looking at the ever-changing post-Soviet social milieus.

In the final chapter I explore the current reshaping of the contested language issue in the post-Maidan intellectual debate. In this section I examine the preliminary outcomes of the still ongoing war in Donbas as an influence on the concept of the Ukrainian literary and social space, by analysing the main narratives of the "crisis" played and enacted by Russian-speaking literary actors, in light of the emerging "postcolonial ethics" stemming from their role in public debates. Here the peculiar cases of Aleksei Nikitin (*Victory Park*, 2014; *The Orderly from Institutskaia Street*, 2016), Aleksandr Kabanov (*In the Language of the Enemy*, 2017) and Vladimir Rafeenko (*The Descartes' Demon*, 2014; *The Length of Days*, 2016) lie at the core of my analysis.

Part I: From Culture to Politics—
Displaced Hybridity/ies (1991–2013)

Chapter 1 The Missing Hybridity: Framing the Ukrainian Cultural Space

At the end of the 1980s, all was still simple and straightforward. On political maps a huge part of the planet was uniformly painted red. This was the monolithic "evil empire," the one and indivisible Soviet Union. But suddenly the country of victorious socialism was tearing apart in colourful scraps. Armenia! Kazakhstan! Uzbekistan! Kyrgyzstan! Tajikistan! And more! And more!... The Western world was in confusion. There used to be one country, now there were many. And each one, apparently, had its own history and culture, hopes and claims, disappointments, misfortunes and blood... How to relate to them? What to expect from them? What do they bring to the world?[32] (Volos 2005: 439)

In the opening lines of the prologue to his novel *Khurramabad* (2000), the Russian writer Andrei Volos (b. 1955, Stalinabad—now Dushanbe) introduces us to the pressing cultural and political issues that have arisen from the collapse of the Soviet Union in 1991. In his novel Volos, the son of Russian immigrants in Soviet Tajikistan, aims to retrace the historical encounter between different languages, cultures and traditions in the former Soviet republic, in order to eventually shed light on the reasons behind the sociopolitical upheaval that shook the Central Asian state in

---

32 "Еще в конце восьмидесятых годов все было просто и понятно. Огромный кусок планеты на политических картах однородно закрашивался красным. Это была монолитная «империя зла,» единый и неделимый Советский Союз. И вдруг страна победившего социализма стала расползаться на разноцветные лоскуты. Армения! Азербайджан! Казахстан! Узбекистан! Киргизия! Таджикистан! И еще! И еще!... Западный мир пришел в замешательство. Была одна страна — стало много. И в каждой, оказывается, — своя история и культура, свои собственные надежды и претензии, свои разочарования, беды и кровь... Как к ним относиться? Чего от них ждать? Что они несут миру?"

the early 1990s.[33] While posing as a cultural mediator of one of the fifteen new nation states, or "colourful scraps," that had arisen from the ashes of the "one and indivisible" USSR, Volos highlights the urgency of engaging with the investigation of the profound cultural and political consequences of the tremendous historical rift that globally affected the region.[34]

It is undeniable that the dissolution of the Soviet system has brought into being a radical transformation that has deeply affected the reconfiguration of the political and cultural mapping of the post-Soviet space. Throughout the 1990s, the elaboration of new national cultural models in the former fifteen union republics took shape on the basis of the ideal "return to (post-ideological) normality": languages, cultures, histories and traditions that had been neglected by Soviet rule could now come to life again after the unexpected *explosion* of the Soviet system. It is no surprise that in his last work, entitled *Culture and Explosion* (*Kul'tura i vzryv*, 1992), the prominent Soviet semiologist Iurii Lotman also devoted his attention to the complex dynamics of cultural change in the territory of the former Soviet Union. In his analysis of the explosive processes of cultural development, still in 1992, Lotman emblematically identified the dynamics taking place in the region as following the traditional concepts of binarism (2009: 171).[35]

Following Lotman's reflections, we can describe the process experienced in most of the newly born post-Soviet states at the dawn of the collapse

---

33 In 1992–1997, in Tajikistan, one of the most violent civil wars in the post-Soviet space erupted, leading to "over 50,000 deaths and more than 250,000 refugees" (Heathershaw 2009: 21).

34 Indeed, in *Khurramabad* Volos' narrative about post-Soviet Tajikistan remains quite open to new ideological projections of the Soviet experience. As Clemens Günther and Svetlana Sirotinina (2019: 88) put it: "Although the novel is not free from traces of Soviet nostalgia, their characters are not longing for a return to the Soviet Union but rather for a utopian Eurasian space in whose hybridity they could peacefully co-exist."

35 Most fundamentally, as the Soviet semiologist further develops in his semiotic theory of culture: "In binary structures, moments of explosion rupture the continuous chain of events, unavoidably leading not only to deep crises but also to radical renewals" (Lotman 2009: 169) [В бинарных структурах моменты взрыва могут разрывать цепь непрерывных последовательностей, что неизбежно ведет к глубоким кризисам, но и к коренным обновлениям (Lotman 2000: 144)].

of the Union as "the moment of exhaustion of the explosion" (*moment izcherpaniia vzryva*), which is "not only the originating moment of future development but also the place of self-knowledge: the inclusion of those mechanisms of history which must themselves explain what has occurred"[36] (Lotman 2009: 15). In such a stage of cultural development, we witness the emergence of rigid binary schemes (i.e. self vs. other; superior vs. inferior; centre vs. periphery) for describing the complexity of much more nuanced realms. Thus, a new system of signification exists to take shape from the overthrow of the old symbolic values of the previous era: such is the case of the post-Soviet region, where the flaws and faults of (Soviet) internationalism came to be contested and overruled by the new (post-Soviet) national revivals arising in the former union republics. In some cases, this gradually brought also the unreflective reactualization of the binary opposition between the (Soviet) colonizer and the (post-Soviet) colonized in national political and cultural debates.[37] Nonetheless, as Lotman (2009: 65) notes in his analysis of the unpredictable outcomes produced by the collision of different systems of signification in the history of culture, more often than not "the newly formed phenomenon appropriates the name of one or other of the colliding structures, such that something which is, in principle, new lies hidden under an old façade."[38]

Similarly, more than a decade later, in her study *Post-Soviet Literature and the Aesthetics of Transculturation* (*Postsovetskaia literatura i estetika transkul'turatsii*, 2004), Madina Tlostanova shed light on the ambivalence of the colonial model in the Soviet era and on its outcomes for the post-Soviet epistemological process. She argues that, while the whole system of signification—including language, customs and festivities of the

---

36 "В сфере истории это не только исходный момент будущего развития, но и место самопознания: включаются те механизмы истории, которые должны ей самой объяснить, что произошло" (Lotman 2000: 23).

37 This was still harshly criticized in 2012 by the British scholar Neil Lazarus. While resisting the idea of the USSR as an imperial power, Lazarus pointed to the alleged "experientially based and viscerally felt 'post-communism' of scholars in the post-Soviet sphere" (2012: 121).

38 "[…] новое явление очень часто присваивает себе наименование одной из столкнувшихся структур, на самом деле скрывая под старым фасадом нечто принципиально новое" (Lotman 2000: 63).

empire—was forged by the Soviet "colonizer," in the USSR, the colonial model "was made complex by the Soviet ideology, which in its discourse and external semiotic manifestations disguised itself as a supranational discourse, becoming a hybrid form of imperial configuration"[39] (Tlostanova 2004: 194). This explains the complex dynamics of the post-Soviet cultural field, where today we deal with "categorical assumptions" that make "the national language and literary canon" an integral "part of state ideology"[40] (Tlostanova 2004: 385) in the new nation states that have arisen since the *explosion* of the USSR.

Most fundamentally, the study of post-Soviet cultures reveals a controversial reception of transcultural subjectivities and phenomena: throughout the recent history of the region the cultural processes of appropriation, which hybrid subjectivities have been subjected to, trace back every attempt at methodological categorization to imperial/colonial binarism. Hybridity thus came to be *blurred* within the complex framework of ethnic groups, religions and languages. Following these lines, Tlostanova (2004: 192) in her study symbolically describes hybrid subjectivities as a "missing actor" (*otsutstvuiushchii akter*) in Imperial and Soviet hegemonic narratives.[41]

---

39 "[…] усложнялась советской идеологией, которая на словах и в своих внешних семиотических проявлениях маскировалась под наднациональный дискурс, в результате сама становясь гибридной формой имперской конфигурации."

40 In her study, Tlostanova extensively argues for the urgency of addressing "the deconstruction of previously categorical assumptions concerning the lasting organic connection of the territory, the state and people, language, literature and nation, according to which the national language and literary canon became part of state ideology" (2004: 385; деконструкция прежде непререкаемых представлений о прочной органической связи территории, государства и народа, языка, литературы и нации, в соответствии с которыми национальный язык и национальная канонизированная литература становились частью государственной идеологии).

41 As Tlostanova puts it: "[…] the hybrid, interethnic and intercultural identification was not recognised or was reduced to a single dominant element, thus greatly simplifying the psychological model and the epistemological configuration of the hybrid subject. The writer was thus forced, unintentionally, to reach out to a well-defined ethnocultural and linguistic model, and rarely had the possibility of finding his own realization as a hybrid subjectivity, in the full sense of the word (2004: 194; […] гибридная межэтническая и межкультурная

Despite these controversial dynamics, if "on the one hand, the official Russian epistemology does not include in the field of its attention and reflection the category of hybridity due to negative attitudes towards mediality and cultural mixing," on the other "the very history of the Russian and Soviet empires with their huge number of examples of mixed marriages, ethnic groups, religions and languages, offers a large number of subjectivities that match the hybrid model"[42] (Tlostanova 2004: 192–193). Thus, even today the creation of new interpretive paradigms for the study of trans-cultural—and transnational—traditions still relies on the deconstruction of the organic bonds of nations with language, territory and literature in the post-Soviet space. I believe that the reflective adoption of postcolonial analytical tools for the study of post-Soviet societies can play a valuable role in achieving a better understanding of the reasons behind the current polarization of cultural practices and political orientations in the region—and namely in this work, in investigating the debate around the position of the "(post-)imperial" Russian language and culture in nowadays Ukraine. It is no surprise that, among the post-Soviet countries, it is especially Ukraine, with its "high degree of cultural, social and political diversity," that arises as "a prime laboratory for the study of modern politics and culture" (Kasianov, Ther 2009: 2).

идентификация отрицалась или сводилась к одному доминирующему элементу, заметно упрощавшему психологический рисунок и эпистемологическую конфигурацию гибридного субъекта. Писатель тем самым невольно был вынужден тяготеть к определенной этнокультурной модели и языковой, редко имея возможность реализовать себя в полном смысле слова как гибридного индивида).

42 "[...] с одной стороны, официальная российская эпистемология не включает в поле своего внимания и осмысления категорию гибридности в силу отрицательного отношения к медиальности и культурному смешению [...] с другой стороны, сама история Российской и Советской империй с их огромным количеством примеров смешанных браков, этносов, религий и языков, представляет большое количество реальных субъектностей, отвечающих гибридной модели."

Ukraine: A Laboratory of Political and Cultural Identity/ies

In his article provocatively entitled "Does Ukraine Have a History?" (1995), Mark Von Hagen, in the early 1990s, described how the "experienced past" of the post-Soviet country was still in search of legitimacy. Retracing the critical historical junctures affecting the configuration of the territory of modern Ukraine, Von Hagen clarified that the question "must be seen as a part of a greater dilemma of eastern and central Europe" (1995: 659): a region that was long subject first to the rule of great dynastic monarchies, that is, to the Polish–Lithuanian Commonwealth, the Tsarist empire and the Habsburg monarchy, and then, after the First World War, to either Nazi Germany or the Soviet Union. By virtue of its position on the map of Europe, Ukraine played the crucial role of a borderland "not only of different state formations" but also "of different civilizational and cultural zones" (Plokhy 2007: 37): on the one hand, this deprived it of "full historiographical legitimacy" (Von Hagen 1995: 660) in light of the statehood it had acquired only recently, while on the other it "contributed to the fuzziness and fragmentation of Ukrainian identity" (Plokhy 2007: 38).

Still nowadays, the heterogeneous historical experiences that took shape in the regions making up contemporary Ukraine hinder the actualization of a shared narrative of the past, which could function to legitimize the new state. In the 1990s, the canonization of the great national history, which was developed in opposition to the hegemonic discourses of the Polish and Russian "neighbours" during the second half of the nineteenth century and revamped in the aftermath of independence, saw the rise of a strongly contested reception.[43]

Mykhailo Hrushevs'kyi (1866–1934) and the so-called populist school of Ukrainian historiography elaborated a national history of the Ukrainian people: its founding ideals were embodied by the myth of Cossack origins and its ideals of freedom and equality. As Andreas Kappeler notes

---

43 As the Ukrainian historian Georgii Kas'ianov (2009: 11) notes: "The year 1991 became the turning point [...] Nationalized history began to fulfill important instrumental functions: legitimize the newly established state and its attendant elite; establish territorial and chronological conceptions of the Ukrainian nation; and confirm the appropriateness of that nation's existence as a legal successor in the consciousness of its citizens and neighbours alike."

(2009: 57): "This national myth was diametrically opposed to the 'aristocratic' values of the Polish nation and 'despotic' nature of Russia." The appropriate metaphor proposed by Mykola Riabchuk in his essay "The Ukrainian Friday and Its Two Robinsons" (*Ukraïns'kyi Piatnytsia i ioho dva Robinzony*, 2013) embodies the complex directions drawn by the Polish and Russian hegemonic discourses throughout the course of modern history to essentialize the Ukrainian alternative as a choice of civilization between the "West" and the "East," that is, between a "European-oriented" system of values and an Eastern Orthodox Slavic one. Eventually, as Yaroslav Hrytsak (2004: 232–233) notes, the post-Soviet Ukrainian historiography adopted the interpretation of Ukraine as a "civilizational borderland," promoting it as "[t]he only major addendum to 'Hrushevs'kyi's scheme'."

Still in the post-Soviet era the "teleological" character (Plokhy 2007: 30) of the Ukrainian national narrative seemed to take shape from the need to "reclaim" one's own past, (re)creating a new (old?) system of signification based on a binary opposition to the experience of imperial oppression. However, while in the early twentieth century the national narrative was there to challenge the "All-Russian" imperial narrative and the hegemonic ambitions of a much more "westernized" Poland (Plokhy 2005), it was in the aftermath of the dissolution of the USSR that the definitive canonization of this "old" paradigm in the "new" state led to the crystallization of the exclusive character of contemporary Ukrainian history.[44]

Despite these controversial dynamics, as Kappeler (2009: 63) notes, "[m]any personalities of Ukrainian history cannot adequately be described as Ukrainians, Russians, Poles or Jews, but their lives and historical roles have to be told as multiethnic or transethnic." Similarly, and even more decisively, in his reconstruction of the Ukrainian cultural experience throughout the centuries, Vitaly Chernetsky (2019: 51) argues that "[i]f there is a recurring theme that can be traced through the history of Ukrainian culture, is

---

44 As Andreas Kappeler put it in 2009: "Ukrainian history was mostly a narrative of suffering and martyrdom under the rule of foreign elites and states. Poles, Russians and Jews living in Ukraine were perceived as agents of foreign rule and oppressors of the Ukrainian people. There was no positive place for them in the Ukrainian national narrative and in the collective memory of Ukrainians, nor is there one today" (2009: 57).

that of hybridity and overlapping/contested identifications." In his analysis of premodern and modern developments, Chernetsky highlights the constant interconnection between the definition of political and cultural identities in Ukrainian imperial, Soviet and post-Soviet history. In particular, the "intertwined yet distinct political and cultural realities" of Ukrainian and Russian communities, territories and languages "produced continual shifts and contestation of cultural identities" (Chernetsky 2019: 51). It is also in light of these dynamics that until "recently, the dilemmas of hybrid and split identification faced by cultural producers with ties to Ukraine more often than not remained unsolved" (Chernetsky 2019: 50).

In contextualizing the Ukrainian cultural legacy, it is worth wondering about the specific cultural positioning of authors such as Nikolai Gogol', Taras Shevchenko, Hryhorii Skovoroda and others who worked *between* languages, traditions, and cultures.[45] As Oleh S. Ilnytzkyj (2003: 322) stressed, "these individuals were products of a cross-cultural experience generally unfamiliar to ethnic Russians, but typical for members of Ukrainian society." This experience was "essentially liminal" and "dualistic in terms of language and institutions" (Ilnytzkyj 2003: 322). Whereas still at the end of the sixteenth century "Ukrainian literary texts were composed in at least three languages (Ruthenian, Polish, and Latin)" (Chernetsky 2019: 53), throughout the nineteenth century, especially, the Imperial cultural system was reconceptualized into distinct national models based on romantic vernaculars as part of an ongoing and ever-changing process, establishing new ideological frontiers between the emerging literary phenomena. The rise of the Ukrainian literary system within the "All-Russian" cultural context was thus "filtered" by the use of the Imperial lingua franca. This phenomenon gave birth to a large body of literature in Russian written by Ukrainian authors, which emerged in a composite self-positioning pattern:

> Some writers, like Vasilii Kapnist, Somov, Narezhnyi and Gogol, maintained their regional Ukrainian identities while embracing Russian national identities;

---

45 Here my research will be mainly focused around the complexity of Ukrainian–Russian relations. An analysis of the colonial history of Polish domination in Western Ukraine and its impact on Ukrainian culture and society, which has been the focus of several studies published in the last decade (e.g. see Korek 2007; Ładykowski 2015), lies outside the scope of this work.

some, like Hryhorii Kvitka-Osnovianenko, Mykola Markevych, and Mykhail Drahomanov, existed as "all-Russian"; and others, like Taras Shevchenko, Panteleimon Kulish, Marko Vovchok and Mykola Kostomarov, enjoyed a more or less separate Ukrainian identity. (Ilchuk 2009: 21)

This artistic phenomenon arose from the contact between the different cultural and identity affiliations held by Ukrainian *in-between* literary actors. As George G. Grabowicz (1992: 232) observed, this literary production "should indeed be considered part of Ukrainian literature," even if "there was an inescapable sense for virtually all these writers that Ukrainian literature was a subset of Imperial, All Russian literature." Nonetheless, the Ukrainian writers who gained success at the "centre" of the empire played the important role of cultural mediators between the Russian and Ukrainian societies. In their literary depictions, the Ukrainian "periphery" was transformed and adapted to make it accessible to Russian readership: "Implicitly if not explicitly, their work tended to minimize or aestheticize the differences between Russia and Ukraine, thus discounting the inherent autonomy or 'otherness' of the Ukrainian historical and cultural experience" (Andriewsky 2003: 184).

The case of Nikolai Gogol'/Mykola Hohol' (1809–1852) definitely embodies the fluid cultural dynamics of his epoch. The definition of his national identity has been at the core of intellectual and political debates in Russia and Ukraine, where his literary experience has been included in both the Russian canon (as Nikolai Gogol') and in the Ukrainian one (as Mykola Hohol'). Reading his works, critics have mainly categorized it according to two different periods: the Ukrainian period (1829–1836), including the works devoted to "national" themes, and the Imperial period (1836–1852). Nevertheless, throughout the last decades a huge body of literature on Gogol' has appeared, focusing especially on the hybrid aspects of this literary figure (e.g. see Grabowicz 1994; Luckyj 1998; Ilnytzkyj 2002; Bojanowska 2007). Edyta M. Bojanowska (2007: 6), in her study entitled *Nikolai Gogol. Between Ukrainian and Russian Nationalism*, stresses how the author's national identity "cannot be framed as an either/or question [...] *Whether* Gogol was a Russian or a Ukrainian is thus the wrong question to ask." The periodization of Gogol''s literary production into two distinct artistic phases seems to address the complex duality of the author's experience by means of abstract ideological terms, ignoring the extraordinary patchwork of language, cultural and political elements involved in the formation of his identity. Gogol"s in-between positioning underlies the ambivalence of the literary space imagined by the author. As Myroslav Shkandrij (2001: 115) stressed, "Gogol brought a Ukrainian consciousness to St. Petersburg, that is, structures of thought and feeling that were deeply critical of Russian society, which he drew upon throughout his creative life." Ilnytzkyj (2002), moreover, has tried to define the artistic experience of Gogol'/Hohol' as the outcome of the intersection between three cultural paradigms: the Ukrainian tradition, the Russian model and the Imperial paradigm. This entails a positioning "between cultures" that, as observed by Yuliya Ilchuk (2009), implies an artistic experience moving in an intermediate space "between languages." It is the presence of Ukrainian and hybrid Russo–Ukrainian forms that confers a "defamiliarizing effect" onto Gogol"s literary language: "Positioned on the 'interstices' of two cultures, Gogol existed in the in-between space of cultural ambivalence that diluted the imaginary essence of the Russian nation through a 'distorted' Russian language" (Ilchuk 2009: 19). Thus, Gogol' gives birth to a *transcultural* identity model, which lies outside the rigid parameters of national canonization:

> [...] I only know that I would grant primacy neither to a Little Russian over a Russian nor to a Russian over a Little Russian. Both natures are generously endowed by god, and as if on purpose, each of them in its own way includes in itself that which the other lacks—a clear sign that they are meant to complement each other.[46] (Gogol' 1952: 418)

Gogol"s/Hohol"s "two-souledness" (*dvoedushie*) reflects the duality of the Ukrainian cultural experience: in the author's epoch, as stated by Grabowicz (1992: 224), "the very idea of what is to be a Ukrainian writer (and indeed a 'Ukrainian') was in a state of becoming." Nonetheless, in those same years the publication of Taras Shevchenko's *The Bard* (*Kobzar*, 1940) would offer to Ukrainian intelligentsia "the articulation of an entire cultural language—a language grounded in the Cossack past, its heroic

---

46 "Знаю только то, что никак бы не дал преимущества ни малороссиянину перед русским, ни русскому пред малороссиянином. Обе природы слишком щедро одарены Богом, и как нарочно каждая из них порознь заключает в себе то, чего нет в другой, — явный знак, что они должны пополнить одна другую."

epics (*dumy*) and folklore, as well as a profound sense of loss and victim-ization" (Andriewsky 2003: 192). The new discourse was then capable of deconstructing and demystifying the entire theoretical framework elaborated by the centre of the Empire. Following these lines, it was the ideologization of literary frontiers between the All-Russian and Ukrainian cultural systems that gradually led to the harsh contestation of dual and hybrid cultural experiences:

> By the fourth decade of the nineteenth century, however, those who still tried to maintain a dual Ukrainian-Russian identity were, increasingly, struggling with the issue of a divided loyalty. George Luckyj has described the choice for Ukrainians as the thorns of a dilemma: Gogol or Shevchenko? Empire or Ukraine? (Shkandrij 2001: 31)

The categorization of Nikolai Gogol"s and Taras Shevchenko's artistic experiences in alternative "literary spaces" makes clear their respective roles in the Ukrainian cultural paradigm through the lens of ideology.[47] As Shkandrij (2001: 108–109) emphasized: "[a]t the same time as Shevchenko was indicating the irreconcilability of Ukrainian and Russian interests, Gogol was attempting to resolve the conflict between his 'two souls'."

Following these lines of thought, it is no surprise "that during the Soviet period practically no efforts were made by Soviet scholars to look at Russian-language literary texts written in Ukraine as a distinct coherent corpus" (Chernetsky 2019: 57). Actually, even in post-Soviet times, the ideological legacy of the Imperial and Soviet experience has led to a failure to assimilate the notable duality of the national culture. This has happened precisely because the prehistory of "hybrid subjectivities" still "underwrites the complex processes of transformation currently underway":

> [...] precisely because Russian political and cultural imperialism has for centu-ries compelled Ukrainian authors to write in Russian, contemporary Ukrainian society possesses a well-developed capacity to accept Russophone linguistic and literary realities as parts of a larger Ukrainian continuum. If Nikolai Gogol's writings are claimed as Ukrainian even if composed in Russian, it follows that

---

47 The controversial reception of Gogol' and Shevchenko has been under the focus of several studies for decades (e.g. Luckyj 1971; Grabowicz 1982). In this sec-tion I touched on some of the crucial points of the issue; however, an in-depth analysis of the debate lies outside the scope of this book.

exclusionary attitudes toward linguistic practices in contemporary Ukrainian literature are illogical. (Chernetsky 2019: 51)

Paradoxically, in the contemporary context, "[e]ven though it is clear to all
that there is a vast difference between a forced or imposed hybridity and
a freely-assumed one, the imperial-Soviet experience has made this issue
a painful one for Ukrainian intellectuals" (Shkandrij 2009). Nonetheless,
today it is just this kind of duality that could open the way to a new epistemological and cultural understanding of the inherent hybridity of post-
Soviet realities.

Shifting Social Dynamics in Post-Soviet Ukraine

As the British historian Andrew Wilson (2000) retraces in his analysis of
contemporary Ukrainian politics, in the aftermath of the Soviet collapse the
ground was finally ready for the emergence of a full-fledged independent
state and "unexpected nation."[48] While adopting this definition, Wilson, in
the preface to his work *The Ukrainians: Unexpected Nation* (2000), symbolically addressed the surprise of the international community at witnessing
the rise of a "new *nation*" in Europe with such "pronounced patterns of
ethnic, linguistic, religious and regional diversity" (Wilson 2000: xi). Still,
in 2016 Volodymyr Kulyk's reflections seemed to confirm the peculiar persistence of this complex background, by which the Ukrainian scholar could
ascertain how throughout the history of independent Ukraine "profound
disagreements on the content of national identity stemmed from dissim-
ilar ethnolinguistic profiles and historical trajectories of different regions"
(2016: 593). Nevertheless, despite the stiff competition emerging in intellectual and political debates, during the last decades, the social dynamics
describing the "content of national identity" were not static but rather
constantly fluid and unpredictably shifting.

---

48 According to the British scholar, after the unexpected *explosion* of the USSR in
    Ukraine, symptomatically "there was no real revolution" (Wilson 2015: 102).
    Wilson identifies the alliance between the Communist elite and the "minority
    nationalist movement" as the key to understanding the reasons behind the
    political opportunity to support Ukrainian independence in 1991. In his view,
    this explains "why the country tried to have two catch-up revolutions in 2004
    [i.e. the Orange Revolution] and 2014 [i.e. the Euromaidan Revolution]."

According to the last national census conducted in 2001,[49] more than 130 ethnic groups live in the territory of Ukraine: among them, Ukrainians (77.8 per cent) and Russians (17.3 per cent) are the largest ones, while other major national groups are Belarusians (0.6 per cent), Moldovans (0.5 per cent), Crimean Tatars (0.5 per cent), Bulgarians (0.4 per cent), Hungarians (0.3 per cent) and Romanians (0.3 per cent). The official state language is Ukrainian (67.5 per cent of citizens indicated it as their mother tongue), but Russian (29.6 per cent) is still spoken by a large portion of the population.

Interestingly enough, "despite a decline in the population as a whole" and the insignificant migration rate of ethnic Russians to the Russian Federation, in 2001 "the number of people who declared their nationality as Ukrainian actually increased since the last Soviet census" (Stebelsky 2009: 77).[50] This was first explained as the result of an "ethnic shift" in the self-identification of Russians, who now came to reidentify themselves as Ukrainians (Kuzio 2003). However, in his comparative analysis of the data reported in the last Soviet census in 1989 and the national one in 2001, Ihor Stebelsky (2009) reflected further on the reasons behind the controversial shift in self-identification among the population of Ukraine. He contested the categories used in the first Ukrainian national census, addressing the subtle nuances around the determination of ethnic and language-based identities in post-Soviet times. Stebelsky argued that in 2001, while many people re-identified as Ukrainians, most of them still declared Russian as their native language. He explained this discrepancy as the result of the Soviet nationalities policies, in which "the Soviet Union allowed for Ukrainian as a separate ethnicity,

---

49 See: http://2001.ukrcensus.gov.ua/eng/results/general/ (08/2019). The second All-Ukrainian population census was postponed several times throughout the second decade of the 2000s. At the time of the writing of this book (July 2019), the new census has been scheduled to be held in late 2020.

50 As Ihor Stebelesky (2009: 77) highlights in his study entitled *Ethnic Self-Identification in Ukraine, 1989–2001: Why More Ukrainians and Fewer Russians?*: "While their numbers [i.e. the numbers of Ukrainians] increased from 37.4 to 37.5 million, or by 122.6 thousand, the number of those who declared their nationality Russian decreased from 11.4 to 8.3 million, or by about 3 million people. As a result, the share of the declared Ukrainians and Russians shifted dramatically, from 72.7 and 22.1 percent in 1989, to 78.1 and 17.3 percent, respectively, in 2001."

but continued to confer a much higher status on the Russian language and culture" (Stebelsky 2009: 78–79). This background led then to a situation where "many Ukrainians have adopted Russian as their preferred language, developed 'multiple' or 'hybrid' identities, and some (notably in Crimea) have become Russian in terms of their ethnic self-identification" (Stebelsky 2009: 79). Following these lines, Stebelsky (2009: 98) significantly emphasized that it was mainly "[s]ociopolitical perceptions of identity" that "probably played a significant role in the way people responded in 2001." Most fundamentally, in post-Soviet Ukraine ethnic identity is no longer a legal category in Ukrainians' internal passports: this suggests that, at the dawn of the 2000s, "the identification of non-Ukrainians as citizens of Ukraine" would emblematically imply a passage "to state or civic identity" (Stebelsky 2009: 80) rather than an ethnic one.

Accordingly, we can also grasp the complexity of the Russian–Ukrainian nexus through combining the ethnic criterion with the linguistic one: looking at contemporary Ukraine through these lenses, we can see three major groups in the country, that is, Ukrainian-speaking Ukrainians, Russian-speaking Ukrainians, and Russian-speaking Russians (Arel, Khmel'ko 1996). Among these, throughout the last decades sociological research has emblematically reported that the last two groups do not represent a cohesive "community," and that their identity/ies are much more fragmented than would be expected.[51]

As outlined in a study conducted by researchers at the Kyiv International Institute of Sociology (KIIS), the definition of the ethnolinguistic structure of Ukraine can be fully comprehended only "when considering the phenomenon of individual bi-ethnicity" (Khmel'ko 2004: 15).[52] According

---

51 In his comprehensive reconstruction of Russians' and Russophones' identity formation in Ukraine, Kulyk (2019a) retraced the origins and nuances of the sociological debate around the issue in the last decades. For the sake of clarity, it is worth noting that here we report only some of the crucial dynamics of the point in question.

52 As the KIIS sociologist Valerii Khmel'ko explained in an interview for Radio Liberty: "[...] after the standard question about nationality—what nationality do you consider yourself—we also ask another question: do you consider yourself only a Ukrainian or only a Russian, or to some extent do you consider yourself both? As a result, it turned out that a quarter of the population consists of

to surveys conducted throughout 1991–2003, Valerii Khmel'ko identified Ukrainian–Russian bi-ethnors as "the second largest ethnic group in
Ukraine" (Khmel'ko 2004: 17). KIIS sociologists thus developed a "scale
of bi-ethnicity," which they projected over the territory of Ukraine:

> The farther westward, the more monoethnic Ukrainians and the fewer Ukrainian-
> Russian bi-ethnors and monoethnic Russians we have. Conversely, the farther
> East and South, the fewer monoethnic Ukrainians, and the more Ukrainian-
> Russian bi-ethnors and monoethnic Russians [...] among monoethnic Ukrainians
> the share of Ukrainophones is more than twice the share of Russophones, while
> among Ukrainian-Russian bi-ethnors, by contrast, the share of Ukrainophones is
> more than four time less than the share of Russophones.[53] (Khmel'ko 2004: 18)

These results were corroborated by other studies undertaken throughout the
first decades of the twenty-first century. According to comparative research
on the citizenship identities of young people in the L'viv and Donbas regions conducted by Antonina Tereshchenko in 2005–2006, it appears that
"only the Donbas region in the East shared the characteristics of the traditional borderland [...] in particular, with respect to cultural hybridity
and undecidability as regards people's identification" (Tereshchenko
2010: 152). Moreover, the results of a 2016 survey, *Changes in the Identity
of Russians and Russophones in Ukraine* (*Zminy identychnosti Rosiian ta
Rosiis'komovnykh v Ukraïni*), further revealed the dynamic evolution of
the idea of nation throughout the 2000s (see UCIPR 2016). As analyst Iulia

---

people who—in one way or another—do not consider themselves monoethnic.
Most of these people [...] are Russian-Ukrainian bi-ethnors" (Fanailova 2014a;
[...] после стандартного вопроса о национальности, кем вы себя считаете по
национальности, задаем еще дополнительный вопрос: считаете ли вы себя
только украинцем или только русским, или в какой-то мере считаете себя так
же и другим. В результате выяснилось, что у нас четверть населения — это
люди, которые в той или иной мере себя считают не одноэтничными. Больше
всего таких людей [...] это русско-украинские биэтноры).

53 "Чим далі на Захід, тим більше моноетнічних українців, і тим менше украïно-
російських біетнорів та моноетнічних росіян. І навпаки, чим далі на Схід і
Південь, тим менше моноетнічних українців, і тим більше украïно-російських
біетнорів та моноетнічних росіян [...] серед моноетнічних українців частка
украïномовних більш ніж вдвічі перевищує частку російськомовних, а серед
украïно-російських біетнорів, навпаки, частка украïномовних більш ніж
вчетверо менше за частку російськомовних."

Kazdobina concludes, "a number of Russian speakers started developing their Ukrainian civic identity long before the start of the current Russian aggression [that is, the war in East Ukraine starting in 2014]," and today, "it seems that for Russian speakers, bilingualism is a way to preserve their identity while at the same time integrating into the Ukrainian political nation, where Ukrainian is gradually replacing Russian as the lingua franca" (Business Ukraine 2017).[54]

The cases reported above suggest that throughout the last decades there has not been a real and static dividing line, based on the ethnolinguistic traits of the population, between the generally assumed social collectivities of "Ukrainians" and "Russians," and "Russian speakers" and "Ukrainian speakers" in Ukraine. Indeed, this dividing line was fluid and subject to hybridizing trajectories and intersections with other identity markers. In an attempt to grasp the fluid character of post-Soviet identity affiliations, Peter W. Rodgers in 2008 recognized the regional category, rather than the ethnolinguistic one, as a suitable parameter for describing contemporary Ukraine. In his study *Nation, Region and History in Post-Communist Transitions: Identity Politics in Ukraine, 1991–2006*, Rodgers provided a tentative model for describing the regional composition of contemporary Ukraine: it was conventionally articulated in ten regions, according to the combination of linguistic, cultural and historical affiliations. He distinguished the Crimean Peninsula from other regions, as being "the only area of Ukraine, with an ethnic Russian majority"—according to the 2001 national census (58.5 per cent)—and the "least supportive of Ukraine's state independence" (Rodgers 2008: 56), possessing a unique degree of political autonomy in the country until the contested annexation to the Russian Federation in March 2014. Then, he identified a southern region, including the areas of Kherson, Odesa and Mykolaïv. These territories, which were absorbed as new industrial centres into the Russian Empire in the late eighteenth century with the status of the province of "New Russia"

---

54 The study was conducted by the Ukrainian Center for Independent Political Research (UCIPR) and based on six focus groups from regions under the control of the Kyiv government (L'viv, Kyiv, Kramators'k, Kharkiv, Vinnytsia and Kherson, April–May 2016).

(*Novorossiiskaia guberniia*), are characterized by a greater diffusion of the Russian language and culture, but "the region today is less urban, and ethnically Russian than other parts of Ukraine to the east" (Rodgers 2008: 57).[55] Rodgers further identifies the north-central region (Poltava, Kirovohrad, Cherkasy, Kyiv, Chernihiv and Sumy), acknowledging its historical specificity: this was part of the Polish–Lithuanian Commonwealth until the mid-seventeenth century, and includes the historical lands that were inhabited by Cossacks. It passed then under Russian control with the Treaty of Andrusovo (1667), which ended the Russian–Polish war. As Rodgers (2008: 57) notes in his classification: "Although these areas were under Moscow's control for a similar period of time as lands to the east and in the south, they have always retained a more 'Ukrainian' political outlook." Significantly, even if in the late Imperial and Soviet eras the main urban centres were predominantly Russified, nowadays the population is mostly made up of Ukrainian-speaking Ukrainians. Rodgers distinguishes then the western region (L'viv, Ternopil' and Ivano-Frankivs'k) from the west-central one (Zhytomyr, Vinnytsia, Khmel'nyts'kyi, Rivne and Volyn'): while both are inhabited mostly by Ukrainian-speaking Ukrainians, the first is usually described as the historical region of Galicia (*Halychyna*), where under Habsburg rule the national movement emerged.[56] In the south-west region (Chernivtsi, Zakarpat'ska oblast'), Rodgers further identifies two distinct regions, Bukovyna and Zakarpattia: both were under Habsburg rule up to 1918 and have a large number of national minorities in their territories, but developed divergent historical experiences, bordering respectively modern Romania and Hungary. Finally, according to Rodger's scheme, we have the east-central region (Zaporizhzhia, Dnipropetrovs'k, Kharkiv) and the eastern one (Donets'k, Luhans'k). Historically, both are industrialized and

---

55 Since 2014, in the aftermath of the contested annexation of Crimea and the war in Donbas, the term "Novorossiia" has emblematically experienced a new resurgence in Russian nationalist circles, based on its dual meaning in announcing a "new Russia" including the territories of the former imperial province (Laruelle 2016).

56 As Rodgers (2008: 60) emphasizes in his classification, "the region has continued to see itself as the 'Piedmont' of Ukraine, as the true keeper of national identity on behalf of the rest of Ukraine and a firm supporter of an 'away from Moscow' stance."

Russified areas, but while the first one shows a distinct attitude towards the convergence of Ukrainian and Russian cultural legacies, the second was instead a true "showcase of socialism" (Rodgers 2008: 63), and today has turned out to be tied to a Soviet regional identity, with a predominantly Russian-speaking population.[57]

Indeed, in his study, Rodgers (2008: 55) significantly identifies the potential flaws in his classification and admits that "drawing regional boundaries in Ukraine is fraught with difficulties," especially because "such boundaries are often more fluid than rigid." Together with Lowell W. Barrington and Erik S. Herron (2004), who previously presented a framework made up of eight distinct regions, Rodgers states that the urgency behind a more nuanced regional classification of Ukraine lies in the need to overcome the essentialization of the "divisions of Ukraine into macroregions such as 'Eastern Ukraine' and 'Western Ukraine'," which "fail to illuminate inherent differentiation among areas with contrasting historical, economic and demographic profiles" (2008: 55).[58] This kind of essentializing approach emerged consistently after the 1994 presidential elections in Ukraine, which saw the victory of Leonid Kuchma, who supported the "upgrade" of the status of the Russian language in the country and a

---

57 As Tanya Zaharchenko argued in 2013, it is especially the contested eastern border of Ukraine with Russia that seems to have developed its own "border culture": "The regional version of Ukrainian identity in the East developed without complete renunciation of the Russian culture, although the area simultaneously produced a multitude of influential intellectuals dedicated to the idea of national revival. The region's geopolitical location resulted in the creation of a material and spiritual culture which absorbed the various dimensions of the national-cultural elements of both countries. But speaking Russian has not turned Russophone Ukrainians into Russians" (2013: 257–258).

58 Similarly, the scholars who contributed to the 2019 volume emblematically titled *Regionalism without Regions: Reconceptualizing Ukraine's Heterogeneity*, edited by Oksana Myshlovska and Ulrich Schmid, once again emphasized the controversial nature of regionalism in Ukraine, especially in the aftermath of the Euromaidan revolution in 2013–2014. Following the results included in this study, when looking at Ukrainian regional diversity, it is worth taking into account also generational and urban–rural divides: this helps understand how today identity markers in Ukraine are highly fragmented and not regionally homogeneous.

political rapprochement with Russia, over the incumbent Leonid Kravchuk, the first president of Ukraine (1991–1994), who promoted Ukrainian as the sole state language and the country's distancing from Russia. In public debates the voting patterns were first explained by "a neat dividing line between Ukrainian speakers to the West and Russian speakers to the East" (Rodgers 2008: 50). The essentialization of internal divisions into a binary scheme expanded then its scope from political to polemical debates in the mainstream media: the so-called two Ukraines discourse portrayed a nation split into a European-oriented, nationalist and Ukrainian-speaking West and a Russian-oriented, Soviet nostalgic and Russian-speaking East.[59] In her commentary entitled *The Myth of Two Ukraines*, Tatiana Zhurzhenko (2002a), at the dawn of the 2000s, observed how this controversial debate was sharpened by the so-called " 'Huntingtonization' of the Ukrainian political discourse," that is, the projection of regional differences into a clash between "two civilizations." Paradoxically, "the most important factor of this 'Hungtingtonization' " of internal divisions was an "external one":

> After the end of the Cold War and the initial euphoria caused by the fall of the Berlin Wall Ukraine found itself "in between" the new emerging geopolitical realities: between an enlarging EU and NATO on the one side, and a rather shaky re-integration of the former Soviet republics, dominated by Russia, on the other [...] This uncertainty has been interpreted ideologically as a conflict of two cultural orientations and two mutually exclusive identities: European culture embodied by Western Ukraine and pan-Slavic or Eurasian culture embodied by Eastern Ukraine. (Zhurzhenko 2002a)

Whereas in the course of Ukrainian history the essentialization of the exclusive character of the national narrative took shape along an oppositional relation to external imperial hegemonic discourses, today the internal regional divisions—be they language, ethnic or historically based— re-actualize when the borders imagined by competing binary discourses

---

59 The origins of the "Two Ukraines" discourse date back to the early 1990s, when the Ukrainian intellectual Mykola Riabchuk started to frame and develop this approach in his analysis of the dynamics of Ukraine's nation-building (e.g. Riabchuk 1992; 2001; 2003a; 2003b). Riabchuk then found in Iaroslav Hrytsak (2002), who responded with his paradigm of "Twenty-Two Ukraines," his major opponent in the debate.

harden.[60] Apparently, it is especially in the field of "literary politics" (Rewakowicz 2018: 2) where the room for "rethinking" the Ukrainian literary canon in light of contemporary sociocultural dynamics has been also hindered by such an epistemological approach.

New (Old?) Cultural Standards in the Post-Soviet Era

In the history of Ukraine, as emphasized by Marko Pavlyshyn (2016a: 78), it is especially literature that has played an important role "vis-à-vis the Ukrainian nation," and even today "the participation of a national literature in nation-building" is taken "as axiomatic" (2016: 79). In the aftermath of the post-Soviet historical rift, the debate was not around "the possibility of a national literature," but on "the shape that it, and its history, should take" (Pavlyshyn 2016a: 79–80). While reframing the new national literary canon, it is no surprise that the question of literary bilingualism was emblematically ignored. This approach follows the dynamics of Ukrainian history, in which "[i]n the absence of a Ukrainian state, and with Ukrainian literary activity taking place in a geographical space shared by representatives of other cultures [...] Ukrainian literary history writing from its inception had little cause or opportunity to do otherwise than focus on phenomena marked by their language as Ukrainian" (Pavlyshyn 2016a: 81). As highlighted by George G. Grabowicz (1992: 221), at the dawn of Ukrainian independence:

> [...] the Russian-language writings of Ukrainian writers are most often treated as something of an embarrassment, like a skeleton in the closet; for some they are a hedging on the writer's national commitment. For many others, including most Western critics, this is largely a *terra incognita*. For virtually all, however, language is seen as determining literature: what is written in Russian belongs in the category of Russian literature.

Nonetheless, the ethnic–linguistic criterion is misleading in determining the demarcation of the Ukrainian canon from the Russian one, especially since the hybrid cultural forms have always been of particular interest for

---

60 Through the lenses of these contradictory dynamics—and in light of the annexation of Crimea to Russia and the conflict in Donbas in 2014—as argued by Zhurzhenko (2014a: 249), today "the popular discourse about Ukraine as a 'divided nation' looks like a self-fulfilling prophecy."

Russian and Ukrainian literatures.[61] As Grabowicz argues, "language, thematic focus, ethnic origin and even territorial ties—may play a greater or less role, the issue of whether a given writer is [...] a Russian or a Ukrainian writer must be resolved with finer tools." Whereas we consider literature as the reflection of the composite sociocultural prism of an era, "if that society is, among other things, bilingual, so too will be its literature" (Grabowicz 1992: 222).

In post-Soviet Ukraine, the presence of a multicultural society characterized by an intense dialogue and contact between its heterogeneous cultural agents generates the need to create new interpretive models aimed at "rethinking" the Ukrainian canon in light of contemporary dynamics. This is especially true as we consider that "at no time in modern history prior to Ukraine's regaining independence in 1991 had there been an opportunity or need to conceptualize, let alone construct, an overarching civic national identity that would encompass the many ethno-cultural groups inhabiting Ukraine" (Pavlyshyn 2016a: 76–77). Thus, today it is also scholars in Ukrainian Studies who face the difficult task of creating new tools that can reflect the novelty of contemporary social and political developments:

> A major task facing Ukrainian Studies, both in and outside Ukraine, is that of rethinking and recasting the canon of national culture [...] An essential component will be the orientation of *ukraïnistyka* towards other cultural or minority segments in Ukraine—the Russians, Poles, Jews and so on. This is now a juridical fact and the form of the political system: Ukraine has defined itself as a multiethnic society and its new passports no longer have the Soviet-era rubric of "nationality." But the central paradigm of *ukraïnistyka* as a whole [...] is implicitly still ethnically Ukrainian [...] A reorientation in a genuinely pluralistic direction [...] would go far toward revitalizing the discipline. (Grabowicz 1995: 686–687)

---

61 As emphasized by Myroslav Shkandrij in his work *Russia and Ukraine: Literature and the Discourse of Empire from Napoleonic to Postcolonial Times*: "Russian writers have often viewed their culture as spanning, confronting, and combining two civilizations, particularly the European and the Asian, both culturally and geographically. Ukrainians have focused strongly on their culture's relationship with its neighbours and on the exploration of taboos [...] writers from the Ukrainian borderland situation often had to face challenges to their identity and political-cultural sympathies and frequently were forced to negotiate compromises." (Shkandrij 2001: 272–273)

Despite the vitality of Ukrainian Studies throughout recent decades, the issues raised by Grabowicz still remain unaddressed. Even today, alternative outlooks on the configuration of the "Ukrainian nation" lie in the different historical narratives of the area, leading to the institutionalization of cultural standards:

> The case of Ukraine after the fall of Soviet power [...] presents a vivid example of a system in which both linguistic and social values have been shifting. The Ukrainian language, which had been marginalized and denigrated relative to Russian, has become increasingly used in public urban contexts and by political and cultural leaders, some of whom had themselves been marginalized in the Soviet system [...] In choices of language use and in debates about language, the previously dominant discourses clash with new discourses and practices elevating Ukrainian. (Bilaniuk 2014: 337)

Along these lines, the language issue still represents a contested benchmark even in defining what belongs—and what does not—to the national literary canon. As Grabowicz asserts, "[i]n the case of Ukrainian literature [...] this confusion, which is essentially based on a dissociation of literature from its social context, has led to radical misconstructions of historical reality" (Grabowicz 1992: 221). Today, we witness the need to move further away from "the Romantic and quasi-metaphysical notion of literature as the emanation (the 'spirit') of a 'nation'" and towards "a more rational, and certainly more empirical definition of literature as a reflection, product and function of a society" (Grabowicz 1992: 221).

Whereas "[d]espite their nationalised, politicised images, both Gogol' and Shevchenko span the Russian-Ukrainian linguistic and cultural divide," as argued by Uilleam Blacker (2014), in the aftermath of the post-Soviet historical rift "across contemporary Ukraine, there are dozens of writers, from sci-fi novelists to prize-winning poets, who operate across the two languages." Among them, we deal here with those authors who belong to "the millions of people" who live outside of the political borders of the Russian Federation and "who consider Russian to be their mother tongue"[62]

---

62 As Sergei Chuprinin (2008: 6) puts it in the preface to his work: "I believe that what is now in front of you gives an absolutely stunning, multi-layered and multi-colored picture of Russian literary life in the modern world, where there are tens of millions of people living outside the Russian Federation who

(Chuprinin 2008: 6). In his study *Russian Literature Today: Abroad* (*Russkaia literatura segodnia: zarubezh'e*, 2008), Sergei Chuprinin presents a real dictionary of this literary production, which was divided by countries and cultural initiatives and realized through the support of local experts. As Chuprinin states, such a venture "is not free from inaccuracies" (*ne svobodna ot nedostatkov*; Chuprinin 2008: 6), especially since an in-depth analysis of Russophone literary phenomena emerging in different geographical areas of the world has not been carried out yet.[63] The artistic and epistemological position of these cultural actors is emblematically described by Tlostanova as a condition of *vnepolozhennost'* (2004: 105): this is a "positioning outside of" the national literary and cultural canons of modernity.

Along these lines, it is no surprise that today the issue of Russian-language literature in Ukraine is still the true bone of contention in the contemporary intellectual debate. In order to understand the peculiar characteristics of this artistic milieu, in the next section we will first analyse the dynamics of the contemporary debate on hybridity, highlighting the influence and impact of the new cultural standards, which were promoted by the controversial nation-building policies in post-Soviet Ukraine, on the making of an "external canon" of today's Russophone literature.

Post-Soviet Russophonia in Ukraine: An Intellectual (and Political) Debate

In the post-Soviet intellectual debate, as argued by Tamara Hundorova (2001: 250) in her study *The Canon Reversed*, "the concept of a 'complete' literature and its role in the cultural sphere were the focus of intense interest in the early 1990's" (2001: 252), whereas this answered "the vision of an

---

consider our language as their native one" (И то, что сейчас перед вами, дает, мне кажется, совершенно ошеломляющую, многослойную и многоцветную картину русской литературной жизни в современном мире, где за пределами Российской Федерации оказались десятки миллионов человек, считающих наш язык родным).

63 Here it is worth mentioning the pioneering studies included in the volume *Global Russian Cultures* (2019) that, as argued in the introduction to this book, one decade later opened the way for a more systematic analysis of *plural* Russian cultural phenomena emerging around the world.

innovative, highly-developed Ukrainian culture that was to arise under the new conditions of national independence and freedom." This was followed soon by "the appeal to a European-type modern Ukrainian literature," which could legitimate "the repossession of the literary canon" (Hundorova 2001: 253) after the collapse of the Soviet regime.

Within this frame of reference, throughout the late 1990s it was especially the great success of Russian-language mass literature that brought again to centre stage the debate on the issue of literary bilingualism in independent Ukraine:

> The reverse canon of the 1990s embraced not only Ukrainian-language but also Russian-language mass literature. The preceding literary canon was monocultural and excluded works by Ukrainian authors written in Russian. In the 1990s Russian mass literature swamped the Ukrainian book market [...] Some Russian-language authors, such as Andrei Kurkov and Marina and Sergei Diachenko, live and work in Ukraine and call themselves Ukrainian writers. (Hundorova 2001: 269)

In light of the rise of this highly successful literary phenomenon in post-Soviet Ukraine, the debate came to be around the definition of the role and position of Russian-language literature within the new national cultural model. In an article provocatively entitled "The Smell of Dead Words: Russophone Literature in Ukraine" ("Zapakh mertvogo slova. Russkoiazychnaia literatura na Ukraine," 1998), the Russian philosopher and politologist Andrei Okara first addressed the issue in the broader public debate. His article was first published in *Nezavisimaia Gazeta* in Russia on February 25, 1998, and then reissued in *Ukraïns'ka Pravda* in Ukraine ten years later, thus offering a wider perspective on the peculiar reception of the question in both the countries. Okara analyses the "peripheral" position of this literary phenomenon, emphasizing its distance from both the Russian literary system and the Ukrainian one. According to the author, it is the same Russophone writers who do not know how to describe their own positioning in the contemporary cultural context:

> It is still not clear how to relate to what is written in Russian in Ukraine: should we consider this literature as a Ukrainian national literature in Russian [*ukrainskaia natsional'naia literatura na russkom iazyke*]? Or as a separate branch of the All-Ukrainian cultural process, i.e. the literature of a national minority? Or maybe as a part of Russian [*rossiiskaia*] culture, i.e Russian [*russkaia*] literature in the New

Abroad? Probably, the writers themselves are tormented in search of identification for their own literary production.[64] (Okara 2008)

According to Okara, the birth of a real literary movement is not possible due to the different tendencies and heterogeneous forms of Russohone literature. He identifies two paths for the potential development of Russophone literature in Ukraine: a high literature and a mass literature. The first is considered of little interest, as it has an absence of real masters. The second is labelled as a mere commercial brand without any aesthetic value.

According to Okara, this bleak outlook relies on the status of the Russian language in Ukraine: a dead language, uprooted from the metropolis and from its natural place of development and characterization. To give life to a "high" literature in Russian, it is necessary to live in the "homeland of the Russian language."[65] Okara thus argues that the "peripheral" role of Russophone literature in the Ukrainian cultural context depends on the same function performed by the Russian language in Ukraine: the cultural "diglossia" of contemporary Ukraine, where "an elite culture" (*elitarnaia kul'tura*) is created in one language and the other language is used only in "everyday life" (*v bytu*), determines respectively the different paths and destinies of Ukrainophone and Russophone literary productions. Eventually, following Okara's reflections, only a "high" literature in Ukrainian can prospectively take shape in post-Soviet Ukraine.

---

64 "До сих пор непонятно, как относиться к написанному по-русски на Украине: считать ли эту литературу украинской национальной литературой на русском языке? Или отдельной ветвью общеукраинского культурного процесса — литературой национального меньшинства? А может частью российской культуры — русской литературой в Новом Зарубежье? Похоже, сами писатели мучаются в поисках идентификации собственного творчества."

65 "In order to write properly in Russian, apparently, you have to be born with a sense of the energy of the Russian language, it is necessary to genetically carry the structure of the Russian language. Eventually, it is necessary to live at least some part of your life in Russia, the homeland of the Russian language." (Okara 2008; Чтобы полноценно писать по-русски, надо, видимо, родиться с чувством энергетики русского языка, надо генетически нести в себе строй русской речи. Надо, в конце концов, хоть какую-то часть своей жизни прожить в России, на родине русского языка).

Okara's article was soon followed by Mikhail Nazarenko's response in his "About the Dead and Living Words" ("O mertvom i zhivom slove," 1998), which originally appeared online in early September of the same year.[66] Nazarenko, a Ukrainian Russian-language writer and professor of history of Russian literature at the Institute of Philology of the Taras Shevchenko National University of Kyiv, dismantled Okara's stance on the grounds of the vitality of Russian language and culture in post-Soviet Ukraine:

> The reality is that for a rather large percentage of Ukrainian citizens the Ukrainian language is the second native language after Russian [...] Clearly, their culture is and will always be on the border between the Russian culture and the Ukrainian one. And here the question is not about the existence of this culture—which is quite evident—but first of all on the self-determination, the self-awareness of this

---

66 The story behind this commentary being published is quite telling in terms of the spontaneous and unsystematic development of Russian-language literature and criticism in Ukraine in the 1990s. As retraced by Nazarenko, at the time the blogosphere had not been developed yet, and online communication went through FidoNet, one of the first worldwide computer networks, where the above-mentioned commentary was first published at the initiative of the Russian-language writers Sergei Diachenko (Kyiv, b. 1945) and Henry Lion Oldie, the pen names of Ukrainian science fiction writers Dmitrii Gromov (Simferopol', b. 1963) and Oleg Ladyzhenskii (Kharkiv, b. 1963). Here I refer to the version included on *Lib.ru*, one of the oldest electronic libraries in the Russian Internet segment—also known as Maksim Moshkow's Library—, which dates back to September 18, 1998. Interestingly enough, the commentary was then included, without the author's knowledge, in a small-circulation book edited by the Russian writer Anna Brazhkina (Rostov-on-Don, b. 1959) and the Crimean Russian-language poet Igor' Sid (Dzhankoi, b. 1963), the organizers of the Russian–Ukrainian literary festival *The Southern Accent* (*Iuzhnii aktsent*, 1999), which was held in Moscow in May 1999. In the volume the editors collected some relevant works devoted to Ukrainian literature that had been authored by literary critics in the Russian Federation and Ukraine throughout the 1990s. The book is still available online (see Brazhkina, Sid 1999) on the official website of the Crimean Geopoetic Club (Krymskii geopoeticheskii klub), a literary circle founded in Moscow in 1995 at the initiative of Sid and that gathered together intellectuals from Ukraine, Russia and other post-Soviet regions with the aim of depoliticizing the literary environment and rediscovering the relations between creativity and geographical places through the lens of "geopoetics" (see Kratochvil 2007).

culture. Until recently it was part of the Russian/Soviet culture, thus no need for self-determination arose.[67] (Nazarenko 1998)

According to Nazarenko, it is precisely the liminal position of Russian-language literature, at the crossroads between two linguistic and cultural systems, that provides the Ukrainian Russophone writer with a peculiar role with respect to the Russian and Ukrainian traditions. In his view, the birth of a "marginal" cultural phenomenon involves a slow process of self-definition within the new literary space:

> So, if before 1991 (the date is, of course, conditional) the Russophone writer of Ukraine [russkoiazychnyi pisatel' Ukrainy] thought to be part of a well-defined system, then now, in order to preserve his own identity, he has to realise his own particular position in relation to the literary processes in Russia and Ukraine [...] Everything new in art is created as usually in marginal areas, "on the margins" of the ossified official culture. There is no other way. Otherwise, the only alternative can be assimilation, or "internal emigration." The Ukrainian school of Russian literature (or the Russian school of Ukrainian literature?) has not taken shape yet, and, probably, will not take shape soon, but, nevertheless, it will arise.[68] (Nazarenko 1998)

Okara's and Nazarenko's positions reflect the two main directions of the cultural debate in the 1990s.[69] Language as an instrument of artistic

---

67 "Реальность такова, что для определенного и довольно большого процента граждан Украины украинский язык является вторым родным — после русского [...] Очевидно, что их культура находится и всегда будет находиться на границе между русской и украинской. И вопрос стоит не о ее существовании — оно очевидно, — но в первую очередь о самоопределении, самоосознании. До недавнего времени она была частью российской/советской культуры и необходимости в самоопределении просто не возникало."

68 "Итак, если до 1991 года (дата, разумеется, условная) русскоязычный писатель Украины мыслил себя частью определенной системы, то теперь он вынужден, чтобы сохранить своеобразие, осознать свое особое положение по отношению к литературному процессу и в России, и на Украине [...] Все новое в искусстве создается, как правило, в маргинальных областях, «на полях» окостеневшей официальной культуры. Другого пути нет. В противном случае — или ассимиляция, или «внутренняя эмиграция.» Украинская школа русской литературы (или русская — украинской?) еще не сложилась и, вероятно, сложится не скоро, но, тем не менее, возникнет."

69 Here it is worth mentioning also Aleksandr Zakurenko's (1997) and Inna Bulkina's (1999) contributions to the debate, while commenting on the

expression and its social role in the new post-Soviet nation are the main issues around which the alternative interpretations of the position of the Russophone phenomenon within the frame of the Ukrainian national canon took shape. There is no doubt that the debate intensified especially in light of the unprecedented freedom and opportunities enjoyed by cultural actors in the national literary arena in the aftermath of the Soviet collapse. As retraced by Ihor Kruchyk in his 2014 article "Children of a Soviet Widow" ("Dity radians'koï vdovy"), "under the new circumstances some writers founded their own publishing houses or journals,"[70] and much more often than in Soviet times we witnessed the publication of Russian-language anthologies and the birth of literary prizes and festivals. Broadly speaking, on the one hand in Ukraine, together with "the possibility of publishing," "the construction of de-ideologised hierarchies" in the literary field became conceivable; on the other in Russia, "magazines and publishing houses began to print 'new Russians' from Ukraine much more intensely than it was in Soviet times" (Kruchyk 2014).[71]

It was throughout the 2000s, then, that the highly controversial internal political debate in Ukraine, together with the deterioration of social and political relations with the Russian Federation under Vladimir Putin, further polarized the intellectual community around the language issue. Whereas at the dawn of the new millennium Taras Kuzio could observe how the Ukrainian "post-Soviet nation- and state-building project" was "therefore bound up with a debate over how this identity will be constituted and in what manner its neighbours will be 'Others'" (2001: 358), it was still language that represented "an important aspect of creating difference for the 'Self' in the relation to the 'Other'" (2001: 348). Within this frame, in the national intellectual and political context we gradually witnessed the formation of "language ideologies" (Kulyk 2007), marking conventional boundaries between the Ukrainophone and the Russophone discourses:

---

publication of the volume *Who Are We? Let's Try to Understand...* (*Kakie my? Poprobuem poniat'*..., 1996), an anthology including Russian-language poetry authored by Ukrainian authors from Kyiv.

70 "Деякі літератори за нових обставин заснували власні видавництва або часописи."

71 "[...] нинішні російські журнали й видавництва заходилися друкувати «нових русських» із України набагато інтенсивніше, ніж це було за радянських часів."

I distinguish these discourses on the basis of respective language ideologies, which represent the language processes of Ukraine as a relationship of interaction/ struggle between the two main languages and their language groups (or rather ethnical-language, following the traditional tie between language and ethnicity, and the absence of a clear distinction between ethnic and language identities in Ukrainian society), and I define them as *Ukrainophone* [*ukrainofonnyi*] and *Russophone* [*rusofonnyi*] [...] The characterising trait of the Russophone and Ukrainophone discourses is their orientation in defense of the interests of their "own" group at the expense of the "other's" interests.[72] (Kulyk 2007: 300)

Thus, the language debate came to be not only "about 'form', but also about 'content'" (Zhurzhenko 2002b: 17). As Zhurzhenko emphasized (2002b: 17), the language debate involved broader cultural perspectives on the content of the national identity, especially whereby gradually "[i]n independent Ukraine a hierarchy of cultures (and languages) has emerged and Ukrainian has turned out not to be dominant." The contested ideologization of culture in the internal political debate led historical memory and language categories to acquire a conventional social relevance, reflecting the interests of competitor groups on a regional and a national scale (Zhurzhenko 2002b; Bilaniuk 2005; Moser 2013). Thus, even if the country's cultural policies were generally "flexible and gradualist" and "the identities and cultural practices associated with them" have been "very fluid" (Giuliano 2019), it was paradoxically after the so-called "revolutionary cycles" in 2004–2005 ("Orange Revolution")—and then in 2013–2014 ("Euromaidan Revolution"), as emphasized by Minakov (2018: 61), that "the Ukrainian political space converted itself into a 'conservative situation'". In this ideological field "created by binary oppositions," it is the state that offers "value orientations for sociopolitical interaction" (Minakov 2018: 58). Deprived of space for ideological opponents, "ongoing political antagonism in Ukraine has come to characterize relations [...] between

---

72 "Я выделяю эти дискурсы именно на основе соответствующих языковых идеологий, представляющих языковые процессы в Украине как взаимо-действие/борьба двух главных языков и языковых групп (точнее, языково-этнических, ввиду традиционного связывания языка с этносом и отсутствия в украинском обществе четкого различения языковой и этнической идентичности), и называю *украинофонным* и *русофонным* [...] Характерная черта украинофонного и русофонного дискурсов — ориентация на защиту интересов «своей» группы за счет интересов «чужой»."

ethno-linguo-cultural groups" (Minakov 2018: 62) supporting two different types of conservatism: "one calling for the preservation of 'national statehood', and another one characterized by a desire to protect Soviet 'achievements' and to overcome ethnicity" (Minakov 2018: 62). The ideological field has thus been alternatively appropriated and used by regional financial–political groups (see Minakov 2019) while promoting their political campaigns, creating the ground for polarization and contestation over opposite identity projects in the Ukrainian public debate. Thus, the Orange Revolution—a series of civil protests taking place primarily in Kyiv from November 2004 to January 2005, which brought about the decision to annul the victory of Viktor Ianukovych in the run-off vote of the 2004 presidential elections following allegations of electoral fraud—first "opened the Pandora's box of identity politics and deepened regional cleavages in Ukraine" (Zhurzhenko 2014a: 255). On the one hand, Viktor Iushchenko's Our Ukraine appropriated and rehabilitated Ukrainian nationalism in the "essentialized" version of Galicia in the West, and on the other Viktor Ianukovych's Party of Regions in the "electoral fortresses of Donetsk and Luhansk drew on neo-Soviet symbols and narratives" (Zhurzhenko 2014a: 255). Until 2014, as Gorbach (2019) emphasized, "this kind of polarization was a game for two players," which "used this tool to easily harvest votes in their respective, more or less equally sized, regions."

It was not by chance that in 2011 Abel Polese, in his study on language and identity in Ukraine, could still wonder: 'Was it really nation-building?' (Polese 2011).[73] State interference in cultural processes made harsher the struggle in the domestic sphere, which came to have a rather contradictory

---

73 In his study, Polese contests the widespread use of the term "nation-building" in academic and political debates emerging after the collapse of Yugoslavia, the USSR and Czechoslovakia. He proposes "a working definition of the term that acknowledges the role different segments of a society play in a nation-building project" (Polese 2011: 37). In his analysis of the controversial dynamics of the language debate in post-Soviet Ukraine, at the eve of the dramatic outcomes of the post-Euromaidan political scene, Polese (2011: 47) argued as follows: "Non-native Ukrainian speakers, or those whose Ukrainian is weak, might feel excluded from a strongly monolingual state as Ukrainian officially is, but are not excluded because Ukraine is monolingual only *de jure*, but not *de facto*."

pattern in terms of state-led policies on the eve of Euromaidan. Thus, if under Leonid Kuchma, the second president of Ukraine (1994–2005), we witnessed an ambivalent course of national cultural policies,[74] it was in the aftermath of the Orange Revolution that under Iushchenko (2005–2010) the new political elite "sought to build an inclusive civic identity but put it on a strong Ukrainian ethnocultural basis" (Kulyk 2016: 593). The tension then reached its zenith during Viktor Ianukovych's presidency (2010–2014), when in July 2012 the new law *On the Fundamentals of the State Language Policy (Pro zasady derzhavnoï movnoï polityky)*—n. 5029-VI, submitted by deputies Serhii Kivalov and Vadym Kolesnichenko, was passed. Eventually, this new bill on the protection of minority languages secured the official use of Russian in many regions "not *alongside* but *instead* of Ukrainian" (Riabchuk 2015: 147).[75] Riabchuk's commentary on the passing of the law clearly reveals the impact of the controversial cultural policies adopted under Ianukovych's presidency on the intellectual debate:

> The bright idea of European bilingualism has been rejected by Ukrainophones because they do not believe it is viable in a lawless post-Soviet country, quite reasonably suspecting that any bilingualism here would be Soviet, rather than European. And Russophones are not interested in European bilingualism because they still enjoy the Soviet-style bilingualism that suits their needs much better. All they need is merely to legitimize their right to ignore Ukrainian and to preclude any possibility of changes. The Kivalov-Kolesnichenko bill is just one of many attempts to ensure the dominance of one group over another. (Riabchuk 2012)

---

74 As argued by Zhurzhenko (2002b: 10): "President Leonid Kuchma came to power in 1994 due to support from Eastern Ukraine. He had promised that the Russian language would be granted a special status and that relations with Russia would become closer, but he later shifted to a more 'pro-Ukrainian' position presenting himself as a promoter of the 'national idea.' However, in Western Ukraine he never gained strong political support because of his image as a 'pro-Moscow' politician. His policy or absence of a clear policy became a subject of criticism from Ukrainian nationalists on the one side and the Russian-speaking intelligentsia on the other."

75 This followed the interference of cultural policies implemented in the Russian Federation, whereby, as remembered by Kruchyk (2014), "[f]or 2009–2011, the Russian Federation has allocated more than 1 billion rubles in support of compatriots" (За 2009–2011 роки Російська Федерація виділила понад 1 млрд. рублів на підтримку співвітчизників) in the so-called Near Abroad.

The proliferation of commentaries and interviews in which contemporary writers and literary critics debated the language issue, in the period shortly preceding the outbreak of the Euromaidan protests in November 2013, highlights the high level at which the political discourse interfered in the cultural one. Between February and March 2013, for instance, Iryna Troskot, lead editor of the web portal *LitAktsent*,[76] gathered together in a debate with some of the main representatives of Ukrainian literature. In her introduction entitled *On the Language and the Debate* (*Pro movu i dyskusiiu*), Troskot describes this venture as an attempt to understand "the importance of the language criterion for defining the author's belonging to the national culture"[77] (Troskot 2013) in light of the urgency of the matter. All the writers taking part in the discussion "write, speak and think in Ukrainian" (Troskot 2013).[78] If on the one hand the poet and prose writer Marianna Kiianovs'ka (b. 1973, Nesterov—today Zhovkva) argues that the language is only "one of the instruments of spiritual transformation"[79] (LitAktsent 2013a)—mentioning many artistic personalities who have worked between different languages and cultures throughout history, on the other Taras Prokhas'ko (b. 1968, Ivano-Frankivs'k) considers it as the product of environmental factors that determine a specific type of mentality. For Prokhas'ko, "literature embodies the life of the language" and its possible articulations: it follows that "for one literature" we will have only "one language"[80] (LitAktsent 2013a). Along the same lines, Liudmyla Taran (b. 1954, Kyiv) attributes to the language a "symbolic power"[81] (LitAktsent 2013b).

---

76 *LitAktsent* is an online platform founded in 2007 by Volodymyr Panchenko (1954–2019), professor at the Kyiv-Mohyla Academy, with the support of the Kyiv publishing house Tempora. It is devoted to providing information on contemporary Ukrainian and foreign literature. See: http://litakcent.com (08/2019).

77 "[…] важливість мовного критерію у визначенні приналежності певного автора до певної національної культури."

78 "Усі письменники […] пишуть, говорять і мислять українською."

79 "Мова є одним зі знарядь духовного перетворення."

80 "[…] література — це, передовсім, життя мови […] Тому принцип: одна мова — одна література є для мене визначальним."

81 "Кожна мова має символічне значення."

In contrast, the reflections offered by Volodymyr Dibrova (b. 1951, Donets'k), a Ukrainian prose writer who moved to the United States in the 1990s, reveal a more complex picture. Dibrova identifies three different approaches to the issue. First, for the literary critic it is a question of a theoretical nature: "the writers who write in a language, but consider themselves, or are considered, belonging to another literary system are today a rare case"[82] (LitAktsent 2013b). Second, for the writer the definition of his identity affiliation is not "a central or significant issue for the purposes of his artistic production"[83] (LitAktsent 2013b). The language is an artistic "instrument," which the writer uses in order to distance himself from his political, ideological and religious convictions (LitAktsent 2013b). Finally, Dibrova argues that it is the perspective of the Ukrainian reader that highlights "the contradiction in terms of the contemporary cultural situation"[84] (LitAktsent 2013b). This is rooted in the belief that todays' factor of consolidation in Ukrainian society is not the State, nor the territory or ethnic origins, but the language itself. Following these lines, Tetiana Maliarchuk (b. 1983, Ivano Frankivs'k), Ukrainian-language and—since 2014—German-language prose writer, underlines how the language question gradually made the same actors of the contemporary cultural scene "soldiers" (*soldaty*) in a "war of words." According to Maliarchuk the question becomes quite complex when the state identifies itself in "language and culture":

> Today's Ukraine is not monocultural. But none of the parties wants to accept it. Among these, the Russian and the Ukrainian sides are the strongest ones [...] These two forces can be defined in terms of relationships that I conventionally divide into assimilation, opposition and collaboration. I hope I will never experience the first of these. The last one would be ideal, but for some reason no one supported the example of Switzerland with its four official languages and dozens of dialects.[85] (LitAktsent 2013c)

---

82 "Письменників, які пишуть однією мовою, а вважають себе (або їх уважають) частиною якоїсь іншомовної літератури, досить мало [...]."

83 "[...] питання про «належність» теж не є головним чи визначальним для його творчості."

84 "[...] уся «суперечливість» [...] нинішньої культурної ситуації."

85 "Нинішня Україна не монокультурна, але жодна зі сторін не хоче з цим змиритися. Російське і українське — її найсильніші культурні гравці [...] Ці

Serhii Zhadan (b. 1974, Starobil's'k) then highlights the contradictions of the language criterion for the definition of the national literary canon, "especially in a country like ours where literature is created in two languages"[86] (LitAktsent 2013c). Zhadan addresses the emblematic case of "the literature written in Russian," pointing out that it "is automatically recognized as part of the cultural heritage of Russian literature, while the same possibility that this body of texts could belong to the Ukrainian culture is ignored in most of the cases"[87] (LitAktsent 2013c). The reasons behind this exclusion can be recognized in the identification of the Russophone literary phenomenon with the remains of the imperial legacy, as argued by Petro Tarashchuk (b. 1956, Vinnytsia). According to the Ukrainian translator and journalist, "the insidious discourses on Ukrainian literary bilingualism are an attack on the Ukrainian language"[88] (LitAktsent 2013d), a new stage of the "linguicide" (*lingvotsyd*) orchestrated over the centuries by Russia. Along these lines, according to Prokhas'ko, the same concept of "Russophone literature of Ukraine [*rosiis'komovna literatura Ukraïny*]" is "nonsense"[89] (*nonsens*; LitAktsent 2013a). The "pro-Ukrainian beliefs" (*proukraïns'ki perekonannia*) of a Russophone writer are not enough to make him an integral part of national literature:

> We can talk about a writer who lives in France and writes in German, but we will not consider him part of French literature. In the same way, we will consider as a Ukrainian writer who writes in that language. For this reason, I cannot consider

---

дві сили можуть перебувати в стосунках, які я для себе умовно розділила так: асиміляція, протистояння, домовленість. До першого варіанту я сподіваюся ніколи не дожити. Останній варіант був би ідеальним, але чомусь нікого приклад Швейцарії з чотирма офіційними мовами і їх десятками діалектів не надихає."

86 "Особливо для такої країни, як наша, де фактично література твориться двома мовами."

87 "[…] література, писана в Україні російською мовою, автоматично зараховується до культурного надбання російської літератури, і сама можливіть припустити, що цей корпус текстів є також частиною української культури — в більшості випадків навіть не розглядається."

88 "Підступні балачки про двомовність української літератури — це замах на українську мову […]."

89 "Але немає такої літератури, як російськомовна література України. Це нонсенс."

the works [...] written in Russian as part of Ukrainian literature, although they may reveal another kind of mentality than that typical of the north of Russia, or express pro-Ukrainian or even nationalistic beliefs. It will not be Ukrainian literature.[90] (LitAktsent 2013a)

A possible answer to Prokhas'ko's stance is offered by the poet Natalka Bilotserkivets' (b. 1954, Kuianivka), who argues for "the distinction between the concept of literature as a purely linguistic phenomenon, and that of national culture as a polyphonic phenomenon"[91] (LitAktsent 2013e). In her opinion, this approach could be useful to free us "from the various speculations about who is to be considered a Ukrainian writer and who is not"[92] (LitAktsent 2013e). Similarly, according to Ostap Slyvyns'kyi (b. 1978, L'viv), a poet and professor of Polish literature at the Ivan Franko National University of L'viv, such speculations around the "indeterminacy" of Russophone literature arise precisely from the clash between "the institutions of the Ukrainian national literature and the Russian one"[93] (*instytutsiï ukraïns'koï ta rosiis'koï natsional'nykh literatur*; LitAktsent 2013 f).

Finally, the question about the role and position of Russian writing in contemporary Ukraine is properly raised by Vira Aheieva and Rostyslav Semkiv, literary critics and professors at the Kyiv-Mohyla Academy, in their articles published in *LitAktsent* following the writers' commentaries. In "Can There Be a 'Russian Literature of Ukraine'?" ("Chy mozhe vidbutysia

---

90 "Можна говорити про письменника, який живе у Франції і пише по-німецьки, але все одно це не буде французька література. Так само український письменник — це є письменник, який працює у цій мові, і тому я, скажімо, не можу вважати українською літературою твори, написані, хай буде з присутністю зовсім іншої, ніж там на півночі Росії, ментальності, незважаючи на те, які є переконання проукраїнські чи можуть бути навіть націоналістичні, [...] це не є українська література."

91 "[...] розрізнення поняття літератури як унікального мовного явища і поняття національної культури як явища поліфонічного [...]."

92 "[...] допомогло б позбутися численних спекуляцій довкола теми, кого вважати або не вважати українським письменником."

93 "Попри всі спекуляції, чи не є це результатом того самого ексклюзивізму, як накинутого ззовні, ІНСТИТУЦІЯМИ української та російської національних літератур, так і такого, що існує в свідомості самих авторів, як випечене там клеймо?"

'rosiis'ka literatura Ukraïny'?"), Aheieva shifts the attention to the role played by the cultural institutions, and in particular to the dynamics of the literary market and cultural policies. Opening her contribution with the assumption that "the home of a writer is his language"[94] (Aheieva 2013), Aheieva identifies the reasons behind the inconsistency of the Russian literature of Ukraine in the failure of Soviet institutions to develop such a cultural paradigm even under conditions of full support. According to Aheieva, today the problem finds its origins in the lack of a true cultural policy in post-Soviet Ukraine: with "state support for the publication of books and the growth of the national literary market," the question concerning the role of Russophone literature "would probably not be of great interest to most of our citizens"[95] (Aheieva 2013).

In his "The Cold War of Language" ("Kholodna movna viina"), Semkiv then investigates the role of Russophone literature through the lens of the new relational dynamics between the old Russian "metropolis" (*metropoliia*) and the Ukrainian "former colony" (*kolyshnia koloniia*). As emphasized in the very title of the article, according to the scholar, today we witness the beginning of a new "cold war" of language: the former "centre" does not renounce its sphere of influence, while in Ukraine the imperial legacy is dangerously tolerated for the sake of "democratic openness" (Semkiv 2013a). Semkiv (2013a) does not deny "the right of a local author to write in the Russian language and to identify himself as a Ukrainian writer," but excludes room for "institutional recognition"[96] (*instytutsiine vyznannia*; Semkiv 2013a): the inclusion of the literary production in Russian in the national canon "cannot take place until the Northern neighbor takes concrete steps of institutional support of our culture within its borders"[97] (Semkiv 2013a). Eventually, Semkiv recognizes the existence of a contemporary Russophone literature in Ukraine, but emblematically describes it

---

94 "[…] батьківщина письменника — це його мова […]."
95 "І якби існувала державна підтримка книговидання та захист книжкового ринку […] то проблеми української літератури російською мовою, ймовірно, цікавили б не надто багатьох наших громадян."
96 "[…] право вітчизняного письменника писати російською і називатися українським автором […]."
97 "[…] доки північний сусід не зробить реальних кроків інституційної підтримки нашої культури в себе […]."

as the "quintessence of the colonial/postcolonial condition" (*kvintesentsiia kolonial'noï/post kolonial'noï sytuatsiï*). The hybridity experienced by the Russophone writer, which is described in the article as a "drama" (*drama*), is seen by Semkiv as the true motivation behind his belonging to the Russian canon: "(unless he declares something different), to him (or to her) the center of gravity will always remain the capital of the old metropolis"[98] (Semkiv 2013a).

In Search of a New Self-Determination

Analysis of the extremely heterogeneous ideas about the frame of the Ukrainian cultural space, which has been under scrutiny in this chapter, may help disclose the reasons behind the polarization of the post-Soviet intellectual debate on Russophonia: the complex prehistory of hybridity and the ideological projection of the present onto the past cultural experience; the persistence of old cultural standards in the face of new sociopolitical realia; and, last but not least, the misuse of cultural categories in the contemporary political debate. All these factors contributed to the current state of displacement of Russophone literature, lying *in-between* the Ukrainian and Russian cultural systems.

As Kruchyk (2014) emphasized, "the Russian literature of Ukraine [*Rosiis'ka literatura Ukraïny*] is currently experiencing a painful period of self-determination."[99] Most fundamentally, this process plays an undeniable role in the demarcation of both the boundaries of the national literary space and the national identity project in Ukraine. Today, the

---

98 "Тому центром тяжіння для нього (неї) завжди (навіть якщо декларується інше) залишатиметься столиця колишньої метрополії."

99 "Російська література України нині переживає болісний період самовизначення." In his study, actually, Kruchyk (2014) gloomily describes the perspectives for the further developments of this process: "If the situation in the Ukrainian literary environment is undergoing at least some kind of reflection, then Russian-language literature has almost no criticism and critics [...] That is, Russian-speaking writers do not have serious instruments of self-reflection" (Якщо ситуація в українському літературному середовищі зазнає хоч якоїсь рефлексії, то російськомовна література майже не має критики і критиків [...] Тобто російськомовні письменники не мають серйозного інструментарію саморефлексії."

alternative conceptualizations of cultural categories in the political discourse are mirrored in a still ambivalent national literary space: interestingly, over the last decades, among Russophone intellectuals a process of reflection has taken shape with the aim of voicing the long-awaited self-determination.

Chapter 2   Post-Soviet (Russophone) Ukraine Speaks Back[100]

"We are four," Golitsyn interrupts him, "and we represent at the very least four nationalities. And do we enjoy drinking any less because of that?"
"Which four nationalities, why four?" interjects Roytman nervously.
"Well, you, Borya. That's one. I'm a russkie. Two. He's from Ukraine. Three. And Horobets makes four."
"And who is Horobets?" Borya is inquisitive.
"What's your nationality, Horobets?" asks Golitsyn demanding the truth.
"Now I'll explain everything," Caesar says raising significantly his index finger.[101]
(Andrukhovych 2008: 41)

In the above-quoted excerpt from *The Moscoviad* (*Moskoviada,* 1993) by Iurii Andrukhovych (b. 1960, Ivano-Frankivs'k), in the decaying capital of the "empire" we witness a dialogue between the protagonist, Otto von F., a Ukrainian poet from the Western regions, and his three friends: Iura Golitsyn, a Russian poet; Boria Roitman, a Jewish poet; and Arnold Horobets', a Russophone playwright from southern Ukraine. In this fragment from Andrukhovych's novel, these characters are drinking in the beer hall on Fonvizin Street, when the conversation turns to the definition of their respective identity statements. Horobets' is the only one who is not able to state his own identity and sense of belonging. Just

---

100 An earlier version of this chapter was published as Marco Puleri, "Ukraïns'kyi, Rosiis'komovnyi, Rosiis'kyi: Self-Identification in Post-Soviet Ukrainian Literature in Russian." *Ab Imperio.* 2014. 2: 367–397.

101 "Нас четверо, — перебиває йому Голіцин, — І ми являємо мінімум чотири нації. І що, нам гірше п'ється від цього? — Яких чотири нації, чому чотири? — нервується Ройтман. — Ну, ти, Боря. Раз. Я русак. Два. Він з України. Три. А Горобець чотири. — А Горобець хто? — допитується Боря. — Яка твоя нація, Горобець? — вимагає правди Голіцин. — Зараз я все поясню, — значуще підносить догори вказівний палець Цезар" (Andrukhovych 2014: 58).

when he is striving to explain his condition, the narration switches to the protagonist's concerns, far from the conversation. Otto von F. comes back to join the conversation with his friends, when Horobets' has already come to the end of his description of his own *obscure* "in-between" identity: " 'And so I'm a half-breed,' finishes Julius Caesar his long and convoluted tale about his ethnicity"[102] (Andrukhovych 2008: 46). Analysing and interpreting the *missing voice* of the contemporary Horobets', we are dealing with the recent developments in the cultural identity process in Ukraine, where the presence of a fluid ethnic, language and historical framework links the identity question to situational and environmental contexts. Focusing on the cultural model pertaining to the region, we thus note the need to reconceptualize the very notion of national identity. As Rory Finnin stressed in December 2013, commenting on the early stage of the Euromaidan protests in Kyiv, if looking at contemporary Ukraine "we take a step back and conceive of 'national identity' thinly as a physics of belonging that coheres a country beyond any one language, or any one ethnicity, or any one faith, or even any one historical experience," we are eventually able to reveal new alternative interpretations for the study of Ukraine's national identity as "one of the most influential and underestimated sociocultural phenomena of its kind in modern European history" (Finnin 2013). Following these lines, if on the one hand we assume that the alleged Ukrainian identity "weakness" is the result of the dialogue and the contrast between heterogeneous and polyphonic ethnolinguistic profiles and historical trajectories of different regions, on the other an alternative reading could lead us to interpret its framework as being based on cultural contact and exchange as a performative "prism of self-articulation."[103]

---

102 "І тому я наполовину, — закінчує Юлій Цезар довгу й заплутану розповідь про свою національну приналежність" (Andrukhovych 2014: 64).

103 As the Ukrainian historian Serhii Plokhii argues: "[...] to the history of imperial expansion we need to oppose the history 'from below', the history of the people who settled and still settle the region. Globally, in a world which consists mainly of former colonies, this history successfully competes with the centralizing, imperial and postimperial one [...]" (Vorozhbyt 2014; ... нам треба протиставити історії імперської експансії історію «знизу», історію людей,

Reflections of the Ukrainian self-consciousness prism are particularly evident in contemporary national literature, as described by Maria Zubrytska: "National identity not only seems to appear to us in the mirror of literature, but actually manifests itself in the textual map" (2006: 403). It is no surprise, then, that contemporary literary production is characterized by a fragmented and composite framework. The interest of writers and readership in national "cultural geography" gave rise to the development of literary strategies involving the description and re-elaboration of the images and symbols of local cultures (see Kokhanovskaia, Nazarenko 2012a). The "materialization of memory" determines new artistic representations of the L'viv myth in *The Tango of Death* (*Tango Smerti,* 2012) by Iurii Vynnychuk (b. 1952, Ivano-Frankivs'k), as well as the envisioning of the Carpathian region in *The UnSimple* (*NeprOsti*, 2002) by Taras Prokhas'ko, or the portrayal of the lands of Volyn' in *Rivne/Rovno* (2002) by Oleksandr Irvanets' (b. 1961, L'viv).

Faced with the question of finding its own identity, contemporary literature elaborated new alternative projects. As Olena Haleta highlighted in 2013 in her analysis of the increasingly popular genre of anthology, literature has become a "testing-ground" for identity experimentation.[104] An important case in point is represented by the anthology entitled *The 27 Regions of Ukraine* (*27 Rehioniv Ukraïny*, 2012), published by Folio. Twenty-seven Ukrainian writers, including Serhii Zhadan, Oksana Zabuzhko (b. 1960, Luts'k) and Mariia Matios (b. 1959, Roztoky), contributed to this volume with short stories or excerpts from their novels dedicated to a specific regional area other than the one where they were born or live. This is a collection of poetry and prose in Ukrainian and Russian

---

які населяли й населяють регіон. Ця історія в усьому світі, який складається переважно з колишніх колоній, успішно конкурує із централізаторською, імперською та постімперською...).

104 "[...] the last twenty years have witnessed the reconstruction of cultural spaces related to the national literature and the construction of new ones; as a result, several centres have taken shape that could justifiably claim the status of literary places. The national literature has faced the problem of taking into account the heritage of totalitarianism and colonialism, which involves coming to terms with its internal space as a multilingual one" (Haleta 2013: 82).

by writers from the Eastern and Western regions: an example of dialogue between the diverse features of modern Ukraine.

Furthermore, as highlighted by Rewakowicz (2018: 152), "for a vast majority of Ukrainian-speaking authors the question is not so much of a language choice but, rather, how effectively to express themselves in the official state language that de facto functions in the bilingual and hybrid cultural space." This brought some writers, such as Bohdan Zholdak (b. 1948, Kyiv) and Pavlo Volvach (b. 1963, Zaporizhzhia) to recreate authenticity through the use of *surzhyk*,[105] a hybrid Russo–Ukrainian form—adopting it "for various aesthetic and/or ideological ends, from comical effects to social critique" (Rewakowicz 2018: 153), while others can "express themselves artistically in Ukrainian and in Russian simultaneously"[106] (Rewakowicz 2018: 160).

Another key factor in contemporary Ukrainian literature is represented by the focus on reflection on the "private past" (*privatnoe proshloe*), in order to enact a process of historical self-consciousness (Kokhanovskaia, Nazarenko 2012a: 206). It is especially the re-elaboration of "historical trauma" that becomes a specific feature in the adoption of particular literary strategies. The definition of "Transit culture" (*Tranzytna kul'tura*),

---

105   As rightly observed by Rewakowicz (2018: 153): "In the post-independence period, *surzhyk* still thrives in everyday communication despite the official status of Ukrainian, mainly because in a de facto bilingual country there are plenty of opportunities to facilitate interference of one language over another, and this time it is also Ukrainian that is impacting Russophones who are attempting to express themselves in the state language and in the process make a variety of errors."

106   Interestingly enough, as emphasized by Kruchyk (2014), the process of changing self-identification a privileged literary-artistic instrument has also involved bilingual authors: "Some of them became more active in Ukrainian (Iren Rozdobud'ko, Ihor Lapins'kyi, Ihor Zhuk, Stanislav Bondarenko, Volodymyr Shovkoshytnyi). Others wanted and managed to master Ukrainian, which they previously learned only passively—Leonid Davydenko, Evgeniia Chuprina (Kyiv), Elina Sventsyts'ka (Donets'k), Vasyl' Chubur (Sumy), Mykola Tyutyunnyk (Luhans'k)" [Одні з них активніше запослуговувалися українською (Ірен Роздобудько, Ігор Лапінський, Ігор Жук, Станіслав Бондаренко, Володимир Шовкошитний). Інші захотіли й змогли опанувати українську, котра раніше в них була у пасиві — Леонід Давиденко, Євгенія

suggested by Tamara Hundorova (2013), fosters understanding of the specific traits of Ukrainian "postcoloniality." We deal with a condition of "transition," conveying a moment of productive self-consciousness. It involves the dynamics of cultural memory in a post-totalitarian society. Reading the post-Soviet Ukrainian novel, we observe a "generation symptom": the past affects the future and uproots the subject from its existence, making it a hostage of its own past. By envisioning transition as a definite cultural model, we can thus determine "the moment of future development" (Lotman 2009: 15). It turns out to be the basis for new symbolic codes in order to interpret the existential and cultural condition:

> *Transit culture* is post-traumatic, but is definitely not 'incomplete' [...] *transit culture* can be perceived as *the loss of something*. However, when transience is understood not as a temporary transition and a movement toward a terminal point, but it is observed from the perspective of the very transitoriness and *within a continuous search for dialogue and correspondence between the self and the world, the body and the environment, the consciousness and the state of being*, then a transit culture becomes self-sufficient and complete.[107] (Hundorova 2013: 12)

In his attempt to describe the main narrative strategies adopted in the post-Soviet Ukrainian and Russian literary productions, Vitaly Chernetsky stresses the specific reception of both cultural contexts to the post-modern and postcolonial discourses.[108] He suggests reading these works as "national

---

Чуприна (Київ), Еліна Свенцицька (Донецьк), Василь Чубур (Суми), Микола Тютюнник (Луганськ)].

107 "*Транзитна культура* є посттравматичною, але зовсім не «неповною» [...] *транзитна культура* може сприйматися як *втрата чогось*. Однак коли розуміти транзитність не як тимчасовий перехід і рух до кінцевого пункту, а сприймати її з погляду самої транзитности й почуватися *всередині постійно встановлюваної відповідности й діалогу між я і світом, тілом та оточенням, свідомістю і буттям*, то транзитна культура стає самоцінною і повною."

108 Hundorova also thoroughly theorized the formation of a postcolonial consciousness in Ukrainian culture—vis-à-vis the Russian one: "In general the construction of a postcolonial consciousness in the post-Soviet space presents itself as an especially interesting process. In particular, the late 20th century Ukrainian postcolonial consciousness, marked by an overcoming of cultural provincialism and marginality, is infected by an imaginary revanchism and resentful emotions born of anti-colonial protest. It is precisely literature that became the means of revising such postcolonial mental models and trying out various forms of cultural identification. The newest Ukrainian literature

allegories," using Jameson's terminology,[109] emphasizing how their private and individual features underlie a political project for social change. Mapping Ukrainian postcolonial writing, Chernetsky identifies some major aesthetic paradigms. We acknowledge "a large body of texts characterized by a spatio-temporal convolution of narrative combined with a view of the world that perceives the mundane and the magical as fused or intertwined" (Chernetsky 2007: 186), which can be defined as "magical realist texts." This type of narrative is described as the result of the contact between the Ukrainian Baroque cultural legacies and a specific concern with the question of History. By "corruption" of the predominant historical discourses, authors such as Valerii Shevchuk (b. 1939, Zhytomyr) and Oles' Ul'ianenko (1962–2010, Khorol) deconstruct "the legacies of colonialism and totalitarianism in contemporary Ukraine, manifested both as collective national psychic trauma and as an ontological crisis" (Chernetsky 2007: 205). Another style of writing that can be observed is characterized by a particular focus on intertextuality and the carnivalesque subversion of the traditional narrative, as in the case of Iurii Andrukhovych[110] and Oleksandr Irvanets': "These texts artfully fuse the playful investigative momentum of postmodernist writing with an incisive critique of both the Russian/Soviet imperialist oppression and the fossilized traditional forms of colonial-era Ukrainian nationalist iconography" (Chernetsky 2007: 207).

---

of the 1990s is engendered by socio-cultural reflection aimed at trying to understand the relationship between the metropolis and the colony, 'one's own' and 'other,' the governing and the governed, the personal and the social, male and female, mono- and polycultural, authentic and stylized, and on the whole signals a new situation: entry into the zone of postcolonial dialogue" (Hundorova 2011).

109 "[...] the story of the private individual destiny is always an allegory of the embattled situation of the public [postcolonial] culture and society" (Jameson 1986: 69).

110 As Hundorova emphasizes in her reading of Andrukhovych's *The Moscoviad*: "Colonization by a stolen and divided past locks into a circle of repetitions and simulations. Such is the fate of the postcolonial subject. In Moscoviada this subject is already trying not so much to restore his own 'I' as obtaining revenge on the empire, by fragmenting it and inverting the 'top' and the 'bottom,' the center and the periphery, and also by engaging in voluntaristic-aggressive renaming of toponyms in the metropolis, in this

Ukrainian national allegories reveal heterogeneous and alternative models in order to reconstruct individual and collective memories, traditions and identities. Interestingly, in the post-Soviet milieu new "peripheral phenomena" are also arising, claiming reterritorialization and recognition of their unsystematic cultural symbolic system:

> Ukrainian literature is very diversified, it has been created in very different conditions, in different political circumstances, in different ideological and cultural situations. Furthermore, let's not forget that in the territory of Ukraine a great body of texts was created and is still being created which are considered to be part of the Russian literature (i.e. the literature written in Russian). However, it can also be considered as part of the Ukrainian literature, if we move away from the monolingual understanding of Ukrainian literature as such. In short, I think that our literature is a very complex and interesting phenomenon, and we hardly can (and ought to) tie it to only one specific tradition.[111] (Besedin 2014)

As emphasized by Serhii Zhadan in the above-quoted excerpt, the diversified perspectives and directions of Ukrainian textual mappings give birth to a composite framework. A challenging research perspective of the dynamics of Ukrainian literature—and "weak" national identity—resides in the analysis of a phenomenon which lies at the margins of the national cultural model.

---

manner assaulting the already powerless late-Soviet body of the empire at its very center. Doubtless, it is precisely the postcolonial world view that feeds these first post-Soviet Ukrainian novels appearing in the 1990s" (Hundorova 2011).

111 "Украинская литература очень разная, она создавалась в очень разных условиях, в разных политических обстоятельствах, в условиях разной идеологической и культурной конъюнктуры. Плюс, вы же не забывайте, что на территории Украины создавался и создаётся огромный корпус текстов, который считается частью русской литературы (то есть литература, написанная на русском). Но при желании её можно считать также частью украинской литературы, если отойти от моноязычного понимания самой украинской литературы. Одним словом, мне кажется, наша литература — это очень сложное и очень интересное явление, вряд ли можно (и нужно) привязывать ее к какой-то одной, конкретно выраженной традиции."

Ukraïns'ka Rosiis'komovna literatura versus *Rosiis'ka literatura Ukraïny*

As stressed by Iurii Lotman in his study titled *Unpredictable Mechanisms of Culture* (*Nepredskazuemye mekhanizmy kul'tury*—first appeared in Italian translation in 1994; then, published in Russian in 2010), every culture creates its own extrasystemic, "marginal" system that involves outsiders who do not belong to its centre and that a strict analysis excludes from its model. When extrasystemic elements occur in the system, we can observe one of the fundamental sources of a transformation of a cultural model from a static into a dynamic one. Through the lens of global dynamics characterizing the post-Soviet cultural area, it is no surprise that Russophone literature (*russkoiazychnaia literatura*) came to be described exactly as "literature ad marginem" by Pavel Bannikov (2015), a contemporary Kazakhstani Russian-language writer. In his essay devoted to the dynamics of contemporary Kazakhstani literature in Russian, Bannikov identified marginality as the characterizing feature of the new emerging subjectivities and literary practices in the contemporary cultural context:

> The Kazakhstani writer who writes in Russian is in the position of an eternal marginal, both in his homeland, where his audience is quite peculiar, and in Russia, where he is often perceived as a "provincial" author by inertia, or where some exotics are expected from him.[112] (2015: 197)

Actually, as emphasized by Dmitriy Melnikov (2017: 1), "[t]his definition plays with hierarchical ideas about the centre and periphery, the superior and inferior," referring "not only to external imperial spatial imagination, but to internal state of affairs in Kazakhstan as well—the Russophone writers are on margins in their own society" (Melnikov 2017: 5). Focusing on the dynamics of the Ukrainian cultural discourse—yet taking into account the intrinsic distance from the Kazakhstani realities, the marginal, extrasystemic elements of national culture can also be identified in the contemporary Russophone literary production. The definition of this cultural

---

112 "Казахстанский писатель, пишущий по-русски, находится в положении вечного маргинала, как на родине, где его аудитория весьма своеобразна, так и в России, где он часто по инерции воспринимается как «провинциальный» автор или где от него ждут экзотики."

phenomenon is still contested, whereby the legacy of old cultural standards framed around the opposition between centre and periphery, "colonizer" and "colonized," lies at the core of the debate. It is no surprise that, in our meeting in 2013, Mykola Riabchuk emblematically described the Ukrainian cultural context as fragmented into two main groups, the "aborigines" and the "creoles":

> I used this term, "creole," just in order to identify those people who speak Russian and have some sort of Russian identity, maybe not an ethnic but a cultural one. Actually, they are not Russians: for me, the most important thing was to signal that they have a new land, a new country, a new state and they have no special sympathy for the "aborigines." They are competitors. Still there are some tensions between the two groups, because it is a question of "supremacy," I would say. With regard to literature, the question is what kind of creole literature should exist. Because Ukrainian literature is of course made by native Ukrainians with their own language, following their own tradition. It is clear what the Ukrainian language literary tradition means, but it represents a difficult matter to define what kind of Russophone literature should exist in Ukraine.[113]

The complex relationships between literatures in Ukrainian and Russian, as recognized by Riabchuk, are the consequence of political and ideological struggles. The "ideological past" of the post-Soviet area, which was characterized by "literature-centricity" (*literaturotsentrizm*), as stressed by Marietta Chudakova (2006), makes the definitions applied to literary phenomena involving terminology and canon more convoluted. In cultural debates, as highlighted in the previous chapter, conceptualizing the phenomenon as Ukrainian literature in Russian—*ukraïns'ka rosiis'komovna literatura*—or Russian literature of Ukraine—*rosiis'ka literatura Ukraïny*, we are required to position our statement. The former term describes the phenomenon as integrated into the Ukrainian literary process, while the latter portrays it in the wider context of Russian literature, interpreting its affiliation with Ukraine only in territorial terms.

Unravelling the conceptual borders between history (*istoriia*) and contemporaneity (*sovremennost'*) turn out to be a key-point in post-Soviet studies. In the USSR, the strict dividing line between one's own (*svoë*) and alien (*chuzhoe*) played an important role. Terms such as *russkoe*

---

113 Excerpt from an interview with Mykola Riabchuk (Kyiv, March 19, 2013).

and *sovetskoe* (ethnically Russian and Soviet) revealed specific ideological nuances, just as the borders between literary processes described as domestic (*otechestvennoe*) and foreign (*zarubezhnoe*) concealed a political position. These criteria were made impartial by the attribution of a specific cultural standard value, or *kul'turnost'*. As noted by Chudakova, in the 1960s we observed the rise of "Russophone literature"—*russkoiazychnaia literatura*—, a new literary process, shared by the Soviet area as a whole:

> [...] it included works of Chingiz Aitmatov, Vasil' Bykov, Rasul Gamzatov, Hrant Matevosian, Jaan Kross and many other writers, who were not Russian by birth, self-identification and subject matter. They were available to the All-Union Russian readers in translations, authorized translations or self-authored Russian texts (here we leave aside the political aspects of this phenomenon). The very concept of "Russophone" enabled the opposition between "Russian" and "Russophone" writers on an ideological basis. This phenomenon reached its zenith in Post-Soviet time, in conditions of freedom of speech.[114] (Chudakova 2006)

Throughout the 2000s, many Ukrainian-speaking and Russian-speaking writers announced their projects of artistic cooperation: Serhii Zhadan and Iurii Vynnychuk collaborated with Russian-speaking writers, such as Andrei Kurkov (b. 1961, Leningrad) and Lada Luzina (b. 1972, Kyiv). Rostyslav Semkiv, in a 2013 article for *Tyzhden'*, expressed his rejection of it, defining it as a "cultural capitulation" (*kul'turna kapituliatsiia*). According to Semkiv (2013b), bilingual projects lead us to lose the meaning of Ukrainian culture, because by considering Ukrainian literature in Russian as an active element of the national culture, we strengthen the colonial dependence on Russia and its literary market. This kind of reaction could be prompted by the "dysfunctional" condition of Ukrainian culture, using Riabchuk's terms:

---

114 "[...] в него включались произведения Ч. Айтматова, В. Быкова, Р. Гамзатова, Г. Матевосяна, Я. Кросса и многих других писателей, не русских по рождению, самоотождествлению и материалу и попадавших к всесоюзному русскочитающему читателю в переводах, авторизованных переводах или собственноручных русских текстах (политические аспекты явления мы оставляем здесь в стороне). Понятие «русскоязычный» дало возможность для противопоставления «русских» и «русскоязычных» писателей уже на идеологической основе. Это явление достигло своего расцвета уже в постсоветское время, в условиях свободы слова."

In this postcolonial situation, the problem of the literary market is really important. My main argument is that Ukrainian culture is dysfunctional. It has good cultural artifacts and phenomena, but they do not function in society adequately, just because society is dysfunctional [...] We have got high culture, which works in small circles of intellectuals, and we have this huge group of Ukrainian-speaking provincial undereducated people, who basically are not connected with high culture at all, or who consume pop culture imported from Russia. These two worlds do not interact, and they can be considered as separated. And the whole gap is filled by Moscow and its imported products in literature, music and cinema.[115]

The reasons behind the grim picture of the cultural field described above by Riabchuk can be found in the significant decline that affected the cultural market in Ukraine in the aftermath of the Soviet collapse. In 2011, while commenting on the situation, the president of the Ukrainian association of publishers and booksellers, Oleksandr Afonin (2011), could observe how in post-Soviet times state institutions' disregard of the "true role of the national book in society" brought, among other effects, "a significant general reduction of the volume of book publishing in Ukraine," that is close "to the lowest level in Europe (less than one book per person)" by circulation, thus making "domestic products unattainable for the average consumer."[116]

This is the result of the uneven transition of the book business from Soviet state control to post-Soviet privatization. Indeed, as Afonin remembers, in the Ukrainian Soviet Socialist Republic (URSR) "[l]ibraries of all levels (up to around fifty thousand), from the school to the trade union ones, had an annual reserved budget for replenishment that guaranteed citizens access to any book printed throughout the year in Ukraine"[117] (Afonin 2011). Furthermore, whereas still in the early 1960s circulation was still

---

115 Excerpt from an interview with Mykola Riabchuk (Kyiv, March 19, 2013).

116 "Ігнорування владою істинної ролі національної книжки в суспільстві призвело до [...] значного сумарного скорочення обсягів книговидання в Україні за накладами до найнижчого в Європі рівня (менш як одна книжка за рік на особу) [...] що робить вітчизняну продукцію недосяжною для пересічного споживача."

117 "Бібліотеки всіх рівнів (їх налічувалося майже 50 тис.), від шкільної до профспілкової, мали річний захищений бюджет для поповнення фондів, який гарантував громадянам доступ до будь-якої книжки, видрукуваної впродовж року на теренах України."

relatively small, it was in the 1970s that we had a real boom of the circulation of domestic production in Soviet Ukraine, which reached its zenith in 1974, when about 104 million copies of Ukrainian-language books were published: indeed, it is worth noticing that the number of book titles and brochures in the URSR was only around three thousand the same year (Ivanko 2010). Generally, as reported in research conducted by Ivan Ivanko (2010) on the dynamics of the book publishing industry in the URSR throughout 1921–1989, we can observe how, on the one hand, the circulation of Ukrainian-language books was always inversely proportional to the number of published titles; and on the other, since the 1960s the rate of Russian-language book titles became firmly predominant, while only in the late 1980s did the circulation of publications in Russian exceed that of those in Ukrainian.

In post-Soviet times, the collapse of the state-controlled book industry had, then, a significant impact on the emerging national cultural scene. As Afonin (2011) bitterly reported, while "[i]n the late 1980s, on the eve of independence, the total circulation of the books printed in a year reached 189,5 million copies and 8449 titles," in 2010 "the total annual circulation was around 45 million copies and 22,55 thousand titles":[118] this brought the average rate of 3.7 books per inhabitant of the URSR to 0.98 per citizen of post-Soviet Ukraine. These data clearly show the structural flaws of the national literary market, whereby we can observe the clear gap between the large number of published books and the inadequate level of distribution (Slavins'ka 2011). This alarming tendency was also triggered by the lack of monitoring and policies of institutional control. Most fundamentally, while on the one hand in Russia it was already in 1995 that the new legal framework exempted the activities of publishing houses from value-added tax (VAT), on the other in Ukraine similar legal measures were approved only in 2001 (Afonin 2011). Throughout the 1990s, this led to the gradual takeover of the Ukrainian market by imported products, mainly from Russia. As emblematically reported in a 2013 study of the Ukrainian

---

118 "Наприкінці 1980-х, напередодні незалежності, сумарний наклад книжок, видрукуваних за рік, сягав 189,5 млн примірників і 8449 назв. [...] Минулого ж, 2010 року сумарний річний наклад був 45 млн примірників і 22,55 тис. назв. за середнього тиражу 1993 екземпляри."

book market, today the domestic production accounts "for approximately 20 to 23 % of the total book consumption in Ukraine, while the combined legal, individual and illegal imports from Russia plus pirated editions are estimated to account for 73 to 74 % of the market" (Book Platform: 6–7). Furthermore, currently there are only two main networks of bookstores in Ukraine, Bukva and IE, and—as shown in a 2018 report issued by the National Academics of Statistics—the publishing market in Ukraine remains highly centralized, having its main centres in Kyiv, Kharkiv and L'viv (Horobets' 2018: 26).

Within this alarming framework, as reflected in data published by the State Book Chamber of Ukraine, among the books published in the country in 2013—the last year before the beginning of the "Ukraine crisis"—16,310 editions were in the Ukrainian language (37,892.9 thousand copies) and 7,198 editions were in the Russian language (27,652.0 thousand copies) out of 26,323 editions in total.[119] Following these lines, the number of Russian-language editions still represents an important portion of the entire book market in Ukraine, even if the structural flaws of the national literary market make it impossible for Russian-language editions in Ukraine to compete with the imports from the Russian Federation, especially in light of the former's low level of circulation.

In light of these dynamics, we are therefore dealing with a system based on *régimes d'engagement*, using Thèvenot's (2006) term. Russophone writers' self-identification statements, involving their belonging to Russian or Ukrainian cultural models, is heavily influenced by their opportunities to publish in the respective literary markets. Cultural institutions, such as Russkaia Premiia,[120] the annual award for Russian-speaking writers living outside the Russian Federation, coordinated by Sergei Chuprinin, director of the Russian literary magazine *Znamia*, thus gradually sharpened the "assimilation" of Ukrainian writers into the Russian market, as happened in 2012 to Vladimir Rafeenko (Donets'k, b. 1969) and Marianna Goncharova (Chernivtsi, b. 1967), and in 2013 to Elena Stiazhkina (Donets'k, b. 1968) and Andrei Poliakov (Simferopol', b. 1968), who

---

119 See: http://www.ukrbook.net/statistika/statistika_2013.htm (08/2019).
120 The award was suspended in 2016 for lack of funding. See: http://russpremia. ru (08/2019).

started publishing their works with large publishing houses and literary journals based in Russia.

In general, as Mikhail Berg remarked about the Russian scene in his study *Literaturocracy: The Problem of Appropriation and Redistribution of Power in Literature* (*Literaturokratiia: Problema prisvoeniia i pereraspredeleniia vlasti v literature*, 2000), in the post-Soviet context we can also observe a strong influence from sociocultural phenomena on the adoption of specific narrative strategies and identity statements by the writers:

> The social status of literature determines the value of the positions in the field of literature and, consequently, the social value of literary practices [...] A status change of literature entails a change of the author's strategies, as happened in the early 1990s, when the status of the literary field in the Russian social context changed so swiftly, that up to now there is still a persistent perception of what happened as a catastrophe.[121] (Berg 2000: 180)

In the current sociocultural context, the reshaping of the value system, related to literary practices, gives birth to a new balance. It has the power to ascribe a given phenomenon to "supremacy" or "marginality."[122] The new evaluation parameters are embodied by the market: the increase in printing and distribution marks the path to a "dominant position."[123]

---

121 "Социальный статус литературы определяет ценность позиций в поле литературы и соответственно социальную ценность литературных практик [...] изменение статуса литературы влечет за собой изменение авторских стратегий, как это и случилось, когда в начале 1990-х годов положение поля литературы в российском социальном пространстве изменилось настолько стремительно, что инерция восприятия до сих пор оценивает произошедшее как катастрофу."

122 "In literature we have the power to publish or to refuse a publication, to recognize the legitimacy of a particular practice or to impose a marginal status on it, to declare one or another practice as dominant or archaic, to expand the field of literature at the expense of other fields (that is, the field of ideology or the field of politics); and of course, the power to name and to be named" (Berg 2000: 10; В литературе есть власть публиковать или отказать в публикации, признать легитимность конкретной практики или навязать ей маргинальный статус, объявить ту или иную практику доминирующей или архаической, расширить поле литературы за счет других полей (скажем, поля идеологии или поля политики); и, конечно, власть называть и быть названным).

123 As Berg puts it: "Since the market became the criterion of relevance in the post-perestroika cultural scene, for literature, in order to fit into the market,

Tatiana Kokhanovskaia and Mikhail Nazarenko stressed the difficult situation of the Ukrainian literary market on the eve of Euromaidan. It was determined by weak commercialization. It did not prevent publishers from publishing new literary works, while at the same time it led writers and critics to address mass readership:

> It is the very Ukrainian-language segment of the Ukrainian literature that benefits from this. It has no competitive pressure from Russian book production (simply the higher the number of copies, the lower the cost. For the Ukrainian editions in Russian it is practically impossible to compete with Russian imports). It follows that the winner is the one who offers the reader something that is missing on the Russian market.[124] (Kokhanovskaia, Nazarenko 2011a: 208)

The complex relationship with the "metropolis," that is, the Russian literary market, and the difficult process of assimilation of *rosiis'komovna* literature into the Ukrainian cultural system are mirrored in the national identity question, as stressed by Andrei Kurkov, a Ukrainian Russian-speaking writer, in our 2013 meeting in Kyiv:

> The question of identity is a source of several arguments, and it is a question which divides the nation, rather than uniting it. Because the main problem is "what do you want in Ukraine: ethnic nation or political nation?" Logically for everybody who is not ethnically Ukrainian, we have a multicultural society, with over thirty-five nationalities: some big ones, like Russians and Tatars, and some smaller ones, like Greeks, Bulgarians, Romanians and others. If we accept that Ukraine is a political nation, then we can go further. But before this achievement, I guess that it is difficult to talk about the national cultural context, because we have different regional cultural identities. (Puleri 2016: 182)

The case of Andrei Kurkov is the result of a particular literary background. The "Kurkov phenomenon" arose in the European literary market, where

---

there was only one way—to increase circulation" (Berg 2000: 206; Так как критерием актуальности постперестроечной культурной сцены стал рынок, то для литературы, дабы вписаться в рынок, оставался один путь — увеличения тиражей).

124 "Именно украиноязычному сегменту украинской литературы это на пользу: нет конкурентного давления российской книжной продукции (что и понятно: чем больше тираж, тем ниже себестоимость — украинским изданиям на русском языке практически невозможно конкурировать с российским импортом). А значит, выиграет тот, кто предложит читателю нечто, отсутствующее на русском рынке."

in the second half of the 1990s his first works were published. Nowadays his books are outstanding post-Soviet bestsellers. Because of his use of the Russian language in his literary works, his identity as a Ukrainian writer has been harshly criticized. Nonetheless, his success in the Western market has gradually facilitated his assimilation process in the Ukrainian literary context. His choice to publish his latest works both in Ukrainian and Russian worked then as a positive factor in the relationship between the two national cultural models.[125]

Most fundamentally, as emerges from the case of Kurkov, the novelty of the post-Soviet developments of Russophone literature mainly lies in the new directions undertaken by the writers' positioning in the global cultural arena. As argued by Chernetsky (2019: 61) regarding the need for new "helpful criteria for approaching Russophone literary production in countries other than Russia," the crucial issue is around the authors' self-identification. While analysing the outcomes of the debate among Russian-language Israeli authors in 1991, Chernetsky's reading of Mikhail Gendelev's manifesto "Russophone Literature of Israel" ("Russkoiazychnaia literatura Izrailia") classifies at least three different groups:

> Russophone writers who primarily identify as members of a global Russian-speaking diaspora; those who primarily identify with Russian literature of the metropole; and a portion of writers who believe that "Israeli realities demand new means of expression, aesthetic models that did not exist earlier in Russian literature." (Chernetsky 2019: 61)

Focusing on the local developments in post-Soviet Kazakhstan, Dmitriy Melnikov in his study (2017) similarly argues that among the main differences between the Russophone literature and the literature of the Russian diaspora we can identify "writers' self-identification—whether or not they [the writers] feel themselves representative of a diaspora whose identity is determined by the sense of attachment to the mother country" (Melnikov 2017: 2). The heterogeneity of Kazakhstani Russophone writers' positions subtends "a complex postcolonial situation that strongly affects the ethnic group associated with metropolia—there are not only Kazakhs

---

125 It was only with the publication of his 2012 book *The L'viv Tour of Jimi Hendrix* (*L'vovskaia gastrol' Dzhimi Khendriksa*) that the author started to publish his works simultaneously in Russian and in Ukrainian translation.

writing in Russian not identifying themselves as Russians, but there are also ethnic Russians (or Slavs) writing in Russian and identifying themselves as other Russians" (Melnikov 2017: 3).

Looking at the Ukrainian literary context, the unprecedented novelty of similar dynamics—where we also witness the emergence of "Ukrainian Russophone" and *other* Russian writers—emblematically contradicts the history of modern literature on Ukraine's territory, whereby "instances in which a writer wrote exclusively or mostly in Russian but identified first and foremost with Ukraine were almost nonexistent until recently" (Chernetsky 2019: 57).

The Self-Identification in Post-Soviet Ukrainian Literature in Russian

> [...] at the moment, Russophone literature in Ukraine [*russkoiazychnaia literatura Ukrainy*] is an uncontested phenomenon: it is impossible [...] to ignore, to restrain or to Ukrainize it for several years [...] What if some, albeit not very beautiful, but still unprecedented flower will sprout from this literary humus?[126]
> (Okara 2008)

Contemporary Ukrainian literary production in Russian reveals diversified features. As in the case of Ukrainian-language literature, we cannot determine universally recognized narrative strategies. A significant segment of works can be ascribed to the fantasy genre, as in the case of Marina (b. 1968, Kyiv) and Sergei Diachenko (b. 1945, Kyiv), while other leading cultural actors focus on allegorical and satirical re-elaboration of their own historical consciousness and belonging.[127] Given the situation of the national literary market already described, the main publication

---

126 "[...] на данный момент русскоязычная литература на Украине — явление безальтернативное, ее никак невозможно [...] игнорировать, ущемлять или пытаться украинизировать за несколько лет [...] А вдруг сквозь этот литературный гумус прорастет какой-нибудь, пусть не очень красивый, но зато еще невиданный цветок?"

127 In her study Rewakowicz (2018) devotes attention to Andrei Kurkov's prose and the fantasy genre, analysing Lada Luzina's and Marina and Sergei Diachenkos' literary works. According to Rewakowicz, the Russian-language authors under scrutiny in her work "function (or functioned) within the Ukrainian cultural space [...] and all have attained a high degree of popularity in their respective genres both at home and abroad" (2018: 143).

channels are represented by anthologies, literary magazines and collections (Kokhanovskaia, Nazarenko 2012a). As argued by Kukulin (2007) in his introduction to a special section devoted to Ukrainian–Russian literary relations in *Novoe literaturnoe obozrenie*, we are dealing with a cultural phenomenon producing different kinds of "hybridization" between the Ukrainian and Russian cultural systems:

> [...] It seems that the Russian literature of Ukraine [*russkaia literatura Ukrainy*] consists of several "sub-literatures" having various types of interaction with Ukrainian and Russian literatures: some authors are oriented towards the style of European postmodernism, others towards the uncensored traditionalist poetry of the 1970s, and still others towards Soviet "village" prose [*derevenskaia proza*]... Each author is included in several contexts, both literary and non-literary, at once: those who write in Russian face Ukrainian-language documents in everyday life, participate in everyday conversations in Ukrainian or "surzhik," etc. "The unit of measurement" of Russian-Ukrainian literary relations becomes first of all the single author, and only then literary groups, periodicals, and so on.[128] (2007: 243)

The relatively unsystematic nature of Russophone literature does not allow for globally determining its autonomy or, alternatively, its independence from/dependence on one of the two cultural systems. In order to grasp its marginal and dynamic nature, we should thus opt for an investigation of the heterogeneous tendencies and affiliations, studying the directions taken by single authors or local and regional periodicals.

In my analysis I will first focus on the Kyiv context, which reveals diverse paths towards the process of diffusion of Russophone literature. The alternative cultural outlooks proposed by two leading literary magazines based

---

128 "[...] русская литература Украины состоит словно бы из нескольких «сублитератур,» поддерживающих разного типа взаимодействия с украиноязычной и с российской литературами: одни авторы ориентируются на стилистику европейского постмодернизма, другие — неподцензурной традиционалистской поэзии 1970-х годов, третьи — «деревенской» прозы... Каждый автор включен сразу в несколько контекстов, как литературных, так и внелитературных: те, кто пишет по-русски, в быту сталкиваются с украиноязычными документами, участвуют в бытовых разговорах на украинском языке или «суржике» и т.п. «Единицей измерения» русско-украинских литературных связей становится прежде всего отдельный автор, и уж только потом — литературная группа, периодическое издание и т.п."

in the capital shed light on the complex self-identification framework of the writers in question. *Sho*,[129] founded in Kyiv in 2005, is a cultural magazine published in both languages—Russian and Ukrainian—which displays a particular approach to the Ukrainian cultural process. Its editorial policy is aimed at emphasizing the features of the new post-independence canon, involving the effects of the Soviet cultural legacy. The magazine is directed by Aleksandr Kabanov (b. 1968, Kherson), a famous Russian-language poet living in Kyiv: he declares himself to be a "Russian poet and a Ukrainian citizen" (*russkii poet i grazhdanin Ukrainy*; Volodarskii 2010). The magazine coordinates the annual poetry festival Kyivs'ki lavry. In order to encourage open dialogue, the contest consists of readings of poems in different languages, such as Ukrainian, Russian and Polish. Furthermore, in the magazine we find a section entitled Sho-Izdat, dedicated to the publication of short stories, poems and excerpts from novels by leading Ukrainian- and Russian-language writers. In the January 2014 issue, there was an interesting project involving a rating of national literary production (*Sho* 2014). An enquiry was carried out through interviews with 77 Ukrainian- and Russian-speaking critics, poets, writers and publishers, who stated their viewpoints on four issues: Ukrainian prose, Ukrainian poetry, Russophone prose and Russophone poetry of Ukraine.[130] With regard to my own analysis, the rating showed the most popular Ukrainian Russophone writers to be the ones who publish their works abroad, mainly in Russia.

---

129 See: https://shoizdat.com/ (08/2019).

130 As argued in 2013 by the editor of the project, Iurii Volodarskii, the terms "Russophone prose of Ukraine" [*russkoiazychnaia proza Ukrainy*] and "Russophone poetry of Ukraine" [*russkoiazychnaia poeziia Ukrainy*] are able to better frame the position of the contemporary literary phenomenon in the Ukrainian cultural space: "For intrinsic reasons, the phrase 'Ukrainian literature' is associated at the same time to both the language and the state [...] But what if we are talking about writings that do not correspond with the language, but with the state, that is about texts written by its inhabitants and full-fledged citizens? It would seem simpler than simple: instead of the ambiguous definition of 'Ukrainian literature', we use the quite transparent phrase "literature of Ukraine" [...] It seems to be clear that everything that is written in the country in any language—Ukrainian, Russian, Hungarian, Crimean Tatar, etc.—refers to the literature of Ukraine" (Volodarskii 2013a).

On the other hand, the literary journal *Raduga*,[131] founded in 1927, embodies an instance of the re-elaboration of the Ukrainian–Soviet legacy. After national independence and a brief period of inactivity, the journal was revamped. The aim of this project is to support Ukrainian literary production in Russian by publishing short stories and novels by contemporary writers. Over the last few years, the editors have coordinated the organization of many literary awards oriented towards Ukrainian Russian-language writers, such as Aktivatsiia Slova and Gogolevskaia Premiia. Iurii Koval'skii, lead editor of *Raduga*, defines post-Soviet Ukrainian literary production in Russian as an "island between Russian and Ukrainian literary markets":

> As for the problems of publishing in Russian, this is quite an old question. The matter is that there has always been a special attitude to the poets and the novelists writing in Russian here in Ukraine (in this case, I am talking about the professional environment—fellow writers, publishers). On the one hand, in their homeland they are considered not quite Ukrainian writers, and on the other, in relation to Russian literature they are seen as very peripheral, that is, "eradicated" from the roots of their language. In both cases, we can see some kind of scorn and estrangement.[132] (Stasov 2009)

In this case, the Russian-speaking literary context works as a "periphery" longing for the "centre," Moscow, enacting processes of cultural exchange and interaction between the two literary worlds. The question concerns the actual scope of a phenomenon inherited from the Soviet legacy, described by the Russophone writer Aleksei Nikitin (b. 1967, Kyiv) as *Moskovskii Pylesos*, literally the "Moscow vacuum-cleaner:"

> This may seem a paradox, but in independent Ukraine we had the chance to talk about a real Russian literature of Ukraine [*Russkaia literatura Ukrainy*]. In Soviet times the powerful "Moscow vacuum-cleaner" was still working. It

---

131 See: http://raduga.org.ua/ (08/2019).

132 "Что же касается проблемы издания на русском языке, то она довольно давняя. И заключается в том, что к поэтам и прозаикам, пишущим у нас на русском, всегда было особое отношение (в данном случае имею в виду профессиональную среду — коллег литераторов, издателей). С одной стороны, их считают не совсем украинскими писателями на своей родине, а с другой — применительно к русской литературе — очень периферийными, так сказать, оторванными от языковых корней. То есть в обоих случаях просматривается пренебрежительность, некое отчуждение."

drew to the capital all the people of value. There were some exceptions, but these were rare, and for each of them we could find specific reasons. Overall, the atmosphere of the literary province under such strict ideological control as that to which the Soviet Ukraine was subjected, was not conducive to the appearance of schools and new tendencies in any language [...] Nowadays the "Moscow vacuum-cleaner" is still working, but through a filter. Many writers have moved abroad and some of them have moved to Russia, but those remaining in Ukraine are more and more numerous.[133] (Besedin 2013: 66–67)

Whereas we are not dealing with rigid ideological separations between cultural phenomena, as happened in Soviet times, today we observe the rise of a literary production emerging from the "liminal" space between the two cultural worlds. Significantly, it is also the appearance of new publishing houses in independent Ukraine that testifies to the vitality of the new dynamics described by Nikitin. With respect to this matter, the case of Laurus, a publishing house founded in Kyiv by Polina Lavrova (b. 1972, St. Petersburg) is quite telling: in the period preceding the outbreak of the Euromaidan protests, it acted as a bridge between the Russian and Ukrainian cultural systems. The editorial policy was originally aimed at publishing Russophone prose authored by Ukrainian writers. As argued by Lavrova in a 2014 interview, due to the complex dynamics characterizing the national literary market and cultural context, throughout the 2010s Laurus took a change of direction:

This is problematic, first, because [...] there are still a number of bookstores that, for example, refuse to hold presentations in Russian. They can even borrow books from publishers and put them on the shelf devoted to foreign literature [...] Second, Ukrainian writers who write in Russian, and there are many of them, have already got over the habit of being published in their homeland. Their

---

133 "Может, это покажется парадоксом, но именно в годы независимости Украины появилась возможность говорить о полноценной русской литературе Украины. В советское время работал мощный «московский пылесос,» который засасывал в столицу всех, кто чего-то стоил. Исключения были, но очень редкие, и у каждого для этого находились особые причины. А в целом атмосфера литературной провинции с ужесточенным идеологическим контролем, какой была советская Украина, не особенно располагала к появлению школ и новых течений в любом языке [...] Сейчас «московский пылесос» продолжает работать, но на него надели фильтр. Немало авторов из Украины уехало и некоторые состоялись в России, но оставшихся все же больше."

manuscripts are taken only by small publishers, since the internal market is complex: you need to take them to Russian-speaking regions. Of course, it is easier for Russian-speaking writers to publish in Russia, where the main part of the copies is dropped off [...] Now the situation is gradually changing, but it is still easier for writers to publish their books in Russia, which is undoubtedly bad for the Ukrainian book market.[134] (Demina 2014)

In spite of this complex picture, as emphasized by Lavrova, it was mainly scientific literature in Russian that found its place in the Ukrainian market. The publication of a book series entitled *Zoloti Vorota* by Laurus achieved resounding success in Ukraine: this included renowned Russian and Ukrainian historians' works, such as Serhii Plokhii's, Aleksei Miller's and Oleksii Tolochko's studies, which were published in both Russian and Ukrainian. Furthermore, the poetry series *Chisla* included collections of poems in the Russian language by the Russian writers Lev Rubinshtein (b. 1947, Moscow) and Oleg Chukhontsev (b. 1938, Pavlovskii Posad), and a new edition of Ukrainian-language poems by Serhii Zhadan, Oleksandr Irvanets' and Petro Midianka (b. 1959, Shyrokyi Luh). With regard to this growing cultural exchange, Andrei Dmitriev (b. 1956, Leningrad), a Russian writer who worked as editor at Laurus, in our meeting in 2013 surprisingly highlighted a veritable "boom" of Ukrainian literature in the Russian market throughout the early 2010s. Interestingly enough, as argued by Nazarenko, who co-authored the section *The Ukrainian Vector* (*Ukrainskii Vektor*) in 2011 in the Russian literary journal *Novyi Mir*, controversial questions arise when this attraction takes the shape of "cultural appropriation:"

---

134 "Однако это проблематично, потому что, во-первых, [...] есть ряд магазинов, которые, например, отказываются проводить презентации на русском языке. Они даже могут взять у издателей книги, поставить на полку иностранной литературы [...] С другой стороны, украинские писатели, которые пишут на русском языке, а их много, уже отвыкли печататься у себя на родине. Их рукописи берут только небольшие издательства, поскольку рынок сложный: нужно везти в русскоязычные регионы. Конечно, проще, русскоязычным писателям печататься в России, где и расходится основная часть тиража [...] Сейчас ситуация понемногу меняется, но писателям все ещё проще публиковать свои книги в России, что несомненно, плохо для украинского книжного рынка."

There are two trends in Russia. On the one hand, we may observe an interest in Ukrainian literature and in the Russophone literature of Ukraine, in light of the differences between what is done here and what happens in the literary process in Russia. On the other hand, we may witness new attempts at cultural appropriation, when Russophone authors are recognized only as Russians.[135]

These controversial dynamics were at the core of the roundtable titled "Russophone Literature of Ukraine: The Poor Relative of a Wealthy Family?" ("Russkoiazychnaia literatura Ukrainy: bednaia rodstvennitsa iz bogatoi sem'i?"), which was organized on the premises of Laurus in February 2013.[136] On this occasion, the speakers agreed in describing the distance between the Russophone literary phenomenon and the Russian one and its autonomous developments in the various regions of Ukraine. In particular, the participation of Russophone intellectuals and writers from diverse cultural centres in Ukraine—such as Zaven Babloian (b. 1971, Moscow) from Kharkiv, who edited the Russian-language editions of Zhadan's, Andrukhovych's and Prokhas'ko's works, and Vladimir Rafeenko (b. 1969, Donets'k), a Russian-language writer from Donets'k—testified to the growing "decentralization" of the phenomenon around the country.

Following these lines, the emblematic title of the article co-authored by the Russophone writer Iurii Tsaplin (b. 1972, Kharkiv) and the Ukrainophone poet Rostyslav Mel'nykiv (b. 1973, Podorozhnie), *The North-East of the South-West: On the Contemporary Kharkiv Literature* (*Severo-vostok iugo-zapada: O sovremennoi Khar'kovskoi literature*), which was published in the Russian journal *Novoe literaturnoe obozrenie* in 2007, embodies the peculiar nuances of the "borderland culture" developed in East Ukraine.[137]

---

135 "В России заметно две тенденции. С одной стороны, интерес к украинской литературе вообще и к Украине русскоязычной, потому что они видят, что здесь делается что-то не совсем так, как в России. А с другой стороны, попытки культурного присвоения, когда русскоязычные авторы объявляются просто русскими [...]." Excerpt from an interview with Mikhail Nazarenko (Kyiv, March 26, 2013).

136 See: http://museumshevchenko.org.ua/post.php?id=277&lang=ru (08/2019).

137 As Volodymyr Kravchenko puts it in his study *Khar'kov/Kharkiv: The Borderland Capital* (*Khar'kov/Kharkiv: Stolitsa pogranich'ia,* 2010), the specific position of the city on the geographic–cultural border with today's Russian Federation has created a fluid and permeable regional identity: "The Ukrainian-Russian border is the most problematic of those who delineate the

According to the authors, literary bilingualism in Kharkiv reflects the liminal position of the city lying at the crossroads of the Ukrainian tradition and the Russian one throughout the course of Imperial and Soviet history. As argued by Mel'nykiv and Tsaplin, this intrinsic dual nature should not be overlooked also when describing recent cultural developments:

> In the opinion of one of the authors of this article, this trend has especially intensified in the last fifteen years, bringing to life the recent formula "Ukrainian Russophone literature" [*ukrainskaia rusofonnaia literatura*] that was actively promoted by the Kyiv writer Andrei Kurkov; those who try to think of themselves in the Russian context inevitably find themselves on the margins of the literary process—due to their "diasporic" existence. From the point of view of the other co-author, this trend has rather weakened. In addition, a) the "Ukrainian Russophone" [*ukrainskaia rusofonnaia*] literature, although it may not be considered by Moscow critics as part of Russian literature, is actually such; b) the marginal position in culture, as agreed, sometimes turns out to be advanced and, ultimately, productive. [...][138] (Mel'nikov, Tsaplin 2007: 267)

---

state and national space of modern Ukraine. The administrative and state borders between Ukraine and Russia almost never coincided with the geography of settlement of the respective ethnic groups [...] Earlier, the Ukrainian-Russian border was not stable and strictly fixed, but it has become so only recently. Therefore, it most often acts as a mental construct having a symbolic character, as well as relevant processes, practices and discourses arising as a result of Ukrainian-Russian relations and having their own symbols and cultural texts" (Kravchenko 2010: 7; Украинско-российская граница — наиболее проблемная из всех, которые очерчивают современное украинское государственное и национальное пространство. Административные и государственные границы между Украиной и Россией практически никогда не совпадали с географией расселения соответствующих этносов [...] Ранее украинско-российская граница не была стабильной и строго фиксированной, а стала такой лишь в последнее время. Поэтому она выступает чаще всего в качестве ментального конструкта, имеющего символический характер, а также в виде соответствующих процессов, практик и дискурсов, возникавших в результате украинско-русских отношений и обладающих собственной символикой и культурными текстами).

138 "По мнению одного из авторов данной статьи, эта тенденция особенно усилилась в последние пятнадцать лет, вызвав к жизни активно пропагандируемую ныне киевским писателем Андреем Курковым формулировку — «украинская русофонная литература»; те же, кто пытается мыслить себя в российском контексте, неизбежно оказываются на обочине литпроцесса — ввиду своего «диаспорного» существования.

The different perspectives on the potential self-determination of Russophone literature held by Tsaplin and Mel'nykiv disclose the situational nature of the issue. While on the one hand authors such as Kurkov can promote the novelty of the phenomenon, introducing the calque *rusofonnaia literatura*—taken from analogous developments in the Anglophone, Francophone and Sinophone literatures,[139] on the other the heterogeneous range of positions assumed by Russian-language cultural actors and their still marginal position in the literary field prevents applying any global definition. Nonetheless, in Kharkiv we can still witness the great success of a veritable school of science fiction (*nauchnaia fantastika*): Henry Lion Oldie, which is the pen name of the Ukrainian authors Oleg Ladyzhenskii (b. 1963, Kharkiv) and Dmitrii Gromov (b. 1963, Simferopol'), and Andrei Valentinov, also known as Andrei Shmal'ko (b. 1958, Kharkiv), publish their works mainly in Russia, but are also considered part of the national cultural context, especially thanks to the results of the editorial initiatives undertaken by the Kharkiv-based Folio, one of the largest publishing houses in contemporary Ukraine. It is also the role played by the literary journal *Soiuz pisatelei*,[140] which boosts the relations between Ukrainian-language and Russian-language intellectuals in East Ukraine. The journal was founded in 2000 by the poet Konstantin Beliaiev (b. 1971, Sosnivka) and is edited now by Iurii Tsaplin and Andrei Krasniashchikh (b. 1970, Poltava). Significantly, *Soiuz pisatelei* includes not only works authored

---

С точки же зрения другого соавтора, тенденция скорее ослабела. Кроме того, а) «украинская русофонная» словесность хоть и может не считаться московскими критиками частью русской литературы, но фактически таковой является; б) маргинальная позиция в культуре, как известно, порой оказывается передовой и, в конечном счете, продуктивной [...]"

139 As highlighted by Gorham (2011: 25), the concept of *rusofoniia* has been only recently coined in the Russian language, and "at least up until the first years of Vladimir Putin's presidency, Russia-friendly sources actually treated the term as a pejorative, used against Russian minorities in newly independent states." Then, while in the late 1990s some commentators began to use the term along the lines of 'Francophonie', throughout the 2000s the concept acquired a political nature in the public debate in the 'Near Abroad'. Naomi Caffee (2013: 22) remembers how other similar terms have been also in use throughout the last decades, as in the case of *russkofonnyi* and *russkofoniia*.

140 See: http://sp-issues.narod.ru/ (08/2019).

by Russian-speaking authors from Ukraine but also Russian-language translations of contemporary Ukrainian literature. Finally, it is worth mentioning another journal which was quite active from 2002 to 2011 in the Donets'k region. *Dikoe Pole* was edited by the literary critic Aleksandr Korablev (b. 1956, Kostiantynivka) with the aim of creating a potential "literary showcase" for local Russophone authors. Already in 2004, the journal hosted a rating of national literary production (Korablev 2004). Here the categories used by the editors widely differed from those adopted by *Sho* in 2014: the rating had up to ten different classifications aimed at identifying the degree of recognition of Ukrainian and "Russian" [*russkie*] writers in the country through interviews with more than 60 experts around Ukraine. Interestingly enough, the 2004 rating disclosed the "dysfunctionality" and intrinsic fragmentation of the national cultural context. As gloomily remembered by Korablev (2004: 211): "Some experts have honestly warned about their bias. Others have limited themselves to just a few nominations [...] Frequently, Ukrainian experts have admitted that they do not fully know some Russian authors, while the Russians have recognized this lack with regard to Ukrainian writers."[141] The different positions on the language question played a decisive role in defining the space for the identification of literary production in Russian, as also emerges from Korablev's reflection in our 2013 meeting:

> I doubt that there may be a Ukrainian Russophone literature [*Ukrainskaia russkoiazychnaia literatura*]. Generally, I prefer [...] to define it as "Russian" [*russkaia*], rather than "Russophone" [*russkoiazychnaia*], literature. Perhaps, it will not be politically correct, but, in any case, it is believed that "Russian" [*russkii*] is both the language and the mentality of those people who live in Ukraine. I cannot see it as a full-fledged phenomenon. I see Russian authors, sometimes very talented. Russian literature must be observed both in its entirety and in its various tendencies, when we can really say that there is something that unites them.[142]

---

141 "Некоторые эксперты честно предупреждали о своей пристрастности. Иные ограничивались несколькими номинациями [...] Нередко украинские эксперты признавались в полном незнании русских авторов, а русские, соответственно, украинских."

142 "У меня есть большие сомнения, что существует феномен русскоязычной литературы Украины. Я, вообще-то, предпочитаю [...] называть её не

At the Intersection of Two Cultural Models

In light of the mentioned dynamics and diverse labels applied to the Russophone literature, it is quite clear that both geographical and language criteria are not sufficient to describe the belonging of this literary production either to the Russian or the Ukrainian canon. Eventually, we may assume, as argued by Kukulin (2007: 244), that:

> The question of whether Russophone literature in Ukraine [*russkoiazychnaia literatura Ukrainy*] is independent or is a part of Russian literature turns out to be rhetorical: there is no undivided Ukrainian literature and Russian literature, but we can rather speak of multi-structured fields.[143]

In order to unravel contemporary cultural heterogeneity and negotiation, it is useful to analyse some complementary features of the literary production of Ukrainian-language writer Serhii Zhadan. The writer, born in Starobil's'k, in the Luhans'k region, lives in Kharkiv, set on the geographical and cultural border with the modern Russian Federation. In his prose works, such as *Big Mac* (2007), *Depesh Mod* (2004) and *Voroshylovhrad* (2010), Zhadan realized a project of the cultural translation of slang spoken by his characters' counterparts coming from the Kharkiv suburbs, from Russian into Ukrainian. As the author noted in our meeting in 2013, here we are dealing with an enrichment of the "multi-structured field" of Ukrainian literature:

> [...] I wrote *Depesh Mod* about Kharkiv, and then *Himn demokratychnoï molodi* and *Voroshylovhrad* about Kharkiv and Luhans'k. The real-life counterparts of my characters speak Russian. It is a particular kind of Russian. It is not the standard one, it is a southern accent variation. But it is Russian. In my works,

---

«русскоязычной», а русской литературой. Может быть, это не совсем политкорректно, но всё равно мы предполагаем, что русский — это и язык, и менталитет этих людей, которые живут в Украине. Так вот, русской литературы как целостного феномена я не вижу. Я вижу русских авторов, иногда очень талантливых. Русская литература — это и целостность, и тенденция, когда можно говорить, что что-то их объединяет." Excerpt from an interview with Aleksandr Korablev (Donets'k, November 8, 2013).

143 "Вопрос о том, является ли русскоязычная литература Украины самостоятельной или это часть русской литературы «вообще», при этом оказывается риторическим: ни единой украинской литературы, ни единой русской не существует, скорее можно говорить о сложноустроенных полях."

I tried to re-create it by specific strategies in *Depesh Mod*, where I used more Russian borrowings [...], and using other literary tools in *Voroshylovhrad*, where I created a particular narrative discourse. It is clearly a compromise. I cannot reproduce my hero's direct discourse, because it would turn out to be Russian literature. For this reason, perhaps, certain excerpts of the Russian editions of my novels look more genuine. Everybody understands that it is their slang. This is the biggest problem of the Ukrainian novel.[144] (Puleri 2016: 240)

However, the complex processes of cultural translation, like those of Zhadan, can be undermined by the tactics of cultural assimilation adopted by literary markets, as happened with the Russian edition of Zhadan's *Depesh Mod* published by Amfora of St. Petersburg, without any clear mention of the fact that we were dealing with a translation.[145] Nonetheless, Zhadan's interest in the creation of a "cross-border" reflection on the historical and cultural transition has been shown in most of his literary projects (Dmitriev 2007). In 2009, the publication of the collection of poems entitled

---

144 "[...] написал «Депеш мод» о Харькове, я написал «Гимн демократической молодёжи» о Харькове, «Ворошиловград» о Харькове и Луганске, и в жизни все мои персонажи, естественно, говорят по-русски. Это русский специфический, это не классический русский, это такой южный акцент, южный вариант. Но это русский. И я эту речь пытался воспроизводить одними методами в «Депеш мод,» где больше русизмов [...], другими методами в «Ворошиловграде,» за счёт какой-то авторской речи. Но, так или иначе, это некоторый компромисс. Я не могу передать прямую речь своего героя, потому что это уже будет русская литература. И, возможно, поэтому мои романы в русских переводах звучат в некоторых местах более естественно. Все понимают, что так они и говорят. Это и есть самая большая проблема украинского романа."

145 In this regard, in 2007 Aleksandr Dmitriev could emphasize the peculiar dynamics characterizing the intersection between the Ukrainian and Russian literary markets: "Today in publishing and marketing strategies, the previous dividing practices can be retrieved and used in a completely opposite way. Instead of exoticizing the already separated and half-forgotten neighbors, one suddenly discovers that 'There are our people who live there,'[...] especially near Donets'k, Kharkiv and Luhans'k, where Zhadan is from" (Dmitriev 2007: 290; Сегодня же в книжно-маркетинговых стратегиях прежние разделительные обычаи могут отыгрываться и полностью противоположным образом: вместо экзотизации вроде совсем уже отделившихся и полузабытых соседей вдруг обнаруживается, что «там же наши люди» [...] особенно под Донецком, Харьковом и Луганском, откуда родом Жадан).

The Boundary: Three Border Poets (*Kordon: Tri pogranichnykh poeta*), was an attempt to create a dialogue between cultures.[146] Serhii Zhadan, Andrei Poliakov and Igor' Sid (b. 1963, Dzhankoi) contributed to this literary experiment, which includes poems characterized by the different styles of the three authors, both in Russian and Ukrainian. Ostensibly, in the post-Soviet cultural context it is poetry that is to convey a distinctive historical contemplation, as stressed by Kukulin in his analysis of the contemporary poetic tendencies in the "multi-structured field" of Russian literature:

> The most noticeable changes in the poetry of the 2000s concern the relationship between the person and "broader history" [*bol'shaia istoriia*], primarily the history of Europe and Russia in the twentieth century [...] I have already had occasion to write about poetry and prose's peculiar "role reversal" in modern Russia: of the two, poetry today is far more intensively working out methods to analyze the historical traumas of the contemporary mind, and it is also pointing to ways those traumas may be healed. (2018: 60)

We can also observe the case of Boris Khersonskii (b. 1950, Chernivtsi), a Russophone poet living in Odesa. In the 1990s, his poems were published in Russian and Ukrainian literary journals, such as *Kreshchatik*, *Oktiabr'*, *Novyi mir*, *Znamia* and *Novoe literaturnoe obozrenie*. In 2006, with the publication of his first collection of poems, *The Family Archive* (*Semeinyi arkhiv*) for Novoe literaturnoe obozrenie, he was placed on the shortlist for the 2007 edition of the Andrei Belyi Prize. In these poems the author narrates the *epos* of the southern Ukrainian Jews in the twentieth century. Khersonskii's works are characterized by an analytical reflection on history and its present reception.[147] The poetic ego attempts to recognize and

---

146 The same Zhadan presented the book as "a way of linguistic and geopolitical transition to adjoining areas": "The book combines poetic practices related to the experience of living in conditions of internal transition. *Kordon* means border as a metaphor, as a way of linguistic and geopolitical transition to adjoining areas. It allows to expand the boundaries of perception and mutual understanding" (Krymskii Klub; Книга объединяет в себе поэтические практики, связанные с опытом проживания в условиях внутренней транзитности. Кордон, граница как метафора, как способ лингвистического и геопоэтического перехода на смежные территории, позволяет расширить границы восприятия и взаимопонимания).

147 As Kukulin (2009) puts it: "In [...] Boris Khersonskii's poems we often see elderly characters who remember all their lives, or a narrator who

interpret the process of human self-consciousness, by narrating the relationship between Man and the Great History, as we can read in this poem dedicated to the description of the "ruins of the empire:"

> The ruins of the empire are not much gloomier
> than the empire itself. It is difficult to judge it
> after the lapse of the best-worst-greatest departed days.
> The Mountains got old. The river went dry,
> got lost in a reed-bed,
> a bronze hand sticks out of the grass,
> it holds a scepter or a sword
> difficult to say, but this is not the point.
> It's better to keep the remains of glory for later.
> Then the statue will be unearthed. Apparently,
> it stood on a footless horse.
> Under its missing hooves lies a missing country.
> And you begin to feel you can remember
> how people used to live, buttoned up their coats
> muffled up in their scarves, won the lotto,
> played checkers, chess, backgammon in some rotten yard,
> where the house doomed to be wrecked could barely stand,
> while old men were sitting at the wooden table.
> A Danube herring was wrapped in yesterday's paper.
> Overhead the fresh-painted firmament was shining.
> Everyone was wondering what it was and it turned out to be death.[148]
> (Khersonskii 2010)

---

reconstructs their lives following some external signs [...] during the twentieth century people began to perceive, think and feel their bodies differently. These changes, as powerfully demonstrates Khersonskii, are much more important than the changes of rulers and the struggle for power" (У [...] Бориса Херсонского, в стихотворениях часто появляются немолодые герои, которые вспоминают всю свою жизнь, или герой-рассказчик реконструирует их жизнь по внешним приметам [...] на протяжении XX века люди стали иначе чувствовать, мыслить, ощущать свое тело. Эти перемены, настойчиво демонстрирует Херсонский, куда важнее, чем перемены правителей и борьба за власть).

148 "Руины империи немногим мрачней / чем сама империя. Трудно судить о ней / по прошествии лучших-худших-великих дней. / Состарились горы. Обмелела река, / затерялась в зарослях тростника, / из травы торчит бронзовая рука, / сжимающая скипетр или меч, / точно не скажешь, и не об этом речь. / Лучше остатки славы на потом приберечь. / Тогда откопают статую. Окажется, что она / на коня безногого водружена. / Под

The "bronze hand" that emerges from the bowels of the earth and the statue that rests on a "footless horse" refer to "a missing country," to a narrative that cannot take shape, and to an attempt to understand the past which can only conclude symbolically with "death." Similarly, Khersonskii's sense of belonging to Odesa brought him to analyse the complex self-identification processes involving the different "myths" that shape the "Odesa Syndrome" (*Odesskii Sindrom*), where emblematically no "single unifying myth" can even exist.[149]

Eventually, the reconstruction of both identity and memory cannot be conveyed by a territorialized message. The lyric hero, as in the following Kabanov poem, is only able to narrate his "deterritorialized *epos*," building alternative "bridges between motherlands:"

> Devoid of blindness, deprived of deafness,
> whispering I raised the bridges
> between two motherlands which don't need me.
> Poetry, my Horde charter,
> my bell, my ripped tongue;
> on whose land will I be found?
> To which generation will I be thrown
> by the literary babble?
> Let the mind be bright and calm.

отсутствующими копытами отсутствующая страна. / И начинает казаться, что ты вспоминаешь то, / чем люди жили-были, застегивали пальто, / кутали горло в кашне, выигрывали в лото, / шашки, шахматы, нарды, в каком-то дворе гнилом, / где дом едва стоял, обреченный на слом, / а старики сидели за дощатым столом. / На вчерашней газете лежала дунайская сельдь. / Над миром сияла свежевыкрашенная твердь. / Все думали, что это было, как оказалось — смерть."

149 "This is the most painful thing. I am certain that, given the heterogeneity of the population of Odesa, the city cannot have one single unifying myth. I think that each ethnic group has created its own myth here [...] So, the official 'Odesa myth' is in fact a partial myth, which belongs to a substantial part, but still only a part of the population of Odesa" (Khersonskii 2011; Самое болезненное. Я уверен, что, при разнородности населения Одессы, у нее не может быть одного, единственного мифа. Думаю, что каждая этническая группа создавала здесь свой миф [...] Так вот, официальный «одесский миф» — это тоже миф частичный, принадлежащий существенной части, но все же только части — населения Одессы).

I scrutinize the sense of the native spheres:
let my sight be one with Homer,
let my ear be one with Beethoven.[150] (2014: 443)

In this excerpt from "The Bridges," we see the need for an "intermediate positioning." The displacement experienced by the lyrical subject is symbolically embodied in his "ripped tongue," his artistic medium, lacking the "two motherlands" which "do not need" him. It is only through the symbolic estrangement conferred by art, ironically embodied by Homer's "sight" and Beethoven's "ear," that the poet can eventually recompose his fragmented ego and "territorialize" his positioning.

From Marginality to Minority

In this chapter we identified the contested process of self-determination in post-Soviet Ukrainian Russophone literature as a crucial issue for understanding the novelty of the phenomenon. At the crossroads between the external assimilation carried out by the Russian discourse, and the alternately inclusive and exclusive dynamics of the Ukrainian literary space, today it is the search for a new "centre" that takes shape:

I am a Ukrainian Russophone writer [*russkoiazychnyi pisatel' Ukrainy*]. A man who grew up in Ukraine, but in the context of the Russian-Soviet culture. I am Ukrainian, but at the same time, as for my cultural background, to a large extent I am also Russian [...] in the current political and cultural situation, it suddenly became important for me to understand where the center of the Slavic world is. What is it? What is its significance? Does it exist at all? Moscow used to play this role before, no doubts about that, but where is this center now? And if it still remained in Moscow, then what is happening now? Why did the Slavic world collapse into fragments?[151] (Puleri 2016: 210)

---

150 "Лишенный глухоты и слепоты, / я шепотом выращивал мосты — / меж двух отчизн, которым я не нужен. / Поэзия — ордынский мой ярлык, / мой колокол, мой вырванный язык; / на чьей земле я буду обнаружен? / В какое поколение меня / швырнет литературная возня? / Да будет разум светел и спокоен. / Я изучаю смысл родимых сфер: / пусть зрение мое — в один Гомер, / пускай мой слух — всего в один Бетховен."

151 "[...] я русскоязычный писатель Украины. Человек, который вырос в контексте Украины, но в русле русской советской культуры. Я украинец, но при этом по своему культурному дискурсу в немалой степени русский человек [...] в нынешней политической и культурной ситуации мне вдруг

The questions posed by Rafeenko in our 2013 meeting clearly reveal the tension towards a new identity and artistic positioning.[152] Most fundamentally, while switching our focus to the narratives produced by Russophone writers in order to provide an answer to their existential enquiry, new research questions emerge: how and whether the representation of their hybrid subjectivities occur in their literary production; or, "on what level they are aware of this particular positioning between ethno-cultural, national, linguistic, religious and other traditions"[153] (Tlostanova 2004: 193).

As argued by Nazarenko (2005: 95), whereas a new full-fledged experiential–expressive paradigm has yet to emerge, in Ukrainian Russophone literature this would most likely privilege narratives focusing on "the man at the crossroads between languages, cultures and epochs."[154] It is also thanks

---

стало важно понять, где центр славянского мира, что это такое, каково его значение? И есть ли он вообще? Раньше эту роль выполняла, безусловно, Москва, но где этот центр сейчас? А если он по-прежнему остался в Москве, то что с ним теперь происходит? Почему произошёл распад славянского мира на осколки?"

152 Interestingly, as we will see in the next sections of the book, Rafeenko's position has changed in the aftermath of the Euromaidan revolution and the war in Donbas in 2014, entering the national cultural space and coming even to consider the space for literary bilingualism in contemporary Ukraine.

153 "[...] как осознают это особое позиционирование между этнокультурными, национальными, языковыми, религиозными и иными традициями."

154 "The Russophone Literature of Ukraine reveals marginal features when compared to both its 'sisters' [...] Its most interesting and valuable trait consists in its point of view on both cultures from the inside and the outside—simultaneously [...] The Russophone literature in Ukraine is in need of finding its own characterising attributes [...] in order to understand its unique, distinct and original nature [...] and it is in need of understanding the tasks to be faced. This is needed in order to realize that its main object is the man at the crossroads between languages, cultures and epochs. At the crossroads, that is at the juncture" (Nazarenko 2005: 94–95; РЛУ [Русскоязычная Литература Украины] оказывается маргинальной по отношению к обеим «сестрам» [...] Если русскоязычной литературе и суждено развиваться, то именно в этой сфере. Взгляд на обе культуры изнутри и извне — одновременно! — интереснее и плодотворнее всего [...] РЛУ должна найти в себе черты, которые присущи только ей [...] Понять свою особость, непохожесть, оригинальность [...] необходимо понимание задач, которые стоят перед РЛУ. И понимание того, что основным ее объектом является человек на перекрестке языков, культур и времен. На перекрестке, а значит — на распутье).

to the peculiar marginal position in between cultural systems that these writers can follow different kinds of interaction with the "multi-structured fields" of Ukrainian and Russian literatures. In the marginal space where Russophone subjectivities write from, new "minor" narratives take shape in order to give expression to that *missing voice* of Andrukhovych's Horobets'.

Chapter 3 A Minor Perspective on National Narrative(s): Deterritorializing Post-Imperial Epistemology

There we have the most important question to face: why is it all the same Ukrainian, and not a Russian enclave in Ukraine? The issue is not simple at all. But to answer this question as simply as possible [...] then, this is because the German-language literature of Prague is also not German, and neither is Austrian literature, while at the same time the Irish English-language literature is not English [...] And what can be said about the American, the Canadian and the Australian literatures? The Belgian literature is not French. The Latin-American literature is neither Spanish nor Portuguese. The language is not the decisive factor. But what, then, is the determinant? It is the theme, the mentality, the traditions or the local colour: it is this we need to understand and contest.[155] (Krasniashchikh 2015: 174)

In his article published in *Novyi Mir*'s September 2015 issue, the Ukrainian writer Andrei Krasniashchikh still endeavours to address the question concerning the "canonization" of the Russophone literary phenomenon emerging in post-Soviet Ukraine. By using the acronym *Rusukrlit*—Russian Ukrainian Literature[156]—the author wants to stress the unsystematic character of the Ukrainian Russophone literature that, as highlighted in the previous chapter, does not let us acknowledge either its autonomy from

---

155 "А теперь самое-самое — почему она все-таки украинская, а не анклав российской в Украине. Вопрос совсем не простой. Но если отвечать на него максимально просто [...] то потому же, почему и пражская немецкоязычная не немецкая, и австрийская не, а ирландская англоязычная не английская [...] Что уж говорить об американской, канадской или австралийской. Бельгийская не французская. Латиноамериканская не испанская и не португальская. Язык — фактор не решающий. А что решающий: тема, ментальность, традиции, колорит — нужно разбираться и спорить."

156 "So then, *rusukrlit*. Or, if we talk about the writers, that is *ruskrainskie* writers" (Krasniashchikh 2015: 173; Итак, русукрлит. Или, если говорить

or dependence on one of the respective cultural systems.[157] According to Krasniashchikh, this is not an isolated case, but from a global perspective these dynamics can also be noted in other "marginal" literary traditions, such as Irish English-language literature, or Latin-American Spanish- and Portuguese-language literatures.

Most fundamentally, an analytical description of "marginal" literary practices can be difficult to establish, unless "one doesn't start with a more objective concept—that of minor literature" (Deleuze, Guattari 1986: 18).[158] In their work devoted to the analysis of Kafka's literary production, entitled *Kafka: Toward a Minor Literature* (*Kafka. Pour une littérature mineure*, 1975), Gilles Deleuze and Félix Guattari strove to theorize the features that characterize the minor artistic paradigm. As these French philosophers observed, throughout his literary experience Franz Kafka (1883–1924) reflected upon "the problem of expression" in art, especially "in relation to those literatures that are considered minor, for example, the Jewish literature of Warsaw and Prague" (Deleuze, Guattari 1986: 16). In their view, a minor literature

---

о писателях, — писатели рукраинские). This wording mirrors the common Ukrainian abbreviation *suchukrlit* (*suchasna ukraïns'ka literatura*, contemporary Ukrainian literature).

157 In his study, Krasniashchikh highlights further the "decentralization" of *rusukrlit*: "So, geographically *rusukrlit* is mainly developed in the east and south of the country, and its centres are Dnipropetrovs'k, Donets'k, Kyiv, Odesa and Kharkiv. As for the prose, the assemblage points are Donets'k, Kyiv, Kharkiv" (Krasniashchikh 2015: 175; Итак, территориально русукрлит сконцентрирован на востоке и юге страны, центрами являются Днепропетровск, Донецк, Киев, Одесса и Харьков. По прозе точки сборки — Донецк, Киев, Харьков).

158 "There has been much discussion of the questions 'What is a marginal literature?' and 'What is a popular literature, a proletarian literature?' The criteria are obviously difficult to establish if one doesn't start with a more objective concept—that of minor literature. Only the possibility of setting up a minor practice of major language from within allows one to define popular literature, marginal literature, and so on. Only in this way can literature really become a collective machine of expression and really be able to treat and develop its contents" (Deleuze, Guattari 1986: 18-19).

comes to be defined as the one "that a minority constructs within a major language" (Deleuze, Guattari 1986: 16). This is the condition experienced by Kafka, a Czech Jew writing in German: it is exactly "the situation of the German language in Czechoslovakia, as a fluid language intermixed with Czech and Yiddish" that "will allow Kafka the possibility of invention" (Deleuze, Guattari 1986: 20). His literary works turns out to be "something impossible" due to "the impossibility of not writing, the impossibility of writing in German, [and] the impossibility of writing otherwise" (Deleuze, Guattari 1986: 16). In these conditions, art becomes the main "line of escape," "because national consciousness, uncertain or oppressed, necessarily exists by means of literature" (Deleuze, Guattari 1986: 16). Thus, according to Deleuze and Guattari, in his search for a new self-positioning a minor writer's main instrument is his own language:

> There is nothing that is major or revolutionary except the minor. To hate all languages of masters. Kafka's fascination for servants and employees (the same thing in Proust in relation to servants, to their language). What interests him even more is the possibility of making of his own language—assuming that it is unique, that it is a major language or has been—a minor utilization. To be a sort of stranger *within* his own language. (Deleuze, Guattari 1986: 26)

On the one hand, due to its being affected with a "high coefficient of deterritorialization" (Deleuze, Guattari 1986: 16), language in minor literatures comes to be the most effective *political* vehicle in order "to express another possible community and to forge the means for another consciousness and another sensibility" (Deleuze, Guattari 1986: 17), especially "if the writer lives on the margin, is set apart from his fragile community." On the other, experiencing a deterritorialized cultural condition entails the need "to write as a dog who digs his hole [...] And to do that, to find his own point of underdevelopment, his own jargon, a third world of his own, a desert of his own" (Deleuze, Guattari 1986: 18).

It is no surprise that since the late 1980s, Deleuze and Guattari's minor paradigm has experienced a controversial return to the centre stage of literary and cultural studies. On the one hand, these French philosophers have been "thoroughly castigated" by Kafka scholars for misappropriating "Kafka's thoughts on minor literature" (Edmunds 2010: 351), thus dismissing their interpretation of him as a minor writer.[159] Nonetheless, on the other hand today it is an indisputable fact that in contemporary criticism the minor paradigm has been gradually adopted (and adapted) for the study of the interrelation between literature and politics in global cultural production (e.g. Lloyd 1987; Chin 2003; Burima 2014; Bharat 2015; Tuckerová 2017).[160] It was especially in light of the urgency for a radical remapping of global literary space on the eve of the new millennium that, in her provocative study entitled *The World Republic of Letters* (*La République mondiale des lettres*, 1999), Pascale Casanova also deployed the concept of "small" literatures.[161] While reinterpreting Kafka's ideas from the perspective of the literatures of "small" nations or languages, Casanova (2004: 279) focused on "the need to speak of literary worlds that exist only in their unequal structural relationship to large ('great') literatures." Significantly, thanks to the adoption of "economic theories of globalization into the literary universe" (Casanova 2004: xii), the French scholar in her work sought "to rediscover a lost transnational dimension of literature that for two hundred years has been reduced to the political and linguistic boundaries of nations" (Casanova 2004: xi).

Similarly, in my view, even today Deleuze and Guattari's take on minor literature still remains a valid starting point for understanding the complex

---

159 Deleuze and Guattari have been mainly criticized for their "mistaken view" that Kafka wrote in a "dialect of German" (e.g. Corngold 1994), that is, the way they envision the German of Prague, and for distorting "considerably Kafka's relationship to German language and literary tradition" (Jamison 2018: 27).

160 This trend has also been the object of criticism by Kafka scholars. E.g. Stanley Corngold (1994: 90) described it as "equally wrong-headed," when compared to Deleuze and Guattari's "mistaken" take on Kafka's German, and as a "critical (read 'politicizing') dialect concerned with the literature of small nations," emerging first "in and around colonial studies" and then "in Central and Eastern Europe" in order to promote "the long suppressed topic of national character."

161 Casanova (2004: 203–204) also criticized Deleuze and Guattari's reading of Kafka's *Diaries* (1949) as being based on an "anachronistic conception of politics," whereby "[t]hey project upon Kafka their view of politics as subversion, or 'subversive struggle,' whereas for him, in the Prague of the early twentieth century, it was identified solely with the national question."

nature of current cultural practices that lie beyond the boundaries of national narratives. According to these two philosophers, "we might as well say that the term minor no longer designates specific literatures but the revolutionary conditions for every literature within the heart of what is called great (or established) literature" (Deleuze, Guattari 1986: 18). Thus, "great literature" is honoured with the role of a "canonical mirror" of the human passions, whereas "the primary feature of any literature that is defined as minor is its exclusion from the canon, an exclusion that may on the face of it be as much on the grounds of purely aesthetic judgments as on those of racial or sexual discrimination" (Lloyd 1987: 20). As David Lloyd puts it in his study devoted to the Irish English-language poet James Clarence Mangan (1803–1849), the minor writer does not long for the recognition of the grades of "representative authority" of the "human experience" (Lloyd 1987: 20), precisely because of his "marginal" perspective. This lack of representativeness lies in "the oppositional relationship of the canon and the state" (Lloyd 1987: 21) and is "the product of the biographical alienation of a German-speaking Czech Jew or of a Creole woman in the postcolonial Caribbean" (Lloyd 1987: 22). It is the symbolic representation of *non-identity* that becomes the key feature of this literary paradigm. Minor literatures thus focus on the crisis of the hegemonic narratives on identity, rewriting the expressive forms of tradition by means of parody and frequent intertextual references. Most fundamentally, the authorial voice interacts with the dynamics of "great (or established) literature" and, at the same time, seeks to subvert them.

Following these lines, in the post-Soviet era the Russophone literary phenomenon can also be read as the ground for performative narratives—just "because it exists in a narrow space, every individual matter is immediately plugged into the political" (Deleuze, Guattari 1986: 16)—especially taking into consideration that "the decomposition and fall of the Empire multiplies the crises, accentuates everywhere the movements of deterritorialization, gives rise to complex archaic, mythic, or symbolist reterritorializations" (Deleuze, Guattari 1986: 25). These voices from the margins have a collective value for overcoming post-imperial epistemology, "precisely because talents do not abound in a minor literature, the conditions are not given for an *individuated utterance* which would be that of some 'master' and could be separated from *collective utterance*" (Deleuze, Guattari 1986: 17).

Moreover, through the lenses of Deleuze and Guattari's theorization, it is paradoxically the quantitatively *major* Russian language that ends up in a *minor* position, as a result of the "revolutionary conditions" for post-Soviet Ukrainian Russophone literature within the heart of the "great (or established)" Russian and Ukrainian literatures. It is along these lines that post-Soviet Russophone literature in Ukraine can be read as a minor perspective on the identity and artistic categories pertaining to both the Russian and the Ukrainian "great" traditions.

First, whereas at the dawn of the new century Mark Lipovetsky (2002) stressed how the crisis of the Russian postmodern narrative was produced by the missing link between postcolonial writing and the contemporary Russian context,[162] in the interstitial space between the Ukrainian and Russian worlds we can thus observe deepening processes of negotiation between the fragments of imperial and colonial discourses. Interestingly enough, as emphasized by Tlostanova regarding the impact of "post-Soviet Russophone literature" (*postsovetskaia russkoiazychnaia literatura*) on global Russian literary developments, although Russophone writing in countries other than Russia is "sensitive to the issue of imperial and colonial relations, there are almost no attempts at language transformation, that is the most important tool of postcolonial discourse" (2004: 322).[163] "[T]he rigid normativeness of the Russian literary language" (*normativnost' russkogo literaturnogo iazyka*; Tlostanova 2004: 322) in the Soviet period determines today "the absence of language variations" (*otsutstvie iazykovoi variatsii*), prompting the authors "to seek new channels of transformation" (*iskat' drugie sposoby variatsii*; Tlostanova 2004: 323). According to Tlostanova, it is "deterritorialization and dehistoricization" (*deterritorizatsiia i deistorizatsiia*; Tlostanova 2004: 390–391), around which transcultural literature globally takes shape, that give rise to the recoding of the traditional

---

162 "As to post-colonial writings and fiction focusing on cultural identity, they are totally suppressed in contemporary Russian literature [...] The problem of cultural relations of Russia with the nations of the former Russian and Soviet Empires had not been even touched, to say nothing about the problem of Russian 'self-colonization' or inner colonization" (Lipovetsky 2002: 71).

163 "[...] чувствительной к проблеме имперско-колониальных взаимоотношений, почти нет попыток языковой трансформации, которая является важнейшим инструментом постколониального дискурса."

models of "great" Russian literature in Russophone literature. Through paradoxical metamorphoses of space and time, it is the "chronotope of betweenness" (*khronotop promezhutochnosti*; Tlostanova 2004: 390) that becomes the fundamental principle for the construction of new narrative strategies aimed at representing the dynamics of individual and collective identity reflection.

Second, within the Ukrainian "transit culture" (Hundorova 2013), Russophone literature produces new symbolic codes in order to interpret the existential and cultural condition of Ukrainian postcoloniality. Russophone *minor* writings create the ground for new "collective utterances" which are "immediately plugged into the political," thus undertaking a path complementary to Ukrainophone "national allegories" (Chernetsky 2007). As Nazarenko significantly observed in our 2013 meeting, while on the one hand "Ukrainian-language literature answers the questions 'what happened? what did we have?', in order to fill the gaps of history," on the other "Russian-language literature in most cases answers the question 'how to live here and now?'"[164] Since in the latter "the past is understood not only as the experience of a community, but also as an individual journey,"[165] the vector that leads "from the present to the future is, to a greater extent, proper to Russian-language literature."[166]

Accordingly, looking in this chapter at the *marginal narratives* produced by the Ukrainian Russophone authors Andrei Kurkov, Aleksei Nikitin and Vladimir Rafeenko, will enable us to approach their literary mosaics by analysing their *minor perspectives* on the new framework of interrelations and connections that arose in the post-Soviet epoch.[167] As Deleuze and Guattari observed in their reading of Kafka's *Diaries* (1949), amongst the

---

164 "Русскоязычная литература во многом решает вопрос «и как нам здесь и дальше жить?», а украиноязычная — «что у нас было?», как заполнение белых и чёрных пятен в истории." Excerpt from an interview with Mikhail Nazarenko (Kyiv, March 26, 2013).

165 "[…] прошлое понимается не только как общественный, но и как индивидуальный опыт." *Ibidem.*

166 "[…] такой вектор от настоящего в будущее для русскоязычной литературы, скорее, сейчас более характерен." *Ibidem.*

167 As already mentioned in the introduction to this book, our focus will be mainly on prose, which better develops "the crowding out and displacement of experiences that are painful to protagonists and narrators alike and that compromise the integrity of their sense of self" (Kukulin 2018: 60). Here it is

goals of a minor literature we can witness the tendency to bring to "the full light of day" those cultural negotiations that in the "great" literature/s take place "down below":

> When Kafka indicates that one of the goals of a minor literature is the "purification of the conflict that opposes father and son and the possibility of discussing that conflict," it isn't a question of an Oedipal phantasm but of a political program [...] "What in great literature goes on down below, constituting a not indispensable cellar of the structure, here takes place in the full light of day, what is there a matter of passing interest for a few, here absorbs everyone no less than as a matter of life and death." (Deleuze, Guattari 1986: 17)

Andrei Kurkov: The Displaced Transition in Mass Literature

In his study on the "problem of success" (*problema uspekha*) in contemporary Russian culture, Mikhail Berg (2004) adopts a postcolonial lens to understand the complex process of redistributing social values in literature. The Russian scholar argues that any "gesture or process" in culture and society is "part of a symbolic exchange, that is the exchange of symbolic values for values that are quite real and symbolic at the same time" (Berg 2004).[168] According to Berg, every cultural or social gesture can be considered as developing through two main stages:

---

worth mentioning other recent studies filling the gaps of the issues lying outside the scope of my research. On the one hand, in her 2016 in-depth study of the bilingual literary community of Kharkiv, Tanya Zaharchenko drew on memory and border studies to describe the "tales of trauma" created by the Russophone prose writers Iurii Tsaplin and Andrei Krasniashchikh, and the Ukrainian-language author Oleh Kotsarev (b. 1981, Kharkiv). Along these lines, Zaharchenko significantly argues that these authors' universe "shifts from their predecessors' all-encompassing country to an individual world of total inner turmoil, unchecked against anything external" (2016: 140). On the other, Kukulin (2016) has extensively devoted his attention to the analysis of the postcolonial condition of the Russian-language poetry of Ukraine—where language variations seem to emerge more consistently—and we will briefly draw on his study in the next chapter of this book.

168 "[...] любой культурный жест или процесс [...] является частью символического обмена, то есть обмена символических ценностей на ценности вполне реальные и символические же."

The first one is its preliminary assessment, as a fact confirming the identity of the subject or violating it. The second one is the formation of a symbolic group, in which this fact, when disclosing a complementary attitude, occupies one of the potential complementary positions, or is displaced and disavowed with the help of psychological models of distancing, when manifesting a negative stance.[169] (Berg 2004)

Following these lines of thought, "success and the strategy for success" (*uspekh i strategiia uspekha*) in diverse sociocultural groups "will be fundamentally different" (*budet printsipial'no otlichaiutsia*), whereby these respond to the claims of different symbolic groups.

By adopting this approach to the analysis of the strategies implemented for "literary success" after the collapse of the Soviet Union, Berg could thus highlight on what levels "the psychological and social instruments of self-affirmation" (*psikhologicheskie i sotsial'nye instrumenty samoutverzhdeniia*) in Russian literature related to the postcolonial discourse. Examining the case of Aleksandra Marinina, the pen name of Marina Anatol'evna Alekseeva (b. 1957, L'viv), author of several bestsellers in post-Soviet Russia, Berg could thus find the reasons behind her success in the Russian market in the need nourished by readers in the Russian Federation to find in her works "a self-justification" (*samoopravdanie*) and "an interpretation of life" (*interpretatsiia zhizni*) that would transform "failure" (*neuspekh*) into "the only right and correct strategy" (*edinstvennaia pravil'naia i tochnaia strategiia*). In Marinina's detective stories, "the evil is the Other, it does not belong to normal Russian life, it comes from outside"[170] (Berg 2004): this responds to the claim for "self-justification" laid out by the Russian readership in the 1990s, living in a postcolonial and postimperial "era of changes that violate the usual identity"[171] (Berg 2004).

---

169 "Первая — его предварительная оценка, как факта подтверждающего идентичность субъекта или нарушающего его. Вторая — образование символической группы, в которой этот факт, при комплиментарном к нему отношении, занимает одну из возможных и также комплиментарных позиций, а при негативном — вытесняется и дезавуируется с помощью психологических приемов дистанцирования."

170 "[…] зло — это Другое, оно не принадлежит обыкновенной российской жизни, а привнесено в нее извне."

171 "[…] в эпоху перемен, нарушающих привычную идентичность."

Differently, in the works of another contemporary "successful" author in the Russian market, Boris Akunin, the pen name of Grigorii Shalvovich Chkhartishvili (b. 1956, Zestafoni), it is possible to witness the adoption of alternative strategies for narrating Russia's present. This happens because, as highlighted by Berg (2004), "in any society which has entered the post-imperial, postcolonial period, including the Russian one,"[172] there are other symbolic groups who "support those initiatives that offer different models for radically overcoming important social borders"[173] (Berg 2004). While by the mid-1990s Russian society was changing, at the meeting point between these highly different symbolic groups (namely, the "dominant" and the "marginal" ones) a new "segment of the market of cultural values" (*segment rynka kul'turnykh tsennostei*) emerged "under the name of 'mass culture'" (*pod nazvaniem 'massovaia kul'tura'*; Berg 2004): this made the cultural gestures of "innovative culture" (*innovatsionnaia kul'tura*) accessible to a broader symbolic group. Boris Akunin, together with other cultural actors such as Viktor Pelevin (b. 1956, Moscow) and Vladimir Sorokin (b. 1955, Bykovo), as mentioned by Berg (2004), thus developed their strategies of success precisely at the symbolic border area with mass culture, where "practices that function and achieve success under the laws of mass culture (that is, primarily, due to circulation) are interpreted in some influential socio-cultural groups as exclusive and elitist practices."[174] Thus, adopting a postcolonial lens, Akunin's strategies, at the border area between mass and innovative cultures, are built around the "negotiation of the fragments" (Lipovetsky 2005: 167) inherited from the post-Soviet historical rift. These narratives take the shape of a "mystery" to be decoded: the traditional path of solving a crime, which is undertaken by the Russian investigator Fandorin in Akunin's novels, runs parallel to a "centrifugal

---

172 "[…] в любом, в том числе в российском обществе, вступившем в постимперский, постколониальный период […]."

173 "[присутствуют группы, которые] поддерживают те культурные инициативы, которые предлагают разные модели радикального преодоления общественно важных границ […]."

174 "[…] функционирующие и добивающиеся успеха по законом массовой культуры (то есть, прежде всего, за счет тиражности), интерпретируются в некоторых влиятельных социокультурных группах как практики эксклюзивные и элитарные."

search" (Lipovetsky 2005: 167) for the Russian national and cultural identity. The dialogue with the past that is shaped along Fandorin's inquiries also emerges as a result of the "echo of contemporary political and cultural clashes" (Lipovetsky 2005: 167). As Lipovetsky (2005: 169) notes, Akunin brings to light and demystifies "the phobias of contemporary Russia," creating figures of criminals and murderers whose identity is "hybrid": an ambivalent product that comes to life as a result of the intersection of "stereotypical expectations" of the Other and the symmetric reflexes of the protagonist's subjectivity.

Similarly to Akunin, Andrei Kurkov developed his strategies for success at the border area between mass and innovative cultures. Born in 1961 in Leningrad, Kurkov moved to Kyiv a few years later, where he established himself as a "successful writer" only in the second half of the 1990s. He is the most renowned Ukrainian author of the post-Soviet era, and his novels are translated into many European languages. However, within the national literary context—or "symbolic group"—his identity has been at times "displaced and disavowed" by critics.[175] Today the author emblematically identifies himself as a representative of the post-Soviet "Russophone" cultural group:

[I am] a Ukrainian writer of Russian origin [*ukrainskii pisatel' russkogo proizkhozhdeniia*], writing in the language of my own origin. I am probably the most common example of Russophonia [*rusofoniia*], because after the collapse of the Soviet Union in some countries Russian-speaking culture [*russkoiazychnaia kul'tura*] turned out to be part of other cultures. In some countries in the post-Soviet space, it has remained a kind of healthy atavism (as in Belarus, in Latvia or in Ukraine), while in other ones it was formed as a result of mass emigration of former Soviet citizens.[176] (Sharyi 2013)

---

175 As Kurkov put it in 2012: "I have always written my novels in Russian, my mother tongue. This means that for the past 15 years I have been under pressure to start writing in Ukrainian. I have refused, even though I am happy with Ukrainian as the sole national language. I just find it easier to write in my mother tongue. For now, I have no desire to become a soldier in this war of words" (Kurkov 2012).

176 "[Это] украинский писатель русского происхождения, пишущий на языке своего происхождения. Я представляю собой, наверное, самый обычный пример русофонии, потому что после распада Советского Союза русскоязычная культура в некоторых странах оказалась частью других

According to Kurkov, Russophone culture is a movement which follows an autonomous path, but one still akin to Russian culture. Along these lines, as the author argued in 2013, even if "a separate Russian-speaking space in Ukraine [*russkoiazychnoe prostranstvo Ukrainy*] has not taken shape yet, because it still needs the internal support of the Russian-speaking representatives of Ukrainian culture,"[177] after all the existence of this space is "an objective process" (*ob'ektivnyi protsess*): today in Ukraine we are witnessing "the formation of a Russian speaking cultural space with its own internal structure, its leaders and consumers"[178] (Sharyi 2013).

In Kurkov's works, it is displacement that emerges not so much as an "echo," but rather as a characterizing value of his own Russophone symbolic group. The writer himself claims to be a "victim of the cocktail mixed by Stalin" (Kurkov 2005), which involved people of different Soviet nationalities in a circle of continuous displacements and internal migrations.[179] As a result of these processes, paradoxically, in the aftermath of the Soviet collapse the author, "[w]ithout emigrating or even moving house," found himself "in a different country called Ukraine"[180] (Kurkov 2005).

культур. Кое-где на постсоветском пространстве она осталась своего рода здоровым атавизмом (как в Белоруссии, в Латвии или на Украине), а в других странах она образовалась как результат массовой эмиграции бывших советских граждан."

177 "Отдельное русскоязычное пространство Украины еще не сформировано, потому что оно нуждается во внутренней помощи самих русскоязычных деятелей украинской культуры […]."

178 "[…] формирование русскоязычного культурного пространства с его внутренней структурой, с его лидерами и с потребителями этой культуры."

179 "I am a victim of a milkshake. A cocktail that was mixed by Stalin some time before I was born. It should have been impossible to drink that stuff, but the USSR gulped it down without a murmur. Stalin took people of various nationalities (there were more than 100 represented in the Soviet Union), put them together in the army, or the Siberian camps, left them to marinate for 10 to 20 years, until their homelands seemed very far away and then sent them to live in another unfamiliar corner of that vast country" (Kurkov 2005).

180 Kurkov's reflections emblematically refer to the "radical crisis of identity" (Laitin 1998: ix) experienced by the Russian speakers in the broader region after the collapse of the USSR. As David D. Laitin puts it in the preface to his 1998 study entitled *Identity in Formation: The Russian-Speaking Populations in the Near Abroad*, Russian speakers then faced "a set of questions about

Kurkov's outsider perspective on post-Soviet Ukrainian society thus revolves around the difficult exchange of symbolic values taking place between the individual and the sociocultural context in which he lives. In the broken mechanism portrayed by Kurkov, the presence of surreal and absurd elements is accepted as a normal feature of everyday life. Along these lines, Sally Dalton-Brown described Kurkov's literary world as follows:

> Kurkov's work remains within the realms of the probable [...] the extraordinary can seem quite commonplace, making the comic and political point that his characters live in denial, or have no real understanding of what is "normal" [...] The acceptance of such "normality" has two unfortunate consequences: Kurkov's characters often seem morally vague and, often, rather passive. Their acceptance of, or indeed preference of the "role" of victim, or the detached role of outsider, perhaps extends into an acceptance of whatever fate offers. (Dalton-Brown 2010: 107–108)

During the 2000s, the publication of the trilogy entitled *Geography of a Single Shot* (*Geografiia odinochnogo vystrela*, 2003), and the novels *The President's Last Love* (*Posledniaia liubov' prezidenta*, 2004), *The Milkman in the Night* (*Nochnoi Molochnik*, 2007) and *The Gardener from Ochakov* (*Sadovnik iz Ochakova*, 2010) reflected the author's interest in the representation of the individual's identity metamorphoses in the face of the recent Ukrainian and Soviet history. Yet the centrifugal search for "social and psychological instruments of self-affirmation" in the changed existential conditions of the post-socialist period mainly emerges in Kurkov's early works. It is in the novels written in the late nineties that the author gives a systematic account of the post-Soviet displacement.[181]

Death and the Penguin (*Piknik na l'du*, 1996)—originally published under the emblematic title *The Death of a Stranger* (*Smert' Postoronnego*)—was

---

who they are and what are they to become": "Are they a people in diaspora, even if it was not they but their country that moved? Would they 'return' to a homeland many of them had never seen? [...] Would they become loyal citizens of the new republics but maintain a Russian identity? [...] Would a new identity form, not quite Russian, but not titular either?" (1998: ix)

181 As argued by Kurkov in our 2013 meeting: "My early novels deal with the question that life is more powerful than individuals, and that individuals are evading life. They are trying to preserve themselves. The question was 'how to survive in our environment,' since the environment is hostile to us. The way can be found also in betraying our main principles" (Puleri 2016: 183).

Kurkov's first novel also to attract the attention of international literary critics (see Kalfus 2001; Benedictus 2002). After the publication of the German-language edition in 1999 by the Swiss publishing house Diogenes, the work became an outstanding bestseller. *Death and the Penguin* is set in post-Soviet Kyiv, and tells the story of a writer in a crisis state, Viktor Alekseevich Zolotarev. Without any chance to publish his novels, the protagonist is hired as a writer of obituaries for a local newspaper: from that moment on, his life is shaken by a series of unpredictable events.

Throughout the novel, Zolotarev's relationship with the surrounding environment becomes the key to understanding how the surreal and the absurd are accepted as normal features of everyday life. Walking through the streets of Kyiv, Zolotarev wonders about the changes that have occurred. In this "suspended" urban dimension, the individual's existential transition and the continuity of the space between present and past are stuck:

> Something was wrong with this life, he thought, walking with downcast eyes. Or life itself had changed, and was as it used to be—simple, comprehensible—only on the outside. Inside, it was as if the mechanism was broken, and now there was no knowing what to expect of a familiar object—be it a loaf of Ukrainian bread or a street pay telephone. Beneath every surface, inside every tree, every person, lurked an invisible alien something. The seeming reality of everything was only a relic of childhood.[182] (Kurkov 2011a: 183)

The symbiotic relationship between the protagonist's *displacement* and the urban space, where "an invisible alien something" is hidden "beneath every surface," paralyses the transition to the present: the internal "mechanism" of signification is now "broken" by the effects of the post-Soviet historical rift. In his analysis of the symbolic representations of urban space in the literary text, Blacker observes (2012: 144) that the buildings, streets and monuments of the city "not only tell of the past," but "physically connect

---

182   "— Что то не то в этой жизни, — глядя себе под ноги, на ходу думал он. — Или это сама жизнь изменилась, оставшись только внешне прежней, простой и понятной. А внутри ее словно сломался механизм и теперь неизвестно, чего ждать от знакомых предметов. От буханки украинского хлеба, от уличного телефонного автомата. Что то чужое и невидимое прячется за всякой знакомой поверхностью, внутри каждого дерева, внутри каждого человека. Все только кажется знакомым с детства" (Kurkov 2001: 203-204). Translated by George Bird.

those who encounter them directly to their referents—the cultures who created and first inhabited them." If we mean Kyiv as a "text," a "chain of signifiers" (Blacker 2012: 141), we may identify "its own referent" in Zolotarev and the former and present inhabitants of the Ukrainian capital. These "are invariably in a state of degradation, of fragmentation, and 'open to narrative elaboration'" (Blacker 2012: 144).

Interestingly, as emerges in Blacker's studies, in the "great" Ukrainian literature today the process of remapping the urban space translates to heterogeneous narrative strategies (Blacker 2008). The proliferation of texts built on a symmetrical relationship between man and the city is influenced by post-communist "spatio-temporal disjunctions" (Blacker 2012: 139), which gave rise to the "discussion of alternative and uncomfortable pasts" in literature. In Kurkov's Kyiv, the Soviet and post-Soviet spatio-temporal dimensions thus overlap: the absurd embodied by the normality of the present emerges from this intersection. In *Death and the Penguin*, it is two characters in particular who are paralysed by the broken dialogue between the present and the past: the penguin Misha and the zoologist Pidpalyi.

The former is Zolotarev's faithful companion, ever since the Kyiv Zoo was forced to give up some of its animals. Throughout the novel, Misha embodies the alter ego of Zolotarev, who is an outcast of the post-Soviet world. The introduction of anthropomorphic animals is a constant feature in Kurkov's literary production, as well as being a specific instrument of political allegory that was widespread in twentieth-century Russian literature.[183] Here the penguin personifies the *homo sovieticus*, who is "paralysed" in

---

183 The brightest example is, of course, Mikhail Bulgakov's *The Heart of a Dog* (*Sobach'e serdtse*, 1925), where the author, who was originally from Kyiv, also depicts the results of the transplantation of human organs into an animal, in order to demystify the Soviet project to create a new *homo sovieticus*. In general, as Dalton-Brown (2010: 111) observes: "The blurring between human and animal has often been used in Russian twentieth-century literature for purposes of political allegory, as in Fazil Iskander's 1982 *Kroliki i udavy* (Rabbits and Boa Constrictors), in which Stalin appears as the Great Python, or in Georgii Vladimov's *Vernyi Ruslan* (Faithful Ruslan, 1975) [...] Iuz Aleshkovskii's *Kenguru* (Kangaroo, 1981), with its animal-victim clearly a metaphor for Soviet victim, outlines the approach adopted by Kurkov [...] namely, the depiction of the animal who evokes empathy."

the post-Soviet present.[184] Misha is symbolically characterized by a state of melancholic depression: he is alone and disoriented, and suffers from a disease that can be cured only with the transplantation of a human heart.

Only the zoologist Pidpalyi is able to understand Misha's world and to identify his disease. Pidpalyi is also an outcast: after the zoo relinquished the penguins to those who could take care of them, his "knowledge" became useless. Most fundamentally, Pidpalyi belongs to "other times" and "other places": he cannot survive the present. Before dying alone and abandoned in a hospital bed, the zoologist asks Zolotarev to set his apartment on fire. In the following passage of the novel, we may witness the depiction of a space which has been left without "its own referent" after Pidpalyi's death:

> There were also photographs on the walls, framed and redolent of the past. The whole furnishing of the flat was of a past age [...] that same recent but already so far distant past of a country that no longer existed. The past believed in dates. And everyone's life consisted of dates, giving life a rhythm and sense of gradation, as if from the eminence of a date one could look back and down, and see the past itself. A clear, comprehensible past, divided up into squares of events, lines of paths taken [...] he [Zolotarev] felt at ease and safe [...] And here he sat amid things and papers that were no longer anybody's—in a whole world left without its creator and master. The old man had wanted no outsiders to have contact with it, or to see the destruction of a cosy little world three or four decades behind the times.[185] (Kurkov 2011a: 140–143)

---

184 As the author emphasized in a 2009 interview: "The penguins came to mind because they remind me so much of the Soviets. They are animals that live in groups. One individual, isolated, cannot survive; it loses its sense of orientation. The group, meanwhile, possesses a certain collective conscience. Each new generation takes the same path as the one before. Everything is programmed in these animals and they function according to the programme only when they are together. If you put a penguin on a deserted island, the programme stops. In 1991, with the breakdown of the Soviet Union [...] the programme directing the Soviet people's collective life disappeared too. Individuals found themselves alone and disoriented" (Kurkov 2009: 22).

185 "[...] На стенах тоже висели фотографии в рамках — от них веяло прошлым. Вся обстановка квартиры принадлежала другой эпохе [...] И такие же фотографии в рамках — та же эпоха, то же недавнее, но такое уже далекое прошлое, прошлое страны, которой уже нет [...] Прошлое верило в даты. И жизнь каждого человека состояла из дат, придававших жизни ритм, ощущение ступенчатости, словно с высоты очередной даты можно было оглянуться и, посмотрев вниз, увидеть само прошлое. Ясное, понятное прошлое, поделенное

Pidpalyi's *private* space, as well as the *public* space in the city of Kyiv, is a "chain of signifiers." At first, the "clear and comprehensible past" that was told by the photographs on the wall gives back to Zolotarev the dimension of his private memory, but once its is deprived of "its own referent", the same photographs then suddenly work as "cultural relicts," to borrow Aleida Assmann's (2011: 335) definition. As highlighted by Assmann, these are stored in the community's "archive," an intermediate space between memory and oblivion: they "are not unmediated," but "are de-contextualized and disconnected from their former frames which had authorized them or determined their meaning" (Assmann 2011: 335). Cultural relicts are thus "open to new contexts and lend themselves to new interpretations," and mainly tend to interact with the canon, which aims to legitimize the historical narrative of a community's past and identity boundaries.

In *Death and the Penguin*, Kurkov stages the heterogeneous dynamics enacted by the interaction between the archive and the canon of his community's cultural memory. The "cultural relicts" recalled by Kurkov may afford "a direct route to the past, to its referents," and at the same time, in their fragmentary nature provide "space for the work of the imagination" (Blacker 2012: 143–144). If, on the one hand, the "relicts" contained in Pidpalyi's archive may initially create in Zolotarev "the illusion of accessing and possessing the past, when the present—as reality—is beyond our control" (Blacker 2012: 142), on the other for the zoologist the only possible option in order to preserve his own memory happens to be the erasure of the same past. Pidpalyi dies because he cannot abandon his own identity: symbolically, it is the Soviet past that burns in his house. Most fundamentally, Pidpalyi's example persuades Zolotarev to opt for his only chance of survival: the adoption of a new identity. In *Death and the Penguin*'s emblematic

---

на квадраты событий и линии дорог [...] Виктор почувствовал себя уютно и защищенно [...] И вот он сидел среди вещей и бумаг, которые уже никому не принадлежали. Среди целого мира, оставшегося без своего создателя и хозяина. Старик не хотел, чтобы к этому миру прикасались посторонние, он не хотел, чтобы кто то видел разрушение этого маленького уютного мира, календарь которого словно запаздывал на три—четыре десятка лет" (Kurkov 2001: 155-159). Translated by George Bird.

conclusion, Zolotarev decides to substitute Misha on the scientific expedition that would take him to Antarctica. Emblematically, the expedition takes place on 9 May, the same date of the celebration of the Soviet "victory day" against Nazi Germany. The protagonist's last line in the novel is revelatory: "So it's me who's the penguin" (Kurkov 2011a: 187).[186] To use Deleuze and Guattari's terms for describing Kafka's metamorphoses, Zolotarev's act of "becoming animal" embodies the individual's "path of escape" from the never-ending cycle of missed "reterritorializations" in post-Soviet Ukraine:

> The acts of becoming-animal [...] are absolute deterritorializations [...] To become animal is to participate in movement, to stake out the path of escape in all its positivity, to cross a threshold, to reach a continuum of intensities that are valuable only in themselves, to find a world of pure intensities where all forms come undone, as do all the significations, signifiers, and signified, to the benefit of an unformed matter of deterritorialized flux, of nonsignifying signs. (Deleuze, Guattari 1986: 13)

In Kurkov's novels we may thus highlight the creation of new "paths of escape" from the condition of "post-Soviet aphasia" described by Serguei Oushakine. In his study on "the historical and cultural specificity of the post-Soviet subject," the anthropologist used this term to describe "a *collective* discursive behaviour" developing a "(1) *regression* to symbolic forms of the previous historical period that has been caused by (2) the society's *disintegrated* ability to find proper verbal signifiers for the signifieds of the new socio-political regime" (Oushakine 2000: 994). According to Oushakine, within this frame the post-Soviet subject is forced "to build his/her new identity on the basis of 'mythic notions retrieved from the past'" (2000: 1003).[187]

---

186 "Я — пингвин [...]" (Kurkov 2001: 253). Translated by George Bird.

187 In his study on contemporary Russia, Oushakine goes further in describing the strategies implemented by the post-Soviet subject: "[...] in the absence of new cultural forms ready to epitomise ongoing social changes, an individual [...] faces basically two (not necessarily alternative) choices. One of them deals with changing patterns of *usage* of the old symbols; this approach can be called the '*paradigm of remake*'. The other is based on changing one's *attitude* to the old symbols; this pattern of symbolic production can be labelled the '*paradigm of revival*'. Both strategies, however, are aimed at keeping the

Along these lines, if in *Death and the Penguin*, the act of becoming animal creates the room for a new *minor* self-determination able to restore "the individual's ability to speak" (Oushakine 2000: 994), it is in *The Good Angel of Death* (*Dobryi angel smerti*, 1997) that Kurkov gives birth to a programmatic deconstruction of the mythical reterritorializations of the Ukrainian past. The novel describes the great journey of the protagonist, Kolia Sotnikov, through the lands of Eurasia. In the beginning of the story, Kolia works as a nightwatchman in a warehouse in Kyiv. He finds by chance in his new apartment a volume of Taras Shevchenko's *Kobzar*, which is symbolically contained within a copy of *War and Peace* (*Voina i mir*, 1869) by the Russian writer Lev Tolstoi. The handwritten comments placed in the margins of Shevchenko's book disclose mysterious clues about a treasure that the great Ukrainian national poet would have buried in the sands of Kazakhstan, during his military service in exile. While the protagonist is excited about the prospect of obtaining a generous reward for finding the "hidden treasure," Petr and Galia, militants of the Ukrainian nationalist party, as well as mysterious members of the Russian and Ukrainian security services, oppose his search for the "sake of the Fatherland." Interestingly, Kolia's adventures in search of the "national spirit" take place amongst the cultural relicts of the Soviet world: the open space of Eurasia works as the intermediate space where new possible meanings for the signification of the post-Soviet Ukrainian cultural system may be found. At the end of the novel, the discovery of a silver box containing Shevchenko's love letters is emblematically a matter of contention for Petr and Kolia:

> "Do you know how much this is worth?" I asked, nodding at the casket.
> "Maybe it's worth plenty, but it doesn't do anything for Ukrainian culture . . ." he said and shrugged, with an expression of profound disappointment on his face.
> "The great Ukrainian poet writes his love letters in Russian . . ."
> "The great Ukrainian poet also wrote several novellas in Russian," I said. "That didn't make him any less great. It simply shows that he belongs to two cultures."
> "What belongs to two cultures doesn't belong to anyone," said Petro, suddenly switching into Russian himself.[188] (Kurkov 2011b: 369–370)

---

old signifier/symbol intact, while changing its signified/content/ context. Both activate the individual's creative ability within the rigid symbolic frames of the previous era" (2000: 1017).

188 "— Ты знаешь, сколько это стоит? — кивнул я на шкатулку. — Можэ, воно щось и стоить, алэ для украйинськойи культуры цэ ничего нэ дае... — и он

Petr's switching from Ukrainian, which is realized by Kurkov through the use of Russian letters to convey the Ukrainian pronunciation (e.g. Вэлыкый украйинськый поэт пышэ любовни запысочки росийською мовою), to Russian (i.e. То, что принадлежит двум, не принадлежит никому) metaphorically deconstructs the ideological narratives behind the language question and the nature of hybridity in Ukraine. This is the same Petr who in another passage of the novel is symbolically "intoxicated" by the "smell of the Ukrainian spirit" emanating from a mummy. The Ukrainian character under the effect of this spell can thus propose new models of transnational belonging:

> "It's a Ukrainian," Petro said in a quiet, pensive voice.
> "How do you make that out?" I asked in amazement.
> "You noticed yourself that he smells of cinnamon. . . And that's the smell of the Ukrainian spirit."
> "I smell like that too [...]"
> "You don't understand," Petro said in an unexpectedly gentle voice. "It's the smell of the spirit, not the nation. It simply means that this spirit entered you. [...]"[189] (Kurkov 2011b: 181)

The hybrid positioning of Kolia, a Ukrainian citizen of Russian origin, makes him, alternatively, a full member or a contested outcast of the Ukrainian nation. His ability to cross cultural systems is often regarded in the novel as a matter of concern. In the following passage, it is an official of the Ukrainian secret services, Colonel Taranenko, who questions the protagonist, labelling him as "*moskal*'"—an ethnic slur for Russian, while

---

пожал плечами. Лицо его выдавало глубокое разочарование. — Вэлыкый украйинськый поэт пышэ любовни запысочки росийською мовою... — Великий украинский поэт написал и несколько повестей по-русски, — сказал я. — От этого он не стал менее великим. Это просто показывает, что он принадлежит двум культурам. — То, что принадлежит двум, не принадлежит никому, — Петр неожиданно перешел на русский" (Kurkov 2000: 372). Translated by Andrew Bromfield.

189   "— Цэ украйинэць, — спокойным задумчивым голосом сказал Петр. — С чего ты взял? — удивился я. — Ты ж сам помитыв! У нього ж запах корыци... А цэ запах украйинського духа. — У меня тоже такой запах [...] Ты нэ розумиеш, — неожиданно мягко произнес Петр. — Цэ запах нэ нацийи, а духа! Цэ просто значыть, що цэй дух якось и тэбэ торкнувся [...]" (Kurkov 2000: 182). Translated by Andrew Bromfield.

the latter tries to defend himself against the accusation of "interfering in matters that are sacred to every Ukrainian":

"Beginning with a presentation by the Rooskies . . ." [...] "No need to tell me your life story, we've read that already. Let's start with something else—what gave you the idea of interfering in matters that are sacred to every Ukrainian?" [...]
"What do you mean?"
"Why, your interest in Taras Grigorievich Shevchenko, of course, on such an international scale, so to speak."
"There's nothing illegal in that, is there?"
"And who said there was? Not me. But I would say that these are rather delicate matters, especially when they extend beyond certain acceptable limits and begin to impinge on the interests of another state . . ." [...]
"I don't see what boundaries I have crossed, apart from geographical ones . . ." I said, forcing the words out with difficulty, since it was not easy to speak in this position either—I was very short of breath. (Kurkov 2011b: 151–152)[190]

Kolia's hybrid position makes him "very short of breath," while addressing the "delicate matters" around the national question. In *The Good Angel of Death*, Andrei Kurkov significantly chooses another anthropomorphic figure, the chameleon—to which the "angel" of the title refers, in order to mirror the complex nature of the protagonist's identity:

The chameleon's appearance had focused my thoughts on him, and I started thinking we ought to give him a name, since he had joined us. I began running through names in my mind, but human names and dogs' names didn't suit him. I had to find some kind of human prototype. But as the chameleon-like political leaders lined up inside my head, I began feeling embarrassed for the poor reptile: why should I want to name him in honour of people unworthy of either love or trust? And so, in order to make amends, I decided to name him in honour of my grandad—Petrovich. The patronymic without a given name sounded far

---

190 "Сперва с представителем «москалей» [...] Биографию свою рассказывать мне не надо, это мы уже читали. Начнем с другого — как это вас угораздило влезть в святые для каждого украинца дела [...] — Что вы имеете в виду? — спросил я. — Ну шо, конечно, ваш интерес к Тарасу Григорьевичу, да еще в таком, можно сказать, международном масштабе. — Ну а что здесь такого запрещенного? — А хто сказал, шо запрещенного. Нет. Я не говорил. Я бы сказал, шо это довольно деликатные дела, особенно, когда они выходят за допустимые пределы и начинают затрагивать интересы другого государства [...] — Я не вижу, за какие пределы, кроме географических, я забрался... — выдавил я из себя с трудом, так как говорить в этой позе было нелегко – не хватало дыхания" (Kurkov 2000: 152-153). Translated by Andrew Bromfield.

more respectable and at the same time more homely than a name without a patronymic.[191] (Kurkov 2011b: 114)

The chameleon embodies the symbolic metaphor of a liminal, open, "unnamed" identity. The "patronimic without a given name" signals the complex historical and cultural background that is still in search of a new signification. Eventually, in the pages of *The Good Angel of Death*, Kurkov's "individuated utterance" comes to be "immediately plugged into the political" (Deleuze, Guattari 1986: 16) and, through the words of Colonel Taranenko, forges the means for "another possible community" (Deleuze, Guattari 1986: 17) built around the transcultural and inclusive nature of the "national spirit":

The national spirit is higher than the national language. It changes a man's attitude to his surroundings, to everything around him and to himself as well. The spirit affects a man of any nationality, arousing only the good in him. But language is only the external sign of nationality. The president and a homicidal maniac can both speak it equally well. If you make language the most important aspect of the national spirit, it will become an instrument of segregation and a modern inquisition.[192] (Kurkov 2011b: 205)

---

191 "Хамелеон своим появлением переключил на себя мои мысли, и я уже думал, что надо бы ему и имя дать, раз он к нам присоединился. Стал перебирать имена, но человеческие или собачьи ему не подходили. Надо было найти какой-нибудь человеческий прототип. Но когда в воображении выстроились в шеренгу хамелеончатые политические деятели, то мне стало неудобно перед пресмыкающимся: что ж это я хочу назвать его в честь людей, ни любви, ни доверия не заслуживающих. И тогда, чтобы исправиться, я решил назвать его в честь своего деда — Петровичем. Отчество без имени звучало куда солиднее и более по домашнему, чем имя без отчества" (Kurkov 2000: 115). Translated by Andrew Bromfield.

192 "Национальный дух выше национального языка. Он изменяет отношение человека к окружающему, ко всему вокруг и к себе самому. Дух воздействует на человека любой национальности, пробуждая в нем только хорошее. А язык — это лишь внешний признак национальности. На нем одинаково хорошо может говорить и президент, и маньяк-убийца. Если язык перевести в самое важное качество национального духа, он станет инструментом сегрегации, современной инквизиции" (Kurkov 2000: 206). Translated by Andrew Bromfield.

Of Other Spaces (and Of Other Times):
Aleksei Nikitin's Literary Heterotopias

In his essay entitled *Of Other Spaces* (*Des Espaces Autres*, 1984), published just after his death, Michel Foucault studied the interactions between the human being and her/his perception of space. According to the French philosopher, "we live inside a set of relations that delineates sites that are irreducible to one another and absolutely not superimposable on one another" (Foucault 1984: 3). This coordinate system defines our consciousness of the space in which we live. However, quoting Foucault, "there are also in every culture, in every civilization, real places [...] that are something like counter-sites, a kind of effectively enacted utopia in which the real sites that can be found within the culture are simultaneously represented, contested, and inverted" (1984: 3). Thus, Foucault discerns the dimension of the *utopia*, a site devoid of any spatial references, from the *heterotopia*, which characterizes those spaces "that are absolutely different from all the sites that they reflect or speak about" (1984: 4). In order to understand their peculiar functioning, he metaphorically describes *heterotopias* as mirrors, which are able to re-signify reality in *other* spatial dimensions (Foucault 1984: 4).

Heterotopic mirroring enacts a process of metamorphosis: an identity transformation that involves both the man and the space. Thus, borrowing Foucault's words, it is possible to envision this spatial trope also as a different kind of textualization in order to reword the "great" cultural narratives: "*Heterotopias* are disturbing, probably because they secretly undermine language [...] as they destroy 'syntax' in advance, and not only the syntax with which we construct sentences, but also that less apparent syntax that causes words and things [...] to 'hold together'" (Foucault 1970: xxviii).

Interestingly, as noted by Chernetsky (2007: 186), while "Ukrainian authors have been no strangers to producing heterotopic texts" in post-Soviet times,[193] it is also late Soviet-Russian literature that developed such a

---

193 "Among those who have developed this paradigm, I would mention first and foremost Yuri Izdryk and Taras Prokhas'ko as having received the greatest critical acclaim, along with some lesser-known authors like Pavlo Vol'vach and Oleksandr Zhovna, as well as Vasyl' Kozhelianko, who balances on the

narrative model, as in the case of Mikhail Kuraev[194] (b. 1939, St. Petersburg). And, most importantly, it is no surprise that this kind of "exploration of ontological possibilities" widely intersects the *minor* artistic paradigm.[195]

It is by means of his depiction of "other spaces" and "other times" that Aleksei Nikitin seeks to recompose the compensatory illusion of his epoch. Born in Kyiv, Nikitin published his first works in the first half of the 1990s in literary magazines, such as *Druzhba Narodov* and *Oktiabr'*. In 2000, he won the Ukrainian Writers' Union Award for the best Ukrainian work in the Russian language, Premiia imeni Vladimira Korolenko, with his *The Fowler's Hand (Ruka ptitselova)*. In 2011–2012 he managed to publish his two works *Istemi* (2011) and *Mahjong (Madzhong*, 2012) with the Russian publisher Ad Marginem and they were nominated for Russian literary prizes like Natsbest and Bol'shaia kniga. In 2014, he won second prize in the IX Russkaia Premiia edition with his work *Victory Park* (2014).

In an attempt to deterritorialize the post-Soviet experience, this Ukrainian Russophone writer constructs his texts as "literary heterotopias." The duality of the spatial dimension portrayed by Nikitin "mirrors" the ongoing metamorphosis of the people who experience this space, a recurring theme in his works that is emblematically described by Krasniashchikh (2015: 177)

---

verge of innovative writing and commercially driven historical fantasy fiction" (Chernetsky 2007: 186).

194 "The experience of Kuraev's characters is that of individuals whose lives were torn apart by twentieth century history. They occupy positions of utter invisibility, positions at the margin [...] They have lived through multiple conflicting identities. In the end, their lives are actually constituted through narrative itself, the heterotopic narrative of mixed, labyrinthine spaces and times. The narrative serves as the topos where the repressed or suppressed fragments of the traumatized memory, both individual and collective, are unearthed and joined together in an attempt to articulate and simultaneously confront the past [...] writing becomes the locus for an attempt to solve the modern crisis of identity" (Chernetsky 2007: 97).

195 As Chernetsky (2007: 91) puts it: "The textual strategy of heterotopia also suggests bringing into the framework of analysis another theoretical concept: Deleuze and Guattari's 'minor literature' (*littérature mineure*) [...] Thus calling a text 'heterotopic' would also imply that it is preoccupied with exploration of those topoi—cultural, social, linguistic—that lie on the margins of the traditionally privileged literary discourses."

as the "mystery of binary human nature" (*taina binarnoi chelovecheskoi prirody*):

> a mystery that cannot be solved, but that we nevertheless need to try to answer, because our attempts at least reconcile with the fact that anyone—absolutely—who today is a friend-comrade-brother or beloved will imperceptibly turn into something foreign and hostile tomorrow.[196]

In his novels, the author focuses on the late Soviet years, retracing the period of transition that preceded the "historical catastrophe." At the core of his literary production lies his hometown, Kyiv. According to Nikitin, this focus is rooted in the need for a proper narrative of the capital in the late eighties and in the nineties.[197] The marginal position of such an historical period in the "great" narratives devoted to Kyiv makes the author's textualization an important practice of resignification. In order to fill this blank space in the collective memory of his community, Nikitin symbolically chooses to follow game dynamics. Thus, in *Istemi* (2011), the "invention" of history lies in the creation of a world made of new imaginary states: in 1984, five students from Kyiv University invented a fictional role-playing game based on historical events and set in the territories of the former Soviet Union. Within the time frame, which runs until 2004, the borders between past and present come to be blurred in the Kyiv heterotopic space.

---

196 "[…] разрешить которую, тайну, невозможно, но пытаться все равно надо, потому как эти попытки хотя бы примиряют с тем, что любой — абсолютно — сегодняшний друг-товарищ-брат, любимая — завтра незаметно для тебя превратится в чужое враждебное."

197 As argued by Nikitin in our 2013 meeting: "About Kyiv in the late eighties and in the nineties we have almost nothing. Moreover, in general, in the Soviet literature, the period of the eighties, the decline of the Soviet Union, is little described. This is a partial, if not complete omission, since many writers are not very fond of the moments that precede the catastrophe. Although, apparently, these moments should be analysed: it is important, because everything can happen again, by and large" (Puleri 2016: 192; О Киеве 80–90-х почти ничего нет. Больше того, вообще в советской литературе вот этот период 80-х годов, заката Советского Союза мало описан. Это если не белое, то светло-серое пятно, потому что многие писатели не очень любят моменты, предшествующие катастрофе. Хотя, казалось бы, надо анализировать, это важно, потому что всё может повториться, по большому счёту).

In the novel, the synthesis of real and fictional elements works on different narrative levels. Furthermore, *Istemi* is also the outcome of a rewriting process: "Do you remember The Black Book and Shwambraniya? That's where we got the idea. Lev Kassil…,"[198] admits the protagonist Davydov during an interrogation in the KGB's offices. This passage refers to the Soviet novel written in 1928–1931 by Lev Kassil' (1905–1970) and based on an autobiographical subject. In *The Black Book and Shwambraniya* (*Konduit i Shvambraniia*), likewise, two boys "invent" their history, setting it in an imaginary country: *Shvambraniia*. Also, the developments that occur in the game reflect the advent of the Revolution in real life, mixing historical characters and settings with fantasy. By intersecting different temporal strata and constructing "other" spaces, Nikitin has the textual instruments with which he is able to recompose the fragmented identity of his characters. In *Istemi*, he aims to represent "history as a black hole […] rather than a utopian repository of Truth" (Chernetsky 2007: 93–94). Nikitin's characters gain awareness of their precarity by means of a constant dialogue with the Ukrainian capital space, which embodies the true heterotopic mirror of their existential condition:

> In the intervening years nothing had changed here. Everything was the same, the street, Castle Hill, the heaviness of the raw evening sky […] Here Was Borichev, the Church of the Mother of God that they'd finished rebuilding ten years earlier. It was a dead place. Here it seemed that everything was the same as it had ever been: the howling dogs, the old snow at the beginning of spring, the incredible colours of the evening sky. Even the smells were the same. Even Castle Hill. But the bridge to the cosmos had been destroyed. It was gone. There was no cosmos. No metaphysics.[199] (Nikitin 2013: 97)

---

198 "Кондуит и Швамбрания. Помните? Идея — оттуда. Лев Кассиль…" (Nikitin 2011: 53). Translated by Anne Marie Jackson (2013: 45).

199 "Здесь ничего не изменилось за прошедшие годы, все осталось таким же: улицы, Замковая, тяжесть сырого вечернего неба […] Вот Боричев, вот церковь Успенья Богородицы, заново отстроенная десять лет назад. Мертвое место. Здесь, вроде бы, все, как всегда: лай собак, старый снег в начале весны, невообразимые цвета вечернего неба. Даже запахи не изменились. Даже Замковая. Но мост в космос разрушен. Его нет. Никакого космоса.

In this excerpt from the novel, Kyiv is portrayed as the victim of its different historical narratives. Davydov's reflections recall the Soviet past and how it strove for the creation of a "bridge to the cosmos" (*most v kosmos*), that is, an artificial alternative to real life under the regime. In contrast, Istemi, the last lord of the Zaporozhzhian Khanate, is Davydov's alternative, the alter ego chosen by the protagonist in the historical game played with his friends:

> Later, sitting up on Castle Hill and looking down at Kiev in May, I knew, with a distinct and vivid certainty, that our biggest problems were behind us and nothing worse would happen. Could there really be something worse than the prison inside the KGB building? [...] I haven't been back up Castle Hill since then. Probably for no good reason. The view from there is marvellous. Marvellous and very precise— no aberrations, no distortions. Now, twenty years on, I can see that the hill was right and I was wrong. But what can you take from me now? [...] I'm now a peddler of fizzy drinks, and my affairs no longer take me to Castle Hill. But back then…Then, Istemi was behind me, and we were equals. Not in everything, but in some ways we were. And Castle Hill knew it.[200] (Nikitin 2013: 56)

Throughout the novel, Kyiv is represented as a universal place. The holy hills of the capital preserve Kyiv's historical prominence, as conveyed by the traditional textualization of the city's secular image.[201] Nevertheless,

---

Никакой метафизики" (Nikitin 2011: 122–123). Translated by Anne Marie Jackson.

200 "Тогда, сидя на Замковой горе и глядя на майский Киев, я понимал отчетливо и ясно, что самые серьезные неприятности позади, и хуже чем было — не будет. Может ли быть что-то хуже внутренней тюрьмы КГБ? [...] С тех пор я не поднимался на Замковую. Наверное, зря. С нее открывается удивительный вид. Удивительный и очень точный. Никаких аберраций, никаких искажений. Сейчас, двадцать лет спустя, я понимаю: права тогда была гора, а я ошибался. Но, что теперь с меня возьмешь? [...] Теперь я торговец водой, и мне больше нечего делать на Замковой. А тогда... Тогда за мной был Истеми, и мы были равны. Пусть не во всем, но в чем-то были. И Замковая признавала это равенство" (Nikitin 2011: 67–68). Translated by Anne Marie Jackson.

201 As argued by Kokhanovskaia and Nazarenko (2012b: 211–212): "The brightest example is Gogol' [...] and philologists have begun to argue about the chthonic and magical nature of Gogol''s Kyiv. Meanwhile, it is enough to look without prejudice at 'Mirgorod' and 'Dikanka' in order to see that to Gogol' Kyiv, as Dikanka itself, is the heart of an ordered existence, a safely protected place [...] And this is not Gogol''s individual perspective. Kyiv was perceived in a similar way by Shevchenko, and not only in his poetry, but also in his prose [...] It is the Ukrainian variant of one of the main ideologemes related to Kyiv. 'Kyiv is

Nikitin's narrative on Kyiv recovers and integrates different traditions. On a first reading, it seems to recall the nostalgic and intimate gaze of its last great narrators in the twentieth century: Mikhail Bulgakov (1891–1940) and Viktor Nekrasov (1911–1987). Both Bulgakov in *The White Guard* (*Belaia Gvardiia*, 1924) and Nekrasov in his *Notes of an Idler* (*Zapiski Zevaki*, 1976) recorded the familiar historical memory of a "lost city." It is however through a deeper glance at Nikitin's Kyiv, where "life has never been snuffed out" (Nikitin 2013: 139),[202] that we can understand how the Russian narrative of the city, which describes Kyiv as fallen in an "eternal dream," and the Ukrainian one, which depicts it as a "holy city," "out of time," can intersect:

> Somewhere in here we witness the main crossroads between the Russian and the Ukrainian images of Kyiv (Gogol', as always, lies at the intersection). If in

---

the second Jerusalem': it is a holy city that, by definition, stands on the hill in the center of the world. This image, which has been secularised for obvious reasons, survived the Soviet power and, becoming a cliché, has come into our days [...]" (Самый яркий пример — Гоголь [...] филологи стали говорить о хтонической и колдовской природе Киева у Гоголя. Между тем достаточно непредвзято взглянуть на «Диканьку» и «Миргород,» чтобы увидеть: для Гоголя Киев, как и сама Диканька, — сердцевина упорядоченного бытия, надежно защищенное место [...] И это — не индивидуальная гоголевская оптика. Таким же видел Киев и Шевченко, причем не только в поэзии, но и в прозе [...] Это украинский извод одной из главных киевских идеологем «Киев — второй Иерусалим»: святой город, по определению стоящий на горе в центре мира. Образ этот, по понятным причинам секуляризовавшись, пережил советскую власть и, превратившись в штамп, дошел до наших дней [...])."

202 See Nikitin 2011: 179. "It's not for no reason that human beings have lived for thousands of years on these high clay banks, not wishing to leave them. Whatever the circumstances—and at times the circumstances were gut-wrenching and life grew utterly unbearable—life has never been snuffed out. Something keeps us here, replenishing us with the force of life. Come what may, the force of life has always been abundant in the Kiev hills (Все-таки не зря последнюю пару тысяч лет на этом крутом и глинистом берегу реки суетятся люди, не желая его оставлять. Как бы ни складывались обстоятельства, а временами они складывались очень кисло и жизнь здесь становилась невыносимой, полностью, все же, она не пресекалась никогда. Что-то держит нас на этом месте, наполняя жизненной силой. Чего-чего, а жизненной силы на киевских холмах всегда было в избытке)." Translated by Anne Marie Jackson (2013: 138–139).

the Russian tradition Kyiv is frozen in an absolute past, has fallen in an eternal sleep (golden or nightmarish), and has turned into a sacred graveyard, then in the Ukrainian tradition the sacred and ancient image of the city instead remains time-less: from this point of view, the modern Kyiv, fussy and profane, is just another link in that unbroken chain that began, following Nestor the Chronicler, already in Apostle Andrew's times. This duality of Kyiv's image is primarily due to the real history of the city, where periods of rapid rise were followed by decades of decline and immersion into an ahistorical stillness. [...][203] (Kokhanovskaia, Nazarenko 2012b: 212)

The duality embodied by Kyiv reflects the *dvoedushie* experienced by Davydov-Istemi. The protagonist's "two-souledness" finds its heterotopic mirror in the textual space created by Nikitin. If in the last pages of *Istemi* Davydov can still glimpse the Castle hill, which is "already disappearing into the night" (Nikitin 2013: 151),[204] it is in Nikitin's second novel that the Kyiv hills are there to convey a warning to its inhabitants. In the urban space imagined by Nikitin in *Mahjong* (*Madzhong*, 2012), the remaining bastions of the national culture are eroded by the new post-Soviet "winds of change":

A gust of wind coming from Dnipro can rip the hat off the careless passer-by in Mariïns'kyi Park. It can tear away the child's balloon, taking it over the crys-talline skies of Kyiv. Don't cry, baby. Don't cry. Get used to it. Not far from here, there are other winds, other hurricanes, which echo. And don't compare the winds coming from Dnipro with the dry and dusty ones that are eroding the country, which are rising from the bustle coming from Hrushevs'kyi and

---

203 "Где-то здесь и проходит принципиальная развилка между русским и украинским образами Киева (Гоголь, как всегда, стоит на распутье). Если в русской традиции Киев замер в абсолютном прошлом, заснул вечным сном (золотым или кошмарным), превратился в священное кладбище, то в украинской — сакральный и древний образ города не находится исключительно в прошлом, скорее остается вне времени. Только с такой точки зрения современный Киев, суетливый и профанный, оказывается лишь еще одним звеном той неразрывной цепи, которая началась, согласно Нестору, еще во времена апостола Андрея. Двойственность образа Киева обусловлена прежде всего реальной историей города, в котором периоды стремительного взлета сменялись десятилетиями упадка и, действительно, погружения во внеисторическую неподвижность [...]."

204 "I was standing opposite Castle Hill, but the hill was already disappearing into night (Я стоял напротив Замковой, но гора уже ушла в ночь)" (Nikitin 2011: 197). Translated by Anne Marie Jackson.

Bankova Streets [...] in Kyiv, as some are wearing away and building up the soil of the historical hill of Shchekavytsia, while Sofia and Lavra are trying to hold on with all their remaining energies. How long is it going to last? [...] and what can be said of us, disunited and weak, who vivaciously argue over trivial matters, invented out of a whole cloth?[205] (Nikitin 2012: 358)

In *Madzhong*, Kyiv is crowded with failed writers, ambitious *bukinisty* and unscrupulous billionaires, all striving to seize a "priceless manuscript." In this novel as well, the game dynamics underlie Nikitin's literary world, and are employed in order to rewrite tradition and to reappropriate History. It is the trilogy of *Mertvye dushi* (*Dead Souls*, 1842) as planned by Nikolai Gogol', the contested father of Ukrainian literature in Russian, that is to be the target of a complex rewriting.[206] Gogol''s project was to write a great epic poem in prose on the Russian Empire, which was to be structured in three parts. It would narrate the journey of the protagonist, Pavel Ivanovich Chichikov, following lines of development close to Dante Alighieri's *Divine Comedy* (*Divina Commedia*, 1321). Legend has it that the second part of the trilogy was destroyed by Gogol' shortly before his death, while the drafting of the third part was never even started. In *Madzhong*, the main plot concerns the fortuitous finding of the fragments of a supposed *Dead Souls* third volume. While the protagonist, Zhenia L'vov, is a failed philologist whose *unfinished* doctoral dissertation was devoted to studying the evolution of Chichikov's developments in Gogol''s *missing* trilogy, the

---

205 "Порыв свежего ветра с Днепра может сорвать шляпу с неосторожного прохожего в Мариинском парке, может выхватить шарик у ребенка и унести его в ясно-голубое киевское небо. Не плачь, детка. Не плачь. Привыкай. Совсем рядом ревут другие ветры, другие ураганы. И не сравниться ветру с Днепра с иссушающими страну самумами, поднятыми шелестом на улицах Грушевского и Банковой [...] срезают и застраивают в Киеве историческую Щекавицу, из последних сил держатся София и Лавра. Долго ли продержатся? [...] то что же говорить о нас, разъединенных и слабых, радостно грызущихся из-за выдуманных, из пальца высосанных пустяков?"

206 Similarly, it is worth remembering that in Andrei Kurkov's *The Good Angel of Death*, which was under scrutiny in the previous section, the plot concerns the search for a mysterious "treasure" belonging to one of the fathers of modern Ukrainian literature: Taras Shevchenko.

demiurges of the story come to be the four players of mah-jong: throughout the novel, their matches open the chapters and their moves upset the balance of the exhausting search for Gogol"s volume. As stressed by the literary critic Viktor Toporov (2012), we witness a "Russian prose built on a Ukrainian subject and clearly oriented towards Western models (Borges, Cortázar, Umberto Eco, Pérez-Reverte—here on this line)."[207] Literature, as well as History, is subject to fate. At the end of the "game," the different narrative levels symbolically intertwine in the "last unnumbered chapter," a spatial dimension where Zhenia becomes the shaman Kara Gergen. Under these guises, the protagonist finally has the power to change the course of "History":

– What's the manuscript?
– "Dead Souls." Nikolai Vasilevich Gogol'. Part Three.
– Great. I sincerely congratulate you.
– Why?
– Because you are in good company now.
– With Gogol'? Thanks.
– If it was just with him…well, what's wrong with your manuscript?
– It does not exist. Ok, it existed before. I read some pages.
– But then, when it came the time to place Hen Tamgan, it turned out that there was no manuscript, didn't it?
– Yes. That's how it turned out […]
– That's all right. Actually, the manuscript does not exist. It does not and never did exist. You have not written it yet.
– Me? That's me who did not write it? […]
– No one wrote it. Neither you nor Gogol'. Nor anybody else.[208] (Nikitin 2012: 381)

---

207 "[…] русская проза — на украинском материале, — и очевидно ориентированная при этом на западные образцы (Борхес, Кортасар, Умберто Эко, Перес-Реверте — вот по этой линии)."

208 "Что за рукопись? — «Мертвые души». Николай Васильевич Гоголь. Том третий. — Прекрасно. От души тебя поздравляю. — С чем? — Ты попал в хорошую компанию. — К Гоголю? Спасибо. — Если бы только к нему… Ладно. Что же не так с твоей рукописью? — Ее нет. Прежде она была. Ее читали, держали в руках. Я сам видел несколько страниц. — А когда пришло время наложить хэн тамган, оказалось, что рукописи нет. Правильно? — Да. Именно так и оказалось […] — Тогда все в порядке. Дело в том, что этой рукописи

"More than everything else, that story looked like a game" (Nikitin 2012: 370), comments the narrator in the last pages of *Mahjong*. In addition to the well-structured stylization of Gogol"s prose in the imaginary passages from the third volume of *Dead Souls*, Nikitin injects his authorial intrusions and historical digressions to consolidate his rewriting of tradition. Thus, the writer can disguise himself as Old Kachalov, one of the mah-jong players, and reappropriate his voice to formulate his "historical truth:"

> The Russian language was created by Ukrainians and it should be recognised abroad as Ukrainian property. Kachalov began with the Primary Chronicle, which was written only three hundred meters from his office, and did not forget anyone. In his list it was not only the theologians from Mohyla Academy, who were invited by Patriarch Nikon to Moscow to put in order the church books, that needed to be included, but also all the renown Ukrainian nobles and raznochintsy who wrote in Russian.[209] (Nikitin 2012: 72–73)

The sarcastic comment made by Kachalov reflects Nikitin's *minor* position on the language and identity issues in Ukraine. According to the author, the Ukrainian contribution to Russian culture throughout the centuries is an indisputable matter: it is not to be envisioned as an Imperial "cultural expansion" (*kul'turnaia ekspansiia*), but rather as an "exchange of authors" (*obmen avtorov*; Puleri 2016: 186). The Russophone writer considers those arguments recognizing the presence of the Russian language in Ukraine as the outcome of a kind of colonial domination to be inappropriate. Instead, Nikitin asserts that we witness a mutual influence between the Russian and Ukrainian systems, which later gave rise to the development of two different cultural models. Furthermore, framing the contemporary "Russian literature of Ukraine" (*russkaia literatura Ukrainy*) as an active element of the Ukrainian artistic production would not limit it from being considered also as a constitutive "part of Russian literature" (*chast' russkoi literatury*;

действительно нет. Нет и никогда не было. Ты ее еще не написал. — Я? Не написал? [...] — Никто не написал. Ни ты, ни Гоголь. Ни кто-то другой."

209   "русский язык создан украинцами и его следует признать собственностью Украины за границей. Качалов начал с «Повести временных лет,» написанной в трехстах метрах от его офиса, и не забыл никого. В записке были перечислены все богословы Могилянской Академии, которых Патриарх Никон пригласил в Москву приводить в порядок церковные книги, а также все известные украинские дворяне и разночинцы, писавшие по-русски."

Melezhik 2013).[210] As Nikitin stressed, to writers, self-identification is an "intimate question" and is affected by multiple factors that have nothing to do with the discourses of tradition (Besedin 2013).

Vladimir Rafeenko: The Ukrainian "Magical Realism"

In his overview of recent developments in *rusukrlit*, Krasniashchikh (2015: 181–182) argues that "[t]he theme of transformation and re-transformation is the cross-cutting and leading one in the work of Donets'k writers, both for those who write magically and postmodernistically, and for those who write in a more or less realistic manner."[211] The fantastic world created by Vladimir Rafeenko in his literary production to "transform" reality seems to belong to the former group of Donets'k writers' stylistic tendencies.[212] As the author argued in our 2013 meeting, broadly speaking, this finds its roots in an aesthetic paradigm that is particularly dear to modern Ukrainian prose:

---

210 In 2013, in an interview with the Russian magazine *Svobodnaia Pressa*, directed by Russian writers Zakhar Prilepin and Sergei Shargunov, Aleksei Nikitin was asked to identify his own sense of belonging. Once more, we are dealing with the difficulties of giving a categorical answer: "Many times I observed the situation involving two writers living in the same country and writing in the same language. One of them feels Russian, and the other one Ukrainian. Actually, we belong to both cultures. Russian literature of Ukraine is a segment of Russian literature and at the same time one of the literatures of Ukraine, which is a part of Ukrainian culture" (Melezhik 2013; Я не раз наблюдал ситуацию, когда встречались два автора, живущие в одной стране, пишущие на одном языке, при этом один ощущает и называет себя русским, другой украинским. На самом же деле мы принадлежим обеим культурам, русская литература Украины — это часть русской литературы и в то же время одна из литератур Украины, часть культуры Украины).

211 "Тема превращения и перепревращения — сквозная, ведущая в творчестве донецких писателей, и у тех, кто пишет магично-постмодернистично, и у тех, кто — в более-менее реалистической манере."

212 In his study, amongst the most prominent Donets'k Russian-language authors Krasniashchikh also analyses the works by Elena Stiazhkina (b. 1968), Nikolai Fomenko (b. 1953, Rossosh'), Sasha Protiag (b. 1978, Voronezh), Sergei Shatalov (b. 1958, Stalino—today Donets'k) and Oleg Zaviazkin (b. 1970, Makiïvka), all developing narratives at the crossroads between realistic and postmodern tendencies.

It seems to me that both the Russophone writers of Ukraine and the Ukrainian writers themselves show an intimate predilection for unrealistic prose. And this is our main difference from the mainstream of Russian prose. In Ukraine, for many talented artists pure realism as such is not perceived at all as an adequate form for literary transformation and vision of the world [...] Ukrainian prose writers, both Russian- and Ukrainian-speaking, are united by a meta-realistic, suggestive view of things.[213] (Puleri 2016: 220)

Along these lines, in "great" Ukrainian literature the narrative strategies adopted by authors such as Shevchuk, Ul'ianenko and Vynnychuk have been compared by Chernetsky (2007: 205) to the aesthetic paradigm known as "magical realism," which emerged in Latin America in the twentieth century. In the literary production of authors such as the Cuban Alejo Carpentier (1904–1980) and the Colombian Gabriel Garcia Márquez (1927–2014), magical realism works as "a mode suited to exploring—and transgressing—boundaries, whether the boundaries are ontological, political, geographical, or generic" (Zamora, Faris 1995: 5). This becomes the cornerstone for developing "the fusion, or coexistence, of possible worlds, spaces, systems that would be irreconcilable in other modes of fiction" (Zamora, Faris 1995: 5–6). In magical realist literature, reality undergoes a process of transformation, where the creation of new narrative models lays the groundwork to reimagine it. The adoption of magical realist narratives can thus play the role of "a kind of liberating poetics" (Faris 2002: 103) able to voice those elements of reality that are usually perceived as "marginal."

Ukrainian cultural tradition reveals strong affinities with this artistic paradigm: this seemingly finds its roots in the legacy of the Baroque, "both as a system of thought and an aesthetic practice."[214] Today's re-evaluation

---

213 "Мне кажется, что и у русскоязычных писателей Украины, и у писателей собственно украинских имеется внутренняя установка на нереалистичную прозу. И это главное наше отличие от русского прозаического мейнстрима. У нас чистый реализм как таковой, большинством талантливых людей вообще не воспринимается, как адекватная форма литературного воссоздания и видения мира [...] Украинских прозаиков, как русскоязычных, так и пишущих на украинском языке, объединяет мета-реалистичный, суггестивный взгляд на вещи."

214 As argued by Chernetsky (2007: 188–189): "An affinity with the Baroque, both as a system of thought and an aesthetic practice, and with allegory,

of the heritage of the Baroque experience is in line with the peculiar trends developed in modern Ukrainian literature, where the impact of Ivan Kotliarevs'kyi's (1769–1838) *Aeneid* (*Eneïda*, 1798), a mock-heroic poem in which Virgil's Trojan heroes are replaced by the Zaporozhzhian Cossacks, is regarded as the archetype of the Ukrainian-language literary tradition. This "great epic burlesque literary fresco," which even managed to convey "a realistic vision of the world" (Pachlovska 1998: 503), then gave birth to an epigonic tradition during the nineteenth century, known as *kotliarevshchyna*.[215]

Nikolai Gogol''s peculiar worldview (Shapiro 1986) further confirms a constant influence of Baroque aesthetics on the authors who worked in the intermediate space between the "great" Ukrainian and Russian literatures. Gogol' is considered one of the major precursors of magical realism, and the legacy of his masterful use of "fantastic elements" within a real and

---

which twentieth century criticism recognized as 'the dominant stylistic law' of the Baroque, constitutes an important strain in their makeup [...] It appears to be fundamentally linked with their liminal position within the context of Western civilization and [...] of the Russian /Soviet Empire and with the critical power that stems from such a position [...] It has been argued that among Slavic cultures, Ukraine is possibly the most Baroque-oriented, and, indeed, the Baroque era (more exactly, the seventeenth century) marked Ukraine's greatest prominence in the Slavic, as well as the Eastern Christian, world. Hence it comes as no surprise that Ukrainian writers of later eras were frequently drawn to portraying and reevaluating this legacy [...]."

215 The reception of this artistic paradigm has always been highly contested in Ukraine, since the exaggerated and farcical characterization of the Ukrainian ethnic elements came to subtend a message of political and cultural "inferiorization" in relation to the empire. As Grabowicz (2003) points out, the parodic-subversive nature of the *kotliarevshchyna* is, in any case, two-fold: this literary paradigm, still remaining totally dependent on the colonial relationship with the literature of the centre, had the function of mocking the same imperial reality.

local frame still can be recognized even in Soviet literary subgenres,[216] such as chimeric prose (*khymerna proza*).[217]

Vladimir Rafeenko's literary production is in line, in many respects, with these trends. According to Rafeenko, Nikolai Gogol' embodies "the origin of the Russian-language literature created by the Ukrainians" (*istok russkoiazychnoi literatury, sozdavaemoj ukraintsami*), and it is thanks to the "magical" and the "marvelous" that the "Gogolian school" (Puleri 2016: 220) could articulate its specificity in the course of the centuries that followed.

The Russophone writer's literary success is fundamentally linked to the last editions of the Russian literary award Russkaia Premiia. After publishing his first works, *The Brief Book of Farewells* (*Kratkaia kniga proshchanii*, 1999) and *The Magis' Holidays* (Kanikuly magov, 2005), in Donets'k, with a relatively low level of distribution, his novel *The Non-Reflexive Verbs* (*Nevozvratnye glagoly*, 2009) entered the longlist for the

---

216 Kokhanovskaia and Nazarenko (2011b: 208) highlight the continuity of Gogolian tradition in Ukrainian literature: "Chimeric prose, as well as magical realism, are deeply rooted in national culture. The new Ukrainian literature, whose origin dates back to Somov, Gogol', Shevchenko and Kulish, was born in the age of romanticism, and even today it seems in general to remain there, actualising its various features over time. Gogol''s tradition has never been interrupted. Another issue is the fact that it could degenerate—and it did degenerate—into a primitive 'sharovarshchyna' [stereotypical cultural forms]" (Химерная проза, как и магический реализм, глубоко укоренена в национальной культуре. Новая украинская литература, у истоков которой стояли Сомов, Гоголь, Шевченко, Кулиш, рождена эпохой романтизма — и до сих пор, в общем-то, в ней остается, актуализируя с течением времени разные ее черты. Гоголевская традиция никогда не прерывалась, другое дело, что она могла выродиться — и вырождалась — в примитивную «шароварщину»).

217 *Khymerna proza* was a literary trend emerging in the 1970s in Soviet Ukraine, and lying "outside the boundaries of realism, and not just the socialist one" (*za ramki ne tol'ko sotsialisticheskogo, no i kakogo by to ni bylo realizma*; Kokhanovskaia, Nazarenko 2011b: 207). It was initiated by Oleksandr Il'chenko's 1958 novel, *The Cossack kin never wanes, or Mamai and the stranger woman* (*Kozats'komu rodu nema perevodu, abo zh Mamai i chuzha molodytsia*). As Chernetsky (2007: 190) emphasizes, the "national character" emerging from these works, which were permeated by "a humorous, or sometimes sarcastic, tone," "reinforced some of the worst colonial stereotypes about Ukraine and the Ukrainians" (Chernetsky 2007: 190).

award in 2008. The favourable recognition of the novel in Russia was then followed by its publication in the Kharkiv-based Russian-language literary journal *Soiuz Pisatelei*. It was the prelude to the publication of the prose poem *Flagrum* (*Fliagrum*, 2011) in *Novyi Mir*; a collection of novellas, *All Summer Long* (*Leto naprolet*, 2012), and the novel *The Moscow Divertissement* (*Moskovskii Divertisment*, 2011) in *Znamia*. The latter work won second prize in the 2011 Russkaia Premiia edition, while the Russophone author was then awarded first prize in 2013 with his novel *The Descartes' Demon* (*Demon Dekarta*, 2013).

In his works, "Orpheus Rafeenko" ("Orfei Rafeenko"; Dais 2013a), with a background in philology and culturology, gives birth to a peculiar interpretation of the Gogolian heritage. The Russophone writer elaborates an aesthetic paradigm that, also due to his metaliterary reflections on the transformative power of the artistic language, has been defined as "magical postmodernism" (*magicheskii postmodernizm*; Dais 2013a). In Rafeenko's artistic world, reality undergoes an alchemical transformation, which takes shape thanks to a postmodern interplay of heterogeneous literary traditions and styles. The minor position of the Donets'k author within the Ukrainian and Russian cultural systems intensifies the process of stylistic deterritorialization, involving what Deleuze and Guattari described as the "machine of expression:"

> Kafka emphatically declares that a minor literature is much more able to work over its material. Why this machine of expression, and what is it? We know that it is in a relation of multiple deterritorializations with language; it is the situation of the Jews who have dropped the Czech language at the same time as the rural environment, but it is also the situation of the German language as a "paper language." Well, one can go even farther; one can push this movement of deterritorialization of expression even farther. (Deleuze, Guattari 1986: 19)

Similarly to Kafka, Rafeenko opts for the language "as it is, in its very poverty," makes "it vibrat[e] with a new intensity" (Deleuze, Guattari 1986: 19). In his works Rafeenko creates a literary world full of intertextual references that is immersed in a constant dialogue with different artistic traditions. This "disjunction between content and expression" (Deleuze, Guattari 1986: 20) brings the reader to enter a universe that is built around the revisiting of Russian and Ukrainian cultural models. Most fundamentally, as argued by Krasniashchikh (2015: 182),

The prose of Rafeenko is rhythmic, lyrical, mythological, but also largely humorous [...], that is a very important quality: real, light, deep, comical humour sets a particular reading mode, and on the level of worldview, perhaps, solves problems (including the "eternal" and "last" ones), leveling the tragedy of being and making it surmountable—as for the heroes, as for the author and the reader.[218]

The work that seems to better exemplify the syncretic tension found in Rafeenko's literary production is *The Moscow Divertissement*, the novel that brought the author to the attention of Russian and Ukrainian literary critics (see Volodarskii 2013b; Bondar'-Tereshchenko 2014). From the subtitle of the work, "novel-Iliad" (*roman-Iliada*), we can already grasp the author's programmatic attempt to revisit the mock-heroic poem of Ukrainian tradition. Here the classical world of the Homeric poem overlaps with the German Romantic model: thanks to the intersection of these myths, Rafeenko can thus give birth to a mystical, fantastic narrative. The "Passage between stories" (*Pereval istorii*)[219] is the magic element used by the author to explore and transgress the boundaries between the Homeric epos and the family idyll found in E. T. A. Hoffmann's story "The Nutcracker and the Mouse King" ("Nussknacker und Mausekönig," 1816). In the phantasmagoria created by Rafeenko, "metamorphosis" (*metamorfoza*) becomes "the true hero" (*glavnaia geroinia*) of *The Moscow Divertissement* (Volodarskii 2013b). The novel is set in Moscow, symbolically depicted as the new Troy, which is under attack by giant rats:

---

218 "Проза Рафеенко ритмична, лирична, мифологична, но в значительной же степени и юмористична [...], это очень важное ее качество: юмор — настоящий, легкий, глубокий, смешной — задает режим чтения, а на мировоззренческом, что ли, уровне, решает проблемы (включая и «вечные,» «последние»), нивелируя трагику бытия, делая ее преодолимой — и для героев, и для автора, и для читателя."

219 See Rafeenko 2013: 51. "there is some sort of Passage between stories: something happened there, and now people and literary characters illegally incarnate into each other and lose the rightful places that Zeus set for them. Now we all, that is, they all somehow move from one world to another, from one time to another, thus becoming, how shall I put it, mutually inverse [...] (...есть какой-то Перевал историй, там что-то случилось, и теперь люди и персонажи незаконно воплощаются друг в друга и утрачивают законные места, положенные для них Зевсом. Теперь все мы, то есть они, как-то перемещаются из одного мира в другой, из одного времени в другое. И стали, как бы это выразиться, взаимообратными...)."

There is always a place in the world one considers prestigious to bombard [...] at the same time in the world there may be a number of places that represent one and the same Troy. Troy, you know, moves around a bit, drifting around the world. Today it is here, and the next day, lo and behold! it is already in another place. It is the phenomenon of the refraction of ideal objects, you know [...] Why is it so important to conquer Troy? Because, on the one hand, Troy is to be blamed. It does not matter why, you can always find faults. Therefore, faults are always pretty abstract.[220] (Rafeenko 2013: 51)

The Russophone writer positions himself in the "heart of the empire" to mock contemporary myths and phobias from within. The main thematic line of the novel is around the war of the Muscovites against the rats, but in the course of the story the same inhabitants of the capital will turn into their enemies, making it impossible to understand "how Moscow will manage to win and at the same time defend itself" (Puleri 2016: 210).[221]

As Rafeenko noted in our 2013 meeting, "the metaphor of Moscow occupied by rats is a metaphor for the modern world" (Puleri 2016: 212).[222] The logic of Pascalian divertissement—that is a "distraction," a diversion of the human conscience—determines a continuous system of refractions, projections of the historical reality in the magic Moscow created by Rafeenko. In *The Moscow Divertissement*, the characters inhabiting the capital are Homeric heroes and anthropomorphic animals that take part in an allegorical masquerade able to highlight the "diverted images" of reality created by national and imperial discourses. In the novel, the same idea of empire is the real *divertissement*:

Hedgehog rose and waved his cigarette. 'Yes, you want, probably, to know what there was in the hall of the Moscow Heart and how the battle ended?! So, I'll tell you: we won! Exactly. We forged ahead as an avalanche, all of us, Russians

---

220 "Всегда в мире есть место, которое считается престижным ткнуть ракетой [...] одновременно в мире может существовать несколько мест, которые являются одной и той же Троей. Троя, понимаешь, перемещается немного, дрейфует по миру. Сегодня она здесь, а послезавтра, глядишь, уже в другом месте. Феномен рефракции идеальных объектов, понимаешь? [...] Почему это так важно — победить Трою? Потому что Троя, с одной стороны, виновата. Тут не важно в чем, вину найти всегда можно. Поэтому вина эта всегда довольно абстрактная."

221 "[...] как Москве победить саму себя, как саму себя защитить от себя самой."

222 "[...] метафора Москвы, занятой крысами — это метафора современного мира."

and non-Russians, right and left, young and old, clever and stupid, men and not men. We advanced toward this riff-raff with bare hands and hearts filled with the exciting beauty of death and love!'[223] (Rafeenko 2013: 170)

The battle, which in the end turns out to be a cinematic farce, is joined by characters drawn from the Russian tradition, such as the hedgehog from Iurii Norshtein's (b. 1941, Andreevka) Soviet animated shorts, or the Russian bear, portrayed as a decayed "king of the woods."[224] The characters inhabiting Rafeenko's Moscow symbolically refer to the "metamorphosis" and decay of Russian culture.[225]

The novel was compared by critics (Bondar'-Tereshchenko 2014; Volodarskii 2013b) to the rarefied narrative emerging in Venedikt Erofeev's (1938–1990) prose poem *Moscow-Petushki* (*Moskva-Petushki*, 1973) and to the fantasmagoric world of the capital depicted in Mikhail Bulgakov's (1891–1940) *The Master and Margarita* (*Master i Margarita*, 1967). Nevertheless, *The Moscow Divertissement* seems to weave an intense

---

223 "Ежик встал, помахал сигаретой. «Да, вы хотите, наверное, знать, что там было в зале Московского Сердца и чем завершилась битва?! Так вот что я вам скажу — мы победили! Точно говорю. Мы шли сплошной лавиной, все — русские и нерусские, правые и левые, молодые и старые, умные и глупые, мужчины и не очень — мы шли на эту серую сволоту с голыми руками и серцами, наполненными пьянящей красотой смерти и любви!» "

224 See Rafeenko 2013: 88. "I did not draw any beautiful picture, compose any verse, or shoot any film! I tormented myself and my family for my entire life with the existential Russian melancholy and periodic drunkenness! Forgive me, my God, have mercy! [Ни картины не написал прекрасной, ни стиха не сочинил, ни фильм не снял! И себя, и семью свою мучил только всю жизнь экзистенциальной русской тоской и периодическим пьянством! Прости меня, Боже мой, помилуй!]."

225 See Rafeenko 2013: 87–90. "'Vatslav, how could you become a hedgehog? How? You, a dancer who was applauded by the whole Europe! [...] Reflected in the mirror I was alone: only me, nothing else! Nothing! No scene, no music, no atmosphere of tragedy and creativity of which a decent life should be colored. Nothing...'" [«Вацлав, как ты мог стать ежом?! Как ты мог?! Ты, танцор, которому аплодировала вся Европа!...Только я сам, сам я там, в зеркале стоял, и ничего больше! Ничего! Ни сцены, ни музыки, ни той атмосферы трагедии и творчества, которой должна быть окрашена всякая порядочная жизнь! Ничего...»]."

dialogue with Iurii Andrukhovych's *The Moscoviad*.[226] On the one hand, in his "horror novel" (*roman zhakhiv*)—the subtitle of the Ukrainian author's work—the position of the protagonist Otto Von F., a Ukrainophone poet from the Western regions of Soviet Ukraine, seems to have clear, well-defined contours; on the other, the ontological crisis staged by Rafeenko's characters, who are in a state of constant metamorphosis, seems instead to break the political and cultural boundaries of modernity. While in *The Moscoviad* the narrator introduced the reader to a "modern Odyssey," to the "archetypal 'journey home'" of a Ukrainian poet (Chernetsky 2007: 224) going back to his Motherland, in Rafeenko's *Divertissement*—emblematically—the narrative does not have a subject or a direction. As an imaginary Patroclus states:

> [...] you are only a character. And a character goes his direction and cannot depart from it. Nowhere? No, my dear, nowhere. Neither to the right nor to the left? No, neither to the right, nor to the left.[227] (Rafeenko 2013: 122)

---

226 Dais (2013a) highlighted the correspondences between the two novels in her review of Rafeenko's *The Moscow Divertissement*: "Andrukhovych's *The Moscoviad* was a sensational novel at the time. The protagonist, the Ukrainian poet Otto Von F., a student at the Literary Institute, performs a tortuous route around the capital, eventually getting to a secret hall under the Red Square, where he faces the symbols of the Empire and, after having taken revenge against them, goes to Kyiv. The battle with the rats, which Rafeenko's heroes, who are gods, humans and animals, have to face, is an echo of the Moscow apocalypse described by Andrukhovych. He describes giant three-metres rats roaming in the Moscow metro (in the 1990s tabloids were really full of similar rumours)" [«Московиада» Юрия Андруховича — нашумевший в своё время роман, в котором главный герой, украинский поэт Отто фон Ф., студент Литинститута, проходит сложным маршрутом по стольному граду, попадая в конечном счете в тайный зал под Красной площадью, где встречает символы империи, расправившись с которыми, уезжает в Киев. Битва с крысами, которую ожидают герои Рафеенко: боги, люди и звери — это отголосок московского апокалипсиса Андруховича, описывающего то, как в московского метро бродят трёхметровые крысы-гиганты (подобными слухами действительна полнилась жёлтая пресса начала 1990-х)].

227 "[...] ты просто персонаж. А персонаж идет по своему пути и не может от него отклониться. Никуда? Нет, милая, никуда. Ни вправо, ни влево? Ни вправо, ни влево."

Rafeenko's narrative exemplifies a reverse, but still—to a great extent—complementary, path to the one undertaken by Andrukhovych in his 1993 novel, thus revealing alternative dynamics for weaving a dialogue with the former "metropolis" in Ukrainian literature.[228] In *Moskoviada*, Andrukhovych exorcises the Ukrainian colonial ghosts, rewriting in Ukrainian the phantasmagoric Moscow of the late 1980s:

> The fact is, for about a year now rumors have been spreading around Moscow, fueled by the tabloids and perhaps by all of the press, that in the depths of the metro there have appeared giant, shepherd-dog-sized rats […] Before they only gave signs of themselves at night. Now they have started appearing even at daytime […] "For the heart of the matter is not in the rats but in the need to exterminate someone […] each rat taken individually, yours truly being no exception, undoubtedly contains a certain particle of evil and thus becomes its active . . . eh . . . promoter […] And this is exactly why there can be no winners or losers in your war, only victims . . ."[229] (Andrukhovych 2008: 125; 127–128)

Yet, Rafeenko takes possession of the "centre" of the empire, rewriting it in Russian from his minor perspective. The "dreamy" dimension of Rafeenko's *Divertissement*, where the rats themselves can speak, responds to the Soviet "nightmare" imagined by Andrukhovych in his Moscow:

> The emperor of rats must be present during all significant events in the life of the pack, but all the decisions are taken without him […] The emperor should be regularly punished for his human conscience! The emperor is not of interest to

---

228 As the author argued in this regard in our 2013 meeting: "My Moscow differs from Andrukhovych's one radically. Andrukhovych's Moscow is the symbol of the terrible Soviet Empire […] My Moscow is not so terrible, there is no more insanity in it than in the rest of the world. But there is, of course, a lot of evil, harshness, cynicism, melancholy and the impossibility of happiness. […] This is a novel-game, a novel-joy, but, in any case, it is not a political satire, as Andrukhovich's novel at times turns into. I cannot say anything bad about *The Moscoviad*, which impressed me a lot at the time. But Andrukhovich's vision is essentially different from mine" (Puleri 2016: 214).

229 "Бо справа в тім, що ось уже протягом року Москвою повзуть чутки, підкріплені жовтою і не лише червоною пресою, ніби в нетрях метрополітену завелися велетенські з добру вівчарку завбільшки, щури […] Раніше вони давали знати про себе лише вночі. Зараз почали з'являтися навіть удень […] Адже справи тут уже не так у щурах, як у потребі когось винищувати […] І саме тому у вашій війні не буде переможців і переможених, а будуть самі лише жертви…" (Andrukhovych 2014: 114–115).

the pack as a warrior leader or a rat. When rats need new rats they will act otherwise.[230] (Rafeenko 2013: 137).

Despite assuming different positions, in both the "great" Ukrainian and the "minor" Russophone literatures, Andrukhovych and Rafeenko undertake a deconstruction of the phobias and the identity complexes of the decaying empire. Interestingly enough, the two authors enter into a dialogue with the former empire through different perspectives and cultural references. While Andrukhovych reflects his own presence in the novel in the displacement experienced by the Ukrainian people in Moscow, Rafeenko in his *novel-Iliad* "enters" Troy, mocking and deconstructing Russian cultural myths:

> I recall from a poem by Andrukhovych, "Here the bus takes me daily right by the jail. They teach me to love this country." Nice lines, damn it.[231] (Andrukhovych 2008: 59) "Hey, son, you'd let me die here, eh? [...]—"Each person has his own fate"—you sighed. "And his path wide open"—he added.[232] (Andrukhovych 2008: 115).
> "Oh, the copper burns on the maple trees, and the bear feels his youth, so beautiful and shaggy, he drinks the honey of love, he drinks the honey of losses..." [...] what a wonderful poem! Really? Do you like it? Yes, of course! It reminds me a little of Esenin, and in general of our good, great and free Russia![233] (Rafeenko 2013: 86). [...] who is your favourite writer? Pushkin. And among the contemporary ones? Pushkin. And among the very contemporary ones? Vladimir Rafeenko. But you do not know him.[234] (Rafeenko 2013: 97)

---

230 "Император крыс должен присутствовать во время всех существенных событий в жизни стаи, но все решения принимаются без него! [...] Император должен быть регулярно наказуем своей человеческой совестью! Император не интересует стаю как воин руководитель или крыса. Когда крысам нужны новые крысы они поступают иначе!"

231 "Згадується з Андруховича: «Я щодня тут їжджу попри в'язницю. Мене вчать любити всю цю країну». Гарні рядки, чорт забирай" (Andrukhovych 2014: 56).

232 "— Синок, ну не подихать же мне, а? [...] — У всякого своя доля, — зітхнув ти. — І свій шлях широкий, — додав він" (Andrukhovych 2014: 105).

233 "«О, как горит на кленах медь, как юность чувствует медведь, как он прекрасен и космат, пьет мед любви, пьет мед утрат...» [...] хорошие ведь стихи! Да? Тебе нравится? Ну конечно! Немного Есенина напоминает, а вообще хорошо, широко, приволье чувствуется наше российское!"

234 "[...] из писателей тебе кто больше всех нравится? Пушкин. А из современных? Пушкин. А из самых самых современных? Владимир Рафеенко. Но ты его не знаешь."

"Each person has his own fate / and his path wide open." Quoting the opening verses of the poem *The Dream* (*Son*) by Taras Shevchenko, in *The Moscoviad*, Andrukhovych attempts to reconstruct the missing link with the Ukrainian tradition in his nightmarish Moscow. In the fantastic world of *The Moscow Divertissement*, Rafeenko's referents are the Russian poets Sergei Esenin (1895–1925) and Aleksandr Pushkin (1799–1837). Here the demystification of Russian cultural myths takes shape through the use of anthropomorphic figures—the Russian bears populating Moscow—reading their poems in Russian: this eventually lays the ground for the final entrance of the same Russophone author into the novel. Most fundamentally, Rafeenko's minor position endows him with the ability to "reappropriate" Russian and to desecrate "the conflict that opposes father and son" (Deleuze, Guattari 1986: 17). From the "wild steppes" of Donbas, the theatre of the war that would dramatically change the history of post-Maidan Ukraine since 2014, the Russophone author can thus project his allegorical vision of the former "center of the Slavic world" (Puleri 2016: 210).

Part II: From Politics to Culture—
After Revolution of Hybridity
(2014–2018)

Chapter 4 Hybridity Reconsidered: Ukrainian Border Crossing after the "Crisis"[235]

> it is very convenient to have a confrontation between the East and the West, a contrast between Ukrainophones and Russophones, between industrial regions and less industrialized ones. It is very convenient to everyone: to patriots and non-patriots, to those who love Russia and to those who love Europe... This is the internal dividing line, and everybody backed it up. Including writers and artists. We need to call things by their proper names.[236] (Nikolaichuk 2015)

Looking at the events that shook his country throughout the "Ukraine Crisis" in 2013–2014, Serhii Zhadan tells about "a war which is not our war" (Nikolaichuk 2015). To unveil the mechanisms for representation of the supposed clash of identities in Ukraine, the writer chose the trope of "crisis." He argued that the terms that have permeated the public debate over the past years—Russophones versus Ukrainophones, terrorists versus fascists, patriots versus compatriots—are just superficial labels that distract intellectuals unable to "call things by their proper names" (Nikolaichuk 2015).

The rhetoric of crisis imposes binary thinking and informs the language used by politicians and intellectuals. It is permeated by the "postmodern

---

235 An earlier version of this chapter was published as Marco Puleri, "Hybridity Reconsidered: Ukrainian Border Crossing after the 'Crisis'." *Ab Imperio*. 2017. 2: 257–286.

236 "[...] дуже зручно мати це протистояння сходу і заходу, протиставлення україномовних і російськомовних, протиставлення індустріальних регіонів і менш індустріальних. Дуже зручно для всіх: і для патріотів, і для непатріотів, для тих, хто любить Росію, для тих, хто любить Європу... Є така внутрішня лінія поділу, і її всі трималися. В тому числі і письменники, і митці. Слід називати речі своїми іменами."

syntax" that, as observed by Aleksandr Rubtsov, is characterized by "the citation of 'ruined' texts, whereas the original meaning is not important and is taken as raw material in creating a new collage" (Rubtsov 2014). Thus, the "revolution of dignity" (Shveda 2014), as the 2013–2014 Euromaidan protests are regarded by Ukrainian citizens, is juxtaposed to the "defence of compatriots" (Laruelle 2015a)—invoked by Putin; the "European values" are set against the "Russian World" that, being endowed by its "cultural distinctiveness" (*kul'turnoe svoeobrazie*), is able to "unit[e] two worlds—the East and the West" (*ob"ediniaiushchaia dva mira—Vostok i Zapad*; MKRF 2015: 4); and, eventually, the "fascists" from Western Ukraine meet their counterpart in the nostalgic "dregs" (*sovki*, nostalgic for everything Soviet) from Donbas (Miller, Wert 2015).

The clash of representations engendered by the language of "crisis" reveals the inability of intellectuals to develop a syntax "which causes words and things (next to and also opposite one another) to 'hold together' " (Foucault 1970: xxviii). In light of the dynamics described in the first part of this book, this entails a serious epistemological crisis that involves the process of self-representation in the post-Soviet space. In this logic, it appears that the epistemological crisis preceded the political one and prompted its escalation, rather than the other way around.

In his analysis of the contemporary Russian social and political discourse, emblematically entitled *Hybridisation of Discourses, or the Sovietisation of the Post-Soviet* (*Gibridizatsiia diskursov, ili Sovetizatsiia postsovetskogo*), Kazbek Sultanov observed how "in the post-Soviet format the reincarnation of *homo sovieticus* and the Soviet narrative takes place"[237] (Sultanov 2017). The post-Soviet "imagined reality" (*voobrazhaemaia realnost'*) can be described as a "depleted vision of the future" (*istoshchivsheesia videnie budushchego*): it employs the "second legitimation" (*vtoraia legitimatsiia*) of the old conceptual attributes, such as "the mythology of the enemy's image" (*mifologiia obraza vraga*), "the apology of exclusivity" (*apologiia*

---

237 "[…] в формате постсоветского состоится реинкарнация *homo soveticus* и
      советского нарратива […]."

iskliuchitel'nosti), and "the exacerbation of traditional binary oppositions" (*obostrenie traditsionnykh binarnykh oppozitsii*; Sultanov 2017). Thus, the flow of authoritative discourse strives to offer new forms of historical creativity to overcome the condition of "post-Soviet aphasia" (Oushakine 2000) experienced in contemporary Russia:

> In the labyrinth of post-Soviet connections, the substantial content of this "flow," taken in its real irreversibility, is marginalized and depreciated by the tautology of meanings, value ambivalence, and hybrid oxymorism, when the authorized mobilization of the Soviet occurs as a mode of self-determination of the present. If hybridization is understood as the combination of different, often alternative, sociocultural formats, as the shifting of narratives and the poetics of the unification of, seemingly, irreconcilable senses, thus the phenomenon of post-Soviet hybridization of discourses can and should be perceived in the historical dimension, revealing the contamination of the mutually exclusive but also paradoxically interrelated temporalities "Soviet-post-Soviet," "colonial-postcolonial." In other words, hybridization appears as a form of historical creativity [...].[238] (Sultanov 2017)

Unlike the Russian top-down direction of ideological innovations, in the Maidan revolution in Ukraine, we witnessed a concrete answer from below to the paralyzing state of aphasia. It is in the absence of new analytical languages to describe Ukrainian post-Soviet society that a performative "historical creativity" took place (through social practices, rather than discourses), as highlighted by Ilya Gerasimov in the introductory essay to the thematic forum *Ukraine and the Crisis of "Russian Studies:"*

> How does this postcolonial and post-postmodern (i.e., post-relativist and post-cynical) collective subjectivity differ from "regular" national subjectivity,

---

238 "В лабиринте постсоветских сцеплений субстанциальная содержательность этого «потока», взятого в его реальной необратимости, маргинализируется, обесценивается тавтологией смыслов, ценностной амбивалентностью, гибридной оксюморонностью, когда санкционированная мобилизация советского выдается за модус самоопределения современности. Если понимать гибридность как совмещение различных, нередко альтернативных социокультурных форматов, как смещение нарративов и поэтику сопряжения непримиримых, казалось бы, смыслов, то феномен постсоветской гибридизации дискурсов может и должен быть воспринят в историческом измерении, обнаруживая контаминацию взаимоисключающих, но и парадоксально взаимотяготеющих темпоральностей «советское – постсоветское,» «коло-

twentieth century style? Several contributors to the forum [...] mention the significance of hybridity as a new phenomenon in Ukraine, or rather as a familiar
phenomenon that has changed its modality—from a sign of marginality and
parochialism to a trendy and mainstream personal quality [...] the overwhelming
role of new Russian-language and culturally Russian Ukrainian patriotism and
nationalism cannot be dismissed. (Gerasimov 2014: 32)

Using Mikhail Nemtsev's (2017) terms, post-Maidan Ukraine clearly testified
to the "modernity of 'Russianness'" (*sovremennost' "russkosti"*), which lies
"in its deterritorialization, in going beyond the coordinates predetermined
by Moscow."[239] This reflects the existence of a window of opportunity in
the post-Soviet area for experiencing the "space of demobilised Russians"
(*prostranstvo demobilizovannykh russkikh*) evoked by the Russian scholar
in his *Five Theses on "Russian" and the "Russian World"* (*Piat' tezisov o
"russkom" i o "Russkom mire"*).[240] Things get particularly complicated in
Ukraine, where, throughout the past decades "Ukrainian elites had to tread
carefully when differentiating between 'our Russians' and 'those Russians'
living in the neighbouring Russian Federation" (Kuzio 2001: 356). The
identification of who is "us" and who is the "other" within the Ukrainian
state, paradoxically, has been influenced by the Russian state-sponsored
process of self-representation, whereas "*who* a Russian is depends on how
one defines *where* Russia is" (Clowes 2011: xii).

Nonetheless, as highlighted by Alexander Morrison (2017), today "there
is little awareness that the Russian-speaking world and the political and
ethnic boundaries of Russianness do not coincide." In post-Maidan Ukraine
evidence of this comes from the new developments in approaching a highly
debated question in the national intellectual milieu, that is, the language
question. In 2015, Kulyk registered the shift in popular opinion during
the period of Euromaidan and the beginning of the war: "for most people,

---

ниальное—постколониальное». Иначе говоря, гибридизация предстает как
форма исторического творчества [...]."

239 "Современность «русскости» состоит в ее детерриториализации — в выводе
за пределы координат, предопределенных Москвой [...]."

240 "[...] the 'Russian World' is the space of demobilized Russians [...]
living anywhere and arbitrarily formulating their own racial, ethnic and
ethnoconfessional identities and preferences" (Nemtsev 2017; «Русский мир» —
это пространство демобилизованных русских [...] живущих где угодно и как

a stronger Ukrainian identity does not mean a worse attitude towards Russian; speaking and /or liking the Russian language has not become generally perceived as incompatible with being Ukrainian, even among those who speak mainly Ukrainian themselves" (2015: 4–5). These developments should be viewed within the broader context of the search for new self-identification under the sign of hybridity in post-Soviet societies.

In light of pre-Maidan cultural developments in Ukraine, which have been under scrutiny in the first part of this book, these reflections help in understanding the complex dynamics that make, using Pavlyshyn's (2016a) terms, "literary history as provocation of national identity" and, at the same time, "national identity as provocation of literary history." On the one hand, questioning the Ukrainian literary space, and positioning Russian-language Ukrainian literature as an integral part of the Ukrainian literary canon, provides the framework for discussing a space for demobilized Russians (or, as proposed by the Ukrainian analyst Ol'ha Mykhailova, for Ukrainian Russians—*Ukrainskie Russkie*[241]) in the new Ukrainian national identity project developing from below. On the other, with the beginning of the Maidan Revolution, many Russian-speaking literary actors took part in the protests and supported the Ukrainian state, while at the same time claiming their ties to Russian language and culture. Tanya Zaharchenko believes that we witnessed the shaping of post-Soviet "hybrid subjectivities:"

Today, the intricate relationship between Russia and Ukraine is, as ever, decisive for the future of this part of the world. And, as ever, it remains largely simplified as either antagonistic or fraternal. Russian-speakers in Ukraine effectively topple this dichotomy. They are the new soldiers of sentiment in a war of calculation.

угодно формулирующих свои расовые, этнические и этноконфессиональные идентичности и предпочтения).

241 The term was firstly introduced to public debate already in March 2014 by the Ukrainian analyst Ol'ha Mykhailova: "Russia, of course, does not recognise the appearance of this new people, and will persistently consider them Russians. This persistence will cost Russia a lot of money spent in promoting the idea of 'protecting the rights of Russians' among people who feel no longer simply Russian, but Ukrainian Russians" (Mykhailova 2014; Россия, конечно, не признает появление этого нового народа, и будет упорно считать их русскими. Это упорство будет стоить ей немалых денег, потраченных на пропаганду идеи «защиты прав русских» среди людей, которые ощущают себя уже не просто русскими, но — украинскими русскими).

Whether they refer to motherland as *Rodina* (in Russian) or as *Bat'kivshchyna* (in Ukrainian) is secondary. (Zaharchenko 2014)

In this chapter we will thus focus on the outcomes of the Euromaidan revolution for the conceptualization of the Ukrainian cultural and social space, by analysing the role of the "crisis" and the main narratives conceptualizing it as produced by Russian-speaking literary actors. Then, we will deal with the "centripetal movements" from Donbas to Kyiv in the wake of the war in East Ukraine. By highlighting the prime examples of Elena Stiazhkina and Vladimir Rafeenko, Russian-language writers from Donets'k, we will follow the *hybridizing* trajectories marked by the dramatic events occurring during the past years.

Dialectic of Transition from Post-Soviet to Post-Maidan: Between Old and New Narratives

In September 2014, in her essay symbolically entitled "From Borderlands to Bloodlands," Tatiana Zhurzhenko wondered about the possible consequences of the dramatic events which Ukraine has undergone since November 2013: the Maidan Revolution in Kyiv, the annexation of Crimea by the Russian Federation, and the war in Donbas. On the one hand, Zhurzhenko observed the arrival of a new historical phase for these "borderlands," marked by dangerous and rigid contrasts between alternative geopolitical, cultural and linguistic affiliations. On the other hand, "the end of ambiguity," as she defined it, gave way to new unpredictable movements in this "hybrid area" shaken by war:

> Certainly, one danger of the current war is that it has encouraged the creation of "enemies" and "collaborators." Yet it has also cleared the intellectual atmosphere and put the debate on Ukrainian identity back to zero. Journalists, academics and writers from eastern Ukraine, many of them Russian speaking but Ukrainian patriots, have had a refreshing effect on the public discourse. (Zhurzhenko 2014b)

The need for an organic narrative of the events following Euromaidan prompted new identity negotiations, especially for those cultural actors who experience everyday life in an intermediate space between the "imagined communities" involved in the conflict. This prompts the formation of a new "civic" identity today, especially in the case of Russian-language cultural actors.

Literature played a particularly important role in the contemplation of the ongoing historical drama. As was highlighted by Il'ia Kukulin in his study on the Russian-language poetry of Ukraine, the "most sophisticated Ukrainian-language and Russian-language writers of Ukraine [...] resist the interpretation of this conflict within the framework of any particular ideology" (2016: 181). This is the case with Andrei Kurkov. In the preface to his *Ukraine Diaries*, first published in German (*Ukrainisches Tagebuch*, 2014) and then in Ukraine only in 2015 (*Dnevnik Maidana*), Kurkov clearly declared his interest in the events that shook his country. In the *Diaries*, the author retraces the main stages of the "Ukraine Crisis," starting with not signing the Association Agreement with the European Union in November 2013 and continuing to the eruption of the conflict in Eastern Ukraine in April 2014. Kurkov decides "to live each day" of the "whirlwind of history" to convey it to Western readers:

> And then, having been led on more than one occasion into the path of a whirlwind of history, I found myself the witness to the dramatic events that arose in November 2013 in Ukraine, events of which we have not yet seen the end. I do not know what will happen next, or what lies in store for me and my family. I only hope that everything will be all right. I am not leaving. I am not shying away from reality. I live each day in the very centre of reality.[242] (2014: 2)

The point of observation is Kurkov's apartment, just a few steps from Maidan Nezalezhnosti, the centre of the revolutionary events. His viewpoint is one of a "Russian citizen of Ukraine" (*Russkii grazhdanin Ukrainy*). At the same time, subtle nuances of identity needed to be explained:

> [...] there is a big difference between "being Russian" [*Russkii*] and "being a Russian" [*Rossiiskii*], although many Ukrainians don't seem to understand that. I am Russian [*Russkii*] myself, after all, an ethnically Russian citizen of Ukraine. But I am not "a Russian" [*Rossiiskii*], because I have nothing in common with Russia and its politics.[243] (Kurkov 2014: 69)

---

242 "И вот, уже не первый раз оказавшись в центре «исторического водоворота,» я снова стал свидетелем драматических событий, начавшихся в Украине в ноябре 2013 года и до сих пор продолжающихся. Я не знаю, чем они закончатся, я не знаю, что ждет меня и мою семью в ближайшем будущем. Я только надеюсь на лучшее. Я не уезжаю. Не прячусь от реальности. Я в ней живу каждый день." (Kurkov 2015: 5).

243 "[...] между словами «русский» и «российский» есть большая разница, которую множество украинцев не замечает. Я ведь тоже русский, этнический

The Euromaidan protests clearly reflected this position. Prominent Ukrainian- and Russian-language cultural actors have been engaged in the "socio-Brownian movement" (*sotsial'no-brounovskoe dvizhenie*; Kurkov 2014: 156) sparked by the protests (see Kratochvil 2014; Pomerantsev 2014). As described by Kurkov in his *Diaries*: "Handwritten or printed poems are stuck to fences and tents, in Russian and Ukrainian"[244] (2014: 90). In fact, throughout 2013–2014 downtown Kyiv became a true open-air theatre, "a space of socio-cultural performance where new kinds of identities were constructed—national, social, political and gender" (Hundorova 2016: 161). The *Artistic Barbican* (*Mystets'kyi Barbakan*), a temporary gallery erected on Khreshchatyk—the main street of Kyiv city centre stretching from Maidan Nezalezhnosti to Bessarabs'ka Square, symbolically embodied the "performative character" of the artistic phenomena that emerged throughout the protests.[245] Between the end of 2013 and the beginning of 2014, several readings and exhibitions took place in the *Barbican*: Russophone and Ukrainophone cultural actors, such as Aleksei

---

русский гражданин Украины. Но я не «российский» потому, что не имею никакого отношение к России, к ее политике [...]" (Kurkov 2015: 28).

244 "На заборах и палатках внутри и снаружи баррикад приклеены листы бумаги с написанными от руки и отпечатанными на принтере стихотворениями. На русском и на украинском языках" (Kurkov 2015).

245 "Among the hundreds of protesters' tents erected in the square, there is one that bears the name Mistetski Barbakan ('Artistic Barbican'). Though an active and fully integrated part of the Maidan, it has a life of its own. There is a permanent exhibition of revolutionary painting there, generally anarchistic and politicised, evoking the poster art of the 1918 Civil War. There are also book launches, concerts by singer-songwriters, readings by poets and writers. Revolution always gives impetus to the arts. It was the same in 1917 and after the October Revolution, and it is the same today" (Kurkov 2014: 89–90) [Среди сотни палаток демонстрантов, стоящих тут внутри баррикад, есть палатка с названием «Мистецький Барбакан.» Она живет своей жизнью, являясь одновременно живой частью Майдана. Здесь работает постоянная экспозиция революционной живописи, в основном очень анархистской и политизированной, похожей на плакатную живопись времен гражданской войны 1918 года, здесь проходят выступления поэтов и писателей, презентации книжек, концерты бардов. Революция всегда дает толчок искусству. Так было в 1917 году во время и после Великой Октябрьской революции, так происходит и сейчас (Kurkov 2015)].

Nikitin, Iurii Andrukhovych and Serhii Zhadan, contributed to this cultural venture by giving lectures and participating in debates. From the brief experience of the *Artistic Barbican*, the publishing house Liuta Sprava[246] was created in 2014: the publisher, Andrii Honcharuk, promotes it as a venture that was born on the barricades of the "Revolution of Dignity" (see ArmiiaFM 2017). The publication of the anthology titled *The Artistic Barbican* (2015), which includes contributions in Ukrainian, Russian and Belarusian by writers, journalists, musicians and bloggers who joined the venture, demonstrates the publisher's intention to make Liuta Sprava the true heir to "revolutionary art."[247]

It is worth noticing that almost all the literary texts that have symbolically become an integral part of the "artistic manifesto" of the protests found their virtual audience in social networks.[248] For example, Ukrainian poet Evgeniia Bil'chenko's (b. 1980, Kyiv) poem in Russian, "Who Am I?" ("Kto ia?"), was posted on Facebook on February 21, 2014 (Bil'chenko 2014). The post was widely circulated on the Web, and then translated into Ukrainian by the poet Halyna Kruk (b. 1974, L'viv) just three days later (Kruk 2014). Thus, throughout 2014 we witnessed the publication of dozens of anthologies and bilingual collections of "Maidan poems." In her analysis of this large literary production, Inna Bulkina observes that a unifying representative model can be found only for the works in Ukrainian: most of these poems have been built around the topos of the mother who mourns her lost son, while the "Russian-language authors reproduce this canon very rarely, and generally in their poems it is difficult to identify and to distinguish a unifying principle in relation to genres

---

246 See: http://www.lutasprava.com/ (08/2019).
247 Amongst the publications of Liuta Sprava, we see Aleksei Nikitin's *povest'* on EuroMaidan, *The Orderly from Institutskaia Street* (*Sanitar s Institutskoi*, 2016), the first work by the Russian-language author to be issued in Ukraine.
248 Social networks and video-sharing platforms, such as Facebook, Vkontakte and YouTube, hosted most of the prose and poetry related to the Euromaidan (see Stahl 2015). This phenomenon has been followed by the publication of a kind of anthologies collecting the fragments of these virtual audiences. This is the case with the Russian-language poet Boris Khersonskii, who collected his most popular works posted in 2014 on Facebook in the volume *Open Diary* (*Otkrytyi dnevnik*, 2015), issued by Dukh i Litera.

and themes"[249] (Bulkina 2016a). In the former case, we deal with clear "biblical allusions" (*biblieiskie alliuzii*), which became a true " 'classic of *suchukrlit'* (contemporary Ukrainian literature)" ("*klassika ukrsuchlita"—sovremennaia ukrainskaia literatura*; Bulkina 2016a), while in the latter, as highlighted by Kukulin, we often witness the authors' attempt to investigate "(dis-)identification poetically" (2016: 176).

In times of crisis, it is worth emphasizing the role played by the literary community as a whole in redefining Ukraine as a coherent political and cultural entity, even though throughout 2014–2015 the intellectual sphere occasionally also experienced political polarization. The Ukrainian historian Andrii Portnov, a native of Dnipropetrovs'k (now Dnipro), followed the diverse phases of the national cultural debate during the war in the Donbas region, stressing the process of estrangement of the "Ukrainian Orient" (*Vostok Ukrainy*) from the national body that was carried on by most of the Ukrainian intelligentsia. According to the historian, the construction of new physical and ideological frontiers found its roots in the "fear of the complexity" (*strakh pered slozhnost'iu*; Portnov 2014) of a composite and heterogeneous national identity. Whereas hegemonic narratives of the "crisis" seem to promote binary ethnic and linguistic contrasts, multicultural participants in the events defy any essentialized divisions. Iana Dubinianskaia (b. 1975, Feodosiia), a Ukrainian bilingual writer, identifies the myth of the language question as "a ghost that nobody had never seen, who lived in the conscience of both Russian and Ukrainian speakers"[250] (Dubinianskaia 2014). According to Dubinianskaia, a native of Crimea, such a problem does not exist, but it conceals deeper identity questions.

The problem of language reveals all its complexity in the context of literary production, particularly due to the factor of territorially and politically marked literary markets, Russian and Ukrainian. In the post-Maidan years, in close correlation with political dynamics, we have witnessed

---

249 "Русскоязычные авторы воспроизводят этот канон довольно редко, в их стихах в принципе трудно найти и выделить столь единый в сюжетном и жанровом отношении слой текстов."

250 "[…] призрак, которого никто и никогда не видел, жил в сознании носителей обоих языков."

reduced opportunities for collaboration between the two literary domains. Nonetheless, this tendency did not cause "a complete rupture of literary connections between the Russian-speaking literatures of Ukraine and Russia, but only the transformation of their forms" (Kukulin 2016: 171). Amongst the most significant ventures undertaken by the Kyivan Russophone community, a major role is played by the bilingual cultural magazine *Sho*, whose editors strive to sustain a difficult dialogue between Ukrainian and Russian cultural actors. During the time of turmoil, the magazine dedicated the ninth annual festival Kyïvs'ki Lavry (2014) that it had organized and sponsored to social poetry, including a selection of verses by Ukrainian-language and Russian-language authors about EuroMaidan and the war in Donbas. In the May 2014 issue, titled *The Temptation of War* (*Iskushenie voinoi*), the magazine collected some of the most interesting works presented at the festival (Slyvyns'kyi 2014; Rissenberg 2014). In the last issue of 2014, titled *Ukraine-Russia. Culture Is Falling to Pieces* (*Ukraina-Rossiia: kul'tura treshchit po shvam*), the editors promoted the idea of a possible dialogue between Ukrainian and Russian literary figures, such as Liudmila Ulitskaia (b. 1943, Davlekanovo) and Lev Rubinshtein on the Russian side (Volodarskii 2014). As a result of this collaboration, we witnessed the publication in Russia of a collection of Ukrainian literary works on the war: *This Summer Sky* (*Nebo etogo leta*, 2015), which was edited by Ulitskaia and the Ukrainian literary critic Iurii Volodarskii. The book includes works by both Russian-language and Ukrainian-language authors, where the latter were translated into Russian by popular Ukrainian litterateurs, such as Zaven Babloian, Elena Marinicheva and Evgeniia Chuprina (Katsun 2015).

Ukraino-Russian cultural relations were at the centre of the 2016 annual Book Arsenal Fair in Kyiv (see Vynnychuk 2016; Liubka 2016), after a proposal to introduce a special license and quota for Russian books. The initiative, originally proposed by the former deputy prime minister Oleksandr Sych in 2014, and then supported by MP Ostap Semerak, came into force on 1 January 2017.[251] The position taken by Boris

---

251 The contested measures promoted in post-Maidan cultural policies will be further discussed in the next chapter.

Khersonskii[252] captures the complex situation experienced by the Russophone cultural actors during the war:

> This war evoked crisis in my worldview and even in my identity. I was active mainly as a Russian-language poet whose works were published by Russian publishing houses; I have been receiving literary awards in Russia; I have been taking part in cultural events in Russia. Now I feel myself a Ukrainian poet who writes in Russian and Ukrainian, and translates poetry not only from Ukrainian into Russian, as it was yet three years ago, but from Russian into Ukrainian as well. I'm diligently studying the Ukrainian language, mastering it on a daily basis despite my elderly age [...] I declined [offers] to participate in cultural events in Russia; I haven't been there and won't visit it until Putin and the concept of the "*russkii mir*" (Russian world) reigns there. (Barskova et al. 2017)

Another Russian-language writer, Andrei Poliakov, took a different stance on the war that offers an interesting perspective on the crisis of post-Soviet identity. In an interview for the Russian Web portal Colta.ru, the Crimean poet, who decided to stay in Simferopol' after its annexation by the Russian Federation, interprets the recent events through the lenses of the region's Soviet past:

> The identity of the people living here remained mainly a Soviet one [...] We are a nation torn apart from the inside [...] Nobody explained to us what it means to be Russian [*russkim*]. I do not know what it means to be Russian. And what to do with the Soviet period of our history? It has not been thought over. There are two possible attitudes to it. The first approach is [the trope] of the Great October Socialist Revolution, the victory of the proletariat, the total triumph. The second approach is to see a total disaster. But both readings are just words, emotions [...].[253] (Morev 2014)

---

252 Significantly, in the aftermath of the "crisis," Khersonskii began to post his poems on Facebook simultaneously in both Ukrainian and Russian (see McGrane 2017; Khersonskii 2016).

253 "[...] идентичность людей, живущих здесь, во многом остается советской [...] Мы, в принципе, изнутри разорванный народ [...] никто не объяснил, что такое быть русским. И я не знаю, что такое быть русским. И что делать с этим советским пластом нашей истории? Он, в принципе, не осмыслен. Есть два варианта отношения к нему. Первый вариант — это Великая Октябрьская социалистическая революция, победа пролетариата, все замечательно. Второй вариант — это катастрофа. Но и то и другое — это просто слова, просто эмоции [...]."

Poliakov's reflections suggest that the war of memories is still a powerful factor in the struggle for Ukraine's future. In the aftermath of the "crisis," the State-sponsored politics of memory increasingly leant towards a national-ized and exclusive representation of the entangled past. As a result, "decom-munization" (*dekomunizatsiia*) as the central element of these politics, using the definition of the historian Georgii Kas'ianov, paradoxically reminded one of "the communist practices" (*komunistychni praktyky*; Kurina 2016). Despite its staunch anti-Soviet stance, judging by the new measures, the post-Maidan political elite was caught in the paradigm of "Sovietization of the post-Soviet." In the words of Serhy Yekelchyk, throughout the recent history of the country, "the real mechanism of constructing a new historical memory for the New Ukraine [...] relied on the tropes inherited from the Soviet discourse of national identity" (2015: 99).

Nonetheless, the emerging new "national utopia" clashed with the grass-roots practices of dis-identification as implemented by Russian-language literary figures. To avoid an escalation of the war of historical memories, Aleksei Nikitin insisted on the need to disentangle the past and the present: "We probably need to look at history not as a prelude to our present [...] we need to know it, but we should move on as if these historical fractures have never occurred"[254] (Fanailova 2014b).

Moving Centripetally: Reconsidering Hybridity

The war in Donbas has inevitably wrought major changes in Ukrainian culture and society. One of the most dramatic results was the evacuation of more than two million refugees from Crimea and Eastern Ukraine.[255] As of June 2019, the Government of Ukraine reported over 1.5 million registered internally displaced persons (IDPs).[256] Moreover, a number of

---

254 "Наверное, надо относиться к истории не как к предисловию к сегодня [...] Это надо знать, но двигаться вперед так, как будто всех этих поражений не было."

255 Still in January 2017, "[a]ccording to government sources in receiving coun-tries, the total number of Ukrainians seeking asylum or other forms of legal stay in neighboring countries" stood at "1,554,497, with the majority going to the Russian Federation (1,226,104) and Belarus (148,867)" (UNHCR 2017).

256 See: https://www.unhcr.org/ua/en/internally-displaced-persons (08/2019).

organizations and businesses had to be relocated. Painful as it is, the process of integration of IDPs in a new place was further complicated by hostile political attitudes and rhetoric in the media (Bezruk 2016). As Oksana Mikheieva and Viktoriia Sereda observed in their study carried out during the early stage of the war in 2014: "The main efforts associated with relocation and adaptation of internally displaced persons were undertaken primarily by public associations. The activities of local government institutions (first of all municipalities) played a secondary role" (2015: 2). The emerging culture of openness to accommodating the Other was "centripetal." It began developing from the contested Ukrainian borders towards the central territories, subsequently taking the form of a broad social process "from below" that could be considered the direct result of the *hybridizing* impetus of the revolution:

> This is the first time in Ukraine, when representatives of various regions met in the process of active cooperation (first in the "Maidan," and later at the time of resettlement from the occupied territories). Direct communication undermines mutual stereotypes, promotes the integration of Ukrainian society. These processes are slow, but overall demonstrate positive trends (Mikheieva, Sereda 2015: 24).

These new trends have shown their sustainability.[257] The new culture of accommodation is, arguably, one of the most impressive results of the dramatic events undergone by Ukraine in the post-Maidan years. Many artists and intellectuals coming from Donbas moved to the capital and introduced the "Ukrainian Orient" to the centre of Ukrainian cultural life. This promises to be a game changer in the Ukrainian public sphere, whereas throughout the 1990s–2000s the "subject of 'two Ukraines' was addressed either from a Galician or from a Kyivan perspective," and the " 'other side', so to say, appeared uncommunicative and unwilling to talk" (Portnov 2017). Creating a new mental map of Ukraine becomes a priority, with Donbas playing the most divisive role (just as it remains a politically contested territory).[258] Yuliya Ilchuk has noted that the rising visibility of

---

257 According to a 2017 report by the Ukrainian Sociology Department, already after three years of war, the majority of IDPs had "no intention to return to the Eastern Ukraine" (Mikheieva 2017: 18).

258 As was underlined by Yuliya Ilchuk: "Lately, there has been a consensus among Ukrainian intellectuals on the urgency of transforming the Donbas myth" (2017: 258).

Ukrainian writers and artists from Donbas transformed the foundational "proletarian myth of the region," thus associating Donbas with a new social identity.[259]

While, on the one hand, Ilchuk argues that the unifying principle of these artists' works "is the search for a shared communication space and their direct access to the audience on occupied territories" (2017: 258), on the other, it is worth noticing that this production is also simultaneously contributing to the transformation of the Ukrainian public discourse. A good example is the cultural centre Izolyatsia,[260] "a non-profit non-governmental platform for contemporary culture, founded in 2010 on the territory of a former insulation materials factory in Donets'k."[261] As stressed by activists affiliated with the centre, the name of the project is derived from the technical term "insulation" (*izoliatsiia*—in the Ukrainian and Russian languages, one word is used for both "insulation" and "isolation"), and thus reflects their mission "to preserve the industrial heritage of the Donets'k region and to simultaneously construct something new, which will inspire social and cultural development in Ukraine."[262] On June 9, 2014, the territory of *Izolyatsia* was seized by the militia of the self-proclaimed Donets'k People's Republic.[263] After the centre was moved to Kyiv, Izolyatsia launched a new project, Donbas Studies, aimed at debunking stereotypical visions and

259 "The most recent cultural and literary initiatives produced by two Donetsk artists, Serhii Zakharov and Angela Dzherikh, and two Luhansk writers, Serhii Zhadan and Olena Stepova [...] represent grassroots attempts to create a political literature and art, both in its classical and contemporary understanding [...] Regardless of whether this art is aligned or not with the ideas of the public, the fact that it carves a space and adds its voice to other voices in public can be considered as the civic practice of artists" (Ilchuk 2017: 258).

260 See: https://izolyatsia.org (08/2019).

261 See: https://izolyatsia.org/en/foundation/ (08/2019).

262 See: http://teh.net/members/izolyatsia/ (08/2019).

263 On 11 May 2014, status referendums were held in the territories of the Donets'k and Luhans'k regions under the control of separatist groups. The controversial results of the pollings, which were held in the midst of war, legitimized the self-proclaimed independence of the Donets'k People's Republics (DNR) and Luhans'k People's Republic (LNR). The independence of the DNR and LNR has not been recognized by any state, except South Ossetia, which is also a de facto state with limited recognition.

myths of Donbas and "creating a comprehensive discussion concerning the region of Ukraine, with an involvement of experts from various fields of knowledge."[264] Within this initiative, in November 2014 Donbas Living Library was launched: it was an interactive project that, according to its members, offered "the public to meet residents of Donbas to introduce the region and its people."[265] It was part of a general mission to create a new Ukrainian and international research environment around Donbas studies, with a special emphasis on promoting cultural and gender studies. Ukrainophone cultural actors, such as Serhii Zhadan, joined the project, and its results were first shown at the Taras Shevchenko National Museum in Kyiv in November 2014.

Amongst the most influential intellectuals from Donbas on the modern Ukrainian cultural scene is Elena Stiazhkina, a Russian-language writer and scholar, who has become a central figure in Ukrainian intellectual debates. It was especially her book *In the Language of God* (*Movoiu boha*), published in 2016 both in Russian—in the literary journal *Iehupets'*—and in Ukrainian translation by the Kyiv-based Dukh i Litera, that received critical acclaim (Shevtsova 2016). Analysing the roots of the war in her home region, Stiazhkina singled out the role of the language of the "crisis:" "Language, words, meanings present the battlefield. In order to survive and to win, we must call things by their proper names"[266] (Stiazhkina 2016).

Stiazhkina formerly taught History of the Slavs at Donets'k National University, which the Ukrainian authorities moved to Vinnytsia in the wake of the war (Chernova 2015). After the very beginning of the conflict, in April 2014, Stiazhkina was awarded the Russkaia Premiia. During the ceremony, which was held in Moscow on April 22, 2014, Stiazhkina read her work *Love* (*Liubov'*), inspired by the events that were shaking Donets'k in those days (see Ostrov 2014). In her prize acceptance speech, based on her previous online publications, Stiazhkina portrayed the difficult situation of a Ukrainian woman of Russian origins who experiences a profound internal conflict:

---

264 See: https://izolyatsia.org/en/project/donbas-studies (08/2019).

265 See: https://izolyatsia.org/en/project/donbass-live-library (08/2019).

266 "Мова, слова, сенси — це поле битви. І щоб вистояти та перемогти у ній, треба називати речі своїми іменами."

Forgive me Russia, and I will forgive you this Sunday. Forgive me, because I wrote, I taught, I loved in Russian. Forgive me because I will continue to dream, to think, to worry in Russian [...] it is, probably, difficult to kill those who speak the same language with you. There is a unique chance to taste it now [...] You'll have to kill us. Both Russian Ukrainians [*russkie ukraintsy*] and those who shout today: "Russia, Russia!"[267] (Stiazhkina 2014)

In her diary, *Country. War. Love* (*Strana. Voina. Liubov'*),[268] which follows the lines of her speech in Moscow, Stiazhkina looks at the dramatic developments of the war in Donets'k and Luhans'k from March until the end of August 2014. Following the escalation of the conflict, the narrator realizes that "The homeland is a child. Not a mother" (*Rodina-ditia. Ne mat'*; Puleri 2014b: 82), thus, unexpectedly, acquiring a new child as a new sense of the homeland:

I am Russian. After the 16th of January I felt like an extremist. After the 20th of February I felt—clearly—a *banderovka*. And since a long time, already from the times of Tuzla spit, I felt Ukrainian. I do not know how it happened that after the sinking of Atlantis, the USSR, in my soul an almost painful, disturbing and sweet feeling was rising and growing: once there was a country and it turned out to be my Homeland.[269] (Puleri 2014b: 75)

The birth of a new idea of homeland recorded by Stiazhkina in her diary reflects the rise of a new subjectivity in contemporary Ukraine. This experience is shared by most of the artists who were shaken and displaced from their hometowns after the outbreak of the war in Donbas in 2014.[270] It is

---

267 "Прости, Россия, и я прощаю тебя в это воскресенье. Прости за то, что писала на русском книги, читала лекции и любила тоже на русском. Прости за то, что и дальше буду мечтать, думать и тревожиться на русском языке [...] Это, наверное, трудно — убивать тех, кто говорит с тобой на одном языке. Уникальный шанс попробовать это на вкус сейчас есть [...] И убивать придется нас. И русских украинцев, и тех, кто сегодня кричит: «Россия, Россия» — тоже."

268 The fragments of the diary have been included in several online publications throughout 2014–2015, and then included in Iurii Vynnychuk et al. 2015.

269 "Я — русская. После 16 января почувствовала себя экстремисткой. После 20 февраля — отчетливо — бандеровкой. И давно, еще с косы Тузлы — украинкой. Я не знаю, как так получилось, что после затонувшей Атлантиды — СССР, в душе появилось и разрослось это чуть болезненное, тревожное и сладкое тоже ощущение: жила-была страна, а оказалось — Родина."

270 As noted by Y. Ilchuk (2017: 269): "in the long run, the people of occupied Donbas will have to answer the question of their identity not on the

also the case of Vladimir Rafeenko, who moved to Kyiv in July 2014. There he started to collaborate with the cultural magazines *Sho* and *Fokus*. In light of his recent relocation to Kyiv, Rafeenko still emphasized the "in-between" position experienced by Russian-language cultural figures from Donbas in independent Ukraine:

> Donbas as a space was excluded from the nationwide context, as it was from the Russian one: I know it well, because I visited Moscow, where they treated me warmly, but there I was still a Ukrainian. And it is normal, because it is a fact of life. But even in Kyiv I was a *"Moskal'"* [...] In Donbas, life formed around cities, and the cities formed around business, to which people and urban culture were subordinated. The Russian language was a tool, the language for international communication, because 10–15 nationalities could live in the same street [...] There is nothing wrong with the cosmopolitanism which has been experienced by Donbas. It is a kind of culture. And Ukraine is a great and very heterogeneous country. It is important not to lose this diversity, because it enriches us, this is our big advantage [...] So it hurts when I read statements on social networks by people I used to respect, where they say "death to Russian," or they ask Russophones how it is to speak the "enemy's language."[271] (Slavins'ka 2015)

In the interview from 2015 quoted above, Rafeenko pointed out the contradictions in the national discourse on Donbas, by focusing on the need to reconsider the value of inclusivity, especially in times of war, since

---

collective but on the individual level [...] While official ideology, whether national Ukrainian or separatist, tries to box people into collective identity, artists focus on the identities of individuals and encourage their audience to take responsibility for their own life and destiny."

271 "Донбас як простір був виключений із загальноукраїнського контексту. Але так само він був принципово виключений і з російського контексту: це я точно знаю, бо бував у Москві, де до мене тепло ставилися, але я все одно був там українець. І це цілком нормально, бо це факт буття. А от в Києві я був «москаль» [...] На Донбасі життя формувалося навколо міст, а міста — навколо підприємств, яким людина та міська культура були підпорядковані. Російська мова там була інструментом, мовою міжнаціонального спілкування, бо на одній вулиці могли жити 10-15 національностей [...] Немає нічого поганого в космополітизмі, який мав Донбас. Це такий різновид культури. Україна — велика країна. Вона дуже різноманітна. І дуже важливо не втрачати це різноманіття, бо це нас збагачує, в цьому наша велика перевага [...] Тому мені боляче, коли я читаю в соціальних мережах висловлювання людей, яких я раніше поважав, де вони кажуть «нехай здохне російська мова» або питають російськомовних, як воно — говорити «мовою ворога.»"

"it happened that almost the entire literary milieu, whose members I used to be on talking with, have left Donets'k: some moved to Kyiv, others to L'viv"[272] (Slavins'ka 2015). The fracture between the "old" and the "new" life is a recurring theme in the poems of Iia Kiva (b. 1984, Donets'k). In 2014, this Russian-language poet moved from Donbas to Kyiv, where she actively participated in the debate on defining the "language/s" of Ukrainian poetry (see Kiva 2016; 2017). In 2018, her collection of poems *Far from Paradise* (*Podal'she ot raia*), including works in both Russian and Ukrainian, was published by the publishing house Kaiala, which was founded in Kyiv in 2015.

The (Political) Acceleration of Cultural Change

> Hybridity means selecting foreign forms that best suit one's own interests in the modern world. (Gerasimov et al. 2016: 25)

The "dynamic transformation of social imagination" (Gerasimov et al. 2016: 20) enacted by the dramatic events in 2013–2014 is forging a new language describing the post-Maidan cultural space. New narratives emerge from the "centripetal dynamics" within the Ukrainian public sphere; new hybrid subjectivities are striving to "affect the content" (Gerasimov et al. 2016: 25) of the public discourse. Paradoxically, thanks to the war we witnessed the acceleration of cultural change in Ukraine: eventually, this also brought the long-awaited fulfilment of the painful self-determination process in Ukrainian Russophone literature. As argued by Krasniashchikh in 2015,

> if two years ago for many of them [the Russophone writers] it would have been an impossible task, today—thanks to the war—everyone clearly identified himself. We can argue that if on this basis for twenty five years (and actually, even more) *rusukrlit* was closer and closer to be born, but the childbirth was always delayed, then over the past year and a half the process has been swiftly completed, and everyone who wanted spoke out about his affiliation to the literature of Ukraine.[273] (2015: 174)

---

272 "[…] так сталося, що майже все письменницьке коло, з яким я спілкувався, виїхало з Донецька та переїхало хто до Києва, хто до Львова."

273 "И если два года назад для многих из них это была бы неподъемная задача, то сегодня — вот уж спасибо войне — все четко самоотождествились.

Along these lines, if the "question of whether Russian authors could be included in Ukrainian literature and the Ukrainian canon used to be painful in the late 2000s," as argued by Kukulin (2016: 168), "the recent political and military events changed the imagination of Ukrainian literature as only Ukrainian-speaking—both in Ukraine and in Russia." Eventually, as emblematically stressed by Inna Bulkina (2016b) in her article "Russian Literature of Ukraine: Yesterday, Today and Tomorrow" ("Russkaia literature Ukrainy: vchera, segodnia, zavtra"), "the new history of Ukraine happens here and now, and, in any case, it will be written also in Russian."[274]

Yet literary processes are emblematic of the trajectory of the Ukrainian (post-imperial) epistemological crisis. Today the major obstacle to the new developments is the inertia of the (post-)Soviet "cult of 'pure forms'" (Gerasimov et al. 2016: 24), which still can be recognized in the language of hegemonic political discourse.[275] Most fundamentally, this reflects a global analytical impasse, whereas nowadays it is still not clear how to "talk about the postimperial political and cultural realities outside the normative nation-centered framework" (Gerasimov et al. 2016: 19). More controversially, as the editors of *Ab Imperio* put it: "One should be surprised not by the fact that a 'national tradition' emerges as a result of forging a new hybrid collective subjectivity, but by how fast that initial hybridity is forgotten" (Gerasimov et al. 2016: 26–27).

Можно сказать, что если по этому признаку — русукрлит двадцать пять лет (а реально — больше) рождался, рождался, рождался и роды затягивались, то за последние полтора года процесс стремительно завершился и все, кто хотел, высказался о своей принадлежности к литературе Украины."

274 "Новая история Украины происходит здесь и сейчас, и, так или иначе, она будет написана и по-русски."

275 In a special issue devoted to the dynamics of social and political imagery in post-imperial order, Ilya Gerasimov, Marina Mogilner, Serguei Glebov and Alexander Semyonov endeavoured to reflect upon the controversial nature of the "surprisingly understudied phenomenon of hybridity" in modern societies. Emblematically, they identified it as doomed to be "a victim of the social imagination centered on the cult of 'pure forms'": "Nationalist discourse marginalizes hybridity as culturally inferior and politically subversive to the goal of national homogenization [...] Anticolonial discourse equally distrusts hybridity as potentially leading to reconciliation with imperial domination" (Gerasimov et al. 2016: 24).

Chapter 5 Values for the Sake of the (Post-Soviet) Nation[276]

It is a question of belonging to different time flows, different orders. According to the coordinates of modernity the nation is tied to political categories. According to those of postmodernity it is the cultural definitions that dominate.[277] (Mykhailova 2014)

When describing the pronounced centrality of national identity in post-Soviet studies, Mark Bassin and Catriona Kelly observed how "each of the fifteen newly independent nation states" which emerged from the collapse of the Soviet Union was "engaged in its own process of so-called 'nation-building', whereby an aspiring leadership seeks to provide—along with novel constitutional arrangements and legal structures—freshly crafted narratives of national belonging" (2012: 7). Most fundamentally, according to the editors of the collective volume *Soviet and Post-Soviet Identities* (2012), the "post-Soviet experience demonstrates [...] that the practice of identity construction is not restricted to these sorts of coordinated exercises in the macro-management of official state ideologies," but "can be driven not from the top but from below, by social sub-groupings within a given national context who are seeking to establish and defend their position in the novel social and political circumstances" (Bassin, Kelly 2012: 7). Thus, the discourse flows on cultural identity enacted by political elites can only work within the realm of a balancing game, in an attempt to adapt social claims to states' strategies. This balance is of

---

276 An earlier version of this chapter was published as Marco Puleri, "Values for the Sake of the (Post-Soviet) Nation: Patriotism(s) and the Search for the 'True' Self in Ukraine." *Southeastern Europe*. 2018. 42, 3: 350–375.

277 "Это вопрос принадлежности разным временным потокам, разным укладам. В ориентирах модерна нация привязана к политическим категориям, в ориентирах постмодерна довлеют культурные определения."

crucial importance, especially in times of national crisis, wherein "culture becomes comprehensive and ubiquitous" (Etkind 2017: 2).

This is the case with the new directions of Ukrainian and Russian nation-building, responding to internal dynamics which have indicatively arisen "from below." Significantly, both countries have recently experienced national crises, or "contestation cycles." If the 2011–2012 Russian protest movement against election fraud "did not formulate a social doctrine and failed to create a social consensus," as observed by Etkind, we still need to recognize that "its impact on national and international politics was immense and remains underestimated" (2017: 1). Evidence for this comes from the recent Russian attempts "to export its national models to Ukraine in the form of federalization and constitutional reforms" (Nikitina 2014: 5): throughout the Ukraine crisis, and especially in the aftermath of the annexation of Crimea to Russia, as observed by Iulia Nikitina, we witnessed how the Kremlin strategy has been precisely proposing that "Russian state-building and nation-building models are more viable than those of Ukraine" (2014: 5). Eventually, the Russian scholar came to argue that the Russian–Ukrainian war showed exactly how "for post-Soviet states, nation-building and state-building are more vital issues than regime type" (Nikitina 2014: 1).

In fact, when dealing with the Ukrainian Euromaidan movement in 2013–2014, we could observe the rise of a concrete alternative in the traditional relations between state and civil society in the post-Soviet area: this movement was organized from below as "a political response to a government and a form of politics" (Kordan 2016: 140) and addressed the need of a society. As claimed in the "Statement of the Civic Sector of Maidan—On the Creation of the Wide Civic Movement of Euromaidan," posted on Facebook in December 2013, the movement was not "to be created on the basis of political party institutions" (Statement of the Civic Sector of Maidan 2013) and, contrary to what could be expected from Nikitina's insights, clearly aimed to obtain a regime change.[278] Furthermore, Kordan (2016: 141) observed that as "a political alternative to the status quo, the

---

278 As stressed by Kordan (2016: 144), here lies "the profound difference between the Orange Revolution and the Maidan," as the former "placed its hope and expectations in politicians and looked to change from above."

Maidan necessarily represented a threat to the established power structures [...] not only in Kiev, but Moscow as well."

Significantly, in the aftermath of the contested annexation of Crimea to Russia and the war in East Ukraine, the national public debates in both these countries were opened to a more dynamic and polyphonic system of interrelations. On the one hand, in the Russian Federation the short-term period of openness following the "Crimea campaign" highlighted the rise of heterogeneous voices in the national political debate, revealing the existence of assertive social subgroupings in the Russian social milieu. Neo-imperialist, nationalist and liberal discourses on Ukraine found their common ground in Russian geopolitical imagination, whereby "Ukraine is not a political subject but an arena of contestation among geopolitical players" (Zhurzhenko 2016). Thus, a large part of the national intelligentsia embraced the "increasingly conservative and nationalistic ideology" (Kolesnikov 2015) proposed by the Kremlin. On the other hand, in the Ukrainian case the events which shook the country in 2014–2015 favoured the emergence of an "anti-Russian nationalist attitude in Ukrainian society," although "until the annexation of Crimea, Maidan as a protest movement was not anti-Russian, even if some segments of it were nationalists" (Zhurzhenko 2016).

Following these lines, we can still observe the strong interrelation of the Ukrainian and Russian cultural and political contexts in redefining the boundaries of their respective identity markers. As a consequence of the still ongoing war in Donbas, today the social claims arisen from the Ukrainian–Russian clash of discourses have been included and interpreted in their respective political elites' discourses in a more nuanced and situational form. Nowadays both countries' political elites have to come to terms with the results of social mobilization: thus, if on the one hand in Ukraine "the danger of radical nationalism should not be denied, though it is a threat to the Ukrainian state in the first place" (Zhurzhenko 2016), on the other "one issue remains sensitive for the Kremlin: Russian nationalism" (Laruelle 2017a). This shows how nation-building is "not only the policies adopted at the national level, but also the way people react to them" (Polese 2011: 40).

Following these lines, this chapter is aimed at deeply analysing the political and cultural narratives which emerged in the aftermath of the recent

Ukrainian–Russian clash of discourses. An accurate tracking of both the policies normativizing the field of culture, on the one hand, and the blurred cultural boundaries on the other, can be insightful in further questioning and defining the fixed constructs of national and cultural identity when looking at the everchanging post-Soviet social milieus.

Towards Shifting Cultural Policies in the Post-Maidan Era

I argue that the main divide in Ukraine is neither Ukrainian/Russian, nor Ukrainophone/Russophone, nor West/East, but essentially Ukrainian/Ukrainian. It runs primarily along the lines of identity inasmuch as each group insists that its members represent "true" Ukrainianness, whereas their opponents represent some sort of historical deviation—either artificially constructed by the "sinister" West's intent to undermine East Slavonic unity, or fabricated by "perfidious" Russia through centuries of colonization, assimilation and political domestication of primordial Ukrainians. (Riabchuk 2015: 139–140)

Looking at the events that shook his country throughout 2014–2015, Mykola Riabchuk observed how it was precisely the rise of an "internal Other" in the body of the Ukrainian state that affected the possibility of consolidating policies of integration into post-Soviet nation-building. The inability of the national political elite to unmake "Soviets into Ukrainians" led them to opt for a "middle way between Baltic-style de-Sovietization and Belarus-style re-Sovietization of national life" (Riabchuk 2015: 145). The complex mosaics of languages, local memories and multiple ethnicities could then be resignified and appropriated by the members of a "civic nation by default" (Shevel 2004) only along the unstable trajectories of the Ukrainian "identity-based and value-driven" (Riabchuk 2015: 139) political divide. At the crossroads between "the post/neo Soviet and the non/anti Soviet" (Riabchuk 2015: 143) Ukraine(s), this ideological contrast played a central role in defining the new national project, whereas "the inherited Soviet Ukrainian identity that had been largely sub-regional and pre-national [...] developed into the alternative form of Ukrainian national identity" (Riabchuk 2015: 146), as opposed to the national "ethno-cultural" stance. Thus, the regionalization of the conflict (i.e. Donbas vs. Galicia; East vs. West) was then the result of the artificial manipulation of these ideological constructs in the internal political debate.

The events which occurred in 2014–2015 provoked a fracture in the framing of national identity "from below," which still needs to be mended and translated into concrete policies by the new political elite. As claimed by Kulyk (2015: 2), by comparing the results of two nationwide surveys conducted by the Kyiv International Institute of Sociology in February 2012 and September 2014, "national identification increased by 10 percent": that is, still in the early post-Maidan months, when describing their primary territorial identification in post-Maidan Ukraine, respondents increasingly preferred to identify as citizens of Ukraine over other local and regional identifications. However, analysing the data from the 2016 nationwide survey conducted by the Razumkov Centre, we see how actually "in the Ukrainian society there is no consensus as to what is better between preserving the cultural characteristics of regional and ethnic groups and supporting cultural unification"[279] (2016: 10).

On the one hand, within the frame of the "rather nationalist agenda for the memory domain" (Kulyk 2017: 1) implemented by the post-Maidan political elite, in April 2015 the Ukrainian Rada approved four contested "decommunization" laws: the law *On the Legal Status and Honouring of Fighters for Ukraine's Independence in the Twentieth Century* (*Pro pravovyi status ta vshanuvannia pam'iati bortsiv za nezalezhnist' Ukraïny u XX stolitti*), n. 2358; the law *On Condemning the Communist and National Socialist (Nazi) Totalitarian Regimes and Prohibiting Propaganda of their Symbols* (*Pro zasudzhennia komunistychnoho ta natsional-sotsialistychnoho—natsysts'koho—totalitarnykh rezhymiv v Ukraïni ta zaboronu propahandy ïkh simvoliky*), n. 2558; the law *On Remembering the Victory over Nazism in the Second World War* (*Pro uvichnennia peremohy nad natsyzmom u Druhii svitovii viini 1939–1945 rokiv*), n. 2539; and the law *On Access to the Archives of Repressive Bodies of the Communist Totalitarian Regime from 1917–1991* (*Pro dostup do arkhiviv represyvnykh orhaniv komunistychnoho totalitarnoho rezhymu 1917–1991 rokiv*), n. 2540. The removal of monuments to communist leaders and the change of the names of streets, towns and villages were implemented

---

279   "[...] в українському суспільстві немає консенсусу стосовно того, що краще — збереження культурних особливостей регіональних та етнічних груп чи культурна уніфікація."

"often as a way to propose continuity between the past and present anti-Russian struggles" (Kulyk 2017: 2). When the then-president Petro Poroshenko enacted the new laws (May 2015), it was no surprise that a vibrant domestic and international contestation erupted (see Stadnyi 2015; Marples 2015): this was especially directed towards the controversial role of the Ukrainian Institute of National Remembrance (see Umland 2017).

On the other hand, in his studies on identity politics in post-Euromaidan Ukraine, Kulyk (2017; 2019a) could highlight how it was paradoxically in the domain of language where there had been no consistent policy.[280] At first glance, there seems to be a contradiction in terms, as still in September 2015 Kulyk could observe that "while many Russian speakers proudly assert their Ukrainian identity, which they link not to ethnic origin or language practices but to civic belonging, public discourse reveals conflicting opinions about the consequences of this identity choice for language use in society" (2015: 2). Generally, by analysing data from the above-mentioned 2014 nationwide survey conducted in early post-Maidan times, it emerged that Ukraine was "not generally perceived as a nation with two languages" (Kulyk 2015: 5). We could also still observe that "46 percent [of the respondents] believed that the primary task of state language policy was to promote the expansion of Ukrainian in all social domains, while 34 percent wanted the state to 'resolve' the issue of the status of Russian (which in the Ukrainian context means 'enhance' rather than 'downgrade')" (Kulyk 2017: 4).

Eventually, in the first years of activity of the parliament elected in October 2014, the debated "language issue" found a concrete answer in terms of new policies only by means of three legislative provisions in 2015/2017: the law *On Civil Service* (*Pro derzhavnu sluzhbu*—December 2015, n. 889-VIII), according to which civil servants are obliged to use Ukrainian when on duty; the law *On amending Certain Ukrainian Bills*

---

280 As emblematically observed by Kulyk (2017: 2): "After an unfortunate attempt immediately after President Viktor Ianukovych's political demise to revoke the supposedly Russification-oriented language law that he insisted on adopting in 2012 for electoral purposes, the post-Euromaidan leadership seemed to conclude that that law was there to stay because abolishing it would ignite a political confrontation playing into the Kremlin hands."

Regarding Quotas of Musical Works in the National Language in Television and Radio Programmes (Pro vnesennia zmin do deiakykh zakoniv Ukraïny shchodo chastky muzychnykh tvoriv derzhavnoiu movoiu u prohramakh teleradioorhanizatsiï—June 2016, n. 1421-VIII), which establishes a compulsory quota for broadcasters of songs (35 per cent) to be played in the state language; and the law *On Amending Certain Ukrainian Bills Regarding the Language of Audiovisual (Electronic) Media (Pro vnesennia zmin do deiakykh zakoniv Ukraïny shchodo movy audiovizual'nykh (elektronnykh) zasobiv masovoï informatsiï*—May 2017, n. 2054-VIII), establishing a minimum of 75 per cent of daily programmes in the state language for nationwide broadcasters and 60 per cent for local ones. As observed by Kulyk, the passing of these bills "demonstrated the considerable weight of Ukrainian-language supporters in the parliament" (Kulyk 2017: 3) elected in 2014. Moreover, in our analysis we should also consider two laws regulating the cultural market, which came to affect language practices: the bill *On Making Changes to Article 15 of the Ukrainian Law "On Cinema" (Pro vnesennia zminy do statti 15 Zakonu Ukraïny "Pro kinematohrafiiu"*—March 2016, n. 1046-VIII), which banned all the films produced by individuals or companies from the "aggressor state" (*derzhava-ahresor*)—that is, from Russia—that were released or screened for the first time after January 2014; and the law *On Amending Certain Ukrainian Bills Regarding the Restricting Access of Foreign Printed Production of anti-Ukrainian Content to the Ukrainian Market (Pro vnesennia zmin do deiakykh zakoniv Ukraïny shchodo obmezhennia dostupu na ukraïns'kyi rynok inozemnoï produktsiï antiukraïns'koho zmistu*—December 2016), which eventually had the result of banning the import of Russian books until the relevant regulations and verification mechanisms had been developed (see Kuchkina 2017).

Even if these provisions were not part of a comprehensive cultural policy, we can still consider this as the ground for opening a new political debate on cultural issues in Ukraine. In fact, the registration of three draft laws on languages submitted by pro-Ukrainization parliamentary deputies in October 2016 and January 2017 testified to the consolidation of new perspectives for nation-building policies in post-Maidan Ukraine: the draft law *On Languages in Ukraine (Pro movy v Ukraïni*, n. 5556), which was submitted by a group of deputies from the Petro Poroshenko Bloc, headed by

Iaroslav Lesiuk; the draft law *On the Functioning of Ukrainian as the State Language and the Modality of Use of Other Languages in Ukraine* (*Pro funktsionuvannia Ukraïns'koï movy iak derzhavnoï ta poriadok inshykh mov v Ukraïni*, n. 5669), initiated by Mykhailo Holovko, a member of the nationalist party Svoboda; and the draft law *On the State Language* (*Pro derzhavnu movu*, n. 5670), which was then submitted by the deputy head of the Committee on Culture and Spirituality Iryna Podoliak, member of Union Self Reliance. In particular, the initiators of the last two draft laws promoted the creation of a special commission for monitoring the observance of the state language law, introducing language inspectors and expensive fines for the desecration of the Ukrainian language.

These provisions opened an intense debate on the possible outcomes after the passing of the laws (see Nitsoi 2017; Masenko 2017). In her commentary entitled *Language Madness* (*Movne bozhevillia*), Iryna Podoliak, author of the contested draft law *On the State Language*, significantly defined the situation where "in the country N live people who do not speak the N language"[281] as the product of the "language madness imposed by totalitarian Russia and its colonial policy"[282] (Podoliak 2017). According to Podoliak, "the official language is one of the foundations of the constitutional system, one of the markers of sovereignty, now and in the near future it is part of national security"[283] (Podoliak 2017). Thus, the draft laws were meant as a response to the need for the creation of a national cultural environment, whereas the use of Russian is still consistent in traditional and digital media (see Holub 2017). In fact, Podoliak's stance reflected the reactive and defensive character of the newly proposed cultural policies.[284] Finally, the approval of the new law *On Education* (*Pro osvitu*—September

---

281 "[...] в країні N живуть люди, які не володіють «енською» мовою."

282 "[...] мовне божевілля, накинуте тоталітарною Росією та її колоніальною політикою."

283 "Державна мова є однією із засад конституційного ладу, одним із маркерів суверенності, а нині та в найближчому майбутньому — елементом національної безпеки [...]"

284 This significantly follows the dynamics of the contested nation-building perspectives traced by the pre-Maidan elite: it is interpreted as a reaction to the "Kremlin's Trojan horses" (*Troians'ki koni Kremlia*; Marusyk 2016), as the contested 2012 law *On the Fundamentals of the State Language Policy* (*Pro zasady derzhavnoï movnoï polityky)* by Serhii Kivalov and Vadym

2017, n. 2145-VIII) confirmed this tendency: the bill, which was signed by the Ukrainian president on September 25, 2017, established a huge reform of the educational system in Ukraine, raising the years of schooling from 11 to 12, and, most importantly, elevated Ukrainian as the main language of instruction, replacing minority languages from secondary school onwards. On the one hand, amongst the law's backers this was expected to "help to eliminate *de facto* segregation of minority-language speakers, thereby unifying Ukrainian society—critical to a strong and vibrant democracy" (Sushko 2017). On the other, the provision provoked the immediate reaction of the governments of Hungary, Romania, Poland and Russia, which criticized the law for limiting the rights of the national minority populations living in Ukraine. Actually, this "poorly timed" bill, which was "presented as an attempt to align Ukraine's school system more closely with European standards" (Sasse 2017), underlay the wider project "to further strengthen the status of the Ukrainian language vis-à-vis Russian." If, according to Balázs Jarábik, this controversial move could "be explained as the ruling elites in a pre-election mode choosing patriotism and resistance against Russian aggression as key campaign themes" (Minakov 2017), in a broader view the "long-term cumulative effect of individual policies that foster exclusion rather than inclusion," as observed by Tetiana Maliarenko, reflected "a worrying tendency in Ukrainian politics and society that does not bode well for the democratic development of the country, for its security and stability, or for prospects of sustainable conflict management and settlement" (Minakov 2017).

Within this complex frame, the expected reconstruction of a full-fledged nation- and state-building process "from the top" implied a high level of contestation. In his commentary entitled "The End of Revolution?" ("Kinets' revoliutsiï?"), the Ukrainian historian Iaroslav Hrytsak (2017) looked precisely at the fluctuating dynamics of "symbolic politics," which echoed the polarization of the pre-revolutionary period. Eventually, even

---

Kolesnichenko has been defined. Interestingly, it was only in February 2018, four years after the then-president Viktor Ianukovych left the country in the aftermath of the protests in Kyiv, that the 2012 law was declared unconstitutional by the National Court.

in post-Maidan times the battle of myths and value-based ideologies came to lie at the core of the national political debate:

> Language and historical battles imply high risks. They relate to symbols. And symbols are always explosive [...] Historical-language discussions are also dangerous by the fact that they divert attention from reality [...] We can take it as a rule: whenever a revolution has exhausted itself, our goverment and our parties click on the historical-language button. This happened with Yushchenko. And, I am afraid that this is happening now.[285] (Hrytsak 2017)

This was the prelude to the electoral campaign that preceded the new presidential and parliamentary elections taking place in the first half of 2019, in which historical-language discussions still played a prominent role.[286] Eventually, it was only in April 2019, four days after the second and final round of the new presidential elections, that we witnessed the passing of the law *On Guaranteeing the Functioning of the Ukrainian Language as a State Language* (*Pro zabezpechennia funktsionuvannia ukraïns' koï movy iak derzhavnoï*, 2704-VIII), which emerged out of the revision of one of the draft laws presented in 2017 (n. 5670-D)—thus embodying the ultimate result of the cultural policies implemented by the first post-Maidan parliament.[287] Under the new law, which does not cover private interactions and religious practices, the functioning of the Ukrainian language finally finds its full-fledged "normative" description as "a tool for unification of Ukrainian society, an instrument for strengthening the state unity and

---

285 "Мовні й історичні баталії пов'язані з високими ризиками. Вони стосуються символів. А символи завжди вибухові [...] Історично-мовні дискусії небезпечні ще й тим, що відвертають увагу від реалій [...] Можна вивести правило: щоразу, коли революція себе вичерпала, наша влада і наші партії натискають на мовно-історичну кнопку. Так було за Ющенка. Так, боюся, є зараз."

286 The developments of Ukrainian politics in 2019 will be further discussed in the concluding section of this volume.

287 Most of the amendments made to the law throughout 2017–2019 have definitely softened the potential impact of its most critical and contested issues (i.e. the introduction of language inspectors has been removed; media operating in foreign languages are not obliged to publish a Ukrainian-language version of their publications, when using Crimean Tatar or any official language of the European Union).

territorial integrity of Ukraine, its independent statehood and national security"[288] (Zakon Ukraïny 2019). Furthermore, as reported in the introduction to the bill, the Ukrainian language is recognized as "the determining
factor and the main marker of the identity of the Ukrainian nation"[289]
(Zakon Ukraïny 2019), and ensuring its proper functioning in the national
society is considered to be "a guarantee for the preservation of the identity
of the Ukrainian nation and the strengthening of the unity of the Ukrainian
state"[290] (Zakon Ukraïny 2019).

The law came into force in July 2019, but most of the normative measures, such as the adoption of a compulsory Ukrainian-language exam for
obtaining Ukrainian citizenship, or the introduction of administrative
fines against those desecrating the state language, will be put into effect by
2021–2022, thus opening the ground for further discussion on the language
issue in the future. Apparently, the 2019 law "does not solve the issue of
how Russian and Ukrainian co-exist as languages" in Ukraine, but—as the
Ukrainian journalist Roman Huba provocatively put it—seems to revolve
around "the following concept: if you're a Ukrainian, that means you're a
Ukrainian speaker" (Huba 2019).

Envisioning Identity Markers after the Ukraine Crisis

When dealing with the perennial "failure to normalize Ukrainian–Russian
relations," a central issue that political and cultural analysts often need to
take into consideration consists in questioning the "unresolved national
identities on both sides" (Kuzio 2001: 351). It is no surprise that Igor'
Torbakov, while studying the recent developments in the Ukrainian and
Russian realms, looked at the "insights offered by scholars of colonial and
postcolonial studies," which "might enhance understandings of Ukrainian-
Russian multifaceted entanglements" (2016: 90). Borrowing methodological

---

288 "[…] функціонування державної мови як інструмента об'єднання українського
     суспільства, засобу зміцнення державної єдності та територіальної цілісності
     України, її незалежної державності і національної безпеки."
289 "[…] українська мова є визначальним чинником і головною ознакою
     ідентичності української нації […]."
290 "[…] є гарантією збереження ідентичності української нації та зміцнення
     державної єдності України […]."

tools from postcolonial studies, Torbakov observed how "Ukraine and Russia exhibit extreme 'hybridity' and ambivalence in several spheres, including social, cultural and political" (2016: 91). This comes to be a crucial point especially when analysing the response of social subgroupings to the recent directions of state cultural policies in both countries. It is in the "intrinsic societal differences that conditioned Ukraine's and Russia's diverging post-Soviet political trajectories" (Torbakov 2016: 96) that we can find the reasons which lie behind the relationship established by state and society in the respective national contexts. This mainly regards "the degree of Ukraine's and Russia's sociocultural homogeneity, the role that regionalism plays in both countries, and Ukrainians' and Russians' attitudes towards the state and revolution" (Torbakov 2016: 96). Most fundamentally, in terms of policies implemented "from the top," we should take into consideration the results of different "processes associated with histories and geopolitics of the two countries" (Torbakov 2016: 90). As suggested by Torbakov, in the case of Russian leadership's perspective on the Russo-Ukrainian conflict, these processes include:

> [...] protracted and painful imperial disintegration and readjustment; immature national/political identity in post-Soviet Russia and Ukraine; and alternating expansion and contraction of the "spheres of identity" in what is usually designated as "historical borderland" between "Russia" and "Europe." (2016: 90)

Following these lines, even if "Russians and Ukrainians seem to differ in their attitudes toward state authority, in their acceptance of trade-offs between unchecked power and social stability, and in their attitudes toward revolutionary upheavals" (Torbakov 2016: 98), over the last years in both countries state policies have been characterized by discontinuity and ambiguity. This is particularly significant, especially since the recent cycles of contestation in the 2010s eventually came to embody a turning point in the struggle for the solution to the national question in post-Soviet Russia and Ukraine.

Regarding the former, observers generally tend to overestimate the Russian role in contested and conflicting world areas by accepting Russian elite self-representation of the country as an internally coherent and cohesive realm—while underestimating the space for contestation in the domestic sphere. Following the internal dynamics which have characterized the Russian Federation throughout the last years, it is worth noticing that the "unexpected" outburst of the protests in Moscow and St. Petersburg in 2011–2012, in the aftermath of the State Duma elections, marked the rise of a new important benchmark to be traced in the national narrative: an "ethnic turn" in the elite's discourse able to distinguish between the "real patriots" and the "other Russians." As observed by Helge Blakkisrud, "in addition to being the biggest manifestations of political opposition since the collapse of the Soviet Union," the 2011–2012 demonstrations embodied "a breakthrough for cooperation across ideological divides, with the Western-oriented liberals overcoming some of their traditional distaste for the Russian ethnonationalists" (2016: 255). In response to this, the Russian elite decided in favour of "co-opting" (Blakkisrud 2016: 255) some of the rhetoric of the latter, while isolating the former. Thus, in order to respond to internal conflicts and public mobilization "from below," throughout the first years of Putin's third mandate we witnessed the ratification of several federal laws which regulated the terms of public discourse, following neo-conservative stances: that is, the federal law *On Amendments to the Code of the Russian Federation on Administrative Offenses and the Federal Law "On Assemblies, Meetings, Demonstrations, Marches and Picketing"* (*O vnesenii izmenenii v Kodeks Rossiiskoi Federatsii ob administrativnykh pravonarusheniiakh i federal'nyi zakon "O sobraniiakh, mitingakh, demonstratsiiakh, shestviiakh i piketirovaniiakh"*—n. 65-FZ, June 2012), restricting the freedom to organize and participate in public assemblies; the federal law *On Amendments to Legislative Acts of the Russian Federation Regarding the Regulation of the Activities of Non-Profit Organizations Performing the Functions of a Foreign Agent* (*O vnesenii izmenenii v otdel'nye zakonodatel'nye akty Rossiiskoi Federatsii v chasti regulirovaniia deiatel'nosti nekommercheskikh organizatsii, vypolniaiushchikh funktsii inostrannogo agenta*—n. 121-FZ, July 2012), limiting the activities of NGOs;[291] the federal law *On Amendments to the Article 148 of the*

---

291 The potential status of "foreign agent"—that is, a label for entities that are funded by a foreign country, promoting its interests, while located in Russia—was extended to international public broadcasters in November 2017 (*O vnesenii izmenenii v stat'i 10-4 i 15-3 federal'nogo zakona "Ob informatsii, informatsionnykh tekhnologiiakh i o zashchite informatsii" i stat'iu 6 Zakona Rossiiskoi Federatsii "O sredstvakh massovoi informatsii"*, n. 327-FZ) and to individual journalists and bloggers operating in the Russian Federation

Criminal Code of the Russian Federation and Certain Legislative Acts of the Russian Federation in Order to Counter the Insult of Citizens' Religious Beliefs and Sensibilities (O vnesenii izmenenii v stat'iu 148 Ugolovnogo kodeksa Rossiiskoi Federatsii i otdel'nye zakonodatel'nye akty Rossiiskoi Federatsii v tseliakh protivodeistviia oskorbleniiu religioznykh ubezhdenii i chustv grazhdan—n. 136-FZ, June 2013), which was inspired by the international scandal following the performance of the punk rock group Pussy Riot at the Christ the Saviour Cathedral in Moscow in 2012 and now sets fines and jail terms for those offending religious feelings; and the federal law *On Amendments to the Federal Law "On the State Language of the Russian Federation" and Certain Legislative Acts of the Russian Federation in Relation to the Improvement of the Legal Regulation in the Use of the Russian Language (O vnesenii izmenenii v Federal'nyi zakon "O gosudarstvennom iazyke Rossiiskoi Federatsii" i otdel'nye zakonodatel'nye akty Rossiiskoi Federatsii v sviazi s sovershenstvovaniem pravovogo regulirovaniia v sfere ispol'zovaniia russkogo iazyka*—n. 101-FZ, May 2014), banning swearing in literature, cinema, arts and media.

These legislative measures came to be legitimate in the symbolic narrative carried out by the Russian elite on the new "clash of civilizations," between traditional Russian values and the "spiritual decay of the West."[292] As observed by Laruelle (2017a), "fostering conservatism provides a much easier ideological framework" for the Kremlin.[293] Throughout the recent

---

in December 2019 (*O vnesenii izmenenii v Zakon Rossiiskoi Federatsii "O sredstvakh massovoi informatsii" i Federal'nyi zakon "Ob informatsii, informatsionnykh tekhnologiiakh i o zashchite informatsii"*, n. 426-FZ).

292 It is not by chance that in his address to the Federal Assembly in December 2013, Putin referred to the philosopher Nikolai Berdiaev (1874–1948), quoting his statements on the decay of Western civilization in the early twentieth century (see Putin 2013).

293 "The presidential administration therefore succeeded in developing an *explicit* but blurry narrative of conservatism—embodied by anti-Westernism, anti-liberalism, and the promotion of so-called traditional moral values—and in offering an *implicit* ideological diversity available for collective consumption. These doctrinal products are elaborated by different groups of ideological entrepreneurs who have room to act [...] Their fragile entrepreneurship must work in permanent negotiation and tension with competing groups and the presidential administration itself" (Laruelle 2017a).

history of the Russian Federation, state actors have been stuck in an ideological impasse, alternatively shifting their focus from a civic *rossiskii* to an ethnic *russkii* understanding of the Russian national idea (see Shevel 2011; Blakkisrud 2016). Even during the Ukraine crisis, Putin's address on the inclusion of Crimea and Sevastopol' as subjects of the Russian Federation in March 2014 was considered a crucial shift to an ethnic conceptualization of the "Russian question."[294] Nonetheless, it is only through the lenses of the highly flexible pattern of conservatism that we can observe how the national question has been recently reframed. Evidence comes from the 2013 Valdai Club meeting, whose results were published in February 2014, on the eve of the Ukraine crisis. The report *National Identity and the Future of Russia* (*Natsional'naia identichnost' i budushchee Rossii*) better testifies to the main core of the new directions undertaken in the Russian "struggle for meanings." In the section emblematically entitled "Culture as the Basis of Russian Identity" (*"Kul'tura kak osnova rossiiskoi identichnosti"*), conservatism and identity find their common ground in "Russian culture" (*russkaia kul'tura*)—as selectively conceptualized by the editors of the report:

> Any attempt to formulate national identity through the ethnic or religious prism contradicts the entire history of *Rossiiskii/Russkii* civilisation [...] Historically in Russia the dominant culture is the Russian (*russkaia*) [...] The Russian (*rossiiskaia*) national identity should be built on the principle of a common cultural field, with vivid national fragments enriching the basic culture [...] We are not a nation-state or an empire. In the long term, the hybrid form of a cultural-civic nation is the closest one to Russia as a country. The links lying in the cultural field, which were codified in the great Russian literature, music, painting, architecture and cinema, are the most lasting integrator for all the people who connect themselves with Russia.[295] (Valdai 2014: 30–31)

---

294 Such is the perspective claimed by the Norwegian scholar Helge Blakkisrud: "[...] Putin went even further in linking the fate of the ethnic Russians and Russian statehood [...] Putin consistently used the term *russkii* rather than *rossiiskii* [...] In other words, bringing the peninsula back under Moscow's control was not only legitimised by Crimea historically having been part of the Russian Empire and the RSFSR—the peninsula was also considered *ethnic* Russian lands" (2016: 259).

295 "Попытка сформулировать национальную идентичность через этническую или религиозную противоречит всей истории российской/русской цивилизации [...] В России исторически доминирующая культура — русская

Eventually, the institutionalization of Russian culture and conservatism as the main benchmarks in defining the national idea came in December 2014, with the ratification of the *Basics of the State Cultural Policy* (*Osnovy gosudarstvennoi kul'turnoi politiki*), which are considered to be "an integral part of the Russian Federation National Security Strategy" (*neot'emlemaia chast' strategii natsional'noi bezopasnosti Rossiiskoi Federatsii*; MKRF 2015: 3). It is exactly this new passage in the contemporary political discourse which leads to the crystallization of the Kremlin's situational narrative in a concrete normative policy. The document follows the main lines of the draft project published in May 2014 by Sergei Ivanov (see MKRF 2014), head of the presidential administration until August 2016. Here, finally the national "cultural code" comes to have a normative value.

As observed by Il'ia Kalinin (2015), "[t]his normativeness has its foundations in the idea of nation and in the approval of unity as the main national value":[296] this creates the ground for the new language of the Russian cultural policy, where "'patriotism' stands for loyalty to the politics undertaken by the state, 'love for the homeland' stands for support of the current elite, 'cultural tradition' stands for tradition of the Russian strong and autocratic statuality […]"[297] (Kalinin 2015). The pragmatic aspect of this extreme change of direction lies in the use of culture for

---

[…] Российская национальная идентичность должна выстраиваться по принципу общего культурного поля, с яркими, обогащающими основную культуру национальными вкраплениями […] Мы не нация-государство и не империя. В долгосрочной перспективе наиболее близкой для России как страны представляется гибридная форма культурно-гражданской нации […] Связи, лежащие в культурном поле, кодифицированные в великой русской литературе, музыке, живописи, архитектуре, кинематографе, — самый прочный интегратор для всех людей, связывающих себя с Россией."

296 "Эта нормативность находит свое основание в идее нации и в утверждении единства как главной национальной ценности."

297 "В этом новом языке российской государственной культуры «патриотизм» означает лояльность к проводимой государством политике, «любовь к Родине» — поддержку правящей элиты, «культурная традиция» — традицию сильной и автократичной российской государственности […]."

strategic interest, "adopting it as the main subject in foreign politics and the bastion of domestic political unity"[298] (Kalinin 2015).

Eventually, the legitimation of conservative stances followed the externalization of the internal conflict *beyond* the borders of the Russian Federation: the "Crimean euphoria" served as a catalyst for new external projections of the Russian idea. Especially, the theorization of *Russkii mir* (Russian World), that is to say, a "civilization" embracing Europe and Asia following shared language and cultural affiliations, works within blurred boundaries. *Russkii mir* was adopted in the 2000s by state actors for a strategic interest, mainly referring to "Russia's policy for its Near Abroad," "Russia's interaction with Russian diasporas in the world" and "Russia's brand, both as a public-relations project and a messianic project" (Laruelle 2015b: 6). It works in parallel with other Russian foreign policy projects, such as the Compatriots' (*Sootechestvenniki*) project directed to the Near Abroad (see Shevel 2011), and the term was emblematically used by Putin in the March 2014 address on Crimea.[299] Since Patriarch Kirill became the head of the Russian Orthodox Church in 2009 and, emblematically, since

---

298 "[…] делая ее аргументом внешней политики и оплотом внутриполитического единства."

299 While supporting the aspiration for self-determination of the Crimean people, the Russian president addressed his Western counterpart, comparing the 2014 annexation of Crimea to German reunification in 1990: "I believe that Europeans will understand me, and first of all Germans. Let me remind you that in the course of political consultations on the unification of the FRG and DDR […] not all the representatives of the countries which are and were then allies of Germany supported the idea of unification. And our country, on the contrary, unequivocally supported the sincere, overwhelming aspiration of Germans for national unity. I am certain that you have not forgotten it, and I expect that German citizens will also support the aspiration of the Russian world [*Russkii mir*], of historical Russia to restore unity" (Putin 2014; Верю, что меня поймут и европейцы, и прежде всего немцы. Напомню, что в ходе политических консультаций по объединению ФРГ и ГДР […] представители далеко не всех стран, которые являются и являлись тогда союзниками Германии, поддержали саму идею объединения. А наша страна, напротив, однозначно поддержала искреннее, неудержимое стремление немцев к национальному единству. Уверен, что вы этого не забыли, и рассчитываю, что граждане Германии также поддержат стремление русского мира, исторической России к восстановлению единства).

the outbursts of the 2011–2012 protests and the re-election of Putin in 2012, the term became "less associated with dispersed people—bearers of 'Russianness'—and more with territories and historical legacies" (Suslov 2016: 295). As observed by Mikhail Suslov, this began to signify, together with the twin concept of Holy Rus, "an ethnically and religious united land-mass, comprised of Russia proper, Belarus, Ukraine, and, depending on the geopolitical appetites of ideologues, parts of other post-Soviet republics" (2016: 295). As observed by Laruelle, even if it "is poorly articulated," the Russian world concept significantly "functions in almost complete harmony with the Kremlin's new conservative agenda," whereas "both repertoires advance the idea or assumption that Russia represents a unique civiliza-tion" (2015b: 20). Over the last years, this double-edged strategy was aimed to consolidate the Russian electorate by means of the codification of a new "social contract":[300] thus, public mobilization could eventually be enacted "from the top." Following Ekaterina Shul'man's (2017) reflections, we could thus consider the "external projection" of the internal conflict throughout Putin's third mandate, that is, the neo-conservative shift and the Ukrainian campaign, precisely as a direct answer to the 2011–2012 protests.

In a broader view, the patriotic shift in Russian state policies not only affected the domestic social balance but also significantly influenced the developments in other post-Soviet states, and namely in Ukraine. Generally, even today the language issue comes to be included in the broader patriotic repertoire that in the aftermath of the Maidan Revolution and the Russo–Ukrainian war was emblematically proposed "from below," and only

---

300 As Andrei Kolesnikov puts it: "Thus March 2014 marked the acceptance of a renewed version of the unofficial social contract [...] In this new rendition of the contract, Crimea and the restoration of the feeling of Russia's great power status (this time without economic accomplishments) were offered in exchange for the unconditional support of the Russian people. The era of symbols and synonyms began. The semantic meaning of the word 'Crimea' came to extend well beyond geography. It contained everything: rectifying historical injustices, an imperial sense of the country's greatness as well as the quick return of a defence-minded outlook, which translated into national unity. When Russians said 'Crimea,' they meant 'Putin,' and vice versa. Whoever did not share in the nationwide euphoria became an outcast" (Kolesnikov 2016).

eventually legitimized "from the top." Most fundamentally, this reveals a quite symmetric pattern in Ukrainian and Russian state–society relations, whereas "the break of the patriots with the liberals makes impossible not only the 'third Maidan', but also any powerful pressure on the authorities on the part of society"[301] (Semenov 2017). Eventually, to both state and civil society, discourses about the "external threat" legitimize illiberal tendencies in the search for those who are "true patriots" and those who are not.

This is particularly significant, especially when looking at the role assumed by radical subgroups in Ukraine and Russia throughout 2017. In February, the members of a Ukrainian far-right nationalist organization attacked an exhibition by the artist David Chichkan at the Centre for Visual Culture in Kyiv. In his exhibition *Lost Opportunities* (*Uteriannye vozmozhnosti*), the artist reflected on the Maidan revolution as a "lost opportunity" for Ukrainian society to accomplish a social revolution. Chichkan was thus considered to be openly criticizing the rather nationalist policies implemented by post-Maidan state actors, mainly in reference to the decommunization process. Thus, if on the one hand the reaction of far-right activists, "accusing him of separatism and playing up to Moscow" (Bezruk 2017) testified to the radicalization of assertive subgroupings in the national social milieu, on the other, as observed by Bezruk, the absence of a "large-scale demonstration of solidarity in support of freedom of expression" revealed how "Ukrainian society's consensus of justification towards people who have turned patriotism into vandalism is becoming more and more tangible" (Bezruk 2017). Liberal and patriotic stances also diverged at the L'viv Book Forum in September 2017. The presentation of the children's book *Maia and Her Moms* (*Maiia ta ïï mamy*) by the Ukrainian writer Larysa Denysenko (b. 1973, Kyiv) was cancelled over fear of possible violence from far-right groups—that in a letter to the organizers and local authorities accused the author of provocatively offending traditional and moral values. Mainly for describing gay and non-traditional families, *Maia and Her Moms* was at the centre of a scandal, "with religious-conservative and nationalist groups lambasting the book and liberals defending it"

---

301 "[…] разрыв патриотов с либералами делает невозможным не только «третий Майдан,» но и любое сколько-нибудь мощное давление на власть со стороны общества."

(Wesolowsky 2017). Indicatively, Ievhen Holovakha described the debate on Denysenko's book as "our Ukrainian *'Matil'da'* (*nasha ukraïns'ka "Matyl'da"*; Iakhno, Hruzdev 2017), referring to the simultaneous debate in Russia around the movie by the prominent director Aleksei Uchitel' on Tsar Nikolai II. In his commentary Holovakha aimed to highlight precisely the paradoxical situation determined by the symmetric search for "spiritual bonds" in Ukraine and Russia.[302] In the latter, the situation is far more complex: as in the case of *Matil'da*, the balancing game enacted by state actors between conservative, religious and imperialist stances revealed alarming ideological gaps in the Russian state discourse.

Uchitel"s movie, which was financed by the Russian culture ministry, tells the story of a love affair between Tsar Nikolai II, who was canonized by the Russian Orthodox church in 2000, and the dancer Matil'da Kshesinskaia, and depicts the tsar in explicit erotic scenes. In August 2017, after receiving official approval for release in Russia, the movie faced calls for a ban from religious and conservative critics invoking the application of the already mentioned federal law on offending the feelings of religious believers (n. 136-FZ, June 2013). In the same month, a Molotov cocktail was thrown into Uchitel"s film studio in St. Petersburg, while radicals torched cars parked on the Moscow street in front of the director's lawyer's office. It was particularly the radical Russian Orthodox Christian movement Christian State-Holy Rus (Khristianskoe gosudarstvo-Sviataia Rus') that played an important role in the public campaign against the movie. Already in January 2017, the movement sent letters to cinemas across Russia to warn them that if *Matil'da* was screened, cinemas would be burned. Most fundamentally, it was the official reaction to this radical movement that was ambiguous: on the one side, Putin and Dmitrii Medvedev condemned the threats of violence, even if the former "also said that artists should not provoke society

---

302 "In Russia, of course, the scale of this is larger, but the psychological foundations and social basis are the same. Unfortunately, both Ukraine and Russia are in the system of the post-feudal past. That is, we have not yet come out of the system of a traditional, semi-dispersed patriarchal society" (Iakhno, Hruzdev 2017; В Росії, звичайно, масштаби цього більші, але психологічні основи та соціальне підґрунтя — однакові. На жаль, і ми, і Росія перебуваємо в системі постфеодального минулого. Тобто ми ще не вийшли з системи традиційного, напіврозкладеного патріархального суспільства).

by producing work that could upset believers" (Bennetts 2017); on the other, such public figures as Natal'ia Poklonskaia,[303] a conservative United Russia MP, took the stage to harshly advocate for the rights of religious believers (see Ufimtseva 2017).

These controversial dynamics reflect how the dialogue between state actors and non-state actors comes to be established in Russia today. Within the frame of the conservative shift, considered as "a deliberate attempt to 'neutralise' liberal Russians" (Bennetts 2017) in the aftermath of the 2011–2012 protests, Orthodox and nationalist radical groups "are permitted to exist by the authorities," representing the "marginal, extreme side of the state's official dialogue" (Bennets 2017).

It was mainly the patriotic mobilization in 2014 that deeply influenced the co-optation of radical actors in the state discourse. Especially, it was amongst the nationalistic and imperialistic segments of the Russian cultural milieu that the Russian intervention in Crimea came then to reconcile the internal fracture between state and non-state actors, as claimed by the fantasy writer and historian of Belarusian origin Kirill Benediktov already in February 2014 (see Benediktov 2014). Benediktov has been amongst the lead editors of the online platform Russkaia Idea: Site on Conservative Political Thought (Russkaia Idea: sait konservativnoi politicheskoi mysli), which was sponsored by the Institute for Socio-Economic and Political Studies (ISEPR), a new and influential think tank founded in 2012, soon after Putin's re-election. According to its editors, the platform "is devoted to the issue of 'political conservatism' in relation to the new ideology for Russia"[304] (Russkaia Idea 2014). As Benediktov observed already in February 2014, on the eve of the Crimean annexation to Russia, "the events of the last days in Ukraine have extremely aroused the creative part

---

303 In the Russian–Ukrainian clash of discourses, the public role of Natal'ia Poklonskaia is particularly significant. She was a Ukrainian prosecutor in Crimea until 2014. During the Crimean crisis, she resigned in March 2014 from Ukrainian service and was appointed prosecutor general of Crimea, then confirmed by the Russian authorities. In Crimea she was on duty until her election to the Russian State Duma in Fall 2016.

304 "Наш сайт посвящен проблематике «политического консерватизма» — относительно новой идеологии для России."

of our society"[305] (Benediktov 2014). Notable fantasy writers such as Sergei Luk'ianenko immediately assumed a pro-Kremlin stance, while it was only in late 2016 that the Russian PEN Centre lost some of its most prominent liberal members, such as Sviatlana Aleksievich and Boris Akunin, who disapproved of the "conformist" and "servile" position taken by the institution (see *Novaia Gazeta* 2017).[306]

The shifting political positions assumed by the segment of Russian imperial nationalists can further shed light on the alternative outlooks endorsed by the intellectual environment throughout the crisis. Amongst Russian intellectuals, the experiences of the writers Eduard Limonov and Zakhar Prilepin, respectively the leader and a prominent member of the National Bolshevik Party (NBP), clearly reflect the subtle nuances of social mobilization in the Russian Federation. In his article emblematically entitled "The Journey of National Bolsheviks towards Putin and Back Again" ("Puteshestvie natsbolov k Putinu i obratno"), Il'ia Azar (2017) retraces the origins and the recent story of one of the most relevant parties of the opposition groups which "have seen their ideological stance challenged during the Ukrainian Crisis" (Laruelle 2017b: 92). The so-called *Limonovtsy*, appearing in the 1990s, and labelled as "imperial nationalists" (Kolstø 2016: 707), "created a vivid youth counterculture around music, aesthetics, dress codes, and street violence targeting official institutions, such as police headquarters and the judicial administration" (Laruelle 2017b: 91). It was in 2014 that the NBP partly reconciled with the Kremlin:

> The National Bolsheviks—once the most vivid of the opposition forces to Putin— after the annexation of Crimea to Russia believed in the revival of the Russian imperial project. They sent around 2000 volunteers to the Donbas along with the "Interbrigada" and fought the war. But the dream of the DNR [Donets'k People's

---

305 "[…] события последних дней на Украине крайне возбудили креативную часть нашего общества."

306 On September 20, 2017, the St. Petersburg PEN centre, a liberal branch of the Russian PEN centre, was elected an independent member of the International PEN Club. This was on the occasion of the 83rd World Congress, which was held in L'viv, to which the leadership of the Russian PEN centre was not invited.

Republic] as a country where National Bolsheviks could engage in politics holding weapons and build new social justice quickly collapsed.[307] (Azar 2017)

While in the aftermath of the Crimean annexation "Eduard Limonov attacked his former allies in the Russian opposition for their failure to welcome Crimea into Russia" (Kolstø 2016: 718), it was the prolonged and bloody war in Donbas that again distanced the NBP from the Kremlin. Differently from Limonov, Zakhar Prilepin has maintained a pro-Kremlin stance. In early 2017, he reached the battlefield in Donbas with his own volunteer battalion (Kots 2017). By calling on the tradition of Russian "literary spetsnaz" (*literaturnyi spetsnaz*),[308] Prilepin's decision emblematically received the public praise of Sergei Lavrov, the Russian minister of foreign affairs (Ukraïns'ka Pravda 2017).

Finally, these dynamics came also to affect the contested field of the Russian-language literature developed at the Ukrainian-Russian borderland.[309] As emphasized by Mikhail Nazarenko (2014), whereas still in the

---

307 "Нацболы — некогда самая яркая из оппозиционных Путину сил — после присоединения к России Крыма поверили в возрождение русского имперского проекта. Они отправили на Донбасс по линии «Интербригад» около 2000 добровольцев и воевали сами. Но мечта о ДНР как о стране, где нацболам дадут заниматься политикой с оружием в руках и строить новую социальную справедливость, быстро рухнула."

308 "In general, when I began to reflect on this topic, this phrase came to my mind: 'We have special forces of Russian literature behind us.' We certainly knew that Gumilev, Lev Tolstoi were serving somewhere... But in fact this list is huge. In Russia, since the eighteenth century, I counted more than a hundred among poets and writers, whose life was directly connected with military service. Over here impostors of Russian literature began to prove that the Russian writer is such a little prick on thin legs which always speaks of children's tears or other touching things" (Kots 2017; Вообще, когда я стал заниматься этой темой, у меня в голове сформулировалась фраза: «За нами стоит спецназ русской литературы.» Мы конечно имели представление, что Гумилев служил где-то, Лев Толстой... Но на самом деле список этот огромен. В России с XVIII века я насчитал более сотни поэтов и писателей, у которых жизнь была напрямую связана с воинской службой. У нас самозванцы русской словесности стали доказывать, что русский литератор — это такой исусик на тонких ножках, который вечно говорит о слезинке ребенка и о прочих трогательных вещах).

309 Here it is worth mentioning also one of the rare reports on the situation in Crimea after its annexation to Russia. In her contribution *Crimea: The Interface*

1990s Ukrainian *fantasty* could remain outside of the realms of politics, writing and publishing for post-Soviet readers in Ukraine and abroad, it was in the 2000s, after the Orange Revolution and even more after the Euromaidan Revolution, that the situation changed: the historical and identity narratives crystallized, and it was also the self-identification of the authors, together with the readership addressed by Ukrainian *fantasty*, that changed. This is the case of the Ukrainian writers who authored books belonging to the series titled "Military and Historical Speculative Fiction" (*voennoistoricheskaia fantastika*), that was launched in 2008 by the Moscow-based publishing house Eksmo/Iauza. As a highly politicized genre, the series creates the ground for projecting Soviet history into the future: this is also testified by the publishing policy at Iauza, simultaneously publishing documentary book series devoted to the Soviet past and history, with a specific focus on the Stalin era, and patriotic *fantastika*.[310] It is no surprise that, as emphasized in the publisher's web page, the main task of the books issued by Iauza is to promote "the education of the military-patriotic spirit of the younger generation in Russia."[311] Amongst the most notable authors of the series we have two writers from Eastern Ukraine, Fedor Berezin (b. 1960, Donets'k) and Gleb Bobrov (b. 1964, Khrustal'nyi). Bobrov's novel *The Era of the Stillborn* (*Epokha mertvorozhdennykh*) and

---

Between Politics and Culture (2019), Tatjana Hofmann argued: "Despite the challenges, the peninsula is by no means of a cultural desert. More than 700 events per year—social, environmental and, in a narrower sense, cultural—are listed on the trilingual Culture Ministry's calendar, including Crimean Tatar and Jewish festivals, memorial events for the victims of deportation [...], First and Second World War remembrance, and literary events, notably the Gumilev Festival and the Voloshin Festival in Koktebel."

310 As Oleksandr Zabirko (2018: 121) argues in his study on contemporary speculative fiction: "While life in the USSR is being perceived here as the pre-thinning condition, the narratives of the series evolve from emotionally and nostalgically romanticizing the Soviet past towards outright resentment. Nostalgia does not mean here the intention to return or regain the lost object but instead refers to a political program which considers the Soviet past as a possible source of a new imperial patriotism (which, although predominantly Russian, is at least potentially an option for other former Soviet republics)."

311 "[...] воспитание военно-патриотического духа в подрастающем поколении России." See: http://yauza.info/ (08/2019).

Berezin's *War 2010: The Ukrainian Front* (*Voina 2010: ukrainskii front*) were published respectively in 2008 and 2009: while the first work is about a hypothetical civil war in Ukraine—and after 2014 acquired the status of a cult novel for his prophetic value, Berezin's novel projects this internal clash in the international arena. As emblematically argued by Oleksandr Zabirko (2018: 123):

> Despite the overall political bias of this *fantastika*, it is still surprising how many writers seized the occasion to take an active part in the war in Eastern Ukraine, grasping the chance to become the heroes of their own stories or rather to turn those stories into self-fulfilling prophecies. Probably, the most striking example is provided by Fedor Berezin, who in 2014 actually made it up to deputy minister of defence of the self-proclaimed Donetsk People's Republic.

At the Crossroads between Normative Measures and Blurred Cultural Boundaries in the Post-Soviet Space

The heterogeneous positions assumed by political and cultural actors in the contested struggle for identity markers in Ukrainian and Russian milieus reveal a controversial framework of tendencies. Generally, there is no doubt that the Euromaidan movement testified to a concrete rift in conceptualising national identity in Ukraine. It is no surprise that it has been significantly interpreted as a "postcolonial revolution" (Gerasimov 2014) or "the birth of a nation" (Goble 2015). It was also as a result of the prolonged Ukraine crisis that, paradoxically, the "undeclared Russo-Ukrainian war has catalysed the growth of Ukrainian civic rather than ethnic nationalism," that, according to Riabchuk, "was quite a rational and reasonable response of a bi-ethnic and bilingual society to the external military threat" (2015: 152).

In terms of a nation-building project born from below, this was a clear response to both the process of othering enacted by the Ukrainian elite and the ideological reappropriation of the *russkie* claimed by the Kremlin. Nonetheless, on the one hand, the difficult process of "deterritorialising," using Nemtsev's terms, the "Ukrainian Russianness" in the all-Ukrainian national discourse still clashes with the new normative measures adopted by the post-Maidan political class; on the other, after Putin's re-election in 2012 and the Ukraine crisis, interestingly enough, the idea of the Russian World implemented by the Kremlin "grew increasingly contentious and tended, on the whole, to fracture the very world it was designed to unify" (Gorham 2019: 201).

Eventually, the militarization of culture represents the latest step in the escalating "war of words" between Ukraine and Russia. Clearly, the war in Donbas also drew a rigid separation line between the Ukrainian and Russian cultural milieus: today the interrelation between the field of culture and the field of politics has become narrow as a direct result of the clash of discourses enacted by the respective political elites.[312]

---

312 The issue was debated by both Russian and Ukrainian cultural actors at the roundtable "Russia–Ukraine: War as a Factor of Politicisation in Literature" ("Rossiia–Ukraina: voina kak factor politizatsii literatury"), which was organized by the editors of the Russian online platform Gefter in April 2017 (see Gefter 2017).

Chapter 6 Towards a Postcolonial Ethics: Rewriting Ukraine in the "Enemy's Language"

The challenges of developing a utopian, postcolonial orientation in Ukraine, or any part of the former Soviet Union, are onerous. They include many tasks: recovering, maintaining, and honoring the memory of individual and collective victims of tyranny, but without the ressentiment against the former colonizer that many exercises in memory may engender; taking adequate account of the crimes and injustices perpetrated against the colonized, while also recognising the extent to which the colonized were themselves involved in these crimes and injustices [...] conceptualizing the past as an often dismal prelude to the future, but not a determinant of it; and, finally seeking models for the harmonious co-existence of former participants in the colonial relationship, even if this quest appears asymmetrical, and the desire for rapprochement one-sided. In Ukraine, all of these "tranquil lakes of the transmontane commune" appear more remote and inaccessible [...] in the midst of a neocolonial war, than at any time since independence.[313] (Pavlyshyn 2016b: 64)

As highlighted by Marko Pavlyshyn above, the "challenges of developing a utopian, postcolonial orientation in Ukraine [...] are onerous," especially today "in the midst of a neocolonial war." It is in the literary arena where the tenor of the debate seems to be "best captured by the term 'anti-colonial'," as being permeated by "cultural phenomena that assert the autonomy, dignity, and value of the colonized and resist the strategies of cultural colonialism" (Pavlyshyn 2016b: 62).

As a result of the prolonged war in Donbas, the strong patriotic mobilization created a fertile ground in Ukraine for ideologizing language

---

313 While describing postcolonialism as a utopian "orientation," Pavlyshyn in his study symbolically refers to the distant shimmer of the "tranquil lakes of the transmontane commune" in Mykhola Khvyl'ovyi's story "I: A Romantic Tale" (*Ia: romantyka*).

and culture—as being the projection of either "patriotic" or "enemy" attributes. Memory and language policies came to represent two controversial domains for the post-Maidan government, whereas "Ukrainian activists have been insisting that in view of the war with neoimperial Russia, Ukraine must cut all ties with the Moscow-led 'Russian World'" (Kulyk 2017: 1). Along these lines, as provocatively emphasized by the Ukrainian Russian-language literary critic Iurii Volodarskii (2017b), "since there is no opportunity to defeat the external enemy, even in the coming years, [...] compensation arises: the search for internal enemies begins."[314]

Today at the core of the debates is found again the eternal language issue, the myth, or better, the political "slogan" (*lozung*; Volodarskii 2017a), as suggested by Georgii Kas'ianov, that makes Russian an instrument of cultural hegemony implemented by the "occupier," the "enemy." Eventually, the misuse of language and historical myths imposed by political elites throughout the "Ukraine crisis," which has been examined in the previous chapter, created the ground for the interrelation between the field of politics and the field of culture, giving birth again to a tense and controversial situation.

These dynamics were actually observed by the Russian writer Dmitrii Bykov, in an article entitled "The Brain of Nations" ("Mozg natsii"), which looks at the recent developments in Russian-Ukrainian cultural relations:

> Maybe one day, Russian performers will still be able to perform in Ukraine, and Ukrainians will be able to do it in Russia. This is normal, like any cultural exchange. But they will have to sing and read in their own languages. The niche of the Russophone poet in Ukraine [*russkoiazychnyi poet na Ukraine*] is gradually disappearing, becoming impossible, since Russian is perceived as the language of the enemy. Whether it is so, it is a separate issue, we will not discuss it here. But during the war the nuances disappear [...] the third position becomes impossible

---

314 "Поскольку возможности победить внешнего врага нет и в ближайшие годы, [...] возникает компенсация, начинается поиск врагов внутренних."

now. For this, much has been done by both sides, and—by and large—this is the logic of history.[315] (Mironova, Bykov 2017)

Contrary to the situation outlined by Bykov, in this chapter we will investigate how the latest developments in the cultural scene show us that, in the case of Ukraine, there is still room for the rise of a "third position" stemming from a "postcolonial orientation."

Demistifying Anticolonial Myths: The "Ukrainian Russians"

There is no doubt that both the social environment and the cultural industry in Ukraine have undergone radical changes in the last few years. Amongst the most significant outcomes of the Euromaidan, according to Pavlyshyn (2016b: 79), is the phenomenon of Russian-language Ukrainian patriotism. Recent sociological research shows the unpredictable trajectories for ethnonational identifications in Ukraine, which have been influenced by recent events. Based on an analysis of mass surveys and focus group and public discourse data, Volodymyr Kulyk concludes in his study that:

> the increasing Ukrainianness of the Russian-speaking part of Ukraine's population means that most of these people do not cease to be Russian-speaking when becoming (more) Ukrainian. Indeed, the share of those using predominantly Russian in their everyday life decreased only marginally for the years of independence [...] Euromaidan and the war, while stimulating attachment to Ukrainian as the perceived national language and alienation from Russian as the perceived language of the aggressor, did not urge a considerable part of Ukraine's population to radically change their language practice. (2019b: 174)

The changing perceptions of such terms as nationality and language eventually come to affect the fluidity of the current framework of ethnonational identifications in Ukraine. Today, reframing the positioning of so-called Ukrainian Russians means changing terms such as language and ethnicity

---

315 "Какое-то время российские исполнители еще смогут выступать на Украине, а украинские — в России; это нормально, как любой культурный обмен. Но петь и читать они вынуждены будут на своих языках. Ниша русскоязычного поэта на Украине постепенно исчезает, становится невозможной, поскольку русский воспринимается как язык врага. Является ли он таковым — вопрос отдельный, обсуждать его мы здесь не будем; но во время войны нюансы исчезают [...] третья позиция становится невозможной. Для этого многое сделали обе стороны, а по большому счету — такова логика истории."

into more fluid identity markers. Considering the relevant share of mixed identifications, we should value "the important role of hybrid identifications as an intermediate state between the clear-cut designations by established categories" (Kulyk 2018a: 135). Most fundamentally, the changing meaning of Ukrainianness "from an ethnic to a civic criterion for membership" (Kulyk 2019b: 169) follows a process of deterritorialization of Russianness. This reflects not only a process of "shedding Russianness" and "recasting Ukrainianness," as emphasized by Kulyk (2018a), but is a clear attempt at recasting Russianness *within the frame of* Ukrainianness.

This may be the reason for Pavlyshyn's recognition of "postcolonial ethics" in Andrei Kurkov's positioning as a Ukrainian author writing in Russian, where "he exemplifies a postcolonial capacity to overcome the colonizer's hauteur without embracing the rancor of the colonized" (Palyshyn 2016b: 72). This emerging "orientation" is highly reflective of the position assumed by Russophone intellectuals and recent literary ventures in Ukraine. It is no surprise that in January 2018 Andrei Kurkov announced the need for *appropriating* Russian as a Ukrainian cultural good:

> The Russian language outside of Russia is an independent phenomenon. But, like in the case of Francophonie 150 years ago, Russia is trying to use the Russian language in its own interests. To limit the ability of Russia to protect the Russian language in Ukraine, it is necessary to recognize Ukrainian Russian-speaking [*ukrainskoe russkoiazychie*] as Ukrainian "cultural property" and to take Ukrainian Russian [*ukrainskii russkii*] under its philological control.[316] (Kurilenko 2018)

The stance taken by Kurkov responds to the need for creating a broader cultural space in Ukraine, including all the members of the Ukrainian civic nation. This is clearly a provocation aimed at responding to the rigid binarism enacted by both the Kremlin-sponsored Russian World concept and the exclusivist positions assumed by the most of Ukrainian-language elite, especially in post-Maidan times. Throughout recent years, the emerging "patriotic"

---

316 "Русский язык вне России является самостоятельным явлением. Но, как и в случае франкофонии 150 лет назад, Россия пытается использовать русскоязычие в своих интересах. Для ограничения возможности России защищать в Украине русский язык нужно признать украинское русскоязычие украинской «культурной собственностью» и взять украинский русский под свой филологический контроль."

position of Russophone intellectuals in Ukraine has gradually become "not enough," as argued by Kulyk (2018b: 66) in his analysis of the images of Russian speakers in social media for the entire year of 2016: "[w]hile most speakers of both Ukrainian and Russian languages increasingly see themselves as Ukrainians, some question the national belonging of those who continue to rely on the Russian language in various social practices." It was in 2017 that the proliferation of articles and commentaries on the language question—in the aftermath of the publication of the aforementioned draft laws on language policy in January that same year—testified again to the high level of interference of the political discourse in the cultural one. Thus, the prominent Ukrainian writer Serhii Zhadan described an ongoing "war against Russian, and not for Ukrainian language" (*borot'ba ne za ukraïns'ku movu, a proty rosiiskoï*; Novoe Vremia 2017), while the literary critic Oleksandr Boichenko (b. 1970, Chernivtsi) answered him by defending "the last remaining territory" (*ostannia terytoriia*) for the Ukrainian language, if compared to the Russian language's geopolitical space which stretches "from Kaliningrad to Petropavlovsk-Kamchatsky" (*vid Kalininhrada do Petropavlovs'ka-Kamchats'koho*; Boichenko 2017). Similarly, in late 2018, after the Ukrainian Rada approved the draft law N.5670-D *On Guaranteeing the Functioning of the Ukrainian Language as a State Language* at first reading, the cultural magazine *Sho* hosted a debate on the language question. In the issue titled *Everything Will Be Ukrainian—or How to Rip Off Russian* (*Vse bude Mova—ili vyrvat' Iazyk*), the editors critically addressed both the Ukrainian- and Russian-language intellectuals who supported the law (Volodarskii 2018a), and moreover did so in light of the complex outcomes that this would create for the publication of Russian-language cultural products.[317]

---

317 The publication of the issue shortly followed the official approval of regional laws restricting Russian-language cultural products in L'viv, Zhytomyr, Ternopil', and Ivano-Frankivs'k oblasts "until Russia stops its occupation of Ukrainian territory" (Krasnikov 2018. See also Unian 2018; Ukraïnska Pravda 2018a, 2018b). After the passing of the new national language bill at first reading in October 2018, the question was mainly around one of the law's articles, which stipulated that all media in Ukraine had to be in Ukrainian. This implied that all the periodicals published in other languages could be issued only if they also produced a Ukrainian version of the same size and content.

Thus, Andrei Kurkov's position is quite exceptional in the national literary scene, especially because of his high visibility in the West, and his decision to publish his works simultaneously in both Ukrainian and Russian.[318] This example of language inclusivity has been followed only recently by other members of the "niche of the Russophone poet," which was rather active in recasting *literary nationness* throughout recent years. This is the case for the two new anthologies recently published, respectively, by the Kharkiv-based Folio publishing house, and the Kyiv-based Lehenda. Aleksandr Krasovitskii, the publisher and editor of the volume *Ukrainian Prose and Poetry in Russian* (*Ukrainskaia proza i poeziia na russkom iazyke*, 2016), emphasized the need for reconsidering "Russian Ukrainian literature" [*Russkaia ukrainskaia literatura*] as an integral part of the great Ukrainian literature, especially in times of war.[319] The anthology includes works of authors who are "bilingual in everyday life" (*v zhizni dvuiazychny*), but whose literary production was usually published in their "native language" (*rodnoi iazyk*; Krasovitskii 2016: 3).[320] This

---

Eventually, in the final version of the law that was approved by the Parliament in April 2019, this norm remained valid only for Russian-language cultural products.

318 As the author retraced in our 2013 meeting in Kyiv: "It happened for the first time with *L'vivs'ka Hastrol Džimi Chendriksa* [*L'vivs'ka Hastrol Dzhiimi Khendriksa—The L'viv Tour of Jimi Hendrix*] (2012). It was an experiment. I agreed with the publishing house, Folio, to have the same diffusion for the two editions, and actually the Ukrainian edition has sold more than the Russian one. This could be explained by the active attitude of Ukrainian-speaking readers in the West rather than the passive one of the Russian-speaking readers" (Puleri 2016: 185).

319 "I am convinced that Ukraine has only one literature, the Ukrainian, which is made in the different languages of the people who inhabit our State" (Krasovitskii 2016: 3; Я убежден в том, что Украина имеет одну литературу — украинскую, но она создается на разных языках народов, населяюших наше государство).

320 As Chernetsky (2019: 67) argues, the "confusion about the book's title" is still "symptomatic" of the "current contradictory, transitory state of the Russophone literary scene in Ukraine": "originally it was to be titled *Russkaia proza i poeziia sovremennoi Ukrainy* (Russian prose and poetry of contemporary Ukraine), but several contributors insisted that the title be changed to *Ukrainskaia proza i poeziia na russkom iazyke* (Ukrainian prose and poetry

would also offer a wider overview of the most prominent contemporary Russian-language authors, from fantasy to poetry, for the Ukrainian readership, which is a challenging perspective, since until 2014 most Ukrainian Russian-language writers only published their works in Russia, and before the outbreak of the war they were more widely read in Russia rather than in Ukraine.[321] Another venture, which was undertaken by Donbas writers, goes significantly further by attempting to revise the canon from the East. As Ivan Dziuba emphasized in the preface, the anthology of Ukrainian writers from Donbas, titled *Poroda* (Rock, or Breed), clearly aims to show how the "Ukrainian Word and the Russian Word" (*ukraïns'ke Slovo i rosiis'ke*

---

in Russian). Whether deliberately or as a result of an oversight, both titles are present in the final work."

321 With regard to the latest developments of the literary market, it is worth mentioning the results of the project Ukrainian Reading and Publishing Data 2018—see: http://data.chytomo.com/en/pro-proekt/ (08/2019). This mapping of the Ukrainian publishing market and readership was organized in 2018 by the web platform Chytomo, together with the publishing house Gutenbergz and the sociological centre Razumkov. As for my research, amongst the most interesting results, we witness that "to the majority of Ukrainians the language question is not determinant in choosing a book," while still 33.3 % of respondents prefer reading books in the original edition, 28.3 % of respondents prefer reading in Russian, 24.2 % in Ukrainian, and to 12 % of respondents it was equally comfortable to read in any language they understand. Whereas the latter data remained quite stable, the only results highly differentiating from the previous survey in 2014 regard the preference for Russian-language books, which decreased by 20 %—see: http://data. chytomo.com/knyzhka-za-tsinoyu-obidu-skilky-ukrayintsi-gotovi-platyty-za-chytannya-ukrayintsi-3/ (08/2019). Furthermore, the latest data published by the State Book Chamber of Ukraine showed that amongst the books published in Ukraine in 2018 (22,612 editions), 16,857 editions were in the Ukrainian language (38,107.4 thousand copies) and 3,253 editions were in the Russian language (6.106.2). The same data in 2013, the last year before the beginning of the Ukraine crisis, reported 16,310 editions in Ukrainian (37,892.9) and 7,198 in Russian (27,652.0) out of 26,323 editions in total—see: http://www. ukrbook.net/statistika/statistika_2013.htm (08/2019); http://www.ukrbook. net/statistika/statistika_2018.htm (08/2019). In general, we see how the total number of book titles published in the Ukrainian market in 2018 has returned

Slovo) can coexist in harmony within the Ukrainian literary space. Dziuba explains further that:

> Maybe [...] this anthology should have appeared earlier. Of course, it would not affect the course of events, but it would have helped the Ukrainian community better understand the nature and the reasons behind what is happening in Donbas, and also—this is not less important—it would have helped see how the Ukrainian Word and the Russian Word in the mouths of the honest and responsible sons of our country sound in unison, when it comes to human dignity and the right to life in freedom. In Ukraine.[322] (Dziuba 2017: 19)

The authors included in *Poroda: An Anthology of Ukrainian Writers of Donbas* (*Poroda: Antolohiia ukraïns'kykh pys'mennykiv Donbasu*), which was edited by Veniamin Beliavskii (Veniamin Biliavs'kyi; b. 1949, Donets'k) and Nikita Grigorov (Mykyta Gryhorov; b. 1994, Donets'k)—both of whom emigrated from Donets'k to Kyiv in 2014, are from the Donets'k and Luhans'k regions, or they spent part of their literary career there. More than 60 authors who write poetry or prose, from the second half of the twentieth century until the present, are taking part in the creation of Donbas regional literature as Ukrainians. Oleh Kotsarev observes that the latest texts are particularly important, because "they manifest the self-identification of the writers as Ukrainian authors and record it for history"[323] (Kotsarev 2018). Russian-language authors such as Nikita Grigorov, Iia Kiva, Elena Stiazhkina and Vladimir Rafeenko, together with Ukrainian-language authors such as Serhii Zhadan, Liubov Iakymchuk (b. 1985, Pervomais'k) and Oleksii Chupa (b. 1986, Makiïvka), can thus help "solidify the Ukrainian myth of Donbas" (*tsementuiut' ukraïns' kyi mif Donbasu*; Kotsarev 2018). This is an important step for encouraging

---

to "pre-crisis" levels, while the overall book circulation still remains low (see Khmel'ovs'ka 2019).

322 "Мабуть, [...] ця Антологія, мала б з'явитися раніше. Звісно, на хід подій вона б невплинула, але допомогла б українській громадськості краще зрозуміти сутність і причини того, що відбувається на Донбасі, а ще — і це не менш важливо — побачити, як українське Слово і російське Слово в устах чесних та відповідальних синів нашої країни звучать в унісон, коли йдеться про людську гідність і право на життя у свободі. В Україні."

323 "[...] вони маніфестують самоідентифікацію письменників як авторів українських. І фіксують її для історії."

the integration process in contemporary Ukrainian society, especially since many cultural actors from Donbas, and also Crimea, were forced to move to the other centres of Ukrainian cultural life. Along these lines, Rafeenko's latest book, *The Length of Days* (*Dolgota dnei*, 2017), which was published in Ukrainian translation by the L'viv publishing house Staroho Leva (*Dovhi chasy*, 2017—translated by Marianna Kiianovs'ka), and in Russian by the Kharkiv-based Fabula, was included in the broader project launched by the latter publishing house aimed at creating a series devoted to "Contemporary Ukrainian Prose," including both Russian- and Ukrainian-language authors. Similarly, for the first time, literary works such as *Victory Park* (2016— translated by Viktoriia Merenkova) and *Mahjong* (2017—translated by Olena Iakymenko), which were previously only available in the Russian market, have been published in Ukrainian, eventually making their author Aleksei Nikitin, a Russophone writer from Kyiv, a "Ukrainian cultural phenomenon."

Transgressing the (National) Code: Recasting History and Language in Light of War

The radical changes that have occurred in Ukrainian society in the last few years lie at the core of most of its cultural production. Euromaidan and the war in Donbas have been the subject of a series of literary works in which intellectuals have tried to analyse and grasp the history of their country according to different perspectives and stances. In this section I will focus on works by Russophone writers based in Kyiv—Aleksei Nikitin, Aleksandr Kabanov and Vladimir Rafeenko.[324] Their works, written and published shortly before and after the start of the "crisis" (i.e. in 2013–2017), provide a challenging way to reflect on the potential room for "postcolonial ethics" within the "niche" of Ukrainian Russophone literature.

Reading Aleksei Nikitin's *Victory Park* (2014), we can see how today new narratives contribute to the formation of pluricentric perspectives on the history of Ukraine in the twentieth century, offering a way out from

---

324 Rafeenko moved from Donets'k to Kyiv only in 2014, in the aftermath of the start of the war in Donbas.

an "anti-colonial" perception of Soviet history in the national canon. As Nikitin argued in a 2016 interview,

> Ukraine is constantly set in rigidly fixed historical frames, constantly correlating it with the past, whereas the experiences of the past were not stories of success. And it is this obsession with bad history, with bad experience, that must be overcome. The success of the Ukrainian movement lies not in clinging to the past, but in finding a new perspective, and giving up negative experience.[325] (In Kyiv 2016)

Significantly, the world in miniature which is contained in Nikitin's 2014 novel mirrors the search for an answer to the "ideological void" (*ideologicheskaia pustota*; Sokhareva 2014) of the Ukrainian capital on the eve of the Soviet collapse. *Victory Park*, which was published in Russia in early 2014—slightly before the start of the war in East Ukraine—and was awarded the Russkaia Premiia that same year, is divided into three sections and is entirely set within a time frame which lasts from Spring to Fall 1984. The author justifies this temporal setting as the only one able to restore the familiar, and at the same time estranging, atmosphere of late Soviet everyday life before the collapse of the regime: as the author emphasized in the preface to the Italian edition, "1984 is the last year of the Soviet Union in its truest form" (Nikitin 2019: 7). Most importantly, *Victory Park* is the fictional re-elaboration of a historical research methodically conducted by its author. It is no surprise that, in introducing the Ukrainian edition of the novel in 2016, the Ukrainian historian Oleksii Tolochko described *Victory Park* as a true "document of Kyiv history" (*dokument kyïvs'koï istoriï*; Tolochko 2016: 3): this should not be mistaken for "an instant picture of a frozen epoch" (*fotohrafichnyi znimok zastyhloho chasu*), but as the first novel to tell the history of Kyiv from an alternative perspective, which is embodied in the novel by the Victory Park in the title, which is set on the left bank of the Dnipro River, at the edges of Kyiv. As Nikitin's

---

325 "Украина постоянно находится в жестко поставленных исторических рамках, постоянно соотносит себя с прошлым, а ситуации прошлого не были историями успеха. И эта зацикленность на дурной истории, на дурном опыте, который надо преодолевать. Успех украинского движения состоит в том, чтобы не цепляться за прошлое, находить новое, отказываться от тяжелого негативного опыта."

narrator puts it in a passage of the novel, Left Bank Kyiv is "the stepchild" of Ukrainian history:

> Everything that Nestor later wrote about, everything that the history teachers told to their bored students, took place on the right bank. There, Prince Vladimir baptized the people of Kyiv, Iaroslav defeated the Cumans and built Saint Sophia's Cathedral, and Iurii Dolgorukii, poisoned by the boyars, died of vomit and spasms. The left bank is the stepchild of history.[326] (Nikitin 2014: 37)

Besides not having been the privileged theatre of the millenarian history of Kyiv, "the left bank was not Kyiv, not even from a juridical point of view"[327] (Nikitin 2014: 38): it is only after the end of the Second World War, and the great "Victory" over Nazism, that Soviet modernity reaches this area. It is no coincidence that Nikitin tells us about the process of building over this territory in Soviet times through the metaphorical representation of an overwhelming military advance. As the narrator puts it, "Kyiv came to these places after the war, unexpectedly and swiftly"[328] (Nikitin 2014: 39). Thus, war is also a central element of the novel, but it works here as a cultural substratum of everyday life in late Soviet times: the novel is emblematically set in a public space, the Victory Park in the title, which was created to commemorate the war, and in a city neighbourhood which arose in the aftermath of the war. This is a tool that enables the author to tell a history which "has not been told yet," the history of "the pacific everyday life of the Soviet Kyivans" (Nikitin 2019: 8). The novel can be thus described as an essential bestiary of late-Soviet life in Kyiv: a bestiary reflecting the Soviet history of the Ukrainian capital "from below," restoring the collective memory of a lost generation. Here the Victory Park also plays the important role of an illusory bond between different layers of the history of Kyiv: on the one hand, the Ocherety neighbourhood, an old fishermen's village embodying the traditional life and customs on the Left Bank of

---

326 "Все, о чем потом писал Нестор, все, что рассказывали скучающим школьникам учителя истории, происходило на правом берегу. Там крестил киевлян князь Владимир, побеждал половцев и строил Святую Софию Ярослав, умирал в блевотине и судорогах отравленный боярами Юрий Долгорукий. Левый берег — пасынок истории."

327 "Левый берег не был Киевом, не был им даже юридически […]."

328 "Киев пришел в эти места после войны, неожиданно и стремительно."

the Dnipro River; on the other, the Komsomol' neighbourhood, a Soviet district which was formed in the aftermath of the Second World War and inhabited by young students, workers and officials from different regions of the Soviet Union. Thus, Victory Park becomes a "no man's land, a neutral boundary that not only separated the Komsomol' district from Ocherety, but also allowed the Kyivans to clarify controversial ideological questions related to the world view, without necessarily attracting the attention of the police"[329] (Nikitin 2014: 44). The main characters of the novel are the regular visitors to the Park, who symbolically represent a kaleidoscope of people, stories, successes and failures characterizing the Soviet experience. As described by the narrator, it was especially the Komsomol' district that embodied the results of the migration processes enacted from the top of the regime, repopulating the city largely with young people coming from Minsk, Baku and Leningrad. These "new Kyivans" had few chances to get acquainted with the multiple and contested narratives of Ukrainian history:

> All of them knew little about Kyiv. What they knew could easily fit the narrow confines of history courses at school, so there was still enough space for urban legends and the most absurd fairy tales. They did not see the former Khreshchatyk or the pre-war Kalinin Square. They did not even know Ukraine, they considered it like Russia, perhaps only a little different and strange.[330] (Nikitin 2014: 42)

Throughout the novel, the reconstruction of the bonds between the old and the new Kyiv is symbolically undertaken by the two protagonists: Bagila, from the Ocherety district, and Pelikan, who lives in the Komsomol' district. Their friendship is also the narrative point of intersection between the three parts of the novel. Ivan Bagila is a university student who experiences the world under the wing of his grandfather Maksim, a renowned and admired member of the Ocherety community. Significantly, it is Maksim

---

329 "[...] той ничейной землей, нейтральной полосой, которая не просто разделяла Комсомольский массив и Очереты, но позволяла им, не привлекая ненужного внимания сил охраны общественного порядка, выяснять спорные мировоззренческие вопросы."

330 "Все они знали о Киеве мало, а то, что знали, запросто умещалось в узких рамках школьного курса истории, так что оставалось достаточно свободного места для баек и совсем уж невообразимых басен. Они не видели ни прежнего Крещатика, ни довоенной площади Калинина. Не знали они и Украины,

who first repudiates his son Semen after his decision to move to Russia, and then suggests that his grandson Ivan enrol in Russian school, in order to handle "the language of power" (*iazyk vlasti*; Nikitin 2014: 68) and to read between the lines. Everybody in Kyiv considers Maksim as endowed with the gift of seeing the future and the mysterious and obscure past of the country, since he had taken part in all the main events of Ukrainian history in the first half of the twentieth century:

> In the first half of the twentieth century, Ukraine turned out to be the most dangerous place in Europe. Here, those who survived were not the strongest ones, but those who were prudent and flexible. A well-developed conservation instinct was worth more than any other natural talent. It is not a surprise that later many people did not dare or simply did not want to tell their children how they lived in the years from the beginning of the First to the end of the Second World War. That is also the story of Maksim Bagila: even the people close to him knew very little.[331] (Nikitin 2014: 66)

Pelikan, from the Komsomol district, is Ivan's best friend. He comes from a family of historians and archaeologists, but significantly decides to reject the family legacy of researching the controversial national history and, while longing for an "exact science," enrols together with Bagila in the Advanced School of Physics and Mathematics.

At the end of the novel, Pelikan's failures and frustration bring him to volunteer for military service in Afghanistan. Thus, it seems that the ideological and existential void of late Soviet Kyiv can be filled only by the distorted echoes of a collective memory that is conveyed "from the top," the memory of a past war which was appropriated by the Soviet official discourse. Emblematically, in his 2014 novel Nikitin also comes to portray the "lyric dimension" of the fragmented lives of those who truly experienced war, and significantly are no longer able to talk, living on the margins of society: between old and new wars, and—namely—between old and new veterans. The so-called *afgantsy*, the veterans coming back from

---

считая ее той же Россией, только разве что немного другой и какой-то странной."

331 "В первой половине двадцатого века Украина оказалась самым опасным местом в Европе. Здесь выживали не сильные, а гибкие и осторожные. Развитый инстинкт самосохранения стоил всех прочих природных талантов. Надо ли удивляться, что многие потом не решались или просто не хотели

the Afghan war, are also amongst the regular visitors to the Park and the main protagonists of the novel:

> They were returning from some wild world, of which we knew almost nothing, and we did not really want to know about. The former "right" veterans once defended and liberated their home, their country, and now they carefully attended solemn rallies, patiently stood in the tribunes and took flowers from the pioneers. They did not quiver with anger and resentment, because they knew what they had fought for, because the entire nation had fought with them. And the veterans of the war in Afghanistan did not have time to understand anything, even after returning home [...] The "Afghans" found each other, recognized each other in the crowd [...] The past gathered them together, and if they simply sat in silence, they were silent about the same thing.[332] (Nikitin 2014: 116)

As described by the narrator, in the memory storage of the Kyiv community *Afgantsy* cannot be considered as the "right" veterans of a glorious war, but only as the "cultural relics" of a silenced experience. They are the "second-class veterans" of a silenced collective memory.[333] Eventually,

---

     рассказывать детям, как жили с начала Первой и до окончания Второй мировой войны. Вот и про Максима Багилу даже самые близкие ему люди знали очень немного."

332 "Они возвращались из какого-то дикого мира, о котором здесь не знали почти ничего, да и не очень хотели знать. Это прежние «правильные» ветераны когда-то защищали и освобождали свой дом, свою страну, а теперь аккуратно ходили на торжественные митинги, терпеливо стояли на трибунах, принимали цветы у пионеров. Их не трясло от обиды и ярости, потому что они знали, за что воевали, потому что с ними вместе воевал весь народ. А афганцы не успели ничего понять, даже вернувшись домой [...] Афганцы находили друг друга, узнавали в толпе [...] Прошлое собирало их вместе, и если они просто сидели молча, то молчали об одном и том же."

333 "At first people pitied them, but pity soon turned into irritation. The 'Afghans' enjoyed some kinds of benefits: they could buy some goods at a lower price and could even skip the queues. But the rapidly impoverishing State of eternal queues could no longer maintain what it had promised to the veterans of all its overt and covert, secret wars. As a result of a long-term habit, civil servants were ready to somehow serve the generation of their parents, old people, veterans of the Second World War. For this reason, the boys returning from Kabul, Herat and Jalalabad were answered from almost every official's mouth: 'It's not us who sent you to Afghanistan'" (Nikitin 2014: 116–117; Сперва их жалели, но жалость быстро сменилась раздражением. Афганцам полагались какие-то льготы, что-то им должны были продавать дешевле, где-то пропускать без

Victory Park shows how fiction can fill the gaps of cultural memory, especially for the "ability to make contact zones effective as literature" (Smola, Uffelmann 2016: 21). At the core of Nikitin's work, significantly, lies the reconstruction of historical topics and everyday cultural experiences, facing the binary "antagonisms between what has been censored and uncensored, the canonical and the apocryphal, the orthodox and the heretical, the central and the marginal, all of which makes for a cultural dynamism" (Assmann 2006: 25). In 2016, Nikitin published a *povest'* inspired by the Euromaidan events, entitled *The Orderly from Institutskaia Street (Sanitar s Institutskoi,* 2016), and put out by the Kyiv publishing house Liuta Sprava.[334] The work tells the story of the poet Iurko Nezhoda and his friend Umanets', who meet in the late 1980s in Kyiv and start a literary journal, while living through harsh economic conditions, until the outburst of Euromaidan. The main narrative follows the story of the Nezhoda family through the events of Ukrainian history of the late nineteenth and the early twentieth century. Nikitin uses this narrative tool for revisiting the memory of the World Wars and destabilizing the national intellectual debate. In his literary work, therefore, history is depicted as a game, as something impossible to grasp in its entirety:

> *The Seven Steps of the Patriot* was the most striking and scandalous document of the radical movement for Ukrainian independence at the turn of the nineteenth and twentieth centuries. Nezhoda compiled the doctrine of the new (and of course, secret) revolutionary organization shortly after the dispersal of the Bohun society. Then, he was not twenty yet. Today *The Seven Steps* can be found in the school curriculum, with comments designed to soften their hard and, by modern standards, quite racist character. They are interpreted with a sullen, inhuman

---

очереди, но стремительно нищающее государство вечных очередей уже не могло выполнить все, что наобещало ветеранам всех своих явных и тайных, засекреченных войн. По многолетней привычке чиновники были готовы кое-как обслуживать поколение своих родителей, стариков, ветеранов Второй мировой но мальчишки, вернувшиеся из-под Кабула, Герата и Джелалабада, едва не из каждой чиновничьей пасти слышали: «А мы вас в Афганистан не посылали»)."

334 The first edition of the *povest'* was published in the journal *Druzhba Narodov*, with the title "Shkil'-mozdil'." See: Nikitin, Aleksei (2016). *Shkil'-mozdil'.* "Druzhba Narodov." 1. Available at: https://magazines.gorky.media/ druzhba/2016/1/shkil-mozdil.html (07/2019).

seriousness [...] Meanwhile, it was more a game than the result of reflections and party discussions. The game of a strong and lively mind, mocking and simultaneously romantic, but still only a game.[335] (Nikitin 2016: 60)

The ludic memory of Petro Nezhoda—Iurko's ancestor who experienced the tumultuous events of the twentieth century—embodies the empty value of historical narratives which still influence the perception of the present. Nikitin confirmed that he used the historical figure of Mykola Mikhnovs'kyi, ideologue and leader of the Ukrainian national movement in the early twentieth century, as a real prototype for Petro Nezhoda: "His story was tragic, like in general the stories of all the Ukrainian political actors of his time"[336] (In Kyiv 2016). The story of the Nezhoda family can thus be read as a deconstruction of the rigid historical narratives of the Ukrainian present. Along these same lines, the position assumed by Iurko Nezhoda, the main character of Nikitin's *povest'*, shows how the solution to the obsession with "family history" can be found only in the aftermath of the Maidan revolution:

What matters now is that our entire country is just depressed by its own history. It drags it on and on, like a burden [...] "It does not matter what it really was," said Nezhoda, "it is important that we understand it now. The past must remain in museums. And in theaters, in cinema, in adventure novels. Cursed, beaten, hundreds of times redeemed and changed to complete inconsistency. Enough to walk around the circle and fall into the old pits [...] We always struggle unsuccessfully with someone, and then we mourn the dead. We fight and then mourn, and again fight and again mourn [...] For centuries, for millennia. And the result

---

335 "*Семь шагов патриота* — самый яркий и скандальный документ радикального движения за украинскую независимость на рубеже XIX и XX веков. Незгода составил этот катехизис новой (конечно же, тайной) революционной организации, вскоре после разгона Богунского общества. Тогда ему еще не было двадцати. Сейчас *Семь шагов* можно найти в школьной программе, правда, с комментариями, призванными смягчить их жесткий, а по современным меркам вполне расистский характер. Их толкуют с угрюмой, нечеловеческой серьезностью [...] Между тем, это была скорее игра, чем результат размышлений и партийных дискуссий. Игра ума сильного и живого, насмешливого и одновременно настроенного до крайности романтически, но все же только игра."

336 "История его была трагична, как в общем и всех украинских деятелей того времени."

is out of the window [...] A bad dichotomy, from which it's already time to get out."[337] (Nikitin 2016: 148–149)

Eventually Iurko Nezhoda and Umanets' escape the "bad dichotomy" of Ukrainian history by joining the Maidan Revolution. As Umanets' concludes, in a country "without a state," "we will do all the necessary with our own hands"[338] (Nikitin 2016: 175). The way out of memory wars comes from understanding the cyclical nature of reoccurring wars and revolutions in these "bloody lands at the crossroads of civilizations" (*krovavye zemli na styke tsivilizatsii*; Rafeenko 2016), as described by Nikitin in a 2016 interview. And this introduces new ground, where one can find a new kind of positioning, a third way:

> It is important to see what is happening now on historical scale, even though on a small one. Cosmopolitan views were always important to me, and it is important to me to preserve them now. Strictly speaking, I never felt myself belonging exclusively to the Ukrainian or the Russian culture. The formation of my personality was influenced by a wide range of philosophers, writers, cultural and historical figures. And I feel that they taught me the right things. For example, the ideas of liberalism [...] And the priority of universal values [...] There remained a fundamental localization, i.e. Kyiv as a place for life. And the Russian language as a tool of thinking: this is exactly a key characteristic of my perception and description of the world, and my relation to it.[339] (Rafeenko 2016)

---

337 "— Важно то, что вся наша страна точно так же придавлена своей историей. Она тащит ее на себе как гирю. [...] — Не важно, как было на самом деле, — отмахнулся Незгода, — важно, что сейчас мы это поняли. Прошлое должно остаться в музеях. В театрах, в кино, в приключенческих романах. Оплаканное, обыгранное, сотни раз перепридуманное, измененное до полного несходства. Хватит уже ходить по кругу и проваливаться в старые ямы. [...] — Мы все время с кем-то безуспешно боремся, а потом скорбим о погибших. Боремся — скорбим, боремся — скорбим [...] Веками, тысячелетиями. А результат вон, за окном [...] Дурная дихотомия, из которой давно уже пора выбраться."

338 "Сейчас Украина — страна без государства [...] мы все сделаем сами" (Nikitin 2016: 175).

339 "Важно видеть происходящее, пусть в небольшом, но историческом масштабе. Затем для меня всегда была актуальна некоторая космополитичность взглядов и для меня важно сохранять её. Строго говоря, я никогда не ощущал себя принадлежащим исключительно к украинской или к русской культуре. На формирование моей личности оказал влияние очень широкий круг философов, литераторов, культурных и исторических деятелей. И

A similar position has been assumed by the Russian-language poet Aleksandr Kabanov, who in his work *In the Language of the Enemy* (*Na iazyke vraga*, 2017) clearly aims to demystify the logics of alienation enacted by the war, engaging in a "critique of reduced self-identification" (Kukulin 2016: 179). The volume collects both poems written in times of turmoil (2014–2017), and selected texts from the author's vast body of literary production, thus offering a broader overview of the poet's reflection on self-identification. The unifying key point is clearly stated in the opening pages of the volume: "Language is not guilty. It is always men who are guilty" (*Iazyk ne vinovat. Vsegda vinovaty liudi*; Kabanov 2017: 3).

In his artistic universe, Kabanov thus translates the forms of cultural tradition, reconverting them into a new "language of objects" (*iazyk predmetov*), where an epos made of "historical and literary figures" (*personazhi istorii i literatury*) and "animated statues" (*ozhivshie pamiatniki*) takes shape (Muratkhanov 2011: 194). At the core of his production lies the demystification of both the Russian and the Ukrainian historical narratives, as we witness in the parodic versions of the biblical exodus in the poems "The Exodus of Muscovites" ("Iskhod moskvichei," 2009), which was included in the 2017 collection, and "The Exodus of Ukrainians" ("Iskhod ukraintsev," 2010):

> [...] and now Ukrainian gas is burning in the hobs,
> now the Chechen special forces are walking along the Arbat, [...]
> there are no true Muscovites in the city.
> Above the boiling MKAD rises Alighieri Dant,
> in his hand he has a red-hot hydrant,
> his people leads to desert clouds [...][340] (Kabanov 2017: 81)
> – Who is that?—will ask strangers from the mist.
> – It's us, Ukrainians,—the elephants will sound in response.

есть ощущение, что они меня научили правильным вещам. Скажем, идеи либерализма [...] И приоритет общечеловеческих ценностей [...] Осталась принципиальная локализация — Киев как место для жизни. И русский язык как инструмент мышления. Именно он — ключевая характеристика моего восприятия мира, описания мира и отношения к нему."

340 "[...] а теперь в конфорках горит украинский газ, / а теперь по Арбату гуляет чеченский спецназ, [...] / не осталось в городе истинных москвичей. / Над кипящим МКАДом высится Алигьери Дант, / у него в одной руке белеет раскаленный гидрант, /свой народ ведет в пустынные облака [...]."

– It's us, Ukrainians,—the pigs will grunt in response.
– It's us, Ukrainians,—will shout a couple of Muscovites,
that we took with us to never, never
forget that we are Ukrainians.[341] (Kabanov 2014: 133)

While reading Kabanov's poems, Muratkhanov (2011: 195) suggests that "terror" (*uzhaz*) emerges after "laughter" (*smekh*), but that both emotions find their common ground in perceiving "the absurdity of existence, the proximity of the end, the exhaustion of history" (*absurd bytiia, blizost' kontsa, ischerpannost' istorii*). Eventually, the recent war and the traumatic events that took place in Ukraine highlight the difficult path experienced by the lyrical subject, while imagining a new place for the "Ukrainian Russians," outside the "bad dichotomy" inscribed in the national code:

The Ilovaisk curve,
Memory with a view of the ruin:
I lived in the language of the enemy,
I died for Ukraine.[342] (Kabanov 2017: 6)

In his reading of Kabanov's poems, Chernetsky (2019: 65) identifies the "main drivers of this writing" in the "[t]reatment of Ukrainophone culture at an ironic distance and identification of Russophone Ukrainian culture with the speaker's trauma." Along these lines, the scholar does not recognize any "gestures" that could "signal success in working through trauma" (Chernetsky 2019: 64), thus giving birth to a potential "postcolonial ethics."

Expressing a different outlook, in an interview with Vladimir Rafeenko, published under the long and telling title "The Posthumous Adventures of a Bell-Ringer: How the Writer R. Left the City of Z for the Country U, and Along the Way He Died and Wrote a Novel" ("Posmertnye prikliucheniia zvonaria: Kak pisatel' R. uekhal iz goroda Z v stranu U, po doroge umer i napisal roman"), a sort of intellectual manifesto of the Ukrainian

---

341 "— Кто это там? — спросят чужие люди из тумана. / — Это мы, украинцы, — протрубят в ответ слоны. / — Это мы, украинцы, — захрюкают в ответ свиньи. / — Это мы, украинцы, — выкрикнет парочка москвичей, / которых мы взяли с собой, чтобы никогда, никогда / не забывать о том, что мы — украинцы."

342 "Иловайская дуга, / память с видом на руину: / жил — на языке врага, / умирал — за Украину." Translation by Vitaly Chernetsky (2019: 64).

Russophone writer from Donbas takes shape. This emblematically mirrors the long journey from marginality to recognition that has been experienced by most Russophone authors throughout recent years in independent Ukraine. Paraphrasing Krigel"s words, R(afeenko) is a Russian-language writer from Donets'k (the city of Z, in his novels), who moved to the capital of the country U(kraine) in the aftermath of the start of the war in his hometown in 2014, and gradually entered the Ukrainian literary scene, experiencing a "new life" as a "true" Ukrainian author.

The divergent editorial destiny of Rafeenko's dilogy of the city of Z highly reflects the interference and impact of political and social dynamics in the process of the literary recognition of Russophone literature, still at the crossroads between pre- and post-Maidan times: the first novel of the dilogy, *The Descartes' Demon* (*Demon Dekarta*), was first published in Russia in 2013, and won the first prize of the Russkaia Premiia the same year; the second novel, *The Length of Days* (*Dolgota dnei*), was first published in 2017 in Ukrainian translation (*Dovhi chasy*—translated by Marianna Kiianovs'ka) by the L'viv publishing house Staroho Leva, and then won the Visegrad Eastern Partnership Literary Award and entered the shortlist for the Shevchenko National Prize in 2018. Interestingly, while commenting on the success of Rafeenko's *The Descartes' Demon* in Russia, the Russian critic Ekaterina Dais (2013b) could still argue in 2013 that the case of the Donets'k writer confirmed once again how, "[a]s usual, the path of the Ukrainian writer to fame lies either through Berlin or through Moscow."[343] However, the publication of *The Length of Days* in 2017 by one of the most prominent Ukrainian publishing houses testifies to the swift and growing recognition of Russophone writers in the Ukrainian cultural context in the post-Maidan era.[344]

Both novels reflect Rafeenko's interest in artistic reflection on the Donbas myth-making throughout the history of independent Ukraine. As the author emphasized, the post-Soviet myth about Donbas' and Donets'k'

---

343 "Как и обычно, путь украинского писателя к известности лежит либо через Берлин, либо через Москву."

344 The original edition in Russian of *The Length of Days* was then issued the same year by the Kharkiv-based publishing house Fabula. In our analysis of the novel, we will refer to this edition.

"wild steppes" revolves mainly around the idea of a "separate territory" (*otdel'naia territoriia*; Pomerantsev, I. 2019), which is detached from both Ukraine and Russia, but still linked to the latter by a "common language" and a Soviet past. This "was created intensively in the Nineties, a feeling of abandonment, neglect, isolation, and hopelessness in fact"[345] (Pomerantsev, I. 2019).

In the first novel, *The Descartes' Demon*, the "wild steppes" of the city of Z are symbolically paralyzed by a sortilege that ties miners to the fate of their enterprise.[346] The title of the work refers to the tradition of Cartesian rationalism and its methodological scepticism: the "doubt" that a "devil" may have surrounded us with deceptions on our path to understanding reality. The protagonist of the novel, Ivan Levkin, becomes the true demiurge of an imaginary and threatening city of miners, as emerges already in the first pages of *The Descartes' Demon*: "After a hot day, almost like in Summer, a northerly wind swoops down on the city of Z and its suburbs. It whips farms, villages [...] circles around haystacks, which during the winter are pitted by goats, cows and demons"[347] (Rafeenko 2014: 9). Levkin's world is "the world of a schizophrenic" (*mir shizofrenika*; Dais 2013b), which gives birth to a reality in which every individual is accompanied by a demon, a metaphysical companion. At the dawn of the opening of the city's factory, the characters move in a world where everything is suspended.[348]

---

345 "Это создавалось интенсивно в 90-е годы, ощущение некоторой оставленности, брошенности, изолированности, такой безысходности на самом деле."

346 "The demon controls everything [...] And he would wipe off the earth the city and all of us, if only we let stop the factory [...] Our forefathers allied with the demon of illusion for coal and steel. And now the demon wants to live here" (Rafeenko 2014: 223–224; Демон всем управляет [...] И он сотрет с лица земли этот город и всех нас, как только мы позволим остановить завод [...] Наши деды и прадеды заключили союз с демоном иллюзий ради угля и стали. И теперь он желает тут жить).

347 "После жаркого, почти летнего дня на город Z и его предместья налетает северный ветер. Он хлещет хутора, поселки [...] кружит вокруг стогов сена, изъеденных за зиму козами, коровами, бесами."

348 "And the snow mounds along the roadsides, at the switchmen's booths, at the columns supporting the bridge and at the porticoes of temples, do not want to melt. No way. In some places snow piled up to the architrave. It is

The only way out from the demon's "illusion" is found in the possibility of *dis-identifying* from the historical narratives:

> What is history, if nothing other than pure fantasy? What is a fact, if nothing other than an interpretation? [...] If you control the illusion, you can get peace. If you reject it, you remain a slave. Save yourselves with love and conscience, guys, I implore you! And nothing else![349] (Rafeenko 2014: 237–238)

In the last pages of the book, the illusory world portrayed in this "novel-dream" (*roman-snovidenie*), the subtitle of The *Descartes' Demon*, is emblematically—and prophetically—shaken by the entrance of the army into the city of Z and the start of the war. It is then in the second part of the dilogy, *The Length of Days*, which Rafeenko wrote in 2014–2015, that the war lies at the core of the events taking place in a literary setting which is reminiscent of "the dimension of García Márquez's Macondo or Faulkner's Yoknapatawpha"[350] (Krigel' 2016).

Rather than being narrowly focused on describing of the war dynamics, this "urban ballad" (*gorodskaia ballada*)—the subtitle of *The Length of Days*—embodies the experience of loss that many people, like Rafeenko, had to undergo in deciding whether to stay or to leave their hometown and their friends. As Rafeenko puts it, "the novel is rather focused on the history of human existence, which has to undergo some metamorphoses together with society [...]"[351] (Pomerantsev, I. 2019). The structure of the book also reflects

---

not possible to pass, either to the priest or to the tourist. It is not even possible to look at the columns or to restore the Corinthian capital. You can just walk around it. Cry and drink. Drink and sing." (Rafeenko 2014: 8; И никак не желают таять снежные холмы по обочинам дорог, у будок стрелочников, у опорных колон мостов и у портиков храмов. Кое-где намело до самого архитрава, не пробиться жрецу, не пройти туристу, не рассмотреть колонн, не реставрировать коринфскую капитель. Только ходить вокруг да около. Плакать и пить. Пить и петь).

349   "Что история, как не фантазия? Что факт, как не его интерпретация? [...] Управляя иллюзией, ты обретаешь мир. Отвергая ее, остаешься рабом. Спасайтесь любовью и совестью, заклинаю, мальчики, и больше ничем другим!"

350   "Город Z разрастается в них до вселенной, становится размером с маркесовское Макондо или Йокнапатофу Фолкнера."

351   "[...] роман скорее сконцентрирован на истории экзистенции человеческой, которая должна претерпевать некоторые метаморфозы вместе с обществом."

the constant "split" between the real and the magical worlds in Rafeenko's literary experience:

> Because it is impossible to understand what is happening only through the lenses of reality. It is impossible to forgive, to accept, and to understand. I needed to create two different bodies in the novel: one of them is made by realistic novellas— maybe, even super-realistic, and sometimes to the limit of the naturalistic; the second one, that is the intersecting line of the novel, is such a postmodern thing [...] In any case, these military events that happened pushed me to this bifurcation.[352] (Pomerantsev, I. 2019)

In one of the novellas, *The Seven Dills* (*Sem' ukropov*),[353] Rafeenko thus explores the complex choices faced by Pashka, the son of a miner, trapped by the ghosts of Soviet historical symbols and memories.[354] In another novella, *Clara's Cat* (*Koshka Klary*), the dilemma faced by the inhabitants of Z becomes clear: "To stay or to leave? This is the question" (Rafeenko 2017: 71). This sense of ambivalence is central for Rafeenko's heroes, who

---

352 "Потому что понять только из реальности то, что происходит, невозможно. Невозможно ни простить, ни принять, ни понять. Мне понадобилось сформировать два тела в романе: одно тело — это реалистические новеллы, может быть даже сверхреалистические, иногда до предела натуралистического. Вторая часть, вторая *линия*, переплетенная линия романа — это такая постмодернистская штука [...] Во всяком случае действительно вот эта военная штука, которая случилась, она меня вынудила к раздвоению."

353 Here the use of the term "dill" (*Ukrop*—in Ukrainian) follows the dynamics of the Russo–Ukrainian information conflict in 2014. It was initially used as a derogatory label for addressing Ukrainians in the public campaign in Russia. During the war, it was appropriated by Ukrainians in its new positive connotation of "Ukrainian resistance" (*Ukraïns'kyi opir*—in Ukrainian).

354 "Pashka dreamt about his stepfather every day. He smiled and related something without beginning or end. Something about the coal, Aleksandr Nevskii, Belka and Strelka and the battle of the Kalka River. In truth, Pashka caught only the general tone, and distinguished the details unclearly, as through a dirty glass. Eventually, he enlisted in the war against the Right Sector and, consequently, for Gogol', Gagarin, and mainly for Matvei Ivanovich" (Rafeenko 2017: 94; Пашка же отчима каждый день видел во сне. Тот улыбался и рассказывал что-то без конца и начала. Про уголь, про Александра Невского, про Белку и Стрелку и битву на Калке. По правде говоря, Пашка улавливал только общий тон, а детали различал мутновато, как через грязное стекло. Ну и в конце концов записался на войну против Правого сектора и, соответственно, за Гоголя, Гагарина, а главным образом — за Матвея Ивановича).

live at the crossroads between empty ideologies and matters of private life, as in the love story portrayed in *Beer and Cigarettes* (*Pivo i sigarety*: a clear allusion to Jim Jarmusch's film *Coffee and Cigarettes*).[355] Significantly, as emerges in the novella *Still Lifes of the War* (*Natiurmorty voiny*), the solution to the fundamental condition of identity crisis during wartime can be found only in the patient combination of different "planets" and "incompatible objects," coexisting in harmony in the hybrid cosmology realized by Arsenii:

> For many years Arsenii created and photographed still lifes [...] everything could appear in Barich's photos. Everything had the right to harmony. And the color or texture was not important [...] but the harmony achieved by combining incompatible objects exactly was. Arsenii began to clearly understand this last summer [...] The most difficult step was in finding the point of balance, the invisible axis that united these items [...] The cycle had a distinctive cosmogonic character. Different planets, different objects: some could be recognized, others could not [...] And then, one early, and surprisingly quiet, morning, Barich suddenly realized that depending on his accurateness is the destiny not only of this cycle, but of his life and death. The fate of the city of Z, of the people living here, the fate of Ukraine, of Europe and, maybe, of the entire world.[356] (Rafeenko 2017: 241–243)

---

355 "I will not be killed, Silin, until you can buy beer and cigarettes in Z. I will not go to your Crimea [...] I know, I know, quickly said Mikhail, we have different beliefs. But now it is not about them. Remain a hundred times Ukrainian, God be with you! Now it's about a question of survival!" (Rafeenko 2017: 81; Меня не убьют, Силин, пока в Z можно купить пиво и сигареты. Не поеду я в твой Крым! Шел бы ты с ним сам знаешь куда. Знаю-знаю, быстро заговорил Михаил, у нас разные убеждения. Но сейчас речь не о них. Оставайся хоть сто раз украинкой, господь с тобой! Речь идет о территории выживания!).

356 "Долгие годы Арсений создавал и фотографировал натюрморты [...] все могло оказаться на фотографии Барича, все имело право на гармонию. А то, что главное — не цвет и не фактура [...] а именно гармония, достигаемая путем совмещения несовместимых предметов, Арсений стал отчетливо понимать в это последнее лето [...] Сложнее всего было найти точку равновесности, невидимую ось, которая объединяла именно эти предметы [...] Цикл носил отчетливо космогонический характер. Разные планеты, разные предметы, узнаваемые и не очень [...] И вот одним ранним, удивительно тихим утром Барич внезапно понял — от того, насколько он сможет быть точным, зависит судьба не только этого цикла, но его жизнь и смерть. Судьба города Z, людей, проживающих здесь, судьба Украины, Европы, а может быть, всего мира."

Whereas the novellas give back to the reader melancholic fragments of the life shaken by war in Donbas and Ukraine, the second "body" of the novel follows the lines of the phantasmagoric transformation of reality in Rafeenko's literary world.[357] Here the bathhouse called The Fifth Rome[358] is the true agent of metamorphosis (and imaginary "purification") in the novel:

> On Tuesday, nobody is in the bathhouse. Silence. On Tuesday here it is clean and comfortable. Quiet, peaceful. On Tuesday you can relax and forget. The bathhouse will protect you from military worries, from hatred and losses. The silent song of water and steam immerses in such a peace that you cannot find it anywhere else. The crumbling echo erases the line between reality and dream. Resentment goes away. Bad events disappear, as they did not exist. Did you steal, kill, hit your mother? Did you blow Crimea and Donbas? Did you draw the death of your aunt? Are you a Nazi? An occupier? A goblin? A separatist with acid instead of blood? Angel Obama, Barack Merkel, Putin-Project? [...] Forget it. There is nothing of this. Only the whistle of the wind, rumbles and water droplets. Listen. Open your heart![359] (Rafeenko 2017: 49)

---

357   The connection between the two parts of the novel is embodied by the writer Veresaev, who programmatically announces in the first section of the novel—entitled *The Bathhouse*—his intention to write short stories about the war: " 'By the way,' Veresaev grinned suddenly, 'ladies and gentlemen, do you know that I began to write stories about the war in the city of Z? After the war I will definitely publish them! [...] the main message of the texts coming out of my pen is the following: You, man, are killed by both your own fellows and the others. And you, poor, live! Anyway, it's your war! Whether you want it or not!' " (Rafeenko 2017: 43; — Кстати, — внезапно усмехнулся Вересаев, — господа и дамы, вы знаете, что я стал писать рассказы о войне в городе Z?! После войны обязательно опубликую! [...] основной месседж текстов, выходящих из-под моего пера, следующий. Тебя, человечек, убивают и свои, и чужие. А ты, бедный, живи! По-любому это твоя война! Хочешь ты или нет!).

358   Here the telling name of the bathhouse reflects the humoristic deconstruction of neo-imperialistic ideologies emerging in Russia: " 'Actually, what does the Fifth Rome mean?'—asked the Chinese, hiding his bayonet in the scabbard—'then, why not the Fourth?'. 'Well, because the fourth is never to be'—explained Gredis" (Rafeenko 2017: 63; А что значит, кстати, «Пятый Рим»? — спросил Китаец, пряча штык-нож в ножны. — Почему уж тогда не четвертый? — Потому, что чевтвёртому не бывать, — пояснил Гредис).

359   "Во вторник в бане никого. Тишина. Во вторник здесь чисто и уютно. Тихо, мирно. Ты можешь расслабиться и забыться во вторник. Баня защитит

In the mysterious bathhouse located at the outskirts of the city of Z, where guests can purify themselves, disappear and be reborn again somewhere else, it is still possible to imagine and grasp the different ideas of "the country U" which emerge from the "margins." At the crossroads between the real and the magic world, the main protagonists of the novel—the philosopher Gredis, the writer Veresaev and the dreamer Liza—can witness the multiple and plural reincarnations of Ukraine. Both for those who decide to stay, as in the case of Gredis and Veresaev, and those who decide to leave, as in the story of the professor Marina Arkad'evna, who eventually returns to Z,[360] one can symbolically access it only by experiencing "life after death":

> To us and you who are in Z, Ukraine is not so much a country, a poor and young state that is torn to pieces by both Russian and local jackals. Ukraine is not a territory at all! [...] Essentially, Ukraine is our heavenly homeland. Almost like life after death![361] (Rafeenko 2017: 29)

The End of the Transition?

In an interview published in August 2018 on Radio Svoboda, Aleksei Nikitin emphasized how the recovery of documents related to our past can

---

360 от военных забот, от ненависти и утрат. Немолчная песнь воды и пара погружает в покой, которого нет больше нигде. Рассыпающееся эхо стирает грань между реальностью и мечтой. Уходят обиды. Пропадают, как и не было их, дурные поступки. Ты украл, убил, ударил мать? Просрал Крым и Донбасс? Нарисовал смерть тети? Нацист? Оккупант? Гоблин? Сепаратист с кислотой вместо крови? Ангел Обама, Барака Меркель, Путин-Проект? [...] Забудь. Ничего этого нет. Лишь ветра свист, лишь пара гул, лишь водяная капель. Прислушайся. Открой сердце свое!"

360 "That's what the country is! And you still tell me about the territory. An affair with the devil, that's what Ukraine is! A love story with metaphysics, being and death! And by no means is it a question about borders which were drawn by an unknown person for some unclear purposes" (Rafeenko 2017: 112; Вот это и есть страна! А ты мне говоришь — территория. Роман с чертом — вот это и есть Украина! Любовь с метафизикой, с бытием, со смертью! А отнюдь не границы, прочерченные неизвестно кем и непонятно с какими целями).

361 "— Украина для нас с тобой, находящихся в Z, — это не столько страна, бедная молодая держава, которую рвут на куски как российские, так и местные шакалы. Украина — это вообще не территория! [...] Украина, в сущности, отечество наше небесное. Почти то же самое, что жизнь после смерти!"

contribute to changing "the picture of the world" (*kartina mira*; Fanailova 2018). This follows Nikitin's growing interest in archival research and family documents as the main sources of his literary production, which led him to undertake his own personal "searches for Ukrainianness" (*poiski ukrainskosti*), using Fanailova's (2018) metaphor, through the recollection of "marginal" individual memories and stories.[362]

Similarly, while in 2013 Rafeenko still wondered about the existence of a new "center of the Slavic world" (Puleri 2016: 210), in a 2018 interview he argued that "nationality is a type of self-determination, and it can only be a conscious choice"[363] (Volodarskii 2018b). It is no surprise that amongst the epigraphs opening the first section of his novel *The Length of Days*, we find an emblematic quotation from the Lithuanian and Soviet intellectual Tomas Venclova: "Nationality is not an issue around origins, but a matter of free choice"[364] (Rafeenko 2017: 8).

Along these lines, as Chernetsky (2019: 66) argued, today "Russian-language Ukrainian writing thus emerges as a rich site for developing a new sociocultural project, exploring its hopes and stumbles, seeking to articulate the pain and the utopian impulse that marked the Euromaidan and the difficult birth of a new Ukraine in the context of ongoing war and crisis." The literary experiences of Nikitin and Rafeenko show us that the rise of hybrid subjectivities in Ukrainian society could potentially become the only way to "transcend both colonial arrogance and anti-colonial rancour" (Pavlyshyn 2016a: 86). It is in this sense (rather than out of cynicism or political escapism) that Il'ia Kukulin can argue that "this anti-ideological criticism can become an important part of the future Ukrainian culture"

---

362 This is the case with his forthcoming book on the life story of a Soviet Jewish boxer, Il'ia Gol'dinov, in 1930s–40s Kyiv, which was mainly reconstructed thanks to thorough research in the SBU (Security Services of Ukraine) archives. Some excerpts from the novel, which at the time of the writing of this book (2019) is still unfinished, have been published in the journal *Vremena* (see Nikitin 2018).

363 "[…] национальность — это вид самоопределения, и оно может быть только сознательным."

364 "Национальность становится не делом происхождения, а вопросом свободного выбора."

(2016: 184). Nevertheless, at the time of the writing of this book (2019) the latest cultural developments signal that the "Russophone Ukrainian literature"—together with the national identity project—is still "in a state of postcolonial transition," but significantly "the outcome of the transition is not yet assured" (Chernetsky 2019: 63).

In Place of a Conclusion
The Future of "Russianness" in Post-Maidan Ukraine

In the years which have followed Euromaidan, there has been a considerable debate amongst scholars in Ukrainian Studies over the new potential role and position of the Russian language and culture in Ukraine. In February 2017, "The Future of Russianness in Post-Maidan Ukraine" was the title of a roundtable organized at the Institute for Human Sciences in Vienna (IWM 2017). Russophone researchers and writers with highly diverse backgrounds participated in the discussion: Andrii Portnov, a Ukrainian historian from Dnipro; Anton Shekhovtsov, a Ukrainian political scientist, originally from Crimea; and Andrei Kurkov, a Ukrainian Russophone writer based in Kyiv. The first questions posed by the moderator, Tatiana Zhurzhenko, were the following: "Do you agree that Russian speaker is a political identity? If yes, do you think that this kind of identity complicates political loyalty to the Ukrainian state?" Responding to these questions, Kurkov dismissed the idea that ethnic Russians and Russian speakers can really be divided into two different groups. The Russophone writer argued that the main issue is around the need for differentiating between cultural and political Russophones: since the Russian language has officially no status in Ukraine, it cannot be considered by everybody as a minority language, especially because it still works as a common language between different ethnic groups in the south and in the west of the country (as remembered by Kurkov, Ukrainian Bulgarians usually speak in Russian to Ukrainian Romanians and Poles). Portnov also agreed, stating that a more or less homogeneous political identity of the entire group of Russian speakers in Ukraine does not exist, since we cannot draw any specific geographical border between Ukrainian and Russian speakers. In Portnov's opinion, the issue mainly concerns the true gap between legal definitions and social life in contemporary Ukraine. Accordingly, Shekhovtsov argued that in the near future, the paradigm of "two cultures-two languages" seems to be the most likely in Ukraine.

Interestingly, the second question posed by Zhurzhenko concerned the potential room for a Russian-language Ukrainian literature, and the possibility for imagining Ukrainian literature as multilingual. Kurkov stated that even if a rich Ukrainian Russian-language literature was created during recent decades, officially it is still not recognized as Ukrainian literature: you cannot find Russian-language authors from Ukraine in school and university textbooks of Ukrainian literature, and the attitude of the leading critics is not to discuss the issue. According to Kurkov, in the coming years there will be more Russian-language authors, but they will not be included in the Ukrainian literature: this highly depends on the fact that, in Kurkov's opinion, Ukraine will not become officially a bilingual country, since that would create a split in civil society. At the end of the debate, Kurkov thus gloomily argued that in the near future the discussion will go on, but the situation will be legally the same.

In spite of this seemingly dim perspective for the Russian language and culture in Ukraine, during the discussion Kurkov could still highlight some undeniable and fundamental changes in the cultural sphere: the latest social developments in Ukraine have encouraged some Russophone authors to increasingly turn to the Ukrainian language in their literary production. As Kurkov mentioned, this is the case with Andrii Kokotiukha (b. 1970, Nizhyn), who already at the 2014 Book Forum in L'viv declared himself to be a "Russophone writer" (*rosiis'komovnyi pys'mennyk*) writing "in two languages" (*dvoma movami*; Dziubak 2014), and Iren Rozdobud'ko (b. 1962, Donets'k), who already in the 2000s decided to write only in Ukrainian (Baziv 2018).

Most fundamentally, today this emerging choice could be motivated by the Russophone writers' striving for official recognition in the Ukrainian literary environment, especially in light of the war and the reduced contacts with the Russian market.[365] As emphasized by Vladimir Rafeenko in

---

365 With respect to the latest political measures affecting the national literary market, it is worth mentioning that in March 2019, the then-president Petro Poroshenko signed the decree *On the application, Lifting and Amendment of Personal Special Economic and Other Restrictive Measures (Sanctions)* (*Pro zastosuvannia, skasuvannia ta vnesennia zmin do personal'nykh spetsial'nykh ekonomichnykh ta inshykh obmezhuval'nykh zakhodiv—sanktsii,* n. 82/2019): this included the introduction of a ban on the import of the

2014: "Today the Russophone [*russkoiazychnyi*] writer of Ukraine only dreams of being heard and recognized in his own country"[366] (Sventakh 2014). In order to reach this goal, Rafeenko has recently written his first work in the Ukrainian language, *Mondegreen. Songs about Death and Love* (*Mondegrin. Pisni pro smert' i liubov*, 2019). The title refers to the psychological phenomenon of mishearing or misinterpreting a phrase as a result of near-homophony, producing a different meaning. As the author stated, "such a struggle between us and our own perceptions accompanies us for all our lives"[367] (Kotsarev 2019). *Mondegreen* is thus a work about the language, that is, an intellectual meta-reflection upon the difficult process of language acquisition and the nature of bilingualism in contemporary Ukraine. Throughout the novel, the protagonist, Haba, an internally displaced person from Russian-speaking Donets'k who has recently moved to Kyiv, gets acquainted with the new Ukrainian-language environment of the capital, developing new meanings and constantly commenting on their intrinsic nature. The first chapter of the novel, titled "About the Essence" ("Pro sut'"), swiftly introduces the reader to the complex nature of the bilingualism experienced by the protagonist:

> Here Haba thought that he was apparently starting to be affected by the polyglot syndrome. As long as he was talking with himself in the native Russian, he was still a man to himself. But as soon as he came to learn the second language, all sorts of things started to fall in his mind. For with much wisdom comes much sorrow.[368] (Rafeenko 2019a: 10–11)

---

books published by nine large publishing houses in the Russian Federation—that were selected according to the number of published "anti-Ukrainian" books—such as Eksmo, AST and Iauza, and a ban on the access to Russian online book retailers, such as LitRes, Labirint and Ozon.ru (see Prezydent Ukraïny 2019).

366 "Русскоязычный писатель Украины в настоящее время только мечтает быть услышанным и замеченным в своей стране."

367 "Така боротьба між нами і нашим власним сприйняттям супроводжує нас все життя."

368 "Тут Габа подумав, що в нього, мабуть, починається синдром поліглота. Доки розмовляв із собою рідною російською, був собі людина людиною. А як другу заходився вивчати, усіляке казна-що на ум почало спадати. Від многія знанія многія і печалі."

The "improvised lecture on the philosophy of language" (*improvizovana lektsiia z filosofiï movy*) offered by Haba, as observed by Tetiana Petrenko in her fascinating review of *Mondegreen*, "is about to arrange for readers a difficult journey through all circles of Donets'k hell and the post-traumatic purgatory"[369] (Petrenko 2019) in Kyiv. In the phantasmagoric world created by Rafeenko, Haba is the same archangel Gabriel, a bond "between God and Men (or at least between two very different worlds)" (*mizh bohom i liud'my—chy prinaimni mizh dvoma duzhe riznymy svitamy*; Petrenko 2019), such as the Russophone and the Ukrainophone ones. He symbolically suffers from mental illness, because "if he hears and interprets something incorrectly, it is only because the elements of one world [...] fall into another through him"[370] (Petrenko 2019).

Mondegrin was met with great acclaim in Ukraine—namely, as Rafeenko noted, by "Ukrainophone friends, apparently, with more joy than the Russophone ones"[371] (Kotsarev 2019)—and has been described as the author's "own anticolonial revolt" (*vlasnyi antykolonial'nyi bunt*; Liubka 2019a) against the Russian aggression. Nevertheless, in an essay published in the period shortly preceding the publication of the novel, Rafeenko further clarified the reasons behind his choice:

> This year I wrote my first novel in Ukrainian [...] I want to tell you why I, a Russophone writer of Ukraine [*rosiis'komovnyi pys'mennyk Ukraïny*], wrote it [...] two things forced me to set myself this daunting task and move toward that goal [...] And the first of these is the exploitation of the Russian and pro-Russian media on the need to protect the Russian-speaking population in Ukraine [...] The second thing that subconsciously pushed me to write this work is the confidence of some part of the naturally good Ukrainian-speaking and clear-eyed Ukraine that in Donbas live the suckers, the cattle, people who are not able to experience culture consciously and professionally, the holy conviction that the people of Donbas are themselves to blame for the misery they encountered [...] But when I finally started working on the text, all of that, to be honest, got away from me [...] I worked a lot with the language, simultaneously studying it,

---

369 "[...] ось-ось влаштує читачам непросту мандрівку усіма колами донецького пекла й посттравматичного чистилища."

370 "[...] якщо він чує й інтерпретує щось неправильно, то лише тому, що елементи одного світу через нього, [...] потрапляють до іншого."

371 "Україномовні приятелі, здається, з більшою радістю, ніж російськомовні."

and since I forbade myself to write in Russian, until I write a Ukrainian novel, I invested in the text completely.[372] (Rafeenko 2019b)

Here the case of Rafeenko is the tip of the iceberg of a broader cultural phenomenon involving other prominent Russophone authors, such as Boris Khersonskii. In his study, Uffelmann (2019: 222) describes Khersonskii as "the most prominent example of the larger set of Ukrainian Russophone poets who thematize the problematics of writing in Russian in Ukraine." According to the German scholar, "Khersonsky's poetry carries out a performative critique of the conception of Russophobia at its fundamental levels, articulating the multiplicity and independence of Russian cultures from the constraints of political entities and national boundaries" (Uffelmann 2019: 226). Most importantly, as Chernetsky (2019: 65) recalled, "Khersonskii has not abandoned writing in Russian" and "emphatically asserts his bilingualism and places essays in Russian and Ukrainian side by side, arranged not by language but by theme." In a recent post on Facebook, Khersonskii addressed the "ethical and aesthetic protest" behind his stance on the language question in Ukraine:

My reaction to what is happening is emotional and personal. From the fact that I began to translate my poems into Ukrainian and to write essays in Ukrainian, it does not follow that I have ceased to be predominantly a Russophone poet and translator [*russkoiazychnyi poet i perevodchik*]. This is, if I may say so, an ethical and aesthetic protest.[373] (Khersonskii 2019)

---

372 "У цьому році я написав перший свій роман українською мовою [...] Хочу розказати, для чого і чому я, російськомовний письменник України, його написав [...] дві речі змусили мене поставити собі це карколомне завдання і рухатися до поставленої мети [...] І перша з них — експлуатація російськими та проросійськими ЗМІ тези про потрібність захисту російськомовного населення в Україні [...] Друга річ, яка підсвідомо штовхала мене до роботи. Це впевненість деякої частки природно доброї, україномовної та ясноокої України, що на Донбасі живуть саме лохи, бидло, люди, які не здатні перебувати в культурі свідомо та професійно, свята впевненість, що люди Донбасу самі винні в тій біді, що їх спіткала [...] Але, коли я нарешті став працювати над текстом, все це, сказати чесно, відійшло від мене [...] Дуже багато працював із мовою, одночасно вивчаючи її, а оскільки заборонив собі писати російською, допоки не напишу українського роману, то вкладався у текст повністю."

373 "Моя реакция на происходящее эмоциональная и личная. Из того, что я начал переводить на украинский свои стихи и писать эссеистику, не

Similarly, in the 2019 issue of the Israeli–Russian journal *Dvoetochie*, devoted to the theme of literary bilingualism,[374] Iia Kiva described the subtle nuances behind her recent decision to switch also to Ukrainian in her artistic production, highlighting the pressing need for self-determination in the aftermath of the war.[375] Most fundamentally, the political acceleration of cultural change brought by war still makes today "writing in Russian into an act, if not dramatic, then at least problematic" (Kiva 2019), thus disclosing a gloomy perspective for the future of Russianness in post-Maidan Ukraine:

> I understand the people who today turn massively to Ukrainian as the language of reading and communication. This is a completely natural desire to detach from Russian aggression, to move away from what is causing pain and danger. But this is not my story. I personally like the idea of inclusive identity: I am a citizen of Ukraine, I have an unequivocal civil position, I have a polyethnic background. I speak Russian and Ukrainian in everyday life, I write mostly in Russian, but also in Ukrainian. At the same time, I am absolutely conscious

---

следует того, что я перестал быть преимущественно русскоязычным поэтом и переводчиком. Это, если так можно сказать, этический и эстетический протест."

374 The issue includes texts of authors who write both in Russian and in other languages (i.e. Ukrainian, French, Polish, Latvian and others). Each publication is accompanied by the authors' answers to the questionnaire, asking about the personal circumstances and reasons behind each author's bilingual practices. Interestingly, the issue works as an interesting picture of Russophone poetry outside Russia.

375 "First, [behind this choice lay] the desire to master and appropriate the cultural space, in relation to which I have all this time been only a recipient. [...] Second, the awareness of the complexity of my own identity in light of war [...]. Third, letting myself write in Ukrainian [...] Fourth, the military experience and civil-political position, which turns writing in Russian into an act, if not dramatic, then at least problematic" (Kiva 2019; С одной стороны, желание освоить и присвоить культурное пространство, по отношению к которому я все это время была лишь реципиентом [...] С другой стороны, осознание сложности своей идентичности на фоне войны [...] С третьей, разрешение себе писать на украинском [...] С четвертой, военный опыт и гражданско-политическая позиция, что превращает письмо на русском в акт если не драматический, то проблематизировавшийся).

that I can become the last generation of Russophone authors of Ukraine.[376]
(Esterkina 2018)

As emphasized by Kiva, the complex issue around "literary code-switching" reveals controversial outcomes for the future of the Russian language and culture in Ukraine: on the one hand, it has the potential to develop stronger ties within Ukraine, especially "across language divides" (Chernetsky 2019: 63); on the other, this could reduce the room for "hybridity" in the country, whereby it accommodates to a well-defined ethnocultural and linguistic model. Here, in light of recent developments, new research questions on the wider prospects for Ukrainian culture in the future arise: Are these new practices of "self-hybridization" signalling the end of the transitory state of hybridity in Ukraine? Are post-Maidan political developments drawing the line towards a new process of cultural homogenization under the sign of the Ukrainian language?

Along these lines, it is no surprise that, on the occasion of his public lecture "Ukraine and the Future of Europe", which was held in Kyiv in June 2019, the US historian Timothy Snyder provocatively emphasized the need for rethinking the Russian language as polycentric, also in order to create the room for a more inclusive approach to the role of Russian culture in Ukraine:

> It is a mistake to think that the Russian culture and language belong exclusively to the Russian Federation. Ukraine has a great opportunity to create its own dictionary of the Russian language. If you do so, you do not only standardise the language and change the way you work with it in Ukraine, but you also introduce your own culture to the world. Not to take this opportunity will be a mistake [...] Create cultural, journalistic environments and resources for the West and the Russians. It is not necessary to think that this will weaken Ukrainian culture,

---

376 "Я розумію людей, які сьогодні масово переходять на українську як мову читання та спілкування. Це цілком природне бажання відмежуватися від російської агресії, віддалитися від того, що завдає біль і несе небезпеку. Але це не моя історія. Мені особисто близька ідея інклюзивної ідентичності: я є громадянкою України, маю недвозначну громадянську позицію, в мене поліетнічне походження, спілкуюся російською та українською в побуті, пишу переважно російською, але й українською теж. Водночас я абсолютно свідома того, що можу стати останнім поколінням російськомовних авторів України."

it is not about rivalry. If we consider Russian exclusively as the language of the Russian Federation, then we lose. It is a world language, so we can decide how to use it properly.[377] (Manucharian 2019)

Paradoxically, these reflections on the *local* developments of Russian culture in Ukraine can help us also reframe the global prospects of "Ukrainianness" and "Russianness" in the post-Maidan era. Two years after the aforementioned discussion in Vienna, a new roundtable on the global framework of Ukrainian literature was organized at the Harriman Institute of Columbia University. In February 2019, writers and scholars participated in the roundtable "Envisioning Ukrainian Literature 2019: Versions and Demarcations", who discussed the "various ways of belonging to Ukrainian literature" (Harriman Institute 2019).[378] Significantly, in addition to the questions related to the *local* developments in Ukraine lying at the core of my research, new *plural* and *global* images of the space of Ukrainian literature were also considered:

What are the different ways that Ukrainian literature can be defined in 2019? Literature written in the Ukrainian language? Literature written by citizens of Ukraine in any language? Literature written in Ukrainian outside of Ukraine? Literature written by Ukrainians living outside of Ukraine, in any language? Literature written about Ukraine in any language? (Harriman Institute 2019)

In a 2018 interview, the US scholar Mark Andryczyk, who moderated the above-mentioned roundtable, came to the conclusion that "there's [not] any one way you could define it" (Kinsella 2019). Similarly to the dynamics characterizing the "archipelago" of Russian culture described by Rubins,

---

377 "Ошибочно думать, что русская культура и язык принадлежат исключительно РФ. У Украины огромная возможность создать собственный словарь русского языка. Так вы не только стандартизируете его, измените способ работы с языком в Украине, но и представите миру собственную культуру. Не воспользоваться этой возможностью — будет ошибкой [...] Создавайте культурные, журналистские площадки и ресурсы для Запада и россиян. Не стоит думать, что это ослабит украинскую культуру, это не соперничество. Если мы считаем русский исключительно языком Российской Федерации, то мы проигрываем. Это мировой язык, а значит мы можем решить, как правильно его использовать."

378 Vasyl' Makhno (b. 1964, Chortkiv) joined the debate, together with a Russophone author based in Kyiv, Aleksei Nikitin, and the scholars Maria G. Rewakowicz, Yuri Shevchuk and Mark Andryczyk.

here we may witness the presence of plural centres of Ukrainian culture, which are "subject to continuous redefinition" (Rubins 2019: 25). If on the one hand the participation in the debate by Vasyl' Makhno, a Ukrainian writer living in New York City since 2000, tells us about the "global dispersion" of Ukrainians and Ukrainian literature worldwide, on the other the success of the Kyiv-born Russophone prose writer Katja Petrowskaja (Kateryna Petrovs'ka/Ekaterina Petrovs'kaia; b. 1970, Kyiv), with her debut novel in German *Maybe Esther. A Family Story* (*Vielleicht Esther. Geschichten*, 2014) embodies the experience of the wave of female authors of Slavic origins, most of them from Ukraine, who have been publishing their works in the German-speaking literary market throughout the last decade, and are being awarded with some of the most prominent literary prizes in Europe.[379]

Similarly to Ukrainian culture, it is also the Russian culture, as argued in the introduction to this book, that has gone global. Thus, borrowing the definition proposed by Platt (2019a: 15), we may argue that "Ukrainian culture is Russian, too, and both are equally global in reach." Most fundamentally, the *local* dynamics of Ukrainian culture give us evidence of the existence in the *global* Russian culture of "interstitial, hybrid practices" (Chernetsky 2019: 62) that follow heterogeneous developments, which are highly influenced by the diversity of *local* incentives and constraints—in the post-Soviet region and worldwide. The cultural change brought by the dramatic political developments in Ukraine in 2014–2015 accelerated the process of self-determination of Ukrainian Russophone literature, and this could prospectively work as a precedent for similar phenomena in the post-Soviet area.

Furthermore, as emphasized by Chernetsky (2019: 62), there is no doubt that the Ukrainian case would "also merit comparison with similar practices elsewhere." This is especially true, whereas we consider that—similarly to

---

379 Such is the case of the Ukrainian author Mariana Gaponenko (b. 1981), born in Odesa and awarded the Adelbert von Chamisso Prize in 2013, and Tetiana Maliarchuk, a Ukrainian-language author born in Ivano-Frankivs'k and living in Vienna, who has been awarded the 2018 edition of the Ingeborg Bachmann Prize with her first novel in German, *Frogs in the Sea* (*Frösche im Meer*). Brigid Haines (2008) emblematically described this phenomenon as an "Eastern Turn" in contemporary German literature.

the field of Ukrainian culture—in the context of Russian literature "no one formula may encapsulate global culture," but it is the global that "may still encapsulate a unity of diversity" (Rubins 2019: 46).[380] In the web of trans-national connections offered by "the ceaseless forces of globalization and technological innovation" (Caffee 2013: 191), the *local* centres of Russian culture are likely to find the way to new global platforms, other than the ones offered by the legacy of Soviet cultural institutions and neo-imperial ventures led by the Russian Federation.[381] If previously "the representatives of the 'smaller peoples' of the USSR could relate to one another only 'via Moscow'," as Kukulin argues, since the 1980s an "aesthetics of postcolo-nial 'glocalization'" (2019: 171) has already been developed by the Riga and Fergana poetic schools. Significantly, Kukulin (2019: 172) highlights further that, similarly to the recent developments in Ukraine, "Russian culture, in the works of both groups, appears as 'younger,' and minor—in precisely the sense of 'minor literature' articulated by Gilles Deleuze and Félix Guattari."

---

380 "Remaining in dialogue with metropolitan culture and the national tradi-tion, local cultures simultaneously transcend them, engage in transnational conversations, and create constellations out of diverse aesthetic and ideological vocabularies" (Rubins 2019: 46).

381 In her dissertation, Caffee (2013: 160) analyses "Russophonia's ever-expanding frontiers in the twenty-first century," devoting her attention to the new emerging "locations" online of contemporary literature written in Russian in the independent post-Soviet states. As the scholar argues with an emphasis on Russophone Central Asian poets: "The emergence of interac-tive, rather than exclusive, forms of Internet publishing continues to shape the digital environments in which contemporary Russophone poets' work is produced and received. Beyond formal literary journals and anthologies, the Tashkent, Fergana, and Musaget writers now publish and engage in dialogue with their readers and each other on open networking sites like Facebook, Twitter, vKontakte, and LiveJournal. Their poetry can also be found on Stikhi. ru, an open poetry database and networking site that allows users to anony-mously post and discuss translations, previously published works, and their own original poetry [...] Stihi.ru has no apparatus for categorizing writers ac-cording to geographic location, ethnicity, nationality, or literary training—the only requirement for participation is the ability to use the Russian-language interface. In this way Stihi.ru and its counterpart Proza.ru can be seen as the ultimate Russophone spaces, having eliminated all external markers of identity except language" (Caffee 2013: 184–185).

Along these lines, the publication of scholarly research devoted to the study of Russian culture outside the Russian Federation is likely to intensify, developing diverse approaches capable of investigating the peculiarities of the *local* centres under scrutiny.[382] Likewise, studies investigating the interference of political discourse in post-Soviet cultural developments should not to be overlooked in the near future. This is happening also in light of the growing tensions in the region: it is no surprise that in the introduction to her recent monograph, *Politics and Literary Tradition: Russian-Georgian Literary Relations after Perestroika* (*Politika i literaturnaia traditsiia: russko-gruzinskie literaturnye sviazi posle perestroiki*, 2018), Elena Chkhaidze emphasizes the emergence of new pressing questions today, particularly in the aftermath of the Soviet collapse and recent geopolitical clashes between the Russian Federation and Georgia.[383]

Finally, at the time of the writing of this book (July 2019), there is no doubt that the recent political developments in Ukraine are also likely to affect the postcolonial transition of Ukrainian culture, which seems to be

---

382 Here it is worth mentioning the prominent studies devoted to the identity and literary dynamics in the Latvian context, which have been undertaken by Platt (2013; 2019b), and to the Kazakhstani Russophone literature in Melnikov's dissertation (2017). Furthermore, the formation of the international group of scholars working on Russophone literatures in the post-Soviet area in March 2019 at the Centre for East European and International Studies (ZOiS) in Berlin is also likely to develop a promising research platform.

383 "After the collapse of the USSR, Russia and Georgia gained independence. The imperial-colonial paradigm of past years has collapsed. This raises a number of questions to which there are no answers yet. What happened to the imperial literary tradition, which included three components (creation of artistic works, research and translation processes), after the collapse of the USSR as a special type of empire [...]? How did the post-Soviet armed conflicts affect the themes and motifs in literature in the Russian and Georgian languages?" (Chkhaidze 2018: 15–16; После распада СССР Россия и Грузия обрели независимость. Имперско-колониальная парадигма прошлых лет разрушилась. Отсюда возникает ряд вопросов, на которые пока нет ответов. Что стало с имперской литературной традицией, включавшей в себя три составляющие (создание художественных произведений, научно-исследовательский и переводческий процессы), после краха СССР как особого типа империи [...]? Как повлияли постсоветские вооруженные столкновения на темы и мотивы в литературе на русском и грузинском языках?).

eternally subjected to constant change in direction and destination. The results of the Spring presidential elections and the July parliamentary elections in 2019 literally turned upside down the national political scene. The outgoing president Petro Poroshenko, who had openly promoted "civic nationalism" in 2014, switched to a more national-patriotic conservatism in his 2019 electoral campaign, using slogans such as "Army. Language. Faith" (*Armiia. Mova. Vira*) and couching "his anti-Russian message in a national identity incorporating elements of Ukrainian ethnicity" (Giuliano 2019)—thus following the perennial dynamics of the political field in Ukraine and winning consensus in the Western regions. Since the first round of the presidential elections, the "internal" enemy surprisingly has happened to be the television actor Volodymyr Zelens'kyi, a Russophone comedian from the central region of Kryvyi Rih, who won over 30 per cent of the votes against the 15.95 per cent of Poroshenko. Significantly, Zelens'kyi won the majority of votes in most of the regions, thus over-coming the traditional polarization between the West and the East, thanks to his anti-system rhetoric which did not openly touch radical positions in the identity field, thus also attracting voters in the East from Iurii Boiko's Opposition Bloc, former deputy prime minister in pre-Maidan Ukraine (see KIIS 2019). Ultimately, the dynamics that saw on April 21 an "outsider" winning the second round of the Ukrainian presidential elections testify to a general political disaffection experienced by Ukrainians, and to the inability of the traditional political elite to translate social claims into new concrete projects.[384] As highlighted by Holovakha on the eve of the second round of the elections, in Ukraine "the Zelens'kyi phenomenon is a kind of 'electoral Maidan'" (*fenomen Zelens'koho—svoeoridnyi "elektoral'nyi Maidan"*), whereas—since "the post-Soviet elite has created a society that does not suit the overwhelming majority of the population"[385]—"people

---

384 The results of the second round of the 2019 Ukrainian presidential elections were approved by the Central Election Commission of Ukraine on April 30, 2019. Volodymyr Zelens'kyi won the 73.22 % of the overall votes (see Tsentral'na vyborcha komisiia 2019a).

385 "Пострадянська еліта створила таке суспільство, яке не влаштовує переважну більшість населення."

again choose a new uncertainty" (*narod znov obyraie novu nevyznachenist'*; Rudenko, Sarakhman 2019).

Whereas sociocultural heterogeneity makes "ethnic polarization or conflict unlikely in Ukraine" (Giuliano 2019), a more pragmatic approach to the ideological field still needs to be framed in the country's political arena. After the publication of the first results of the second round on April 21, the newly elected President Zelens'kyi addressed the people of the other post-Soviet states, claiming that in light of the Ukrainian example, "everything is possible" (Interfax Ukraine 2019) now in post-Soviet politics: actually, today the potential novelty of his recent election is still to be framed. Interestingly, as highlighted by Peter Pomerantsev (2019), the controversial paradox of the Ukrainian presidential elections lies in the fact that "part of Zelens'kyi's appeal is that he offers a way for people who still feel close to Soviet and Russian pop culture to become politically European."[386] These dynamics were gloomily observed in the aftermath of the first round of the presidential elections by the Ukrainian writer Taras Prokhas'ko (2019), who interpreted the results as clearly showing that even in Ukraine today the mainstream trend leans towards the model of "the Russian-speaking consumer pop-culture country [*rosiis'komovna spozhyvats'ka pop-kul'tural'na kraïna*]."

Despite a political scenario in constant evolution, at the end of April the outgoing parliament approved the controversial bill 2704-VIII, *On Guaranteeing the Functioning of the Ukrainian Language as a State Language*, thus still reflecting the dynamics and political priorities of the country in the aftermath of the Maidan Revolution.[387] Today, also in light of the extraordinary results achieved by the party of the newly elected

---

386 "This process can upset those who have risked, sacrificed, and staked much on the project of Ukrainian national liberation over the centuries. But it is also potentially subversive for Putin's cultural model of the Russian world too: it opens a space where you can take the positive associations of Soviet culture and fuse them with a desire for democracy" (Pomerantsev, P. 2019).

387 In the aftermath of the passing of the law, Natalia Kudriavtseva bitterly highlighted the intrinsic contradiction between today's language use in Ukraine and the reiterative misuse of the language question in the national political discourse: "The new law clearly prioritizes protection of the rights of the language: of the law's seven tasks positioning language as a major avenue

president, Servant of the People (*Sluha narodu*), in the 2019 parliamentary elections,[388] in "Ukraine's Post-Post-Maidan Era" (Edwards 2019) it is still unclear whether this complete change in the internal political balance will kick into higher gear the social and cultural dynamics of the post-Maidan era or will bring Ukraine back to the pre-Maidan status quo. These doubts are also shared by the Ukrainian intellectuals participating in the debate on the future destination of Ukrainian postcolonial transition: thus, the writer Andrii Liubka (2019b) can describe the new developments under the label of a "counterrevolution of meanness" (*kontrrevoliutsiia nytsosti*)—counterposing the 2014 "revolution of dignity,"[389] whereas the sociologist Volodymyr Ishchenko highlights the "positive side of Zelensky," who "has offset the political contradictions between pro-Russian and pro-Europe, between Russian-speaking and Ukrainian-speaking" (Edwards 2019) in Ukraine.

---

of constructing identity and a driving force in nation-state building, only the last one mentions the 'language needs' of Ukrainian citizens and Ukrainians living abroad. The law launches a state program to promote the learning of Ukrainian through a network of free language courses available to all. Of special significance is the purity of the language, whose 'vulgarization' and 'intended distortion' in official documents will incur liability under the new law" (Kudriavtseva 2019).

388 The parliamentary elections were extraordinarily convened for July 21, after the new president, Volodymyr Zelens'kyi, dissolved parliament on May 21, during his inauguration. The final results were published by Ukraine's Central Election Commission on July 26, 2019: Volodymyr Zelens'kyi's party won 43.16 % of the overall votes, and for the first time since Ukrainian independence, a single party is set to end up with a majority in the parliament (see Tsentral'na vyborcha komisiia 2019b).

389 "Instead of the idea of affirming the Ukrainian language as a state language, instead of a course of decolonization, of the right to have their own history and church, the majority of Ukrainians chose a pro-Russian government. It is not a pro-Putin government, but just a pro-Russian one: it is people who consider Russian language and culture as part of their own identity, and who consider Russians as brothers" (Liubka 2019b; Замість ідеї про утвердження української мови як державної, замість курсу на деколонізацію, права на свою історію й церкву більшість українців обрала собі проросійську владу. Так, не пропутінську, але таки проросійську: людей, для яких російська мова, культура — частина ідентичності, а росіяни — брати).

Yet, as we have retraced in our analysis of the sociocultural evolution of the country throughout the last decades, "[t]he people of Ukraine long ago moved beyond a simple Russian-Ukrainian dichotomy—in their identities, their everyday practices, and their political attitudes" (Giuliano 2019). Today, as highlighted by Elise Giuliano (2019) in March 2019, "it's time to see whether Ukraine's leaders can keep up with them."

Bibliography

Afonin, Oleksandr (2011). "Manikiur dlia ukraïns'koho knyhovydannia." *Tyzhden'*. June 21. Available at: http://tyzhden.ua/Economics/24370 (06/2019).

Aheieva, Vira (2013). "Chy mozhe vidbutysia 'rosiis'ka literatura Ukraïny'?" *LitAktsent*. March 15. Available at: http://litakcent.com/2013/03/15/chy-mozhe-vidbutysja-rosijska-literatura-ukrajiny/ (05/2019).

Alexievich, Svetlana (2015). "On The Battle Lost." *The Nobel Prize*. Translated from Russian by Jamey Gambrell. December 7. Available at: https://www.nobelprize.org/prizes/literature/2015/alexievich/25408-nobel-lecture-2015/ [in Russian: "O proigrannoi bitve." https://www.nobelprize.org/prizes/literature/2015/alexievich/25414-nobel-lecture-by-svetlana-aleksievitch-in-russian/] (04/2019).

Alisharieva, Akbota et al. (2017). "Kazakhstanskii Russkii: Vzgliad so storony." *Ab Imperio*. 4: 231–263.

Andriewsky, Olga (2003). "The Russian–Ukrainian Discourse and the Failure of the 'Little Russian Solution', 1782–1917." In Kappeler, Andreas et al. (eds.). *Culture, Nation and Identity: The Ukrainian–Russian Encounter, 1600–1945*. Edmonton: Canadian Institute of Ukrainian Studies Press. 182–214.

Andrukhovych, Iurii (2014). *Dva Romany: Moskoviada. Roman zhakhiv. Perverziia*. Ivano-Frankivs'k: Lileia-NV [En. ed.: Andrukhovych, Yuri (2008). *The Moscoviad*. Translated by Vitaly Chernetsky. New York: Spuyten Duyvil].

Andrukhovych, Iurii (2017a). "Iedinaia krayna." *Zbruch*. August 18. Available at: https://zbruc.eu/node/69747 (04/2019).

Andrukhovych, Iurii (2017b). "Prynyzhenym i obrazhenym, chy to pak Unizhennym i obizhennym." *Zbruch*. September 1. Available at: https://zbruc.eu/node/70211 (04/2019).

Andrukhovych, Iurii (2017c). "A teper uzhe spravdi pro movu." *Zbruch*. September 8. Available at: https://zbruc.eu/node/70469 (04/2019).

Arel, Dominique; Khmel'ko, Valerii (1996). "The Russian Factor and Territorial Polarization in Ukraine." *The Harriman Review*. 9, 1–2: 81–91.

Armiia FM(2017). "'Nas tsikavyt' okopna literatura'—Vydavets' Andrii Honcharuk." October 10. Available at: http://www.armyfm. com.ua/nas-c%D1 %96kavit-okopna-l%D1 %96teratura---vidavec-andr%D1 %96j-goncharuk/ (07/2019).

Assmann, Aleida (2011). "From 'Canon and Archive'." In Olick, Jeffrey K. et al. (eds.). *The Collective Memory Reader*. Oxford-New York: Oxford University Press. 334–337.

Assmann, Jan (2006). *Religion and Cultural Memory: Ten Studies*. Translated by Rodney Livingstone. Stanford: Stanford University Press.

Azar, Il'ia (2017). "Puteshestvie natsbolov k Putinu i obratno." *Novaia Gazeta*. March 12. Available at: https://www.novayagazeta.ru/ articles/2017/03/12/71752-puteshestvie-natsbolov-k-putinu-i-obratno (07/2019).

Bannikov, Pavel (2015). "Literatura ad marginem." *Novyi Mir*. 12: 196–203.

Barrington, Lowell W.; Herron, Erik S. (2004). "One Ukraine or Many? Regionalism in Ukraine and its Political Consequences." *Nationalities Papers*. 32, 1: 53–86.

Barskova, Polina et al. (2017). "Forum: Poetry In a Time of Crisis." 3 *Poetry International*. January 11. Available at: https://pionline.wordpress. com/2017/01/11/poetry-in-a-time-of-crisis-forum/ (06/2019).

Bassin, Mark; Kelly, Catriona (2012). "Introduction." In Bassin, Mark; Kelly, Catriona (eds.). *Soviet and Post-Soviet Identities*. Cambridge: Cambridge University Press. 3–16.

Baziv, Liubov (2018). "Iren Rozdobud'ko, pis'mennytsia: 'U pryfrontovykh mistakh ie taki patrioty, shcho dai Bozhe nam takymy buty'." *Ukrinform*. April 11. Available at: https://www.ukrinform.ua/rubric-culture/2437775-iren-rozdobudko-pismennica.html (07/2019).

Benedictus, Leo (2002). "Paperbacks." *The Guardian. The Observer*. March 17. Available at: http://www.theguardian.com/books/2002/ mar/17/features.review/print (06/2019).

Benediktov, Kirill (2014). "Esli zavtra voina." *Vzgliad*. February 22. Available at: https://vz.ru/columns/2014/2/22/673796.html (07/2019).

Bennetts, Mark (2017). "From Here to Eternity." *Eurozine*. September 4. Available at: www.eurozine.com/from-here-to-eternity/ (07/2019).

Berg, Mikhail (2000). *Literaturokratiia. Problema prisvoeniia i pereraspredeleniia vlasti v literature*. Moskva: Novoe literaturnoe obozrenie.

Berg, Mikhail (2004). "Postkolonial'nyi diskurs i problema uspekha v sovremennoi russkoi literature." *Personal'nyi sait Mikhaila Berga.* Available at: http://mberg.net/pstk/ (06/2019).

Besedin, Platon (2013). "Aleksei Nikitin: Ischeznovenie liubogo iazyka— utrata dlia strany." *Sho.* 9–10: 62–69.

Besedin, Platon (2014). "Vyrosshie iz shineli Gogolia i Makhno: Ukrainskii pisatel' Sergei Zhadan o literature i sobytiiakh v strane." *Svobodnaia Pressa.* May 3. Available at: http://svpressa.ru/society/article/86247/?aam=1 (06/2019).

Besters-Dilger, Juliane (2009). "Introduction." In Besters-Dilger, Juliane (ed.). *Language Policy and Language Situation in Ukraine.* Frankfurt/Main: Peter Lang. 7–13.

Bezruk, Tetiana (2016). "Ukraine's Ministry of Internal Hatred." *openDemocracy.* October 14. Available at: https://www.opendemocracy.net/od-russia/tetiana-bezruk/ukraine-s-ministry-of-internal-hatred (06/2019).

Bezruk, Tetiana (2017). "Liberal Democracy: A Hard Choice for Ukraine." *openDemocracy.* June 13. Available at: https://www.opendemocracy.net/en/odr/liberal-democracy-hard-choice-for-ukraine/ (07/2019).

Bhabha, Homi K. (1994). *The Location of Culture.* London-New York: Routledge.

Bharat, Meenakhsi (2015). "'Major' and 'Minor' Literatures: Indian Cases." In D'haen, Theo; Goerlandt, Iannis; Sell, Roger D. *Major Versus Minor? Languages and Literatures in a Globalized World.* Amsterdam-Philadelphia: John Benjamins Publishing Company. 253–262.

Bilaniuk, Laada (2005). *Contested Tongues: Language Politics and Cultural Correction in Ukraine.* Ithaca (NY)-London: Cornell University Press.

Bilaniuk, Laada (2014). "Criticism and Confidence: Reshaping the Linguistic Marketplace in Post-Soviet Ukraine." In Zaleska Onyshkevych, Larissa M. L.; Rewakowicz, Maria G. (eds.). *Contemporary Ukraine on the Cultural Map of Europe.* London-New York: Routledge. 336–358.

Bil'chenko, Evgeniia (2014). "Kto ia?" *Facebook.* February 21. Available at: https://m.facebook.com/story.php?story_fbid=633031300065317&id=100000753587068 (06/2019).

Blacker, Uilleam (2008). "Representations of the Urban Environment in Contemporary Ukrainian Literature." *eSharp.* Special Issue – Reaction and Reinvention: Changing Times in Central and Eastern Europe.

5–21. Available at: https://www.gla.ac.uk/media/media_92497_en.pdf (06/2019).

Blacker, Uilleam (2012). "Text, City, Image: Recovering Others' Pasts in Literature in Poland, Russian and Ukraine." *Przeglad Humanistyczny*. 6: 139–147.

Blacker, Uilleam (2014). "Blurred Lines: Russian Literature and Cultural Diversity in Ukraine." *The Calvert Journal*. March 17. Available at: https://www.calvertjournal.com/articles/show/2176/russian-culture-in-ukraine-literature (05/2019).

Blakkisrud, Helge (2016). "Blurring the Boundary Between Civic and Ethnic: The Kremlin's New Approach to National Identity Under Putin's Third Term." In Blakkisrud, Helge; Kolstø, Pål (eds.). *The New Russian Nationalism. Imperialism, Ethnicity and Authoritarianism 2000–15*. Edinburgh: Edinburgh University Press. 249–274.

Boichenko, Oleksandr (2017). "Zovsim ostannia terytoriia." *Zbruch*. March 7. Available at: https://zbruc.eu/node/63133 (07/2019).

Bojanowska, Edyta M. (2007). *Nikolaj Gogol: Between Ukrainian and Russian Nationalism*. Cambridge-London: Harvard University Press.

Bolton, Kingsley; Kachru, Braj B. (2006). *World Englishes: Critical Concepts in Linguistics*. 1–6. London-New York: Routledge.

Bondar'-Tereshchenko, Igor' (2014). "Gorkii rafinad. V romannoi mire Vladimira Rafeenko." *Novoe literaturnoe obozrenie*. 125: 292–298.

Book Platform. "Publishing and Bookselling in Ukraine. Results of a Survey on Book Publishing and Distribution, 2012–2013." Available at: http://bookplatform.org/images/activities/47/publishing_study_ukraine_en.pdf (07/2019).

Brazhkina, Anna; Sid, Igor' (1999). "'Iuzhnii Aktsent': Sbornik russo-ukrainskoi kritiki." *Liter.net. Geopoeticheskii server Krymskogo kluba*. May 26. Available at: http://liter-net.1gb.ru/ukr/critique.html (06/2019).

Brubaker, Rogers (1996). *Nationalism Reframed: Nationhood and the National Question in the New Europe*. Cambridge: Cambridge University Press.

Bulkina, Inna (1999). "Russkii Kiev: Provintsiia ili diaspora?" *Znamia*. 2: 148–154.

Bulkina, Inna (2016a). "'Stikhiia Maidana': russkaia i ukrainskaia 'maidannaia poeziia'." *Gefter*. April 1. Available at: http://gefter.ru/archive/18008 (06/2019)

Bulkina, Inna (2016b). "Russkaia literatura Ukrainy: vchera, segodnia, zavtra." *Gefter*. March 9. Available at: http://gefter.ru/archive/17745 (06/2019).

Burima, Maija (2014). "Comparative Literature and a 'Small Nation': The Latvian Experience." *Interlitteraria*. 19, 2: 261–275.

Business Ukraine (2017). "Russian Language in Ukraine." 11/05/2017. Available at: http://bunews.com.ua/society/item/the-russian-language-in-ukraine (04/2019).

Caffee, Naomi (2013). *Russophonia: Towards a Transnational Conception of Russian-Language Literature*. PhD diss. University of California, Los Angeles. Available at: https://escholarship.org/uc/item/3z86s82v.

Casanova, Pascale (2004). *The World Republic of Letters*. Translated by M. B. DeBevoise. Cambridge (MA)-London: Harvard University Press [or. ed. (1999). *La république mondiale des lettres*. Paris: Seuil].

Charnysh, Volha (2015). "Belarus, Ukraine, Russia React to Alexievich's Nobel Prize." *Belarus Digest*. October 13. Available at: https://belarusdigest.com/story/belarus-ukraine-russia-react-to-alexievichs-nobel-prize/ (04/2019).

Chernetsky, Vitaly (2007). *Mapping Postcommunist Cultures: Russia and Ukraine in the Context of Globalization*. Montreal: McGill Queen's University Press.

Chernetsky, Vitaly (2019). "Russophone Writing in Ukraine: Historical Contexts and Post-Euromaidan Changes." In Platt, Kevin M. F (ed.). *Global Russian Cultures*. Madison (WI): The University of Wisconsin Press. 48–68.

Chernova, Oleksandra (2015). "Elena Stiazhkina: Net nikakikh 'donetskikh'." *Insider*. June 11. Available at: http://www.theinsider.ua/politics/5578879a66571/ (06/2019).

Cheskin, Ammon; Kachuyevski, Angela (2018). "The Russian-Speaking Populations in the Post-Soviet Space: Language, Politics and Identity." *Europe-Asia Studies*. 71, 1: 1–23.

Chin, Rita (2003). "Toward a 'Minor Literature'? The Case of *Ausländerliteratur* in Postwar Germany." *New Perspectives on Turkey*. 29. 61–84.

Chkhaidze, Elena (2018). *Politika i literaturnaia traditsiia: russko-gruzinskie literaturnye sviazi posle perestroiki*. Moskva: Novoe literaturnoe obozrenie.

Chudakova, Marietta (2006). "Russkaia Literatura XX veka: Problema granits predmeta izucheniia." *Toronto Slavic Quarterly*. 18. Available at: http://www.utoronto.ca/tsq/18/chudakova18.shtml (06/2019).

Chuprinin, Sergei (2008). *Russkaia literatura segodnia: Zarubezh'e*. Moskva: Vremia.

Clowes, Edith W. (2011). *Russia on the Edge. Imagined Geographies and Post-Soviet Identity*. Ithaca (NY): Cornell University Press.

Corngold, Stanley (1994). "Kafka and the Dialect of Minor Literature." *College Literature*. 21, 1: 89–101.

Dagnino, Arianna (2013). "Transcultural Literature and Contemporary World Literature(s)." *CLCWeb: Comparative Literature and Culture*. 15, 5: 1–10. Available at: https://docs.lib.purdue.edu/cgi/viewcontent.cgi?article=2339&context=clcweb (04/2019).

Dais, Ekaterina (2013a). "Orfei Rafeenko." *Russkii Zhurnal*. May 8. Available at: http://www.russ.ru/Mirovaya-povestka/Orfej-Rafeenko (06/2019)

Dais, Ekaterina (2013b). "Lemur Sofiia i donetskii Demiurg." *Russkii Zhurnal*. July 29. Available at: http://www.russ.ru/Mirovaya-povestka/Lemur-Sofiya-i-doneckij-Demiurg (06/2019).

Dalton-Brown, Sally (2010). "Laughter of the Lost: Andrei Kurkov's Comedies of Displacement." *Slovo*. 22, 2: 104–118.

Datsiuk, Serhii (2017). "Ukraïnizatsiia ta vyrishennia rosiis'koho pytannia." *Ukraïns'ka Pravda*. September 15. Available at: https://blogs.pravda.com.ua/authors/datsuk/59bb9df1328c3/ (04/2019).

Del Gaudio, Salvatore (2011). "O Variativnosti russkogo iazyka na Ukraine." *Izvestiia Rossiiskoi akademii nauk. Seriia literatury i iazyka*. 70, 2: 28–36.

Deleuze, Gilles; Guattari, Félix (1986). *Kafka. Toward a Minor Literature*. Translated by Dana Polan. Minneapolis (MN)-London: University of Minnesota Press [or. ed. (1975) *Kafka. Pour une littérature mineure*, Paris: Minuit].

Demina, Nataliia (2014). "Polina Lavrova. 'Ia chitala vse vremia'." *Polit.ru*. April 5. Available at: http://polit.ru/article/2014/04/05/lavrova_about_books/ (06/2019).

Dmitriev, Aleksandr (2007). "Mii Zhadan, abo Nebo nad Khar'kovom." *Novoe literaturnoe obozrenie*. 85. 289–310.

Dubasevych, Roman (2016). "Ukraine's Sleepwalking into the 'Russian World'." In Smola, Klavdia; Uffelmann, Dirk (eds.), *Postcolonial Slavic Literatures After Communism*. Frankfurt/Main: Peter Lang. 133–159.

Dubinianskaia, Iana (2014). "Problema, kotoroi u nas net." *Forbes-Ukraina*. July 31. Available at: http://forbes.net.ua/woman/1375602-problema-kotoroj-u-nas-net (06/2017).

Dziuba, Ivan (2017). "Perevidkryttia Donechchyny." In Biliavs'kyi, Veniamin; Gryhorov, Mykyta (upor.). *Poroda. Antolohiia ukraïns'kykh pys'mennykiv Donbasu*. Kyiv: Lehenda. 1–19.

Dziubak, Anastasiia (2014). "Literatura i viina: notatky iz Forumu Vydavciv-2014." *Nova gazeta*. September 17. Available at: http://novagazeta.kr.ua/index.php/podii/kultura/257-literatura-i-viina-notatky-iz-forumu-vydavtsiv-2014 (07/2019).

Edmunds, Lowell (2010). "Kafka on Minor Literature." *German Studies Review*. 33, 2: 351–374.

Edwards, Maxim (2019). "Welcome to Ukraine's Post-Post-Maidan Era." *Foreign Policy*. July 24. Available at:: https://foreignpolicy.com/2019/07/24/welcome-to-ukraines-post-post-maidan-era/# (07/2019).

Esterkina, Inga (2018). "Poetesa Iia Kiva: Ani Putin, ani Rosiia ne maiut' kopiraitu na rosiis'ku movu." *Glavkom*. October 3. Available at: https://glavcom.ua/interviews/poetesa-iya-kiva-ani-putin-ani-rosiya-ne-mayut-kopiraytu-na-rosiysku-movu-533225.html (07/2019).

Etkind, Alexander (2017). "Introduction: Genres and genders of protest in Russia's petrostate." In Beumers, Birgit et al. (eds.). *Cultural Forms of Protest in Russia*. Abingdon-New York: Routledge. 1–15.

Fanailova, Elena (2014a). "Vostok Ukrainy. Sotsiologiia strakhov." *Radio Svoboda*. May 8. Available at: https://www.svoboda.org/a/25376829.html (04/2019).

Fanailova, Elena (2014b). "Bogema na barrikadakh. Chast' 11. Pisatel' Aleksei Nikitin." *Radio Svoboda*. August 19. Available at: http://www.svoboda.org/a/26537627.html (07/2019).

Fanailova, Elena (2018). "Dokumenty meniaiut kartinu mira. Pisatel' v arkhivakh SBU." *Radio Svoboda*. August 26. Available at: https://www.svoboda.org/a/29447756.html (07/2019).

Faris, Wendy B. (2002). "The Question of the Other: Cultural Critiques of Magic Realism." *Janus Head*. 5, 2: 101–119.

Finnin, Rory (2013). "Ukrainians: Expect-the-Unexpected Nation." *Center for Research in the Arts, Social Sciences and Humanities*. December 20. Available at: http://www.crassh.cam.ac.uk/blog/post/ukrainians-expect-the-unexpected-nation (06/2019).

Fitzpatrick, Sheila (2015). *Tear Off the Masks! Identity and Imposture in Twentieth-Century Russia*. Princeton (NJ): Princeton University Press.

Foucault, Michel (1970). *The Order of Things: An Archaeology of Human Sciences*. Translated by A. M. Sheridan Smith. New York: Pantheon Books [or. ed. (1966). *Les Mots et les Choses*. Paris: Éditions Gallimard].

Foucault, Michel (1984). *Of Other Spaces: Utopias and Heterotopias*. Translated by Jay Miskowiec. Available at: http://web.mit.edu/allanmc/www/foucault1.pdf (06/2019).

Frank, Susi K. (2016). " 'Multinational Soviet Literature': The Project and Its Post-Soviet Legacy in Iurii Rytkheu and Gennadii Aigi." In Smola, Klavdia; Uffelmann, Dirk (eds.). *Postcolonial Slavic Literatures After Communism*. Frankfurt/Main: Peter Lang. 191–217.

Gefter (2017). "Kruglyi stol 'Rossiia-Ukraina: voina kak factor politizatsii literatury'." April 21. Available at: http://gefter.ru/archive/21994 (07/2019).

Gerasimov, Ilya (2014). "Ukraine 2014: The First Postcolonial Revolution. Introduction to the Forum." *Ab Imperio*. 3: 22–44.

Gerasimov, Ilya; Mogilner, Marina (2015). "Deconstructing Integration: Ukraine's Postcolonial Subjectivity." *Slavic Review*. 74, 4: 715–722.

Gerasimov, Ilya et al. (2016). "Forms and Practices of Envisaging a Postimperial Order: Hybridity as a New Subjectivity." *Ab imperio*. 4: 19–28.

Giuliano, Elise (2019). "Is the Risk of Ethnic Conflict Growing in Ukraine? New Laws Could Create Dangerous Divisions." *Foreign Affairs*. March 18. Available at: https://www.foreignaffairs.com/articles/ukraine/2019-03-18/risk-ethnic-conflict-growing-ukraine (05/2019).

Goble, Paul (2015). "The Birth of a Nation." *The Interpreter*. February 26. Available at: www.interpretermag.com/the-birth-of-a-nation/ (07/2019).

Gogol', Nikolai V. (1952). *Polnoe sobranie sochinenii*. T. 12. Moskva: Izdatel'stvo Akademii Nauk.

Gorbach, Denys (2019). "Voting hard: Ukraine braces for a fateful presidential election." *openDemocracy*. March 20. Available at: https://www.opendemocracy.net/en/odr/voting-hard-ukraine-braces-fateful-presidential-election/ (05/2019).

Gorham, Michael (2011). "Virtual Rusophonia: Language Policy as 'Soft Power' in the New Media Age." *Digital Icons*. 5: 23–48. Available at: https://www.digitalicons.org/wp-content/uploads/issue05/files/2011/05/Gorham-5.2.pdf (04/2019).

Gorham, Michael (2019). "When Soft Power Hardens: The Formation and Fracturing of Putin's 'Russian World'." In Platt, Kevin M. F (ed.). *Global Russian Cultures*. Madison (WI): The University of Wisconsin Press. 185–206.

Grabowicz, George G. (1982). *The Poet as Mythmaker. A Study of Symbolic Meaning in Taras Ševčenko*. Cambridge (MA): Harvard Ukrainian Research Institute.

Grabowicz, George G. (1992). "Ukrainian–Russian Literary Relations in the Nineteenth Century: A Formulation of the Problem." In Potichnyj, Peter J. et al. (eds.). *Ukraine and Russia in Their Historical Encounter*. Edmonton: Canadian Institute of Ukrainian Studies Press. 214–244.

Grabowicz, George G. (1994). "Hohol' i mif Ukraïny." *Suchasnist'*. 9 (401): 77–96.

Grabowicz, George G. (1995). "Ukrainian Studies: Framing the contexts." *Slavic Review*. 54, 3: 674–690.

Grabowicz, George G. (2003). "Between Subversion and Self-Assertion: The Role of Kotliarevshchyna in Russian-Ukrainian Literary Relations." In Kappeler, Andreas et al. (eds.). *Culture, Nation, and Identity: The Ukrainian-Russian Encounter (1600–1945)*. Edmonton: Canadian Institute of Ukrainian Studies Press. 215–228.

Günther, Clemens; Sirotinina, Svetlana (2019). "Beyond the Imperial Matrix: Literary Eurasianisms in Contemporary Russian Literature." In Friess, Nina; Kaminskij, Konstantin (eds.). *Resignification of Borders: Eurasianism and the Russian World*. Berlin: Frank & Timme GmbH. 67–95.

Haines, Brigid (2008). "The Eastern Turn in Contemporary German, Swiss and Austrian Literature." *Journal of Contemporary Central and Eastern Europe*. 16, 2: 135–149.

Haleta, Olena (2013). "Literary CombiNation: Memory and Space in Contemporary Ukrainian Anthologies." *Australian and New Zealand Journal of European Studies*. 5, 2: 71–82.

Harriman Institute (2019). "Envisioning Ukrainian Literature 2019: Versions and Demarcations, Part I." February 19. Available at: https://harriman.columbia.edu/event/envisioning-ukrainian-literature-2019-versions-and-demarcations-part-i (07/2019).

Hart, Jonathan (1997). "Translating and Resisting Empire: Cultural Appropriation and Postcolonial Studies." In Ziff, Bruce; Rao, Pratima V. (eds.). *Borrowed Power. Essays on Cultural Appropriation*. New Brunswick (NJ): Rutgers University Press. 137–168.

Hausbacher, Eva (2016). "On the Slate of Memory: Postcolonial Strategies in Transcultural (Migration) Literature." In Smola, Klavdia; Uffelmann, Dirk (eds.). *Postcolonial Slavic Literatures After Communism*. Frankfurt/Main: Peter Lang. 413–432.

Heathershaw, John (2009). *Post-Conflict Tajikistan: The Politics of Peacebuilding and the Emergence of Legitimate Order*. London and New York: Routledge.

Hofmann, Tatjana (2019). "Crimea: The Interface between Politics and Culture." *ZOiS Spotlight*. 10/2019. March 13. Available at: https://en.zois-berlin.de/publications/zois-spotlight/crimea-the-interface-between-politics-and-culture/ (07/2019).

Holub, Andrii (2017). "Chysla pro slova. Chy hotove suspil'stvo do peretvoren' u movnii politytsi." *Tyzhden'*. May 5. Available at: http://tyzhden.ua/Society/191481 (07/2019).

Horobets', Olena O. (2018). "Statystychnyi analiz knyhovydannia v Ukraïni ta sviti." *Statystyka Ukraïni*. 81, 2: 22–29.

Hrytsak, Iaroslav (2002). "Dvadtsiat' dvi Ukraïny." *Krytyka*. 4: 3–6.

Hrytsak, Yaroslav (2004). "On Sails and Gales, and Ships Sailing in Various Directions: Post-Soviet Ukraine." *Ab Imperio*. 1: 229–254.

Hrytsak, Iaroslav (2015). "The Postcolonial Is Not Enough." *Slavic Review*. 74, 4: 732–737.

Hrytsak, Iaroslav (2017). "Kinets' revoliutsiï?" *Gazeta.ua*. February 10. Available at: https://gazeta.ua/articles/grycak-jaroslav/_kinec-revolyuciyi/751588 (07/2019).

Huba, Roman (2019). "Why Ukraine's New Language Law Will Have Long-Term Consequences." *OpenDemocracy*. May 28. Available at: https://www.opendemocracy.net/en/odr/ukraine-language-law-en/ (10/2019).

Hundorova, Tamara (2001). "The Canon Reversed: New Ukrainian Literature of the 1990s." *Journal of Ukrainian Studies*. 26, 1–2: 249–270.

Hundorova, Tamara (2011). " 'Internal Colonization'—Re-colonization." *Krytyka*. September. Available at: https://m.krytyka.com/en/articles/internal-colonization-re-colonization. [available also in Ukrainian: " '*Vnutrishnia kolonizatsiia'—povtorna kolonizatsiia.*" http://krytyka.com/ua/articles/vnutrishnya-kolonizatsiya-povtorna-kolonizatsiya] (06/2019).

Hundorova, Tamara (2013). *Tranzytna kul'tura. Symptomy postkolonial'noï travmy*. Kyïv: Grani-T.

Hundorova, Tamara (2016). "Ukrainian Euromaidan as Social and Cultural Performance." In Bertelsen, Olga (ed.). *Revolution and War in Contemporary Ukraine. The Challenge of Change*. Stuttgart: ibidem-Verlag. 161–179.

Iakhno, Olena; Hruzdev, Stanislav (2017). "Sotsioloh Ievhen Holovakha: Divchynka Maia—tse nasha ukraïns'ka Matil'da." *Glavcom.ua*. September 22. Available at: http://glavcom.ua/ interviews/sociolog-jevgen-golovaha-divchinka-mayya-ce-nasha-ukrajinska-matilda-438930.html (07/2019).

Ilchuk, Yuliya (2009). *Gogol's Hybrid Performance: The Creation, Reception and Editing of Vechera na Khutore Bliz Dikanki (Evenings on a farm near Dikan'ka, 1831–32)*. PhD diss. University of Southern California. Available at: http://digitallibrary.usc.edu/cdm/ref/collection/p15799coll127/id/283554 (04/2019).

Ilchuk, Yuliya (2017). "Hearing the Voice of Donbas: Art and Literature as Forms of Cultural Protest during the War." *Nationalities Papers*. 45, 2: 256–273.

Ilnytzkyj, Oleh S. (2002). "Cultural Indeterminacy in the Russian Empire: Nikolai Gogol as a Ukrainian Post-Colonial Writer." In Morris, Paul D. (ed.). *A World of Slavic Literatures. Essays in Comparative Slavic*

Studies in Honour of Edward Mozejko. Bloomington (IN): Slavica. 153–171.

Ilnytzkyj, Oleh S. (2003). "Modeling Culture in the Empire: Ukrainian Modernism and the Death of the All-Russian Idea." In Kappeler, Andreas et al. *Culture, Nation and Identity: The Russian-Ukrainian Encounter (1600: 1945)*. Edmonton: Canadian Institute of Ukrainian Studies Press. 298–324.

In Kyiv (2016). "Sanitar s Institutskoi." March 24. Available at: http:// inkyiv.com.ua/2016/03/sanitar-s-institutskoy/ (07/2019).

Interfax Ukraine (2019). "Zelensky to all states of former USSR: look at us, everything is possible." April 21. Avalaible at: https://en.interfax.com. ua/news/general/582660.html (07/2019).

Ivanko, Ivan (2010). "Knyhovydannia v URSR. Skil'ky ukraïns'koiu i skil'ky rosiis'koiu." *Istorychna Pravda*. November 9. Available at: https://www. istpravda.com.ua/articles/2010/11/9/3586/ (07/2019).

IWM (2017). "The Future of Russianness in Post-Maidan Ukraine." February 13. Available at: https://www.iwm.at/events/event/the-future- of-russianness-in-post-maidan-ukraine/ (07/2019).

Jameson, Fredric (1986). "Third-World Literature in the Era of Multinational Capitalism." *Social Text*. 15: 65–88.

Jamison, Anne (2018). *Kafka's Other Prague: Writings from the Czechoslovak Republic*. Evanston (IL): Northwestern University Press.

Johnson, Steve (2017). "Russian Language in Decline as Post-Soviet States Reject It." *Financial Times*. April 13. Available at: https://app.ft.com/ content/c42fbd1c-1e08-11e7-b7d3-163f5a7f229c?sectionid=world (04/2019).

Kabanov, Aleksandr (2014). *Volkhvy v planetarii*. Kharkiv: Folio.

Kabanov, Aleksandr (2017). *Na iazyke vraga*. Kharkiv: Folio.

Kachru, Braj B. (1992). "World Englishes: Approaches, Issues and Resources." *Language Teaching*. 25,1: 1–14.

Kachru, Braj B. et al. (2006). "Introduction: The World of World Englishes." In Kachru, Braj B. et al. (eds.). *The Handbook of World Englishes*. Chichester: Wiley-Blackwell. 1–16.

Kalfus, Ken (2001). "Open Season." *The New York Times*. November 11. Available at: http://www.nytimes.com/2001/11/11/books/open-season. html (06/2019).

Kalinin, Il'ia (2015). "Kul'turnaia politika kak instrument demodernizatsii." *Polit.ru*. February 15. Available at: http://polit.ru/article/2015/02/15/cultural_policy/ (07/2019).

Kamusella, Tomasz (2018). "Russian: A Monocentric or Pluricentric Language?" *Colloquia Humanistica*. 7: 153–196.

Kappeler, Andreas (2003). "Mazepintsy, Malorossy, Khokhly: Ukrainians in the Ethnic Hierarchy of the Russian Empire." In Kappeler, Andeas et al. (eds.). *Culture, Nation, and Identity: The Ukrainian–Russian Encounter (1600–1945)*. Edmonton: Canadian Institute of Ukrainian Studies Press. 162–181.

Kappeler, Andreas (2009). "From an Ethnonational to a Multiethnic to a Transnational Ukrainian History." In Kasianov, Georgiy; Ther, Philipp (eds.). *A Laboratory of Transnational History. Ukraine and Recent Ukrainian Historiography*. Budapest-NewYork: CEU Press. 51–80.

Kasianov, Georgiy (2009). "Nationalized History: Past Continuous, Present Perfect, Future..." In Kasianov, Georgiy; Ther, Philipp (eds.). *A Laboratory of Transnational History. Ukraine and Recent Ukrainian Historiography*. Budapest-NewYork: CEU Press. 7–23.

Kasianov, Georgiy; Ther, Philipp (2009). "Introduction." In Kasianov, Georgiy; Ther, Philipp (eds.). *A Laboratory of Transnational History. Ukraine and Recent Ukrainian Historiography*. Budapest-NewYork: CEU Press. 1–4.

Katsun, Iuliia (2015). "Ukrainskie pisateli sozdali sbornik o voine dlia rossiian." *Komsomol'skaia pravda v Ukraine*. November 1. Available at: http://kp.ua/culture/517699-ukraynskye-pysately-sozdaly-sbornyk-o-voine-dlia-rossiian (06/2019).

Khersonskii, Boris (2010). "Nad konturnoi kartoi." *Kreshchatik*. 1. Available at: https://magazines.gorky.media/kreschatik/2010/1/nad-konturnoj-kartoj.html (07/2019).

Khersonskii, Boris (2011). "Odesskii Sindrom." *Kreshchatik*. 1. Available at : https://magazines.gorky.media/kreschatik/2011/1/odesskij-sindrom.html (07/2019).

<Khersonskii, Boris> Khersonsky, Boris (2016). "On The Languages of Ukrainian Poetry." *Odessa Review*. December 2. Available at: http://odessareview.com/languages-ukrainian-poetry/ (06/2019).

Khersonskii, Boris (2019). "Svoiu pozitsiiu v otnoshenii iazykovoi problemy v Ukraine…" *Facebook*. June 17. Available at: https://www.facebook.com/borkhers/posts/2538022026232608 (07/2019).

Khmel'ko, Valerii (2004). "Lingvo-etnichna struktura Ukraïny: rehional'ni osoblyvosti ta tendentsiï zmin za roky nezalezhnosti." *Kyïvs'kyi mizhnarodnyi instytut sotsiolohiï*. 1–19. Available at: http://www.kiis.com.ua/materials/articles_HVE/16_linguaethnical.pdf (04/2019).

Khmel'ovs'ka, Oksana (2019). "Knyhovydannia-2018: stop-kryza i pererozpodil liderstva." *Chytomo*. March 4. Available at: https://www.chytomo.com/knyhovydannia-2018-stop-kryza-j-pererozpodil-liderstva/.

KIIS (2019). "Khto za koho proholosuvav: demografija natsional'noho ekzyt-polu." April 9. Available at: http://kiis.com.ua/?lang=ukr&cat=reports&id=850&page=1 (07/2019).

Kinsella, Ali (2019). "Interview: Mark Andryczyk on Ukraine's literary process." *The Ukrainian Weekly*. May 11. Available at: http://www.ukrweekly.com/uwwp/interview-mark-andryczyk-on-ukraines-literary-process/ (07/2019).

Kiva, Iia (2016). "Molodaia Ukrainskaia Poeziia." *Literratura*. December 31. Available at: http://literratura.org/poetry/2053-molodaya-ukrainskaya-poeziya.html (06/2019).

Kiva, Iia (2017). "V kakuiu nam storonu." *Literratura*. March 5. Available at: http://literratura.org/poetry/2158-iya-kiva_v-kakuyu-nam-storonu.html (06/2019).

Kiva, Iia (2019). "Iia Kiva: Iia Kiva." *Dvoetochie*. 32. June 13. Available at: https://dvoetochie.wordpress.com/2019/06/13/iya-kiva/ (07/2019).

Kokhanovskaia, Tat'iana; Nazarenko, Mikhail (2011a). "Ukrainskii Vektor. Schastlivoe detstvo i trudnoe otrochestvo." *Novyi Mir*. 10: 207–214.

Kokhanovskaia, Tat'iana; Nazarenko, Mikhail (2011b). "Ukrainskii Vektor: Sny o minuvshem." *Novyi Mir*. 6: 206–212.

Kokhanovskaia, Tat'iana; Nazarenko, Mikhail (2012a). "Ukrainskii Vektor: Istoriia s geografiei. Poezd N. 112 i drugie marshruty." *Novyi Mir*. 12: 203–212.

Kokhanovskaia, Tat'iana; Nazarenko, Mikhail (2012b). "Ukrainskii Vektor: Istoriia s geografiei. Kievskie gory i nory." *Novyi Mir*. 10: 209–217.

Kolesnikov, Andrei (2015). "Russian Ideology After Crimea." *Carnegie Moscow Center*. September. Available at: https://carnegieendowment. org/files/CP_Kolesnikov_Ideology2015_web_Eng.pdf (07/2019).

Kolesnikov, Andrei (2016). "Why Russians Say Yes." *EastWest*. December 29. Available at: https://eastwest.eu/en/eastwest-69/why-russians-say-yes (07/2019).

Kołodziejczyk, Dorota; Şandru, Cristina (2012). "Introduction: On Colonialism, Communism and East-Central Europe – Some Reflections." *Journal of Postcolonial Writing*. 48, 2: 113–116.

Kolstø, Pål (1996). "The New Russian Diaspora – an Identity of Its Own? Possible Identity Trajectories for Russians in the Former Soviet Republic." *Ethnic and Racial Studies*. 19, 3: 609–639.

Kolstø, Pål (2016). "Crimea vs. Donbas: How Putin Won Russian Nationalist Support – and Lost it Again." *Slavic Review*. 75, 3: 702–725.

Korablev, Aleksandr (2004). "Literaturnaia Ukraina." *Dikoe Pole*. 5: 208–223.

Kordan, Bohdan S. (2016). "Maidan and The Politics of Change: Meaning, Significance, and Other Questions." *East/West: Journal of Ukrainian Studies*. III, 1: 137–154.

Korek, Janusz (ed.) (2007). *From Sovietology to Postcoloniality: Poland and Ukraine from a Postcolonial Perspective*. Huddinge: Södertörns högskola.

Kosmarskaya, Natalya; Kosmarski, Artyom (2019). " 'Russian Culture' in Central Asia as a Transethnic Phenomenon." In Platt, Kevin M. F (ed.). *Global Russian Cultures*. Madison (WI): University of Wisconsin Press. 69–93.

Kots, Aleksandr (2017). "Zakhar Prilepin sobral v DNR svoi batal'on." *Komsomol'skaya Pravda*. 13/02/2017. Available at: http://www.kp.ru/ daily/26642.5/3661046/ (07/2019).

Kotsarev, Oleh (2018). "Antolohiia 'Poroda' zasvidchuie: literatura Donbasu—chastyna ukraïns'koï." *Teksty.org.ua*. February 16. Available at: http://texty.org.ua/pg/article/editorial/read/82942/Antologija_Poroda_ zasvidchuje_literatura_Donbasu__chastyna?a_srt=&a_offset= (07/2019).

Kotsarev, Oleh (2019). "Volodymyr Rafieienko, avtor knyhy 'Mondegrin': 'My vse shche rostemo, i dai nam Bozhe kolys' nareshti vyrosti'." *Yakaboo. Knyzhkovyi blog.* 03/06/2019. Available at: https://blog.yakaboo.ua/rafeenko/ (07/2019).

Krasniashchikh, Andrei (2015). "Rusukrlit kak on est'." *Novyi mir.* 9. 173–197.

Krasnikov, Denys (2018). "Bilingual magazine becomes first victim of Lviv Oblast moratorium on Russian." *Kyiv Post.* October 13. Available at: https://www.kyivpost.com/business/bilingual-magazine-becomes-first-victim-of-lviv-oblast-moratorium-on-russian.html (07/2019).

Krasovitskii, Aleksandr (2016). "Ot sostavitelia." In *Ukrainskaia proza i poeziia na russkom iazyke.* Kharkiv: Folio. 3–5.

Kratochvil, Alexander (2007). "Geopoetic Models in Postmodern Ukrainian and Czech Prose." *Journal of Ukrainian Studies.* 32, 1: 63–77.

Kratochvil, Alexander (2014). "The Writers and the Maidan." *Euxeinos.* 13: 32–36.

Kravchenko, Vladimir (2010). *Khar'kov/Kharkiv: Stolitsa Pogranich'ia.* Vilnius: Evropeiskii gumanitarnyi universitet.

Krigel', Mikhail (2016). "Posmertnye prikliucheniia zvonaria. Kak pisatel' R. uekhal iz goroda Z v stranu U, po doroge umer i napisal roman." *Dlinnyi Fokus.* May 13. Available at: https://focus.ua/long/350379/ (07/2019).

Kruchyk, Ihor (2014). "Dity radians'koï vdovy." *Krytyka.* 08/2014. Available at: https://krytyka.com/ua/articles/dity-radyanskoyi-vdovy (05/2019).

Kruk, Halyna (2014). "Khto ia?" *Facebook.* February 24. Available at: https://www.facebook.com/halyna.kruk/posts/10152136990691919 (07/2019).

Krymskii Klub. "Kordon (Tri pogranichnykh poeta)." Available at: http://liter-net.1gb.ru/Kordon/ (06/2019).

Kuchkina, Anastasiia (2017). "V Ukraine na tri mesiatsa polnost'iu zapretili vvoz knig iz RF. Dazhe 'dlia sebia'." *Vesti.* January 26. Available at: http://vesti-ukr.com/strana/221840-v-ukraine-na-tri-mecjatsa-vveli-polnyj-zapret-na-vvoz-knih-iz-rf-dazhe-v-ruchnoj-kladi (07/2019).

Kudriavtseva, Natalia (2019). "Ukraine's Language Law: Whose Rights are Protected?" *Wilson Center: Focus Ukraine.* July 8. Available at: https://www.wilsoncenter.org/blog-post/ukraines-language-law-whose-rights-are-protected (07/2019).

Kukulin, Il'ia (2007). "Evropeiskii dialog: ukrainskaia i russkaia slovesnost'. Ot redaktora." *Novoe literaturnoe obozrenie*. 85: 242-245.

Kukulin, Il'ia (2009). "Obmen roliami." *OpenSpace.ru*. April 27. Available at: http://os.colta.ru/literature/projects/9533/details/9536/page1/ (06/2019).

Kukulin, Ilya (2016). " 'The Long-Legged Time Is Fording the War': The Postcolonial Condition of the Russian-Language Poetry of Ukraine." In Smola, Klavdia; Uffelmann, Dirk (eds.). *Postcolonial Slavic Literatures After Communism*. Frankfurt/Main: Peter Lang. 161-187.

Kukulin, Il'ia (2018). "To Create a Person When You Aren't One Yet...." *Russian Studies in Literature*. 54, 1–3: 58–83.

Kukulin, Ilya (2019). "Russia as Whole and as Fragments." In Platt, Kevin M. F (ed.). *Global Russian Cultures*. Madison (WI): University of Wisconsin Press. 151–182.

Kulyk, Volodymyr (2007). "Iazykovye ideologii v ukrainskom politicheskom i intellektual'nom diskurskakh." *Otechestvennye Zapiski*. 1: 296–316.

Kulyk, Volodymyr (2015). "One Nation, Two Languages? National Identity and Language Policy in Post-Euromaidan Ukraine." *PONARS Eurasia*. September. 1–9. Available at: http://www.ponarseurasia.org/sites/default/files/policy-memos-pdf/Pepm389_Kulyk_Sept2015_1.pdf (06/2019).

Kulyk, Volodymyr (2016). "National Identity in Ukraine: Impact of Euromaidan and the War." *Europe-Asia Studies*. 68, 4: 588–608.

Kulyk, Volodymyr (2017). "Memory and Language: Ukraine's Divergent Policies on Two Controversial Issues." *PONARS Eurasia*. Policy Memo n. 462. March. Available at: http://www.ponarseurasia.org/sites/default/files/policy-memos-pdf/Pepm462_Kulyk_March2017_1.pdf (07/2019).

Kulyk, Volodymyr (2018a). "Shedding Russianness, Recasting Ukrainianness: The Post-Euromaidan Dynamics of Ethnonational Identification in Ukraine." *Post-Soviet Affairs*. 34, 2–3: 119–138.

Kulyk, Volodymyr (2018b). "Between the 'Self' and the 'Other': Representations of Ukraine's Russian-speakers in Social Media Discourse." *East/West: Journal of Ukrainian Studies*. V, 2: 65–88.

Kulyk, Volodymyr (2019a). "Memory and Language: Different Dynamics in the Two Aspects of Identity Politics in Post-Euromaidan Ukraine." *Nationalities Papers*. 1–18. DOI: https://doi.org/10.1017/nps.2018.60 (12/2019).

Kulyk, Volodymyr (2019b). "Identity in Transformation: Russian-speakers in Post-Soviet Ukraine." *Europe-Asia Studies*. 71, 1: 156–178.

Kurilenko, Aleksandr (2018). "Andrei Kurkov: 'Ukraina dolzhna sdelat' russkii iazyk svoei kul'turnoi sobstvennost'iu'." *Ds News*. January 10. Available at: http://www.dsnews.ua/politics/andrey-kurkov-putinu-ne-vazhno-chto-dumayut-ukrainskie-russkie--02012018220000 (07/2019).

Kurina, Aksin'ia (2016). "Istoryk Heorhii Kas'ianov: Sposoby zdiisnennia dekomunizatsiï nahadaiut' komunistychni praktyky." *Ukraïns'ka Pravda*. May 7. Available at: http://life.pravda.com.ua/society/2016/05/7/211912/ (06/2019).

Kurkov, Andrei (2000). *Dobryi angel smerti*. Kharkiv: Folio [En. ed.: Kurkov, Andrey (2011b). *The Good Angel of Death*. Translated by Andrew Bromfield. London: Vintage Books].

Kurkov, Andrei (2001). *Piknik na l'du*. Kharkiv: Folio [En. ed.: Kurkov, Andrey (2011a). *Death and The Penguin*. Translated by George Bird. London: Vintage Books].

Kurkov, Andrei (2005). "My War of Words." *The Evening Standard*. March 21. Available at: https://www.questia.com/newspaper/1G1-130581460/my-war-of-words (06/2019).

Kurkov, Andrei (2009). "A Wall Comes Down, a World Is Born." *The UNESCO Courier*. 9: 22–23. Available at: https://unesdoc.unesco.org/ark:/48223/pf0000189799 (06/2019).

Kurkov, Andrei (2012). "Ukraine's War of the Words." *The Guardian*. July 5. Available at: http://www.theguardian.com/commentisfree/2012/jul/05/ukraine-war-of-words-russian?newsfeed=true (06/2019).

Kurkov, Andrei (2015). *Dnevnik maidana*. Kharkiv: Folio [En. ed. Kurkov, Andrey (2014). *Ukraine Diaries. Dispatches from Kiev*. Translated by Sam Taylor. London: Harvill Secker].

Kuzio, Taras (2001). "Identity and Nation-building in Ukraine: Defining the 'Other'." *Ethnicities*. 1: 343–365.

Kuzio, Taras (2003). "Census: Ukraine, More Ukrainian." *Russia and Eurasia Review*. 2, 3: 7–10. Available at: https://jamestown.org/program/census-ukraine-more-ukrainian/ (11/2019).

Ładykowski, Paweł (2015). "Poland and Its Eastern Neighbours: A Postcolonial Case Study." *Baltic Journal of European Studies*. 5, 1 (18): 109–132.

Laitin, David D. (1998). *Identity in Formation: The Russian-Speaking Populations in the Near Abroad*. Ithaca (NY)-London: Cornell University Press.

Laruelle, Marlene (2015a). "Russia as a 'Divided Nation,' from Compatriots to Crimea: A Contribution to the Discussion on Nationalism and Foreign Policy." *Problems of Post-Communism*. 62, 2: 88–97.

Laruelle, Marlene (2015b). *The "Russian World." Russia's Soft Power and Geopolitical Imagination*. Washington: Center on Global Interests.

Laruelle, Marlene (2016). "The three colors of Novorossiya, or the Russian nationalist mythmaking of the Ukrainian crisis." *Post-Soviet Affairs*. 32, 1: 55–74.

Laruelle, Marlene (2017a). "Putin's Regime and the Ideological Market: A Difficult Balancing Game." *Carnegie Endowment for International Peace*. March 16. Available at: http://carnegieendowment.org/2017/03/16/putins-regime-and-ideological-market -difficult-balancing-game-pub-68250 (07/2019).

Laruelle, Marlene (2017b). "Is Nationalism a Force for Change in Russia?" *Daedalus*. 2: 89–100.

Lazarus, Neil (2012). "Spectres Haunting: Postcommunism and Postcolonialism." *Journal of Postcolonial Writing*. 48, 2: 117–129.

Lipovetsky, Mark (2002). "Explosive Compromises of Russian Postmodernism." In Albertazzi, Silvia; Possamai, Donatella (a cura di). *Postcolonialism and Postmodernism. Atti del convegno tenuto a Bologna il 5/10/2001*. Padova: Il Poligrafo. 57–74.

Lipovetsky, Mark (2005). "The Missing Link: Postcolonial Discourses in Post-Soviet Culture." In Albertazzi Silvia et al. (a cura di). *Post-scripta. Incontri possibili e impossibili tra culture*. Padova: Il Poligrafo. 155–174.

LitAktsent (2013a). "Pys'mennyky pro movu: Marianna Kiianovs'ka i Taras Prokhas'ko." February 21. Available at: http://litakcent.com/2013/02/21/pysmennyky-pro-movu-marianna-kijanovska-i-taras-prohasko/ (05/2019).

LitAktsent (2013b). "Pys'mennyky pro movu: Liudmyla Taran i Volodymyr Dibrova." March 13. Available at: http://litakcent.com/2013/03/13/pysmennyky-pro-movu-ljudmyla-taran-i-volodymyr-dibrova/ (05/2019).

LitAktsent (2013c). "Pys'mennyky pro movu: Serhii Zhadan i Tania Maliarchuk." February 27. Available at: http://litakcent.com/2013/02/27/pysmennyky-pro-movu-serhij-zhadan-i-tanja-maljarchuk/ (05/2019).

LitAktsent (2013d). 'Pys'mennyky pro movu: Natalka Sniadanko i Petro Tarashchuk." March 1. Available at: http://litakcent.com/2013/03/01/ pysmennyky-pro-movu-natalka-snjadanko-i-petro-taraschuk/ (05/2019).

LitAktsent (2013e). "Pys'mennyky pro movu: Iurii Vynnychuk i Natalka Bilotserkivets'." March 8. Available at: http://litakcent.com/2013/03/08/ pysmennyky-pro-movu-jurij-vynnychuk-i-natalka-bilocerkivec/ (05/2019).

LitAktsent (2013 f). 'Pys'mennyky pro movu: Ostap Slyvyns'kyi i Andrii Sodomora." February 25. Available at: http://litakcent.com/2013/02/25/ pysmennyky-pro-movu-ostap-slyvynskyj-i-andrij-sodomora/ (05/2019).

Liubka, Andrii (2016). "I tak paimut." *Zbruch*. April 27. Available at: http://zbruc.eu/node/50839 (06/2019).

Liubka, Andrii (2019a). "Volodymyr Rafeienko i ioho mova." *Den'*. May 17. Available at: https://day.kyiv.ua/uk/blog/suspilstvo/volodymyr-rafeyenko-i-yogo-mova (07/2019).

Liubka, Andrii (2019b). "Revoliutsiia hidnosti—Kontrrevoliutsiia Nitsosti." *Zbruch*. July 23. Available at: https://zbruc.eu/node/90992 (07/2019).

Lloyd, David (1987). *Nationalism and Minor Literature. James Clarence Mangan and The Emergence of Irish Cultural Nationalism*. Berkeley (CA), Los Angeles (CA), London: University of California Press.

Lotman, Iurii M. (1994). *Cercare la strada. Modelli della cultura*. Translated by Nicoletta Marcialis. Venezia: Marsilio [ru. ed. (2010). *Nepredskazuemye mekhanizmy kul'tury*. Tallin: TLU Press].

Lotman, Iurii M. (2009). *Culture and Explosion*. Marina Grishakova (ed.). Translated by Wilma Clark. Berlin: De Gruyter [or. ed. (2000) *Semiosfera: Kul'tura i vzryv; Vnutri mysliashchikh mirov; Stat'i. Issledovaniia. Zametki*, S. Peterburg: Isskustvo-SPB].

Luckyj, George S. N. (1971). *Between Gogol' and Ševčenko: Polarity in the Literary Ukraine, 1798–1847*. Munich: Wilhelm Fink Verlag.

Luckyj, George S. N. (1998). *The Anguish of Mykola Hohol a.k.a. Nikolaj Gogol*. Toronto: Canadian Scholars' Press.

Manucharian, Diana (2019). "Snaider: Pochemu Ukraine nuzhen Zelenskii i pravo na russkii iazyk." *Liga*. June 23. Available at: https://biz.liga. net/pervye-litsa/all/article/snayder-pochemu-ukraine-nujen-zelenskiy-i-pravo-na-russkiy-yazyk?fbclid=IwAR3nVfx3eLGBG4aOeorbhmsYnp WkbMJGxVWEsWy78evqVMyciBAk8S3H9eA (07/2019).

Marples, David R. (2015). "Open Letter from Scholars and Experts on Ukraine Re. The So- Called 'Anti-Communist Law'." *Krytyka*. 04/2015. Available at: https://krytyka.com/en/articles/open-letter-scholars-and-experts-ukraine-re-so-called-anti-communist-law (07/2019).

Marusyk, Taras (2016). "'Movnyi zakon' Kivalova-Kolesnichenka. Troians'ki koni Kremlia." *Radio Svoboda*. September 6. Available at: https://www.radiosvoboda.org/a/28099057.html (07/2019).

Masenko, Larysa (2017). "Movni zakonoproekty. Pryvyd 'nasyl'nytskoï ukraïnizatsiï' u dyskusiiakh." *Radio Svoboda*. January 28. Available at: https://www.radiosvoboda.org/a/28263923.html (07/2019).

McGrane, Sally (2017). "A Craftsman of Russian Verse Helps Ukraine Find Its New Voice." *The New York Times*. April 10. Available at: https://www.nytimes.com/2015/04/11/world/europe/a-russian-poet-helps-ukraine-navigate-its-new-identity.html (06/2019).

Melezhik, Leonid (2013). "Russkii ili russkoiazychnyi: samoidentifikatsiia pisatelia vne Rossii." *Svobodnaia Pressa*. November 4. Available at: http://svpressa.ru/culture/article/76791/?rss=1 (06/2019).

Melnikov, Dmitriy (2017). *Toward Russophone Super-Literature: Making Subjectivities, Spaces and Temporalities in Post-Soviet Kazakhstani Russophone Writing*. Thesis, Nazarbayev University. Available at: https://nur.nu.edu.kz/handle/123456789/2454 (04/2019).

Mel'nikov, Rostislav; Tsaplin, Iurii (2007). "Severo-vostok iugo-zapada (o sovremennoi kharkovskoi literature)." *Novoe literaturnoe obozrenie*. 85. 263–288.

Mikheieva, Oksana (2017). "Report based on the results of focus group discussions conducted within the framework of 'Strengthening Electoral Preparedness and Political Participation in Ukraine' Project." *Sociology – UKU*. 1–19. Available at: http://sociology.ucu.edu.ua/wp-content/uploads/2017/02/FGD_eng.pdf (06/2019).

Mikheieva, Oksana; Sereda, Victoria (2015). "Contemporary Refugees in Ukraine: Causes of Displacement, Strategies of Resettlement, and Problems of Adaptation." *Sociology – UKU*. December. 1–24. Available at: http://sociology.ucu.edu.ua/wp-content/uploads/2015/12/Contemporary-Refugees-in-Ukraine-2014.pdf (06/2019).

Miller, Alexei; Wert, Paul W. (2015). "The 'Ukrainian Crisis' and Its Multiple Histories." *Kritika: Explorations in Russian and Eurasian History*. 16, 1: 145–148.

Minakov, Mikhail (2017). "The Language Issue in Ukraine, Again." *Focus Ukraine.* September 26. Available at: https://www.wilsoncenter.org/blog-post/the-language-issue-ukraine-again (07/2019).

Minakov, Mikhail (2018). *Development and Dystopia: Studies in Post-Soviet Ukraine and Eastern Europe.* Stuttgart: ibidem-Verlag.

Minakov, Mikhail (2019). "Republic of Clans: The Evolution of the Ukrainian Political System." In Magyar, Bálint (ed.). *Stubborn Structures: Reconceptualizing Post-Communist Regimes.* Budapest-New York: CEU Press. 246–287.

Mironova, Anastasia; Bykov, Dmitrii (2017). "Mozg natsii." *Novaia Gazeta.* January 22. Available at: https://www.novayagazeta.ru/articles/2017/01/23/71248-yazyk-vraga-podhodit-tolko-dlya-listovok (07/2019).

MKRF (2014). "Osnovy gosudarstvennoi kul'turnoi politiki (Proekt)." *Ministerstvo Kul'tury Rossiiskoi Federatsii.* May 16. Available at: http://kremlin.ru/events/administration/21027.

MKRF (2015). "Osnovy gosudarstvennoi kul'turnoi politiki." *Ministerstvo Kul'tury Rossiiskoi Federatsii.* Available at: https://www.mkrf.ru/upload/mkrf/mkdocs2016/OSNOVI-PRINT.NEW.indd.pdf (06/2019).

Moore, David C. (2001). "Is the Post- in Postcolonial the Post- in Post-Soviet? Toward a Global Postcolonial Critique." *PMLA.* 116, 1: 111–128.

Morev, Gleb (2014). "Andrei Poliakov: 'Ia ne znaiu, chto takoe byt' russkim'." *Colta.ru.* May 29. Available at: http://www.colta.ru/articles/literature/3386 (06/2019).

Morrison, Alexander (2017). "Russian Beyond Russia." *EurasiaNet.* April 20. Available at: http://www.eurasianet.org/node/83296 (04/2019).

Moser, Michael (2013). *Language Policy and the Discourse on Languages in Ukraine under President Viktor Yanukovych (25 February 2010–28 October 2012).* Stuttgart: ibidem-Verlag.

Muratkhanov, Vadim (2011). "Apokalipsis segodnia." *Novyi Mir.* 11: 194–196.

Mykhailova, Ol'ha (2014). "Ukrainskie russkie." *Ukraïns'ka Pravda.* March 26. Available at: http://life.pravda.com.ua/columns/2014/03/26/160035 (06/2019).

Myshlovska, Oksana; Schmid, Ulrich (eds.) (2019). *Regionalism Without Regions: Reconceptualizing Ukraine's Heterogeneity.* Budapest-New York: CEU Press.

Nazarbaev, Nursultan (2017). "Vzgliad v budushchee: modernizatsiia obshchestvennogo soznaniia." *Khabar*. April 12. Available at: https://24. kz/ru/specprojecty/statya-n-nazarbaeva-vzglyad-v-budushchee-modernizatsiya-obshchestvennogo-soznaniya (04/2019).

Nazarenko, Mikhail (1998). "O mertvom i zhivom slove." September 18. Available at: http://lib.ru/OLDI/rec_okara.txt (05/2019).

Nazarenko, Mikhail (2005). *Real'nost' chuda (O knigakh Mariny i Sergeia Diachenko)*. Kyiv: Moi Kompiuter.

<Nazarenko, Mikhail> Nazarenko, Mykhailo (2014). "Vtecha z utopiï." *Krytyka*. 3–4: 26–27.

Nemtsev, Mikhail (2017). "Piat' tezisov o 'russkom' i o 'russkom mire'." *Gefter*. March 1. Available at: http://gefter.ru/archive/21334 (06/2019).

Nemtsev, Mikhail (2019). "Rethinking the Russian World." *Riddle*. April 8. Available at: https://www.ridl.io/en/rethinking-the-russian-world/ [also in Russian: "K deterritorializatsii Russkogo Mira." https://www.ridl.io/ru/k-deterritorializacii-russkogo-mira/] (04/2019).

Nikitin, Aleksei (2011). *Istemi*. Moskva: Ad Marginem [En. ed. (2013). *Istemi*. Translated by Anne Marie Jackson. London: Peter Owen Ltd.].

Nikitin, Aleksei (2012). *Madzhong*. Moskva: Ad Marginem.

Nikitin, Aleksei (2014). *Victory Park*. Moskva: Ad Marginem [It. ed. (2019). *Victory Park*. Traduzione di Laura Pagliara. Roma: Voland].

Nikitin, Aleksei (2016). *Sanitar s Institutskoi*. Kyiv: Liuta Sprava.

Nikitin, Aleksei (2018). "Banda Salivenko (glava iz novogo romana)." *Vremena*. 4, 8: 151–164.

Nikitina, Yulia (2014). "Russian Approaches to State- and Nation-Building in Russia's Ukraine Policy." *PONARS Eurasia*. Policy Memo No. 348. September. Available at: http://www.ponarseurasia.org/sites/default/files/policy-memos-pdf/Pepm348_Nikitina_Sept2014.pdf (06/2019).

Nikolaichuk, Solomiia (2015). "Tse ne nasha viina,—Zhadan." *Kanal 24*. February 10. Available at: http://24tv.ua/tse_ne_nasha_viyna__zhadan_n541404 (06/2019).

Nitsoi, Larysa (2017). "Try zakonoproekty pro movu. Vybir Krashchogo." *Radio Svoboda*. January 29. Available at: https://www.radiosvoboda.org/a/28265535.html (07/2019).

Novaia Gazeta (2017). "Iasen pen." January 15. Available at: https://novayagazeta.ru/articles/2017/01/15/71151-yasen-pen?print=true (07/2019).

Novoe Vremia (2017). "Zhadan: U nas vidbuvaiet'sia borot'ba ne za ukraïns'ku movu, a proty rosiis'koïi." February 4. Available at: https:// nv.ua/ukr/ukraine/politics/zhadan-u-nas-vidbuvajetsja-borotba-ne-za-ukrajinsku-movu-a-proti-rosijskoji-587361.html (07/2019).

Okara, Andrei (2008). "Zapakh mertvogo slova-2." *Ukraïns'ka Pravda*. February 25. Available at: http://blogs.pravda.com.ua/authors/ okara/47c2adf2d8235/ (05/2019).

Ostrov (2014). "Pisatel'nitsa iz Donetska v Moskve ob'iasnila tomu, kto khochet zavoevyvat': 'Ukrainu ubit' nel'zia'." April 24. Available at: http://www.ostro.org/general/society/news/443332/ (06/2019).

Oushakine, Serguei (2000). "In the State of Post-Soviet Aphasia: Symbolic Development in Contemporary Russia." *Europe-Asia Studies*. 52, 6: 991–1016.

Oushakine, Serguei (2016). "Neighbours in memory. Svetlana Alexievich: the first major postcolonial author of post-Communism." *Times Literary Supplement*. November 18: 10–12.

Pachlovska, Oxana (1998). *Civiltà letteraria ucraina*. Roma: Carocci.

Pavlyshyn, Marko (1992). "Post-Colonial Features in Contemporary Ukrainian Culture." *Australian Slavonic and East European Studies*. 17, 1–2: 41–55.

Pavlyshyn, Marko (2016a). "Literary History as Provocation of National Identity, National Identity as Provocation of Literary History: The Case of Ukraine." *Thesis Eleven*. 136, 1: 74–89.

Pavlyshyn, Marko (2016b). " 'The Tranquil Lakes of the Transmontane Commune:' Literature and/Against Postcoloniality in Ukraine After 1991." In Smola, Klavdia; Uffelmann, Dirk (eds.). *Postcolonial Slavic Literatures After Communism*. Frankfurt/Main: Peter Lang. 59–82.

Petrenko, Tetiana (2019). "Mova, shcho drimaie v tobi: 'Mondegrin' Volodymyra Rafieienka." *Chytomo*. June 24. Available at: http://www. chytomo.com/mova-shcho-drimaie-v-tobi-mondegrin-volodymyra-rafieienka/ (07/2019).

Pidgora, Nikita (2017). "Ukraine's Displaced Universities." *openDemocracy*. March 3. Available at: https://www.opendemocracy.net/od-russia/nikita-pidgora/ukraine-s-displaced-universities (06/2019).

Platt, Kevin M. F. (2013). "Eccentric Orbit: Mapping Russian Culture in the Near Abroad." In Turoma, Sanna; Waldstein, Maxim (eds.). *Empire*

De/Centered: New Spatial Histories of Russia and the Soviet Union. Aldershot-Burlington (VT): Ashgate. 271–296.

Platt, Kevin M. F. (2019a). "Introduction: Putting Russian Cultures in Place." In Platt, Kevin M. F (ed.). *Global Russian Cultures*. Madison (WI): University of Wisconsin Press. 3–17.

Platt, Kevin M. F. (2019b). "Distance and Proximity in the Baltic 'Near Abroad'." In Platt, Kevin M. F (ed.). *Global Russian Cultures*. Madison (WI): University of Wisconsin Press. 94–112.

Plokhy, Serhii (2005). *Unmaking Imperial Russia: Mykhailo Hrushevsky and the Writing of Ukrainian History*. Buffalo (NY): University of Toronto Press.

Plokhy, Serhii (2007). "Beyond Nationality." *Ab Imperio*, 4: 25–46.

Podoliak, Iryna (2017). "Movne bozhevillia." *Tyzhden'*. May 5. Available at: http://tyzhden.ua/Columns/50/191480 (06/2019).

Polese, Abel (2011). "Language and Identity in Ukraine: Was it Really Nation-Building?" *Studies of Transition States and Societies*. 3, 3: 36–50.

Pomerantsev, Igor' (2014). "Ukraina. Pisatel' i voina." *Radio Svoboda*. September 26. Available at: http://www.svoboda.org/a/26603977.html (07/2019).

Pomerantsev, Igor' (2019). "Kak russkii pisatel' stal ukrainskim." *Radio Svoboda*. June 28. https://www.svoboda.org/a/30023818.html (09/2019).

Pomerantsev, Peter (2019). "Zelensky, the Post-Soviet Man." *The American Interest*. May 6. Available at: https://www.the-american-interest.com/2019/05/06/zelensky-the-post-soviet-man/?fbclid=IwAR17hKX4lCPfq1g7cXymvL08F2Z45YVC-Csuw5JhjZARa51a1vhfbfmIv2I (07/2019).

Portnikov, Vitalii (2015). "Akh, svoia li, chuzhaia…" *Grani.ru*. October 9. Available at: http://graniru.org/opinion/portnikov/m.244887.html (04/2019).

Portnov, Andrei (2014). "Ukraina i ee 'dal'nii i 'blizhnii' vostok." *Uroki istorii. XX vek*. July 31. Available at: https://urokiistorii.ru/article/52153 (06/2019).

Portnov, Andrii (2015). "Post-Maidan Europe and the New Ukrainian Studies." *Slavic Review*. 74, 4: 723–731.

Portnov, Andrii (2017). "The Arithmetic of Otherness: 'Donbas' in Ukrainian Intellectual Discourse." *Eurozine*. June 1. Available at: http://www.eurozine.com/the-myth-of-the-two-ukraines/ (06/2019).

Prabhu, Anjali (2007). *Hybridity: Limits, Transformations, Prospects*. Albany (NY): State University of New York Press.

Prezident Rossii. (2015). "Kontseptsiia 'Russkaia shkola za rubezhom'." November 4. Available at: http://kremlin.ru/acts/news/50643 (04/2019).

Prezydent Ukraïny (2019): "Ukaz prezydenta Ukraïny n. 82/2019." March 19. Available at: https://www.president.gov.ua/documents/822019-26290 (07/2019).

Prokhas'ko, Taras (2017). "Chy ty spysh ukraïns'koiu?" *Zbruch*. August 31. Available at: https://zbruc.eu/node/70184 (04/2019).

Prokhas'ko, Taras (2019). "Kontemporal'nyi hegemon." *Zbruch*. April 4. Available at: https://zbruc.eu/node/88285 (07/2019).

Pucherová, Dobrota; Gáfrik, Róbert (2015). "Introduction: Which Postcolonial Europe?" In Pucherová, Dobrota; Gáfrik, Róbert (eds.), *Postcolonial Europe? Essays on Post-Communist Literatures and Cultures*. Leiden-Boston (MA): Brill. 11–23.

Puleri, Marco (2014a). "Ukraïns'kyi, Rosiis'komovnyi, Rosiis'kyi: Self-Identification in Post-Soviet Ukrainian Literature in Russian." *Ab Imperio*. 2: 367–397.

Puleri, Marco (2014b). "'C'era una volta un paese, ed era...la mia Patria'. Voci dai 'margini': Diari di guerra da Donec'k." *LEA – Lingue e Letterature d'Oriente e d'Occidente*. 3: 65–84.

Puleri, Marco (2016). *Narrazioni ibride post-sovietiche: Per una letteratura ucraina di lingua russa*. Firenze: Firenze University Press.

Puleri, Marco (2017a). "Between Kafka and Gogol'. 'De-territorialising' National Narrative(s) in Post-Soviet Ukrainian Literature in Russian." In Pieralli, Claudia et al. (a cura di). *Russia, Oriente slavo e Occidente europeo: fratture e integrazioni nella storia e nella civiltà letteraria*. Firenze: Firenze University Press. 357–376.

Puleri, Marco (2017b). "Hybridity Reconsidered: Ukrainian Border Crossing After the 'Crisis'." *Ab Imperio*. 2: 257–286.

Puleri, Marco (2018). "Values for the Sake of the (Post-Soviet) Nation: Patriotism(s) and the Search for the 'True' Self in Ukraine." *Southeastern Europe*. 42, 3: 350–375.

Putin, Vladimir (2013). "Poslanie Prezidenta Federal'nomu Sobraniiu." *Prezident Rossii*. December 12. Available at: http://www.kremlin.ru/events/president/news/19825 (07/2019).

Putin, Vladimir (2014). "Obrashchenie Prezidenta Rossiiskoi Federatsii." *Prezident Rossii*. March 18. Available at: http://kremlin.ru/events/president/news/20603 (07/2019).

Rafeenko, Vladimir (2013). *Moskovskii divertisment*. Moskva: Tekst.

Rafeenko, Vladimir (2014). *Demon Dekarta*. Moskva: Eksmo.

Rafeenko, Vladimir (2016). "Ukraina—krovavie zemli na styke tsivilizatsii,— Aleksei Nikitin." *Fokus*. September 21. Available at: https://focus.ua/culture/355421/ (07/2019).

Rafeenko, Vladimir (2017). *Dolgota dnei*. Kharkiv: Fabula.

<Rafeenko, Volodymyr> Rafieienko, Volodymyr (2019a). *Mondegrin*. Chernivtsi: Meridian Czernowitz.

<Rafeenko, Volodymyr> Rafieienko, Volodymyr (2019b). "Ostannia liubov." *NV*. April 25. Available at: https://nv.ua/ukr/opinion/ostannya-lyubov-50013684.html (07/2019).

Razumkov Center. (2016). "Konsolidatsiia Ukraïns'koho suspil'stva: shliakhy, vyklyky, perspektyvy. Informatsiino-analitychni materialy do fakhovoiï dyskusiï." December 16. Available at: razumkov.org.ua/upload/Identi-2016.pdf (07/2019).

Rewakowicz, Maria G. (2018). *Ukraine's Quest for Identity: Embracing Cultural Hybridity in Literary Imagination, 1991–2011*. Lanham (MD) et al.: Lexington Books.

<Riabchuk, Mykola> Ryabchuk, Mykola (1992). "Two Ukraines?" *East European Reporter*, 5, 4: 18–22.

Riabchuk, Mykola (2001). "Dvi Ukraïny." *Krytyka*, 5, 10: 10–13.

Riabchuk, Mykola (2003a). *Dvi Ukraïny: real'ni mezhi, virtual'ni viiny*. Kyiv: Krytyka.

Riabchuk, Mykola (2003b). "Ukraine: One State, Two Countries?" *Eurozine*. September 16. Available at: https://www.eurozine.com/ukraine-one-state-two-countries/ (05/2019).

<Riabchuk, Mykola> Ryabchuk, Mykola (2010). "The Ukrainian 'Friday' and the Russian 'Robinson': The Uneasy Advent of Postcoloniality." *Canadian–American Slavic Studies*. 44: 7–24.

Riabchuk, Mykola (2012). "Playing with ambiguities: Ukraine's language law." *openDemocracy*. June 28. Available at: https://www.opendemocracy.net/en/odr/playing-with-ambiguities-ukraines-language-law/ (05/2019).

Riabchuk, Mykola (2013). "Ukraïns'kyi Piatnytsia i ioho dva Robinzony." *Krytyka*. November. Available at: http://krytyka.com/ua/articles/ ukrayinskyy-pyatnytsya-i-yoho-dva-robinzony>. (06/2019).

Riabchuk, Mykola (2015). " 'Two Ukraines' Reconsidered: The End of Ukrainian Ambivalence?" *Studies in Ethnicity and Nationalism*. 15, 1: 138–156.

Rissenberg, Il'ia (2014). "Psalom Voskhozhdeniia. Son…" *Sho*. 5–8: 21–23.

Rodgers, Peter W. (2008). *Nation, Region and History in Post-Communist Transitions: Identity Politics in Ukraine, 1992–2006*. Stuttgart: ibidem-Verlag.

Rubins, Maria (2019). "A Century of Russian Culture(s) 'Abroad': The Unfolding of Literary Geography." In Platt, Kevin M. F (ed.). *Global Russian Cultures*. Madison (WI): University of Wisconsin Press. 21–47.

Rubtsov, Aleksandr (2014). "Postmodernizm v politike—prosto beda." *Nezavisimaia Gazeta*. March 25. Available at: http://www.ng.ru/ stsenarii/2014-03-25/14_chaos.html (06/2019).

Rudenko, Ievhen; Sarakhman, El'dar (2019). "Ievhen Holovakha: Fenomen Zelens'koho—svoieridnyi 'elektoral'nyi Maidan'." *Ukraïns'ka Pravda*. 18/04/2019. Available at: https://www.pravda.com.ua/ articles/2019/04/18/7212520/ (07/2019).

Russkaia Idea (2014). "O proekte." Available at: http://politconservatism. ru/about (07/2019).

Sasse, Gwendolyn (2017). "Ukraine's Poorly Timed Education Law." *Carnegie Europe*. October 2. Available at: http://carnegieeurope.eu/ strategiceurope/73272 (07/2019).

Saunders, Robert A. (2014). "The Geopolitics of Russophonia: The Problems and Prospects of Post-Soviet 'Global Russian'." *Globality Studies Journal*. 40: 1–22. Available at: https://gsj.stonybrook.edu/ wp-content/uploads/2014/07/0040Saunders.pdf (04/2019).

Semenov, Denis (2017). "Za mig do razryva. Kto i kak raskalyvaet Ukrainu." *Fokus.ua*. May 27. Available at: https://focus.ua/opinions/373368/ (07/2019).

Semkiv, Rostyslav (2013a). "Kholodna Movna Viina." *LitAktsent*. March 22. Available at: http://litakcent.com/2013/03/22/holodna-movna-vijna/ (05/2019).

Semkiv, Rostyslav (2013b). "Kul'turna kapituliatsiia. Iak mitsnishaie rosiis'ko-ukraïns'ka literaturna druzhba." *Tyzhden'*. August 5. Available at: https://tyzhden.ua/Society/85477 (06/2019).

Shapiro, Gavriel. (1986). "Nikolai Gogol' and the Baroque Heritage." *Slavic Review*. 45, 1: 101–119.

Sharyi, Andrei (2013). "Pisatel' Andrei Kurkov—o peresechenii prostranstv." *Radio Svoboda*. April 10. Available at: http://www.svoboda.org/content/article/24953564.html (06/2019).

Shevel, Oxana (2004). "Citizenship and nation-building in Ukraine." Paper presented at the workshop 'Understanding the Transformation of Ukraine: Assessing What Has Been Learned, Devising a Research Agenda'. University of Ottawa. October 15–16. Available at: https://wikis.uit.tufts.edu/confluence/download/attachments/23235422/Shevel_Danyliw04.pdf.

Shevel, Oxana (2011). "Russian Nation-building from Yel'tsin to Medvedev: Ethnic, Civic or Purposefully Ambiguous?" *Europe–Asia Studies*. 63, 2: 179–202.

Shevtsova, Lesia (2016). "'Movoiu Boha': povist', iaka dopomozhe pobachyty dvi storony konfliktu na Donbasi." *Drug Chytacha*. October 12. Available at: http://vsiknygy.net.ua/shcho_pochytaty/review/46881/ (06/2019).

Shkandrij, Myroslav (2001). *Russia and Ukraine: Literature and the Discourse of Empire From Napoleonic to Postcolonial Times*. Montreal-Kingston: McGill-Queen's University Press.

Shkandrij, Myroslav (2009). "The Postcolonial Moment in Ukrainian Writing." *Postcolonial Europe*. April 29. Available at: http://www.postcolonial-europe.eu/pl/studies/70-the-postcolonial-moment-in-ukrainian-writing.html (05/2019).

Sho (2014). "Litso tvorcheskoi natsional'nosti." 1–2: 80–92.

Shul'man, Ekaterina (2017). "Prisoedinenie Kryma—otvet vlastei na protesty 2011–2012 godov." *Snob*. March 22. Available at: https://snob.ru/selected/entry/122061?preview=print (07/2019).

Shveda, Yuriy (2014). "The Revolution of Dignity in the Context of Social Theory of Revolutions." *Religion & Society in East and West*. 5–6: 20–22.

Slavins'ka, Iryna (2011). "Tsifry ta Bukvy." *Sho*. 5–6: 92–93.

Slavins'ka, Iryna (2015). "Ukraïns'kyi pys'mennyk z Donets'ka: Ideiu separatyzmu na Donbasi masovo pidtrymuvaly til'ky militsiia, SBU ta prokuratura." *Ukraïns'ka Pravda*. July 1. Available at: http://life.pravda.com.ua/society/2015/07/1/196534/ (06/2019).

Slyvyns'kyi, Ostap (2014). "Khaiku revoliutsii. Naïlia." *Sho*. 5–8: 8.

Smola, Klavdia; Uffelmann, Dirk (2016). "Postcolonial Slavic Literatures After Communism: Introduction." In Smola, Klavdia; Uffelmann, Dirk (eds.). *Postcolonial Slavic Literatures After Communism*. Frankfurt/Main: Peter Lang. 9–25.

Smola, Klavdia; <Uffelmann, Dirk> Uffel'mann, Dirk (2017). "Postkolonial'nost' postsovetskikh literatur: Konstruktsii etnicheskogo (Vvedenie)." *Novoe literaturnoe obozrenie*. 144: 420–428.

Sokhareva, Tat'iana (2014). "Vechera na khutore bliz promzony." *Gazeta.ru*. May 14. Available at: www.gazeta.ru/culture/2014/05/14/a_6032653.shtml (07/2019).

Stadnyi, Iegor (2015). "Shcho nam ne skazaly pro dekomunizatsiiu?" *Ukraïns'ka Pravda*. April 20. Available at: http://www.pravda.com.ua/columns/2015/04/20/7065289/ (07/2019).

Stahl, Henrieke (2015). "Poesie als politische Partizipation: Der virale poetopolitische Diskurs um Anastasija Dmitruks Videogedicht 'Nikogda my ne budem brat'jami' auf YouTube." *Zeitschrift für Slavische Philologie*. 71, 2: 441–477.

Stasov, Bogdan (2009). " *'Raduzhnaia' li zhizn' u zhurnala?"* *Literaturnaia gazeta*. 35. Available at: http://old.lgz.ru/article/10028/ (06/2019).

Statement of the Civic Sector of Maidan (2013). "Statement of the Civic Sector of Maidan. On the Creation of the Wide Civic Movement of EuroMaidan." *Facebook*. December 22. Available at: https://www.facebook.com/hrom.sektor.euromaidan/posts/643089239063346 (07/2019).

Stebelsky, Ihor (2009). "Ethnic Self-Identification in Ukraine, 1989–2001: Why More Ukrainians and Fewer Russians?" *Canadian Slavonic Papers/Revue Canadienne des slavistes*. LI, 1: 77–100.

Stiazhkina, Elena (2014). "Prosti, Rossiia, i ia proshchaiu." *Ostrov*. March 2. Available at: http://www.ostro.org/general/politics/articles/438984/ (06/2019).

<Stiazhkina, Elena> Stiazhkina, Olena (2016). "Svoï imena." *Deutsche Welle*. August 19. Available at: http://dw.com/p/1JlE1 (06/2019).

Sultanov, Kazbek (2017). "Gibridizatsiia diskursov, ili Sovetizatsiia postsovetskogo." *Gefter*. February 10. Available at: http://gefter.ru/archive/21122 (06/2019).

Sushko, Oleksandr (2017). "An Inclusive Ukrainian Education." *Project Syndicate*. October 3. Available at: https://www.project-syndicate.org/commentary/ukraine-education-law-foreign-hostility-by-oleksandr-sushko-2017-10 (07/2019).

Suslov, Mikhail (2016). " 'The 'Russian World' Concept in Online Debates During the Ukrainian Crisis." In Suslov, Mikhail; Bassin, Mark. *Eurasia 2.0: Russian Geopolitics in the Age of New Media*. Lanham (MD): Lexington Books. 295–316.

Sventakh, Anna (2014). " 'Feodal'no-promyshlennyi idiotizm kak filosofiia vlasti.' Pisatel' Vladimir Rafeenko—o svoei maloi rodine—Donetske, predvoennom i voennom." *Den'*. October 2. Available at: http://m.day.kyiv.ua/ru/article/ukraincy-chitayte/feodalno-promyshlennyy-idiotizm-kak-filosofiya-vlasti (07/2019).

Tereshchenko, Antonina (2010). "Highlighting Place and Space in Studies of Youth Citizenship Identities." *Educação, Sociedade & Culturas*. 30: 145–160. Available at: https://www.fpce.up.pt/ciie/revistaesc/ESC30/n30a11.pdf (04/2019).

Thévenot, Laurent (2006). *L'action au pluriel. Sociologie des régimes d'engagement*. Paris: La Découverte.

Tlostanova, Madina (2004). *Postsovetskaia literatura i estetika transkul'turatsii. Zhit' nikogda, pisat' niotkuda*. Moskva: Editorial URSS.

Tolochko, Oleksii (2016). "Nezastiglyi Chas." In <Nikitin, Aleksei> Nikitin, Oleksii. *Victory Park*. Per. Viktoriia Merenkova. Kharkiv: Fabula. 2–3.

Toporov, Viktor (2012). "O literature s Viktorom Toporovym: Ne lez', podskazchik, k igrokam." *Fontanka.ru*. May 30. Available at: http://www.fontanka.ru/2012/05/30/070/ (06/2019).

Torbakov, Igor (2016). "Ukraine and Russia: Entangled Histories, Contested Identities and a War of Narratives." In Bertelsen, Olga (ed.). *Revolution and War in Contemporary Ukraine: The Challenge of Change*. Stuttgart: ibidem-Verlag. 89–120.

Troskot, Iryna (2013). "Pro movu i dyskusiiu." *LitAktsent*. February 25. Available at: http://litakcent.com/2013/02/25/pro-movu-j-dyskusiju/ (05/2019).

Tsentral'na vyborcha komisiia (2019a). "Protokol tsentral'noï vyborchoï komisiï pro rezul'taty povtornoho holosuvannia z vyboriv prezydenta Ukraïny." April 30. Available at: https://www.cvk.gov.ua/info/protokol_cvk_30042019.pdf (07/2019).

Tsentral'na vyborcha komisiia (2019b). "Pozacherhovi vybory narodnykh deputativ Ukraïny." July 26. Available at: https://www.cvk.gov.ua/pls/vnd2019/wp300pt001f01=919.html (07/2019).

Tuckerová, Veronika (2017). "The Archeology of Minor Literature: Towards the Concept of the Ultraminor." *Journal of World Literature*. 2, 4: 433–453.

UCIPR (2016). "Zminy identychnosti Rosiian ta Rosiis'komovnykh v Ukraïni: 'Velikyi i mogutnii' vidstupaie." Available at http://bit.ly/2uX2zet (04/2019).

Uffelmann, Dirk (2019). "Is There Any Such Thing as 'Russophone Russophobia'?" In Platt, Kevin M. F (ed.). *Global Russian Cultures*. Madison (WI): University of Wisconsin Press. 207–229.

Ufimtseva, Kseniia (2017). "Nechego prikasat'sia k pomazannikam bozh'im!" *Znak*. September 28. Available at: https://www.znak.com/2017-09-28/poklonskaya_uchitel_ne_imel_prava_menyat_scenariy_matildy_i_brat_nemca_na_rol_carya (07/2019).

Ukraïns'ka Pravda (2017). "Lavrov: Prilepin na Donbasse nalazhivaet normal'nuiu zhizn'." February 21. Available at: http://www.pravda.com.ua/rus/news/2017/02/21/7136032/ (07/2019).

Ukraïns'ka Pravda (2018a). "Eshche v odnoi oblasti Ukrainy zapretili ves' russkoiazychnyi kul'turnyi produkt." October 25. Available at: https://www.pravda.com.ua/rus/news/2018/10/25/7196278/ (07/2019).

Ukraïns'ka Pravda (2018b). "Tret'ia oblast' v Ukraine zapretili Rossiiskii kul'turnyi produkt." 6/11/2018. Available at: https://www.pravda.com.ua/rus/news/2018/11/6/7197438/ (07/2019).

Umland, Andreas (2017). "The Ukrainian Government's Memory Institute against the West." *New Eastern Europe*. March 7. Available at: http://neweasterneurope.eu/2017/03/07/the-ukrainian-government-s-memory-institute-against-the-west/ (07/2019).

UNHCR (2017). "Ukraine. UNHCR Operational Update." January 1–31. Available at: http://reliefweb.int/report/ukraine/ukraine-unhcr-operational-update-1-31-january-2017 (06/2019).

Unian (2018). 'Shche v odnii oblasti Ukraïny zaboronyly fil'my ta pisni rosiis'koiu movoiu." December 7. Available at: https://www.unian.ua/society/10367526-shche-v-odniy-oblasti-ukrajini-zaboronili-filmi-ta-pisni-rosiyskoyu-movoyu.html (07/2019).

Valdai. (2014). 'Natsional'naia identichnost' i budushchee Rossii. Doklad Mezhdunarodnogo diskussionnogo kluba 'Valdai'." February. Available at: vid1.rian.ru/ig/valdai/doklad_identichnost_RUS_ISBN.pdf (07/2019).

Volodarskii, Iurii (2010). "Aleksand Kabanov: Ia Russkii poet, grazhdanin Ukrainy." *2000.ua*. February 12. Available at: https://www.2000.ua/v-nomere/aspekty/slovo/aleksandr-kabanov-ja-russkij-poet-grazhdanin-ukrainy_arhiv_art.htm (06/2019).

Volodarskii, Iurii (2013a). "Svoi ili chuzhie." *Korrespondent*. August 12. Available at: http://blogs.korrespondent.net/blog/2379/3216985-svoy-yly-chuzhye (06/2019).

Volodarskii, Iurii (2013b). "Chudesa prevrashchenii." *Sho*. 9–10: 87.

Volodarskii, Iurii (2014). "Liudmila Ulitskaia: 'Ia ne liubliu nikakuiu vlast'…" *Sho*. 11–12: 86–90.

Volodarskii, Iurii (2017a). "Mify zamedlennogo deistviia. Istorik Georgii Kas'ianov o Bandere, russkom iazyke i shchelchkakh istorii." *Fokus*. February 10. Available at: https://focus.ua/society/366016/ (04/2019).

Volodarskii, Iurii (2017b). "Torzhestvo nenavisti." *TSN.UA*. May 5. Available at: https://ru.tsn.ua/blogi/themes/politics/torzhestvo-nenavisti-853692.html (04/2019).

Volodarskii, Iurii (2018a). "Predstav'te sebe." *Sho*, 12–2 (158–160): 90.

Volodarskii, Iurii (2018b). "Vladimir Rafeenko: Bol' i sovest' Donbassa." *Shoizdat*. July 2. Available at: https://www.sho.kiev.ua/vladimir-rafeenko-bol-i-sovest-donb/ (07/2019).

Volos, Andrei (2005). *Khurramabad*. Moskva: Zebra.

Von Hagen, Mark (1995). "Does Ukraine Have a History?" *Slavic Review*. 54, 3: 658–673.

Vorozhbyt, Ol'ha (2014). "Serhii Plokhii: Istoryky maiut' pereity vid propahandy mistsevykh 'pravd' do napysannia istoriï natsiï, de figuruvatymut' usi rehiony, vkliuchno iz Krymom." *Tyzhden'*. 03/05/2014. Available at: http://tyzhden.ua/Society/108399 (06/2019).

Vynnychuk, Iurii (2016). "Iazyk voroga." *Zbruch*. April 24. Available at: http://zbruc.eu/node/50648 (06/2019).

Vynnychuk, Iurii (2017). "Nestrymni zhakhittia translitu." *Zbruch*. September 10. Available at: https://zbruc.eu/node/70530 (04/2019).

Vynnychuk, Iurii et al. (2015). *2014. Khronika gody. Blogi. Kolonki. Dnevniki*. Kharkiv: Folio.

Wesolowsky, Tony (2017). "In Ukraine, Children's Book Featuring Lesbian Parents Met With Threats, Fears of Violence." *Radio Free Europe*. 14/09/2017. Available at: https://www.rferl.org/a/ukraine-childrens-book-lesbian-parents-threats-fear-lgbt-homophobia/28735738.html (07/2019).

Wilson, Andrew (2000). *The Ukrainians: Unexpected Nation*. New Haven (CT)-London: Yale University Press.

Wilson, Andrew (2015). "Ukrainian Politics since Independence." In Pikulicka-Wilczewska, Agnieszka; Sakwa, Richard (eds.). *Ukraine and Russia: People, Politics, Propaganda and Perspectives*. Bristol: E-International Relations. 101–108.

Yekelchyk, Serhy (2015). "National Heroes For a New Ukraine: Merging the Vocabularies of the Diaspora, Revolution and Mass Culture." *Ab Imperio*. 3: 97–123.

Zabirko, Oleksandr (2018). "The Magic Spell of Revanchism: Geopolitical Visions in Post-Soviet Speculative Fiction (Fantastika)." *The Ideology and Politics Journal*. Issue 1 (9). 66–134. Available at: https://ideopol. org/wp-content/uploads/2018/11/_____2018 %201.%209.%20 ENG.%20Zabirko.%20Demodernization%20Form.pdf (07/2019).

Zaharchenko, Tanya (2013). "Polyphonic Dichotomies: Memory and Identity in Today's Ukraine." *Demokratizatsiya*. 21, 2: 241–270.

Zaharchenko, Tanya (2014). "A Ukrainian Thesaurus in Russian." *King's Review*. May 15. Available at: http://kingsreview.co.uk/articles/ ukrainian-thesaurus/ (06/2019).

Zaharchenko, Tanya (2016). *Where Currents Meet: Frontiers in Post-Soviet Fiction of Kharkiv, Ukraine*. Budapest-New York: CEU Press.

Zakon Ukraïny (2019). "Pro zabezpechennia funktsionuvannia ukraïns'koï movy iak derzhavnoï." *Verkhovna Rada Ukraïny.* April 25. Available at: https://zakon.rada.gov.ua/laws/show/2704-19 (11/2019).

Zakurenko, Aleksandr (1997). "'Kievskaia shkola': Vstupitel'nyi ili vypusknoi eksamen?" *Novyi Mir.* 1. 232–237.

Zamora, Lois Parkinson; Faris, Wendy B. (1995). "Introduction: Daiquiri Birds and Flaubertian Parrot(ie)s." In Zamora, Lois Parkinson; Faris, Wendy B. (eds.). *Magic Realism: Theory, History, Community.* Durham-London: Duke University Press. 1–11.

Zhurzhenko, Tatiana (2002a). "The Myth of Two Ukraines. A Commentary on Mykola Riabchuk's 'Ukraine: One State, Two Countries'?" *Eurozine.* September 17. Available at: https://www.eurozine.com/the-myth-of-two-ukraines/ (05/2019).

Zhurzhenko, Tatiana (2002b). "Language Politics in Contemporary Ukraine: Nationalism and Identity Formation." In Bove, Andrew (ed.). *Questionable Returns.* Vienna: (IMW Junior Visiting Fellows Conferences). 12. 1–24. Available at: http://www.iwm.at/wp-content/uploads/jc-12-02.pdf (04/2019).

Zhurzhenko, Tatiana (2014a). "A Divided Nation? Reconsidering the Role of Identity Politics in the Ukraine Crisis." *Die Friedens-Warte.* 89, 1–2: 249–267.

Zhurzhenko, Tatiana (2014b). "From Borderlands to Bloodlands." *Eurozine.* September 19. Available at: http://www.eurozine.com/from-borderlands-to-bloodlands/ (06/2019).

Zhurzhenko, Tatiana (2016). "Hybrid Reconciliation." *Eurozine.* April 8. Available at: http://www.eurozine.com/hybrid-reconciliation/ (07/2019).

Zubrytska, Maria (2006). "Mirrors, Windows and Maps: The Topology of Cultural Identification in Contemporary Ukrainian Literature." *The Slavic and East European Journal.* 50, 3: 403–408.

Index

Postcolonial Perspectives on Eastern Europe

Edited by
Alfred Gall, Mirja Lecke, and Dirk Uffelmann

Advisory Board:
Clare Cavanagh (Evanston, Ill.), Alexander Etkind (Florence), Marina Mogilner (Chicago, Ill.),
Nikola Petković (Rijeka), Mykola Ryabchuk (Kyiv), Izabela Surynt (Wrocław)

www.peterlang.com